TOWARD
LIBERTY

TOWARD LIBERTY

THE IDEA THAT IS CHANGING THE WORLD

25 YEARS OF PUBLIC POLICY FROM THE CATO INSTITUTE

EDITED BY DAVID BOAZ

CATO INSTITUTE
Washington, D.C.

Library of Congress Cataloging-in-Publication Data

Toward liberty : the idea that is changing the world : 25 years of public
policy from the Cato Institute / edited by David Boaz.
    pp. cm
    ISBN 1-930865-27-9 (cloth : alk. paper) – ISBN 1-930865-26-0 (pbk :
alk paper)
    1. Liberty. 2. Free enterprise. 3. Policy sciences. I. Boaz, David, 1953- II.
Cato Institute.

JC 585 .T67 2002
320'.6--dc21   2002024634

Cover design by Amanda Elliott.
Printed in the United States of America.

CATO INSTITUTE
1000 Massachusetts Ave., N.W.
Washington, D.C. 20001

Contents

Contents

Introduction: The Idea That Is Changing the World

by David Boaz

Jimmy Carter. Tip O'Neill. Energy czars. Gas lines. Raging inflation. ABC-NBC-CBS. Mao Tse-tung. The Soviet Union. Apartheid.

It was a different era.

What wasn't so obvious at the time was that it was the end of an era.

In 1977 the Soviet Union seemed a permanent fixture. So did communism in China. Here at home, the Democrats had retaken the White House after Nixon's usurpation. The permanent majority was back in control in Washington. Ninety-one percent of television viewers watched the big three networks. Despite the turmoil of the 1960s and early 1970s, baby boomers thought that communist domination of half the world and Democratic control of Washington were just the natural order of the universe.

In the 1970s Henry Kissinger was quoted as saying that he thought of the United States as Athens and the Soviet Union as Sparta. "The day of the U.S. is past and today is the day of the Soviet Union. My job as secretary of state is to negotiate the most acceptable second-best position available." Kissinger denied saying that, but another leading intellectual-statesman, Senator Daniel Patrick Moynihan, stated a similar view openly in 1976, at the time of the American bicentennial: "Liberal democracy on the American model increasingly tends to the condition of monarchy in the 19th century; a holdover form of government, one which persists in isolated or particular places here and there, and may even serve well enough for special circumstances, but which has simply no relevance to the future. It is where the world was, not where it is going. Increasingly democracy

David Boaz is executive vice president of the Cato Institute and author of *Libertarianism: A Primer.*

is seen as an arrangement peculiar to a handful of North Atlantic countries."

How wrong they were. Under the surface things were changing. Some of the very weaknesses that led Kissinger and Moynihan to their pessimism—such as the federal government's disastrous triple play of Vietnam, Watergate, and stagflation—had eroded the confidence in government built up by the New Deal, World War II, and the prosperous 1950s. The ideas that Ayn Rand, Milton Friedman, F. A. Hayek, and others had been propounding for a generation were taking root. Politicians such as Margaret Thatcher and Ronald Reagan, who had read some of those dissident authors, were planning their challenges to the failing welfare-state consensus.

Even less obvious, Soviet leaders had lost confidence in the Marxist ideology that justified their rule, a fact that would have profound consequences in the coming decade. And in China, Mao had just died, and his old comrade Deng Xiao-ping was maneuvering for power. His victory would have consequences that no one could foresee in 1977.

Politics isn't everything, of course. In 1976 Steve Jobs and Steve Wozniak incorporated the Apple Computer Company, on April Fool's Day. Two other young men, Bill Gates and Paul Allen, had created a company to develop software for the new personal computers, and in 1978 Microsoft Corporation's sales topped $1 million. Around 1978 an Atlanta businessman came up with the idea of an all-news cable channel; Ted Turner launched the Cable News Network on June 1, 1980.

And the Cato Institute opened its doors in January 1977.

25 Years of Change

Twenty-five years later, the world has changed so much that we may hardly remember what 1977 was like. Reagan and Thatcher moved public policy in the direction of lower taxes, less regulation, and privatization. They had an even bigger impact on political culture in their countries and around the world. They both symbolized and galvanized a new appreciation for markets and entrepreneurship. Reagan's optimism—along with the mountains of facts painstakingly accumulated by Julian Simon and other scholars—helped to dispel the doom and gloom of the 1970s.

Reagan and Thatcher did little to challenge the welfare state. But by strengthening the economy and helping more people appreciate the benefits of entrepreneurship and investment, they contributed to a growing demand for reform:

- Economic deregulation (begun under President Carter) made the airline, trucking, railroad, oil, natural gas, telecommunications, and financial-services industries more efficient.
- Tax-rate reductions set off economic booms in both countries, and more people became homeowners and investors.
- Americans came to believe that welfare was trapping millions of people in dependency. What Jonathan Rauch called a "demosclerotic" political system did not change easily, but in 1996 a welfare reform bill was finally passed.
- The Social Security system proved even more impervious to challenge, but by 2001 some 70 percent of Americans told pollsters they approved of privatization.

Abroad, the changes have been even more dramatic. The only thing more certain than Social Security was that the world was divided into communist and noncommunist parts. But the changes that began with Deng's rise to power in 1977–78 and the first stirrings of Solidarity in Poland in 1980 would change the face of the world in little more than a decade. The end of communism did not usher in nirvana, of course. Russia remains mired in poverty and corruption, with its commitment to political and economic liberalism still uncertain. The other former Soviet republics are in most cases even worse off. (But isn't it amazing that the Soviet Union peacefully let go, not just of its client states, but of its internal republics? How we used to scoff at the idea that those "republics" were anything but administrative divisions and Potemkin nations.) The European countries that were once under the thumb of the USSR are doing somewhat better. East Germany is once again simply eastern Germany, part of a prosperous and democratic nation, though poorer than western Germany. Poland, Hungary, the Czech Republic, and the Baltic nations are making fairly rapid transitions to liberal capitalism, while the southeastern European nations—which had little national experience of democracy or capitalism—lag behind.

As we worry about the sluggish pace of Russian reform, one of our problems is CNN. In a world of 24-hour news, we're impatient for change. The communists are gone, so why aren't you capitalists yet? But our own progress toward freedom took time—more than 500 years from Magna Carta to the U.S. Constitution, eight years from victory at Yorktown to the inauguration of an elected president, 90 years from the stirring phrases of the Declaration of Independence to the abolition of chattel slavery. Of course, modern communications and technology might make some transitions quicker. As Johan Norberg notes, "From 1780 it took England 58 years to double its wealth. A hundred years later Japan did it in only 34 years, and another century later it took South Korea only 11 years." We can see which systems have succeeded or failed, and Russia need not repeat the mistakes of earlier democracies, but change still takes time.

China's economic development has been astounding. Since Deng Xiao-ping allowed farmers to benefit from incentives and to assume more responsibility, agricultural production has soared. The resulting surplus food production has allowed workers to move into other lines of work. State-owned enterprises were given more independence, and Chinese citizens were allowed to set up village and even private enterprises. Economic reform has accelerated over the past 20 years. When I attended the Cato Institute's first conference in Shanghai in 1988, the huge city had almost no tall buildings. From the 16th floor of the Shanghai Hilton, you looked across miles of hovels to the Sheraton in the distance. There were few stores and restaurants in 1988, and they had little to sell. In 1997, when I arrived at 10 o'clock at night for Cato's second conference in China, again at the Shanghai Hilton, I took a stroll around the neighborhood. Even at that late hour, I encountered an enterprising people—there were stores, restaurants, fruit stands, bars, nightclubs, farmers selling produce from their trucks. And the city's skyline, if not yet Manhattan, had certainly blossomed to the scale of Houston. The differences were obvious and dramatic.

But there was another difference as well. At our 1988 conference students and professors wanted to talk about market reforms and democracy; they followed Milton Friedman around like a guru. In 1997 the participants were more subdued; they wanted to talk about business models and market institutions, but they clammed up when the Americans turned the discussion to free speech and political reform. It seemed as if the leaders of China had made a bargain with the people: stop talking about democracy, and we'll let you get rich. Not the worst bargain in history, but certainly one that we hope won't last forever. And indeed the history of authoritarian capitalist countries suggests that it won't; increasing affluence and the habit of making their own decisions will lead people to demand more political rights.

Neoliberalism Rules?

Yes, things have indeed changed. Today, just 25 years after the laments of Kissinger and Moynihan, the conventional wisdom is that the Anglo-American model of democratic capitalism is the only viable model left in the world. Scholars such as Daniel Yergin (*The Commanding Heights: The Battle between Government and the Marketplace That Is Remaking the Modern World*) and Robert Skidelsky (*The Road from Serfdom: The Economic and Political Consequences of the End of Communism*), who are not known as free-market enthusiasts, write books assessing the triumph of capitalism. Indeed, Francis Fukuyama speculates that democratic capitalism may constitute the "end point of mankind's ideological evolution" and hence the "final form of human government"—occasional challenges such as Islamic fundamentalism notwithstanding.

This newly ascendant (or resurgent) liberalism is often labeled "neoliberalism," especially by its critics. Fidel Castro holds conferences in Havana on the threat of neoliberalism. Venezuelan strongman Hugo Chavez campaigns against "savage neoliberalism." Amazon.com lists 41 books on neoliberalism, typically with titles like *Profit over People: Neoliberalism and Globalization* or *The Limits of Capitalism*. The 23,000 references found by Google are worse: "For Humanity and against Neoliberalism." "Globalization and Corporate Rule." "The Poverty of Neoliberalism." "Capitalist neoliberalism has caused wars and mass starvation, collapsed economies, pushed millions of people out of work, forced millions of small peasant farmers off the land, weakened labor unions, resulted in elementary school and health clinic closings, while concentrating the wealth and power in fewer and fewer hands."

Paul Mattick writes more soberly in the *New York Times*, "[Adam] Smith is the totemic ancestor of the free market idea itself, the system that since the fall of Communism in the East and the triumph of fiscal conservatism in the West supposedly rules the world under the name of neoliberalism." But who ever actually claimed to rule "under the name of neoliberalism"? As Mario Vargas Llosa writes in this volume, the term is a "macabre scarecrow."

5

We are seeing a revival of true liberalism. In the 18th and 19th centuries, liberalism—the philosophy of individualism, free markets, limited and representative government, peace, and religious toleration—swept through England, the United States, and most of Europe and made inroads in other parts of the world. Liberalism

- abolished the age-old institution of slavery;
- established religious toleration;
- launched the progressive liberation of women, racial and religious minorities, and gays;
- replaced superstition with science;
- toppled monarchs or subordinated them to elected parliaments;
- overturned economic privilege;
- protected property rights for everyone;
- replaced mercantilism with markets; and
- replaced arbitrary power with limited, constitutional government.

The last two points deserve elaboration. We usually think of mercantilism as an economic doctrine: the "economic system of the major trading nations during the 16th, 17th, and 18th centuries, based on the premise that national wealth and power were best served by increasing exports and collecting precious metals in return," according to the *Columbia Encyclopedia*. But mercantilism was actually part of a broader idea, the idea that the sovereign must direct the entire society, with responsibility for the moral, religious, and economic life of the nation. The liberal revolution rejected that broad statist conception, not just its narrow economic aspect. Instead of a king, the representatives of the people should govern. And government, instead of assuming responsibility for every aspect of society, should be restricted to providing a framework in which people would pursue their own ends.

The result was an unprecedented and unimaginable increase in living standards. The *Nation* magazine, which was then a truly liberal journal, wrote in 1900, "Freed from the vexatious meddling of governments, men devoted themselves to their natural task, the bettering of their condition, with the wonderful results which surround us." In the preliberal era, economic growth was virtually nonexistent. The economic historian Angus Maddison estimates that there was no growth at all in per capita income in the first millennium and growth of some 0.17 percent in the developed countries in the period 1500–1820.

But from 1820 to 1900 gross domestic product per capita almost tripled in Western Europe and more than tripled in the United States. Life expectancy rose in the developed world (it rose even more in the 20th century). Years of education per person quadrupled in Great Britain and the United States. Millennia of backbreaking labor and often-lifelong isolation gave way to the steam engine, the railroad, the telegraph, the telephone, electricity, the internal combustion engine.

The 20th century seemed to reverse the gains of liberalism. The world was beset by tyrants and mass murderers, and even the democratic countries succumbed to the hubris of central planning. Even during that period, though, the massive capitalist engine set in motion by liberalism kept working, and living standards continued to rise in most of the world. By the end of the century, the last dictators were falling and people were becoming disillusioned with the welfare-and-regulation state. There was no longer any serious argument in favor of socialism, protectionism, or capital controls (though plenty of unserious ones on those 23,000 Google pages). From Great Britain and Sweden to Estonia and Hungary to Mauritius and New Zealand to Mexico and Uruguay, people decided they wanted to join in the new global prosperity. Intellectuals and activists railed against globalization, but people opted for it almost every chance they got.

If "neoliberalism" means a return to the liberalism that changed the developed world beginning in the 18th century, then it is surely to be welcomed. Those who want a return to mercantilism and statism are profoundly on the wrong side of history. Of course, the critics of neoliberalism often lump institutions such as the World Bank and the International Monetary Fund in with free trade and freedom of investment. And those institutions are a better target for their criticisms. As Ian Vásquez notes in this volume, at best they pursue liberal goals through illiberal means. The IMF, the World Bank, the U.S. Agency for International Development, the Export-Import Bank, and similar institutions all involve compulsory transfers from Western taxpayers to developing-world governments. Their constructivist, top-down approach to reform inevitably undermines liberal goals. Whether or not the agencies' economic advice is good—often it is not—they are understandably resented by citizens who believe that their nations' policies are being determined in Washington or Geneva. Western governments would do far more good in the developing world if they offered less aid and more trade. In an era of generally free trade, the strongest forms of protection are reserved for the products in which poor nations could best compete—agricultural products, steel, textiles.

The transfer agencies aside, neoliberalism would seem to be liberalism—the policy of free markets, free trade, free speech, and limited government—extended to the entire world and to new technologies. And it's about time the poor and oppressed people of the world enjoyed the blessings of liberty.

Continuing Challenges

It would be wrong to proclaim victory for liberalism. In many ways government has continued to get bigger and more intrusive over the past 25 years. Despite the philosophical revolution often attributed to Ronald Reagan, faith in big government has not disappeared. Government spending in real terms continues to rise (though not in percentage of GDP over the past few years). Despite the deregulation of the 1980s, government continues to interfere in many aspects of our lives more intimately than even the preliberal governments of Europe. Governments now regulate everything from where our children will attend school and how we must save for retirement to what size our oranges may be and what we can say to our coworkers. The rise of identity-group politics has revived a primitive form of collectivism, which liberalism always challenged, and led to new government discrimination on the basis of race and gender and to new attempts to regulate speech.

The mercantilist notion that the sovereign is responsible for our religious lives is largely gone, but anti-liberal elements on both right and left still want the government to take responsibility for our moral decisions. Pre-Enlightenment thinkers from Plato to Filmer would recognize the impulse to regulate pornography, hate speech, smoking, and drug use. The drug war in particular has led to manifold violations of our civil liberties as politicians and law enforcement officials try to enforce ever more futile prohibitions. More than a million people are arrested every year for drug use, and our jails and prisons are increasingly filled with drug-law violators. Prohibition infringes on property rights through the civil forfeiture laws. It gives us entrapment, wiretapping, racial profiling, mandatory minimum sentences, and inner cities under siege. And it's no surprise that the leading opponents of prohibition have always been liberals (or what we now call libertarians)—H. L. Mencken, Milton Friedman, Thomas S. Szasz, Gov. Gary Johnson, the editors of the *Economist*.

In the latter part of the 20th century in the North Atlantic welfare states, there was increasing concern about the high cost and unsustainability of a massive system of transfers. Earlier retirement combined with longer life expectancies was one source of the impending bankruptcy of social security systems. In the United States, the number of workers being taxed to support each retiree has fallen from 15 to 3 and will fall in just 20 years to a ratio of 2 workers per retiree—an impossible burden. Japan and Western Europe face even more daunting situations. The dramatic expansion of stock and mutual-fund ownership in the United States also led millions of Americans to believe that they could manage their own investments and that investments could give them a better retirement than Social Security promised.

Americans—beginning with those at the Cato Institute—pointed out that privatization would give people more freedom, more control over their own assets, and more retirement income. Many Americans noticed that Chile had privatized its social security system in 1980. Joe Klein visited Chile in 1994 for *Newsweek* and returned to report on the success of the privatization, which he called "perhaps the first social policy idea to emanate from the Southern Hemisphere"— yet another facet of globalization. Today some 90 countries from Mexico to China are studying social security privatization, and more than half of them have sent government representatives to the Cato Institute for research.

Even President Clinton told friends about the Chilean experience, and his economic advisers studied similar reforms. His perjury and impeachment may have derailed a dramatic shift in the American retirement system. If so, it was a great loss not only for future retirees but for Clinton himself, who desperately wanted history to remember him for some great accomplishment. Privatizing Social Security remains a great challenge for liberals.

In the developing world, the sins of "neoliberalism" are often attributed to "globalization." In an earlier era, the left championed internationalism over nationalism and complained that the capitalist countries excluded most of the world from their prosperous club. To-day, the same anti-capitalist ideologues deplore the extension of mar-kets to the non-Western world. If "globalization" means the ongoing trend toward the freer flow of trade and investment across borders and the resulting integration of the international economy, how can that be a bad thing? It is particularly odd to note that many of the same people who deplore the effects of U.S. trade sanctions on Iraq want the same policy—protectionism—applied to the whole world.

Some opponents of globalization have a clear vested interest: they don't want cheap goods coming into rich countries from poorer countries. Others are simply hostile to capitalism in all its manifesta-tions. Still others display an ill-informed nostalgia for the quaint vil-lages in which happy peasants in their traditional costumes make their traditional arts and crafts. How much more fulfilling that must be than working for Nike or Kathie Lee Gifford! And yet, to the hor-ror of the anti-globalization activists in Oxford and Ann Arbor, the actual peasants flock to the Nike factories. And no wonder: multina-tional companies pay about twice the average wage offered by do-mestic manufacturers in low-income countries. Global incomes are rising because of the increased efficiencies of a greater international division of labor—and rising most clearly in the poor countries that were previously outside the world trading system.

Anti-globalizers complain that foreign investment exploits the poor and makes them poorer. But 81 percent of U.S. foreign invest-ment goes to other high-income countries. Another 18 percent goes to middle-income countries such as Brazil, Mexico, Indonesia, and Thailand, leaving only 1 percent for the poorest countries. Clearly, the poorest countries are precisely the ones least engaged with the international economy. Since labor would be cheap in those coun-tries, we can assume that multinational corporations have good rea-sons for avoiding them. The poorest countries typically lack prop-erty rights, the rule of law, and other institutions necessary for economic enterprise. Liberalism has made few inroads in those countries, but we can hope that the 21st century will see the blessings of liberty penetrate to the last corners of the earth.

That hope goes hand in hand with the free world's newest chal-lenge—the threat posed by weapons of mass destruction in the hands of terrorists. Some of us may note ruefully that our warnings about the dangers of an interventionist foreign policy were well-founded. However, the United States and the West clearly must respond to the attacks of September 11 and other instances of terrorism. The Bush administration promptly offered a vigorous but measured response, carefully planned and focused on the perpetrators of the September 11 atrocities and those who harbor them. But the war against terrorists will not end soon. It will require improvements in U.S. intelligence, further military operations, and a determination to be persistent but not rash. It may require a rethinking of immigration policies, to ensure that we weed out those who would make war on us without closing our borders to people who want to work, trade, and lead lives of liberty and dignity. And since the defense of freedom is always a war of ideas as well as sometimes a military conflict, it clearly requires a renewal of our commitment to the first principles of the American republic, a cause that the Cato Institute has advanced for the past 25 years.

Conclusion

The past 25 years have seen great changes. Those changes have reflected mostly what the Marxists call "objective conditions"—demographic, economic, and geopolitical realities. However, those changes have also come about because people have advocated them. Liberalism arose first because people struggled for liberty—thinkers such as John Locke, David Hume, Adam Smith, and Mary Wollstonecraft described an alternative to the old paradigm of command from above. Journalists and pamphleteers such as John Trenchard and Thomas Gordon, the authors of *Cato's Letters*, and Thomas Paine applied those ideas to contemporary challenges. Statesmen and activists such as the Levellers, the American revolutionaries, and the abolitionists struggled for liberty and limited government.

Today's advocates of liberty build on that foundation. The ideas of liberty have been further developed in our time by myriad thinkers—George Orwell, Karl Popper, Isaiah Berlin, Alexander Solzhenitsyn, Hannah Arendt, Jorge Luis Borges, F. A. Hayek, Ludwig von Mises, Ayn Rand, Milton Friedman, Václav Havel, Robert Nozick, Thomas Sowell, and others. Millions of people around the world have been inspired by their vision. Millions more have recognized the failures of statism in the 20th century and supported candidates, movements, and policy proposals that would constrain the state and expand liberty.

Both the reality of the world—the failure of communism, the impending bankruptcy of social security systems, the prosperity brought about by markets—and the efforts of liberal and libertarian campaigners have brought about the changes that we see today. As the essays in this book demonstrate, the Cato Institute has played its own small part in that transition. We pioneered the idea of Social Security privatization (even while, unbeknownst to us, José Piñera was implementing a similar plan in Chile). We provided support for F. A. Hayek in his later years, during which he wrote *The Fatal Conceit* and lectured around the world. We challenged the Soviet empire by smuggling books into Russia and Poland. We held conferences on free markets and political liberty in Shanghai in 1988 and Moscow in 1990, quite possibly the first public events to address such ideas in either country's history. We demonstrated in scholarly articles that the Constitution grants only limited and defined powers to the federal government and distributed more than 2 million copies of the Constitution to Americans. We challenged the war on drugs in books and studies for more than a decade. We pointed out the costs and risks of America's interventionist foreign policy and made the case for an alternative policy better suited to a peaceful republic. We produced what Milton Friedman called "a steady stream of thought-provoking reports challenging big government and all of its works." And if we've become "Washington's hottest think tank," to quote the *Boston Globe*, perhaps it's simply because libertarian ideas are, as even antiliberal scholars Stephen Holmes and Cass Sunstein admit, "astonishingly widespread in American culture."

The essays in this volume indicate the breadth of our concerns over the past 25 years, though they are of course only a small fraction of the thousands of studies, books, journal articles, op-eds, and essays that Cato scholars have produced. In addition to our own staff, the other authors in this book convey a sense of the issues we've addressed: Karl Popper on the failure of communism, Peter Bauer on economic development, Helen Suzman on the end of apartheid, F. A. Hayek on money and information, Milton Friedman on markets in China, Mario Vargas Llosa on "neoliberalism," Carolyn Weaver and José Piñera on social security. It will be a challenge to do more and better in the next 25 years.

Often it's the opponents of political and economic liberalism who make the most noise. The street protests and violence of the anti-globalization activists from Seattle to Genoa may give the impression of a mass uprising against liberal capitalism. But that would be an error. The anti-globalizers are violent because they're frustrated, and they're frustrated because they're losing. Everywhere governments will allow it, people are choosing open markets and open societies—the free flow of information, commerce, trade, and investment and responsibility for their own lives.

But the triumph of liberalism is by no means inevitable. There never was a golden age of liberty, and there never will be. Although we do seem to have left behind some of the worst forms of government, we can't help but remember that during the past century we have endured communism, fascism, and national socialism. Armed with modern technology, those regimes proved to be the most brutal in history. And they arose at another time when liberal thinkers thought that prosperity and international trade would ensure peace and harmony.

Still, every generation should learn from those that have gone before. By now we should have learned that people can run their own lives better than distant bureaucrats can, that competition works better than monopoly and markets better than central planning, that the freedom to choose is about more than economics, that taxing enterprise makes no more sense than subsidizing irresponsibility, that war is sometimes necessary but always enormously destructive, that limited government is one of the greatest achievements of humanity because it makes possible so much else. If the world is learning those lessons, then the 21st century looks bright indeed.

PART I

IDEAS AND CONSEQUENCES

Interview with F. A. Hayek

Policy Report: What role can a public policy institute, like the Cato Institute, play to limit the size of government and increase individual freedom?

Hayek: Well, I can't speak about particular institutes, but the one institution of that sort which I have watched from the beginning and for the existence of which I am in some sense responsible is the Institute of Economic Affairs of London, which was created by Antony Fisher. He thought you could sway mass opinion. What I insisted and what was strictly followed by the Institute was not to appeal to the large numbers, but to the intellectuals. My conviction is that, in the long run, political opinion is determined by the intellectuals, by which I mean, as I once defined it, the second-hand dealers in ideas—the journalists, schoolmasters, and so on. In fact, socialism is very largely an affair of the intellectuals and not the working class.

So the Institute began publishing little brochures or pamphlets dealing with a few political issues on a level intelligible to the intelligent, but not technically educated, person. They are not writing for the economist, nor for the general public, but for the educated man, represented by schoolmasters and journalists and so on.

It has taken a long time to prove its success. And for a time I did wonder whether or not I was thinking correctly. I now think it has become the most powerful maker of opinion in England. By now, book shops usually have a special rack of Institute of Economic Affairs pamphlets. Even people on the left feel compelled to keep informed of the Institute's publications. And I think that if you are looking for a program here in the United States, you can do no better than to study the Institute's publications catalogue.

F. A. Hayek (1899–1992) was the 1974 Nobel laureate in economics and author of numerous books, including *The Road to Serfdom*. This interview was conducted by the staff of the Cato Institute on December 1, 1982, just before Hayek launched Cato's Distinguished Lecturer Series.

Cato Policy Report, February 1983

PR: Do you think monetarism has failed? And what would be wrong with enforcing a monetary rule that limited the growth of high-powered money?

Hayek: I don't know what monetarism is. If monetarism just means a good old-fashioned quantity theory, of course it has not failed. If it means the particular version of Milton Friedman, I think it has because he imagines that he can achieve—ascertain—a clear quantity relationship between a measurable quantity of money and the price level. I don't think that is possible. In fact, just about 40 years ago in the opening sentences of my book, *Prices and Production,* I wrote that it would be a great misfortune if people ever cease to believe in the quantity theory of money. It would be even worse ever to believe it literally. And that's exactly what Milton Friedman does. He imagines that it is possible to prescribe to the monetary authorities a definite rate at which "the" quantity of money must be allowed to increase. I must say that I don't know what "the" quantity of money in a measurable sense is. It has become so complex. There is a distinction between M1, M2, and so on. I don't think there is such a simple relationship.

When you mean by monetarism that you can instruct the monetary authorities—the Federal Reserve System—to adjust the quantity of money to keep the price level stable, I believe that is correct. But they have to find out by experimentation what they have to do to keep the price level stable. If you understand correctly what Milton Friedman believes, that you can tell them to increase some particular observable quantity by 3% a year, I think it is nonsense. I say this although Friedman is a great friend of mine, and I admire most of his views, but his quantitative approach to economics seems to me to involve a gross oversimplification of what things really are like.

PR: What steps would you recommend to return the United States to stable economic growth and prosperity?

Hayek: What I can say about the United States is exactly the same that I've been preaching in England since Mrs. Thatcher has been in power. It is politically possible to cause, by braking inflation, 20% unemployment for six months. It is not politically possible to create 10% unemployment for three years. If you do it quickly even a very high rate of unemployment can be tolerated. If you try to do it slowly and gently, you are bound to fail, because people in the long run will not put up with it. But they will accept it if it comes quickly.

I think every termination of inflation, which is without doubt the most important thing to do, has to be done much more quickly than it has been done in England. It wasn't Mrs. Thatcher's fault; she knew she couldn't get her cabinet to follow her view. She admits as much. In fact, I heard her say, "My one mistake was to go on much too slowly. I ought to have done it much more quickly."

I think the same thing is in a measure true of the United States. You have done much better. You have, since Reagan came into power, reduced inflation very considerably. But one thing I might add is that reducing inflation is of little use unless you bring it down to zero inflation. Anybody who argues that a little inflation is all right is completely wrong because inflation stimulates things only as it accelerates. If you rely on a little inflation, you are bound to increase it. You are driven into increasing inflation. So the aim must be not to reduce inflation, but as rapidly as possible to get back to a stable price level.

PR: One thing that some of the Reagan advisors have talked about is applying a cost/benefit test to regulations. Is it possible to measure costs and benefits and is cost/benefit analysis a sufficient program for deregulation?

Hayek: If you take "measure" literally, certainly not. But so far as you can estimate them roughly, they must be your guide. I think what you soon arrive at is that for practically all regulations the costs are greater than the benefits. It is simpler to argue against regulations as such than to pretend that you can single out those where clearly the costs are greater than the benefits. There is good sense behind the cost/benefit argument, but I don't think it's of great practical value.

PR: What reforms would you propose in our monetary system?

Hayek: Well, I have despaired of ever again finding a way of restraining government abuse of any money which it issues. My proposal to denationalize money was always in a sense utopian because governments will never freely allow competition in this business. I believe there are ways around this, and my present view—which I hope before long to state in detail—is that there is probably a possibility of not issuing currency but starting with credit accounts under some other name—say, call the unit a "stable" and promise to redeem it with enough of whatever current monies are required to buy a certain list of raw materials. So it doesn't involve issuing any circulating money, but it enables the holder to keep a stable unit in the form of a credit. Once you've succeeded in this, the next step would be issuing credit cards on these accounts. And then you have circumvented the whole monopoly of government.

Since it is politically impractical to deprive the government of its monopoly, you have to circumvent it.

PR: Other than monetary reform, what sort of limits or constraints do you think it is feasible to put on government in a Western democratic society?

Hayek: I think it requires a change in the constitutional arrangement. We have really to redo in a different manner what the world tried to do in the 18th century when they hoped that the principle of the separation of powers was *intended* as a restriction on democracy. It hasn't done so. I think we have to invent a new way.

PR: Professor Hayek, when did you realize the important incentive and information functions played by market prices?

Hayek: Well, it's a very curious story, in a way, that I was led to put the emphasis on prices as a signal of what to do. It was an essay I wrote in 1936 called "Economics and Knowledge." That was originally written to persuade my great friend and master, Ludwig von Mises, why I couldn't accept all of his teaching. The main topic of the essay was to show that while it was perfectly true that what I called the logic of choice—analysis of individual action—was, like all logic, an *a priori* subject, Mises' contention that all the analysis of the market was an *a priori* thing was *wrong*, because it depended on empirical knowledge. It depends on the problem of knowledge being conveyed from one person to another.

Now, curiously, Mises, who was so very resentful generally of critiques by his pupils, even praised my article, but he never seemed to recognize to what extent it meant a diversion from his own fundamental conception. And I never got him to admit what I really imagined to be the case, that I refuted his contention that the analysis of the market economy was an *a priori* function, that it was a fully empirical matter. What was *a priori* was a logic behind it—a logic of individual action—that when you pass from the action of one individual, there occurs a causal process of one person acting upon another and learning. And this could never be *a priori*. This must be empirical. And pursuing this thought is how it started. This led me to investigate how important the prices forming on the market were as guides to individual action. And it is since that date, since what originally was a criticism of my master, Mises, that I have developed this idea of the guide function of prices which I regard as more and more important, which I have applied in its effect on price fixing, on rent restriction, on capital investment.

All through, what it comes to is that we can achieve a condition of correspondence of separate effort only if we rely on prices as guides which tell people what to do.

I am personally convinced that the reason which led the intellectuals, particularly of the English-speaking world, to socialism was a man who is regarded as a great hero of classical liberalism, John Stuart Mill. In his famous textbook, *Principles of Political Economy*, which came out in 1848 and for some decades was a widely read text on the subject, he makes the following statement as he passes from the theory of production to the theory of distribution: "Once the product is there, mankind—socially or individually—can do with it whatever it pleases." Now, if that were true I would admit that it is a clear moral obligation to see that it is justly distributed. But it isn't true, because if we did do with that product whatever we pleased, it would never be there again. Because if you ever did it once, people would never produce those things again.

PR: Professor Hayek, we're hearing much today about the threat to world trade through new rounds of protectionism. What advice would you have to political leaders and also to the people of Western countries who might be concerned about new protectionist measures?

Hayek: Perhaps I am over-optimistic—but one thing has been understood, at least by the more responsible people, that nothing did more to intensify the depression of the 1930s than the return to protectionism. I have not yet found anybody who, once he was reminded of this fact, would still continue to believe that it might be necessary to reintroduce protection.

PR: In your recent interview with the *New York Times* you said, "Keynes was one of the most intelligent people I knew, but he understood very little economics." How do you account for his great influence in policy-making circles as well as in the academic community?

Hayek: Well, that is a very profound problem. He was in complete agreement with the philosophical movement which had invaded that generation, what I'd call intellectualist or constructivist ideas derived from many decades of French philosophers. These ideas taught: Don't believe anything which you cannot rationally justify. This was at first applied to science, but then was equally applied to morals. "Do not regard as binding upon you any morals which you cannot intellectually justify." Now that meant in the person of Keynes two things which he himself stated. He admitted publicly that he had always been an amoralist. And that involved the famous statement—in the long run we are all dead. Now the great merit of traditional morals is that they have evolved and developed by long-run effects which people never foresaw and understood. And the merits of the institution of private property and of saving are that in the long run those groups that adhered to them prospered.

Similarly, the function of the market system, the benefits of it, are effects beyond our vision—beyond our comprehension. Now, any philosopher who says, "I should admit only what I can rationally justify," must exclude effects which are not foreseeable, must refuse to acknowledge a moral code which has been evolved because of its de facto effect. The utilitarian theorists believed, and Mises strongly believed, that man had chosen his morals with an intelligent understanding of the good effects. But that is wrong. Most of the effects of the moral we can't foresee. They are beyond our vision.

The effect is that on the market especially we can serve people whom we do not know. We can profit from the services of people we do not know. In short, we can form an order of activities far exceeding our comprehension. The same is true in our action for the future. Our morals teach that saving is a good thing, because it will help future generations, but that is not a thing we know from experience. All we do know is that those social groups in which saving was a virtue have prospered, and they gradually displaced the others. We simply must realize that our traditional morals are not to be approved because we can show how they are beneficial to us, but only because they have been proved in a process of selection.

By selection I sometimes speak of the natural selection of religions: those religions which preached the right morals survived and enabled the group to multiply. It is not the intelligence of our ancestors that has left us with more efficient morals, but—as I like to express it to shock people—our ancestors were really the guinea pigs who experimented and chose the right ways which have been transmitted to us. It was not necessarily their superior intelligence.

Rather, they happened to be right, so their successes multiplied, and they displaced the others who believed in the different morals.

So the difference between Keynes and me is really based on different beliefs about the foundation of ethics. Keynes believed— asserted—"I am only prepared to believe in such rules the effects of which I can see." But, in fact, civilization has formed by man learning to conform to rules of action, the effects of which were far beyond his vision. I've just come up with a new formulation which I rather like, that the invention or the development of the market amounts to the invention of a new sense organ in effect, similar to the evolution of sight in addition to the sense of touch. The sense of touch gives information only about the immediate environment as far as we can feel. The formation of the sense of sight in the evolution of animals enables us to take account of a much wider environment, but one still visible to our senses. Now, the market has become a sort of, as the biologists call it, extrasomatic or external sense organ, which informs us of things of which we are not aware physically. We cannot see the benefits of our action. We cannot see where our benefits come from, but we have developed a mechanism that serves as an organ of information operating very similarly to the sense organs, but enabling us to adjust our action to events which are beyond our sensory perception.

PR: What flaws do you see in current free-market economic thinking?

Hayek: I have two defaults in my activities which I frequently regret. The one is that when Keynes, after I had devoted so much time to criticism of his *Treatise on Money*, thought out his general theory and told me no one believed in what I spent so much time to criticize, I did not return to the charge and never systematically attacked the *General Theory*.

And the second thing which I regret is that when Milton Friedman, who was a close colleague and friend, preached positivist economics, I did not attack his positivist economics. Positivist economics is really based on the same idea that we can form appropriate policy on the assumption of complete knowledge of all the relevant facts. In fact, the achievement of the market system is that we can do much better than we would do if we relied only on what we positively know. We can make use of this signaling system, as I call the market, which informs us of things which we cannot directly perceive or which are only transmitted to us—and that applies both spatially and temporally. We learn to adjust ourselves to the events which are beyond our vision spatially, which happen on other continents, and we learn to adjust ourselves to things which will happen in the distant future which we cannot see. The mathematical economists in particular talk of the "given" knowledge, the "given" data. Note how the use is placed to cause reduplication: "Given data" means "given" "givens." If they suspect that things are not really given to them, they reassure themselves by calling them "given data"; in fact the data are hypothetical assumptions. Nobody knows all of the data. They only become operative and enable us to form an appropriate order by this transmission system of the market, where through many relays and changes what happened somewhere in New Zealand still affects my action by affecting wool prices or land prices and guiding me in what to do.

So it's all a guide, as I put it before, an information system, something which, incidentally, Adam Smith said over 200 years ago. In many respects I find more wisdom in Adam Smith than in most of the later classical economics (not to speak of the famous mathematical economics) which is very beautiful and very true if you assume all of the data are known, but becomes nonsense when you remember that these data are not known to anybody.

PR: Do you think that positivism as a methodology, as a way of thinking, tends to incline economists toward believing that they can fine-tune and intervene in the economy to achieve predictable results?

Hayek: Yes, very much. I started as a positivist myself, in the Ernst Mach group in Vienna. I gradually changed—and in spite of Mises' argument against positivism, I would say that even Mises was still at heart a positivist who had not completely freed himself from its assumptions, which in a way really go back to René Descartes. The whole basic idea of positivism—that our knowledge is based on given observations of the external world—goes back to Descartes.

PR: Professor Hayek, just one last question. What should be the role of the economist as a policy advisor?

Hayek: You can either be an economist or a policy advisor. Now, just let me in conclusion tell you another story of which I have only become recently aware. You know I have moved about a great deal from country to country, but certainly it drew my attention that in each case I've cleared out as soon as I was threatened to be used for government purposes. In Austria, at the end of the '20s or beginning of the '30s, I was just for the first time called to sit on a government committee. Within six months I was out of the country.

In England I took a little longer. At the age of 19 years I had been for the first time used on a mission of the colonial office and six months later had left the country. In the United States, where I was for 12 years in Chicago, it never got quite as far because by the time I was asked to sit on a government committee I had already committed myself to leave the country. By moving around the world I have avoided that corruption which government service regularly involves.

And more sadly, I have seen in some of my closest friends and sympathizers—I won't mention any names—who completely agreed with me, how a few years in government corrupted them intellectually and made them unable to think straight.

I suppose you all know the famous story of the one-handed economist. An American chief of one of the big corporations advertised for a one-handed economist. His associates were very puzzled as to what he meant. He replied, "Oh, I want a person who doesn't say, 'on the one hand and on the other.'" And I'm afraid that all the people who have been in government service have become two-handed economists who think in terms of one hand and the other. If one has kept out of government service, one remains a one-handed economist who believes there is a clear way in which we ought to proceed, but one maintains this conviction only so long as one stays out of government. All my friends who have gone into it and stayed for any length of time have, in my sense, been corrupted.

Liberalism in the New Millennium

Mario Vargas Llosa

A short time ago, the town council of El Borge, a tiny town in the Spanish province of Málaga, held a plebiscite of its thousand inhabitants. The citizens were asked to decide between two alternatives: humanity or neoliberalism. The result of the poll was 515 votes for humanity and 4 votes for neoliberalism. Since that time, I have not been able to chase those four votes from my thoughts. In the face of such a dramatic dilemma, those four musketeers did not hesitate to charge against humanity in the name of the macabre scarecrow of neoliberalism. Were they four clowns or four sages? Was this a "Borgean" joke or was it the only sign of sense in the entire farcical plebiscite?

Not long after, in Chiapas, an International Congress against Neoliberalism was convened by Subcomandante Marcos, the latest hero of the frivolous, media-driven politics of the West. Among the attendees were numerous Hollywood luminaries, a belated Gaullist (my friend Regis Debray), and Danielle Mitterrand, the incessant widow of President François Mitterrand, who gave her socialist benediction to the event.

Those are quaint episodes, but it would be a grave error to write them off as the insignificant fluttering of human idiocy. In truth, they are but the tense and explosive extremes of a vast political and ideological movement, solidly rooted in sectors of the left, center, and right, and united in a tenacious distrust of liberty as an instrument for the solution to the problems of humanity. They have built up their fears into a new phantom and called it "neoliberalism." In the mumbo jumbo of sociologists and political scientists, it is also known as the "only thought," a scapegoat on which to hang both present calamities and those of the past in world history.

Brainy professors from the universities of Paris, Harvard, and Mex-

Mario Vargas Llosa is a novelist and former candidate for president of Peru.

Global Fortune: The Stumble and Rise of World Capitalism, ed. Ian Vásquez (Cato Institute, 2000). Translated by Tom Jenney.

ico pull their hair out trying to show that free markets serve for little more than making the rich richer and the poor poorer. They tell us that internationalization and globalization only benefit the giant multinationals, allowing them to squeeze developing countries to the point of asphyxiation and entirely devastate the planetary ecology. So it should not surprise us that the uninformed citizens of El Borge or Chiapas believe that the true enemy of mankind—guilty of all evil, suffering, poverty, exploitation, discrimination, abuses, and crimes against human rights committed on five continents against millions of human beings—is that terrifying, destructive entelechy known as neoliberalism. It is not the first time in history that what Karl Marx called a "fetish"—an artificial construction, but at the service of very concrete interests—acquired consistency and began to provoke such great disruptions in life, like the genie who was imprudently catapulted into existence when Aladdin rubbed the magic lamp.

I consider myself a liberal. I know many people who are liberals, and many more who are not. But, throughout a career that is beginning to be a long one, I have not known a single neoliberal. What does a neoliberal stand for? What is a neoliberal against? In contrast with Marxism, or the various kinds of fascism, true liberalism does not constitute a dogma, a closed and self-sufficient ideology with prefabricated responses to all social problems. Rather, liberalism is a doctrine that, beyond a relatively simple and clear combination of basic principles structured around a defense of political and economic liberty (that is, of democracy and the free market), welcomes a great variety of tendencies and hues. What it has not included until now, nor will include in the future, is that caricature furnished by its enemies with the nickname neoliberal.

A "neo" is someone who pretends to be something, someone who is at the same time inside and outside of something; it is an elusive hybrid, a straw man set up without ever identifying a specific value, idea, regime, or doctrine. To say "neoliberal" is the same as saying "semiliberal" or "pseudoliberal." It is pure nonsense. Either one is in favor of liberty or against it, but one cannot be semi-in-favor or pseudo-in-favor of liberty, just as one cannot be "semipregnant," "semiliving," or "semidead." The term has not been invented to express a conceptual reality, but rather, as a corrosive weapon of derision, it has been designed to semantically devalue the doctrine of liberalism. And, as we enter the new millennium, it is liberalism—more

27

than any other doctrine—that symbolizes the extraordinary advances that liberty has made in the long course of human civilization.

We should celebrate the achievements of liberalism with joy and serenity, but without triumphalist hubris. We must be clear in understanding that although the achievements of liberalism are notable, that which remains to be done is more important still. Moreover, as nothing in human history is fated or permanent, the progress obtained in these last decades by the culture of liberty is not irreversible. Unless we know how to defend it, the culture of liberty can become stagnant and the free world will lose ground to the forces of authoritarian collectivism and tribalism. Donning the new masks of nationalism and religious fanaticism, those forces have replaced communism as the most battle-hardened adversaries of democracy.

For a liberal, the most important thing to occur in this century was the defeat of the great totalitarian offensives against the culture of liberty. Fascism and communism, each in its moment, came to threaten the survival of democracy. Now they belong to the past, to the dark history of violence and unspeakable crimes against human rights and rationality, and there is no indication that they will rise from their ashes in the immediate future. Of course, reminiscences of fascism linger in the world. At times, ultra-nationalist and xenophobic parties, much like Jean Marie Le Pen's National Front in France or Jörg Haider's Liberal Party in Austria, attract a dangerously high level of electoral support. Also, there exist anachronistic vestiges of the vast Marxist archipelago, represented today by the flagging specters of Cuba and North Korea. Even so, those fascist and communist offshoots do not constitute a serious alternative—less still a considerable threat—to the democratic option.

Dictatorships still abound, true enough, but in contrast to the great totalitarian empires, they lack messianic aura and ecumenical pretensions; many of them, like China, are now trying to combine the monolithic politics of the single-party state with free-market economics and private enterprise. In vast regions of Africa and Asia, above all in Islamic societies, fundamentalist dictatorships have arisen that have returned those countries to a state of barbaric primitivism in matters concerning women, education, information, and basic civic and moral rights. Still, whatever the horror represented by countries like Libya, Afghanistan, Sudan, or Iran, they are not challenges that the culture of liberty needs to take seriously: the backwardness of the ideology they profess condemns those regimes to fall ever farther behind in the race of modernity—a swift race, in which the free countries have already taken a decisive lead.

Despite the gloomy geography of persistent dictatorships, liberals have much to celebrate in these last decades. The culture of liberty has made overwhelming advances in vast regions of Central and Western Europe, Southeast Asia, and Latin America. In Latin America, for the first time in history, civilian governments—born of more or less free elections—are in power in nearly every country. (The exceptions are Cuba, an explicit dictatorship, and Peru, a subtle dictatorship.) Even more notably, those democracies are now applying—sometimes with more gritting of teeth than enthusiasm, sometimes with more clumsiness than skill—market policies, or at least policies that are closer to a free economy than to the interventionist and nationalizing populism that traditionally characterized the governments of the continent.

Perhaps the most significant thing about that change in Latin America is not the quantity, but the quality. Although it is still common to hear intellectuals who have been thrown out of work by the collapse of collectivist ideology howling at neoliberalism, their howls are like those of wolves to the moon. From one end of Latin America to the other, at least for now, a solid consensus exists in favor of the democratic system and against dictatorial regimes and collectivist utopias. Although that consensus is more restricted with regard to economic policy, Latin American governments are also bowing to liberal economic doctrine. Some governments are embarrassed to confess that, and others—including some real Tartuffes—cover their bases by spewing out volleys of rhetoric against neoliberalism. Nevertheless, they have no other recourse than to privatize businesses, liberalize prices, open markets, attempt to control inflation, and try to integrate their economies into international markets. They have come to learn—the hard way—that in today's economic environment, the country that does not follow those guidelines commits suicide. Or, in less terrifying terms—that country condemns itself to poverty, decay, and even disintegration. Many sectors of the Latin American left have evolved from being bitter enemies of economic liberty to embracing the wise confession of Václav Havel: "Though my heart may be left of centre, I have always known that the only economic system that works is a market economy. . . . This is the only natural economy, the only kind that makes sense, the only one that can lead to prosperity, because it is the only one that reflects the nature of life itself."

Those signs of progress are important and give historical validity to liberal theses. By no means, however, do they justify complacency, since one of the most refined (and rare) certainties of liberalism is that historical determinism does not exist. History has not been written so as to negate any further appeal. History is the work of men, and just as men can act rightly with measures that push history in the direction of progress and civilization, they can also err, and by conviction, apathy, or cowardice, allow history to slide into anarchy, impoverishment, obscurantism, and barbarism. The culture of democracy can gain new ground and consolidate the advances it has achieved. Or, it can watch its dominions shrink into nothingness, like Balzac's *peau de chagrin*. The future depends on us—on our ideas, our votes, and the decisions of those we put into power.

For liberals, the war for the progress of liberty in history is, above all else, an intellectual struggle, a battle of ideas. The Allies won the war against the Axis, but that military victory did little more than confirm the superiority of a vision of man and society that is broad, horizontal, pluralist, tolerant, and democratic over a vision that was narrow-minded, truncated, racist, discriminatory, and vertical. The disintegration of the Soviet empire before the democratic West validated the arguments of Adam Smith, Alexis de Tocqueville, Karl Popper, and Isaiah Berlin concerning the open society and the free economy, and invalidated the fatal arrogance of ideologues like Karl Marx, V. I. Lenin, and Mao Zedong, who were convinced that they had unraveled the inflexible laws of history and interpreted them correctly with their proletarian dictatorships and economic centralism. We should also remember that the West achieved its victory over communism at a time when its societies were full of inferiority complexes: ordinary democracy offered scant "sex appeal" next to the fireworks of the supposedly classless societies of the communist world.

The present battle is perhaps less arduous for liberals than the one that our teachers fought. In that battle, central planners, police states, single-party regimes, and state-controlled economies had on their side an empire that was armed to the teeth, as well as a formidable public relations campaign, conducted in the heart of democracy by a fifth column of intellectuals seduced by socialist ideas. Today, the battle that we must join is not against great totalitarian thinkers, like Marx, or intelligent social democrats like John Maynard Keynes but, rather, against stereotypes and caricatures that attempt to introduce doubt and confusion in the democratic camp; hence the multiple offensive launched from various trenches against the monster nicknamed neoliberalism. The battle is also against the apocalyptics, a new species of skeptical thinker. Instead of opposing the culture of democracy, as did Georg Lukacs, Antonio Gramsci, or Jean-Paul Sartre, the apocalyptics are content to deny it, assuring us that democracy does not really exist and that we are dealing with a fiction, behind which lurks the ominous shadow of despotism.

Of that species, I would like to single out an emblematic case: that of Robert D. Kaplan. In a provocative essay, he maintains that, contrary to the optimistic expectations about the future of democracy heralded by the death of Marxism in Eastern Europe, humanity is actually headed toward a world dominated by authoritarianism. In some cases, this authoritarianism is undisguised; in others, it is masked by institutions of civil and liberal appearance. For Kaplan those institutions are mere decorations. The real power is—or will soon be—in the hands of giant international corporations, the owners of technology and capital that, thanks to their ubiquity and extraterritoriality, enjoy almost total impunity in their actions.

"I submit that the democracy we are encouraging in many poor parts of the world is an integral part of a transformation toward new forms of authoritarianism; that democracy in the United States is at greater risk than ever before, and from obscure sources; and that many future regimes, ours especially, could resemble the oligarchies of ancient Athens and Greece more than they do the current government in Washington."

His analysis is particularly negative with regard to the possibility that democracy may be able to find root in the developing world.

According to Kaplan, all Western efforts to impose democracy in countries that lack a democratic tradition have resulted in terrible failures. Some of those failures have been very costly, as in Cambodia, where $2 billion invested by the international community have not advanced legality or liberty even a single millimeter in the ancient kingdom of Angkor. The result of those efforts in places like Sudan, Algeria, Afghanistan, Bosnia, Sierra Leone, Congo, Mali, Russia, Albania, or Haiti has created chaos, civil wars, terrorism, and the resurgence of ferocious tyrannies that apply ethnic cleansing or commit genocide against religious minorities.

Kaplan looks with similar disdain upon the Latin American process of democratization. The exceptions are Chile and Peru. The fact that the first experienced the explicit dictatorship of Augusto Pinochet and the second is going through the oblique dictatorship of Alberto Fujimori and the armed forces guarantees, in his view, stability to those countries. By comparison, the so-called rule of law is incapable of preserving that stability in Colombia, Venezuela, Argentina, or Brazil where, in his judgment, the weakness of civil institutions, the excesses of corruption, and the astronomical inequalities are pushing "a backlash from millions of badly educated and newly urbanized dwellers in teeming slums, who see few palpable benefits to Western parliamentary systems."

Kaplan wastes no time in circumlocutions. He says what he thinks with clarity, and what he thinks is that democracy and the developing world are incompatible: "Social stability results from the establishment of a middle class. Not democracies but authoritarian systems, including monarchies, create middle classes." He cites the examples of the Asian Pacific Basin (his prime exponent is the Singapore of Lee Kuan Yew) and Pinochet's Chile. Although he does not mention it, he could have also cited Francisco Franco's Spain. The present-day authoritarian regimes he sees creating middle classes and making democracy possible are the China of "market socialism" and Fujimori's Peru (a military dictatorship with a civilian puppet as figurehead). Those are the models of development that he sees as forging "prosperity from abject poverty." For Kaplan the choice in the developing world is not "between dictators and democrats" but between "bad dictatorships and slightly better ones." In his opinion, "Russia may be failing in part because it is a democracy and China may be succeeding in part because it is not."

I have taken the space to review these arguments because Kaplan has the merit of saying out loud what others—many others—think but do not dare to say, or only say in whispers. Kaplan's pessimism with respect to the developing world is great; but it is not less than that inspired in him by the developed world. Once the efficient dictatorships have developed the poor countries and the new middle classes seek to gain access to Western-style democracy, they will only be chasing a mirage. Western democracy will have been supplanted by a system (similar to those of Athens and Sparta) in which oligarchies—the multinational corporations, operating on the five continents—will have snatched from governments the power to make significant decisions for society and the individual. The oligarchies will exercise that power without accountability, because power comes to the giant corporations not by electoral mandate but through their technological and economic strength. In case the reader is unaware of the statistics, Kaplan reminds us that out of the top 100 economies in the world, 51 are not countries, but businesses, and that the 500 most powerful companies alone represent 70 percent of world commerce.

Those arguments are a good point of departure for comparison with the liberal vision of the state of things in the world here on the cusp of the new millennium. In the liberal vision, the human creation of liberty, even with the abundant disorder it has caused, is the source of the most extraordinary advances in the fields of science, human rights, technical progress, and the fight against despotism and exploitation.

The most outlandish of Kaplan's arguments is that only dictatorships create middle classes and bring stability to countries. If that were so, the paradise of the middle classes would not be the United States, Western Europe, Canada, Australia, and New Zealand, but Mexico, Bolivia, or Paraguay. Latin American history is a veritable zoo of petty tyrants, strongmen, and maximum leaders. Juan Domingo Perón—to give but one example—nearly destroyed the middle class of Argentina—a middle class that until his rise to power was vast, prosperous, and had developed its country at a faster pace than most of the European countries. Forty years of dictatorship have not brought Cuba the least prosperity, but have reduced it to the status of an international beggar; to keep from starving, Cubans have been condemned to eat grass and flowers, while their women prostitute themselves to capitalist tourists.

Of course, Kaplan can say that he is not talking about all dictatorships, but only the efficient ones like those of Pacific Asia and those of Pinochet and Fujimori. I read his essay—coincidentally enough—just when the supposedly efficient autocracy of Indonesia was crumbling, General Suharto was renouncing his office under pressure, and the Indonesian economy was collapsing. Shortly before that, the ex-autocracies of Korea and Thailand had collapsed and the famous Asian Tigers had begun to vanish into smoke, like something out of a Hollywood super-thriller. Apparently, those market dictatorships were not as successful as Kaplan thought. They are now gathered on their knees before the International Monetary Fund, the World Bank, the United States, Japan, and Western Europe, asking to be saved from total ruin.

From the economic point of view, the dictatorship of General Pinochet was successful, and up to a certain point (that is, if efficiency is measured only in terms of the rate of inflation, the fiscal deficit, official reserves, and the growth rate of gross domestic product), so is Fujimori's dictatorship. Even so, we are talking about a very relative efficiency. When we leave the comfortable security of an open society (the United States, in Kaplan's case) and examine those regimes from the perspective of those who have suffered the crimes and outrages of dictatorship, that relative efficiency vanishes. In contrast with Kaplan, we liberals do not believe that ending economic populism—or snapping the neck of inflation—constitutes the slightest progress for a society if, at the same time that prices are freed, public spending is cut, and the public sector is privatized, a government causes its citizens to live in abject fear. Progress does not run roughshod over the rights of citizens. Progress does not deprive citizens of a free press or deny them recourse to an independent judiciary when they are abused or defrauded. Progress does not permit that citizens be tortured, expropriated, disappeared, or killed, according to the whim of a country's ruling gang. Under liberal doctrine, progress is simultaneously economic, political, and cultural. Or, simply, it is not progress. That is for practical as well as moral reasons. Open societies, in which information circulates without impediment and in which the rule of law governs, are better defended against crises than satraps. That was demonstrated by the Mexican PRI (Institutional Revolutionary Party) regime several years ago and more recently by General Suharto in Indonesia. The role performed by the lack of genuine legality in the authoritarian countries of the Pacific Basin has not been sufficiently underlined in the current crisis.

How many efficient dictatorships have there been? And how many inefficient ones? How many dictatorships have sunk their countries into prerational savagery, as is happening today in Algeria and Afghanistan? The great majority of dictatorships are of the inefficient variety; efficient ones are the exception. Is it not reckless to opt for the recipe of dictatorship to achieve development—to hope that such a regime will be efficient, decent, and transitory—and not the contrary? Are there not less risky and cruel paths to economic progress? Indeed, there are, but people like Kaplan do not wish to see them.

In countries in which democracy flourishes, the culture of liberty is not necessarily a longstanding tradition. It was not a tradition in any of the current democracies until, after many setbacks and trials, those societies chose that culture and moved forward, perfecting it along the way, until they made that culture their own. International pressure and aid can be a factor of the first order in a society's adoption of democratic culture, as demonstrated by the examples of Germany and Japan, two countries as lacking in democratic tradition as any in Latin America. In the short time since the end of World War II, they have joined the advanced democracies of the world. Why, then, would developing countries (or Russia) be unable to free themselves from the authoritarian tradition? Why would they be unable to do as the Japanese and Germans did, and make the culture of liberty theirs?

Contrary to the pessimistic conclusions that Kaplan reaches, globalization opens up a first-class opportunity for the democratic countries of the world—and especially for the advanced democracies of America and Europe—to contribute to expanding tolerance, pluralism, legality, and liberty. Many countries are still slaves to the authoritarian tradition, but we should remember that authoritarianism once held sway over all of humanity. The expansion of the culture of liberty is possible as long as the following occur:

(a) We have a clear belief in the superiority of this culture over those that legitimize fanaticism, intolerance, and racism, and that legitimize religious, ethnic, political, or sexual discrimination.

(b) We adopt coherent economic and foreign policies, orienting them in such a way that at the same time as they encourage democratic tendencies in the developing world, they penalize and discriminate automatically against those regimes that, like China's or the civilian-military crony-state of Peru's, promote liberal policies in the economic field but are dictatorial in their politics.

Unfortunately, contrary to Kaplan's position, the kind of discrimination in favor of democracy that brought so many benefits to countries like Germany, Italy, and Japan a half century ago has not been applied by the democratic countries of today to the rest of the world. When it has been applied, it has been done in a partial and hypocritical manner, as in the case of Cuba.

With the advent of the new millennium, however, the advanced democracies of the world have a stronger incentive to act with firm and principled conviction in favor of democracy. That incentive comes from the existence of a new danger, a danger that Kaplan mentions in his essay. In apocalyptic terms, Kaplan prophesies the emergence of a future nondemocratic world government composed of powerful multinational corporations that operate without restraint in all corners of the globe. That catastrophic vision points to the real danger of which we are conscious. The disappearance of economic borders and the proliferation of world markets stimulate fusion and alliance between businesses as they attempt to compete more effectively in all areas of production.

The formation of giant corporations does not constitute in and of itself a danger to democracy as long as democracy is a reality, that is to say, as long as there are just laws and strong governments. (For a liberal, "strong" means "small and effective," rather than "big.") In a market economy that is open to competition, a big corporation benefits the consumer because its scale enables it to reduce prices and multiply services. It is not in the size of a business in which danger lies; the danger lies in monopoly, which is always a source of inefficiency and corruption. As long as there are democratic governments that command respect for the law—governments that will even prosecute Bill Gates if he transgresses that law—there is no danger. As long as democratic governments maintain markets that are open to competition and are free of monopolies, then there is nothing to fear from giant corporations, which frequently serve society by spearheading scientific and technological progress.

The capitalist firm has the nature of a chameleon. In a democratic country, it is a beneficent institution of development and progress. However, in countries in which there is no rule of law, no free markets, and in which everything is resolved by the absolute will of a leader or a ruling clique, the capitalist firm can be a source of catastrophe. Corporations are amoral, and they adapt with ease to the rules of the game in the environment in which they operate. If in many developing countries the behavior of multinationals is reprehensible, the ultimate responsibility rests on those who fix the rules of the game in economic, social, and political life. We cannot blame firms for following those rules in their quest for profits.

From that reality, Kaplan extracts this pessimistic conclusion: the future of democracy is gloomy because in the coming millennium the giant corporations will act in the United States and Western Europe with the same impunity that they currently do in, say, the Nigeria of the late Colonel Abacha.

In truth, there is no historical or conceptual reason for such an extrapolation. Instead, we should reach the following conclusion: it is imperative that all countries today under dictatorship evolve quickly toward democracy and develop the kind of free legal order that can demand of corporations that they act decently and equitably, as they are required to do in the advanced democracies. Without the globalization of legality and liberty, economic globalization presents a serious danger for the future of civilization—and, above all, for the planetary ecology. The great powers have a moral obligation to promote democratic processes in the developing world. They also have a practical obligation. With the evaporation of borders, the greatest guarantee that economic forces will benefit all people is to ensure that throughout the world economic life flows within the limits of liberty and competition, and is guided by the incentives, rights, and restraints imposed by democratic society.

None of that will be easy, and none of it will be achieved in a short time. For liberals, however, it is a great incentive to know that we are working toward an attainable goal. The idea of a world united around a culture of liberty is not a utopia but a beautiful and achievable reality that justifies our efforts. As Karl Popper, one of our greatest teachers, said,

"Optimism is a duty. The future is open. It is not predetermined. No one can predict it, except by chance. We all contribute to determining it by what we do. We are all equally responsible for its success."

Disregard of Reality

Peter Bauer

According to Hegel, the Owl of Minerva spreads its wings only at dusk. The later stages of one's career should be propitious for discerning tendencies and forces at work in society. Earlier preoccupations with specific studies can be helpful for subsequent reflection on wider issues but meanwhile absorb time and attention.

High Hopes and Emerging Doubts

Like many of my contemporaries, fellow undergraduates and young academics alike, in my early days I expected much from economics, both in public policy and in intellectual interest. The great advances in the subject and the high intelligence of my academic colleagues seemed to confirm these hopes. Nevertheless, from about the early 1950s increasing claims for economics by its practitioners ran parallel with my own increasing doubts and reservations.

I came to realize for instance that economists systematically exaggerate the impact of their ideas. In an oft-quoted passage in *The General Theory,* Keynes insisted that in the long run the world is governed by little else than the ideas of economists and political philosophers. If this were true, the world would have enjoyed the benefits of free trade for at least one hundred years. Apart from being obviously unsustainable, Keynes's opinion is also naively parochial in attributing exclusive influence to the ideas of economists and political philosophers. He neglects the impact of the

Peter Bauer is Emeritus Professor of Economics at the London School of Economics and Political Science and a fellow of the British Academy. This article is a slightly amended version of comments he made at a regional meeting of the Mont Pèlerin Society in Prague, November 1991, on papers provided by Václav Klaus and Michael Novak.

Cato Journal, Vol. 7, No. 1 (Spring–Summer 1987)

founders and leaders of religious movements, including the Buddha, Christ, Mohammed, and of military commanders such as Alexander the Great, Julius Caesar, and Napoleon.

The ideas of economists do affect the wider scene; like other ideas they have consequences. As Milton Friedman has reminded us, economists can suggest possible options to politicians. But we must not delude ourselves by overstating our influence, whether in the short period or over the longer run.

Well before my retirement I came to be increasingly perplexed by what was going on in economics. I observed, in particular, a widespread disregard of evident reality, in which I include neglect of basic propositions of the subject. Impressive advances coexisted with alarming retrogression.

Unexpected Transgressions

It was in the 1950s that I first noticed the disregard of reality in economics. It was notable in two contexts: the dollar problem and the vicious circle of poverty.

For well over a decade in the 1940s and 1950s economists wrote about an indefinitely persistent and inescapable worldwide shortage of dollars. Some of these contributions and predictions were ostensibly sophisticated. In fact, they systematically ignored the rate of exchange, that is, the price of the dollar, as well as major determinants of this price such as interest rates and financial policy. This neglect of basics soon met the fate it deserved. In the later 1950s the shortage of dollars vanished and, indeed, was replaced by a glut. Many leading economists, and not just some amateurs and novices, had overlooked that supply of and demand for dollars depend on price. This particular discussion subsided with the end of the dollar shortage. But its method of approach soon resurfaced in the idea, which is still with us, that poor countries face inescapable balance of payments difficulties.

The theory of the indefinite dollar shortage was not an example of tentative steps in the construction of exciting, and potentially fruitful, theorems or analytical instruments. Nor did the ostensibly elaborate analyses hinge on novel assumptions about expectations or dynamic processes. Rather, the episode was nothing but a serious transgression.

I now come to the vicious circle of poverty. According to this notion, stagnation and poverty are necessarily self-perpetuating: poor people generally and poor countries or societies in particular are trapped in their poverty and cannot generate sufficient savings to escape from the trap. This notion became a cornerstone of mainstream development economics. It was the signature tune of the advocates of foreign aid throughout the 1950s. Yet it is in obvious conflict with simple reality. Throughout history innumerable individuals, families, groups, societies, and countries—both in the West and the Third World—have moved from poverty to prosperity without external donations. All developed countries began as underdeveloped. If the notion of the vicious circle were valid, mankind would still be in the Stone Age at best.

These episodes also alerted me to the role of intellectual and political fashion in much of economics. Prominent, distinguished practitioners seem often to find it difficult to resist the vagaries and winds of fashion, even when these are ephemeral or blow them off course.

I have recently reread part of the literature of these two subjects with a mixture of incredulity, embarrassment, and amusement. It looked as if the queen of the social sciences was being dethroned by her entourage.

The two examples I have taken represent unequivocal examples of intellectual retrogression made possible by the disregard of reality. In the interwar years the role of the rate of exchange in the supply of and demand for currencies was routinely recognized. And before World War II, no one would have suggested that poor societies or countries were doomed to stagnation. Historians, anthropologists, administrators, and economists then discussed in detail the impact and implications of rapid changes in less developed countries (LDCs).

Alongside these instances of evident retrogression there took place major advances in economics, including advances in international trade theory and the theory of foreign exchanges, both closely related to the lapses.

There were dissenters from the most widely articulated opinion. This was particularly so in the case of the dollar problem, but applied also to the vicious circle. Some of the dissenters had high academic credentials, yet their views did not have much impact in academic circles and did not reach a wider public. This was because on the contemporary scene, also in academe, a voice is rarely effective without an echo. Dissenters find this difficult to secure unless their dissent is modish. The exponents of the dollar problem and the vicious circle of poverty, especially the latter, were supported and encouraged by articulate groups in the academies and the media. Dissent was crowded out.

These two episodes first prepared me to question received opinion, even when endorsed by the great and the good. Since the 1950s there has been an overdose of examples where reality is simply ignored or brushed aside.

Let me take a further example. Since World War II, many academics (as well as clerics, public figures, politicians, and spokesmen of the official international organizations) have argued that commercial contacts between the West and LDCs inflict economic damage on the peoples of the Third World. Sometimes it is said that Third World poverty is the result of Western neglect; but more often it is claimed that poverty results from Western oppression, exploitation, and manipulation of international trade. These widely canvassed opinions are not confined to Marxist-Leninists. (One should really say Leninists, since Marx was at times lyrical about the achievements of capitalism in transforming backward societies.) Yet as is abundantly evident throughout the Third World, the poorest and most backward societies and areas are those which have fewest commercial contacts with the West, and the most advanced are those with the most extensive and diversified contacts, including contacts with those bogeymen, the Western multinationals. Throughout the Third World the level of economic attainment declines as one moves away from regions with most Western contacts, to the aborigines and pygmies at the other end of the spectrum.

Those interested in the survival of ideas may like to know that the notions of the vicious circle of poverty and of the malign economic effects of commercial contacts with the West are alive and well.

Advances in Economics

Over the period in which I have been active in academic economics I have seen remarkable advances and also, as I have just noted, lapses which amount to blatant retrogression.

Advances in knowledge are what is expected from an academic discipline, especially when it has enjoyed a large expansion of resources and of opportunities. Even a necessarily incomplete list of significant advances must include various contributions to price theory, including the recognition of transaction costs; to the role and nature of the firm, including the economics of vertical integration; to the concept and implications of social cost; to the theory of interna-

41

tional trade and the theory of the foreign exchanges; to the analysis of the diffusion and use of knowledge; to the economics of property rights; and to the economics of political and bureaucratic processes. Some of these advances have been helpful far outside economics and have been useful to historians, anthropologists, political scientists, and demographers.

Such advances go a long way to support the sanguine expectations of my early days. So do the intellectual capacity and technical competence of so many practitioners. My academic colleagues in recent years have been no less bright and competent than were most of my teachers a generation ago. If I am now perplexed, it is because I have encountered a plethora of instances of retrogression stemming from the disregard of reality.

The retrogressions are of a quite different order from what went on in economics in the past. The writings of nineteenth-century and early twentieth-century economists were often unsophisticated, even naive. But they were not in such evident conflict with reality as is so much of the more recent literature.

The Emperor Inverted

Mathematization of the subject has perhaps been the most conspicuous thread running through economics since I first entered it. In the 1930s one could read the journals without much knowledge of mathematics, with the exception only of *Econometrica* and the *Review of Economic Studies*. Today one is regarded as unqualified without some knowledge of mathematics, and especially of its language. As economics deals very largely with functional relationships and dynamic processes, some understanding of mathematics is undoubtedly valuable in many contexts ranging from the proper understanding of the concept of elasticity to the appreciation of feedback effects. And it is often convenient to express in mathematical form inferences and conclusions derived from reasoning and empirical evidence. The appropriate procedure is, however, to reason to mathematics, rather than from mathematics. But as highly qualified practitioners have argued, mathematical methods and formulations have run riot in economics without proper appreciation of their limitations. The major limitations have been pointed out by outstanding scholars with technical mathematical credentials, including Marshall, Pigou, Keynes, Leontief, Stigler, and their observations have often been pointed, specific, and pertinent. Those of Norbert Wiener, one of the great figures of modern mathematics, were particularly vigorous. In one of my books I have referred at some length to his *God and Golem, Inc.,* published posthumously in 1964. Yet these critical observations have made little impact. Reading the journals one gets the impression that economics has become little more than a branch of applied mathematics and one that can be successfully pursued with little reference to real-life phenomena.

Another conspicuous development in economics since I first studied the subject has been the use of econometric methods. Much useful work has been done with these methods. But far better qualified people than myself have demonstrated their frequent abuse and the misapplication or misinterpretation of their results.

Here I want to draw attention only to some of the ways in which mathematical economics and the use of econometrics have contributed to the disregard or neglect of evident reality. Their use has led to unwarranted concentration in economics on variables tractable to formal analysis. As a corollary, it has led to the neglect of influences which, even when highly pertinent, are not amenable to such treatment. Similarly, it has encouraged confusion between the significant, on the one hand, and the quantifiable (often only spuriously quantifiable), on the other. It has contributed to the neglect of background conditions and historical processes where they are indispensable for understanding. For instance, differences in income and wealth, both domestic and international, cannot be considered helpfully without attention to their antecedents and background.

Belief in the well-nigh universal applicability of testing by econometric methods has led to inappropriate claims for these methods. It has also smothered other forms of reasoning and inference. What has become of the traditional method of direct observation, reflection, tracing of connections, reaching tentative conclusions, and referring these back to observation and to established propositions of the discipline, or to findings of cognate disciplines? Such procedures are no less informative than quantitative analysis. For instance, with the traditional approaches the economist was much more likely to be aware of the gap between theoretical concepts and the available information.

The acceptance of quantitative methods as the most respectable procedure has permitted the burgeoning of incompetent or inappropriate econometric studies, including those based on seriously flawed data. Conversely, studies based on direct observation or detailed examination of slices of history are apt to be dismissed as anecdotal, unscholarly, or unscientific, even if they are informative. All too often their findings are dismissed as no more than casual empiricism or expressions of opinion. Moreover, in what passes for high-level discourse, insistence on the obvious can be made to sound trivial and therefore not worth saying. In short, preoccupation with mathematical and quantitative methods has brought with it a regrettable atrophy of close observation and simple reflection.

I have just asked the rhetorical question of what has happened in economics to the traditional sequence of observation, reflection, inference, tentative conclusion, and reference to established propositions, and to findings of other fields of study. Being rhetorical, the question can be answered readily. This type of reasoning and its vocabulary have contracted greatly throughout the subject and have virtually disappeared in large parts of it. And the traditional method has retreated not because it has been proved less informative than the methods that have replaced it. It has retreated because it has been castigated as being less rigorous than its more modish successors, largely because it less resembles the procedures of the natural sciences, especially those of physics.

I think that in the course of this shift of approach pertinent differences between the study of nature, especially physics, and economics have not been sufficiently recognized. Some differences may be only of degree, others are sufficiently pronounced to be more nearly differences in kind.

Natural scientists seek to establish uniformities about phenomena and relationships which are substantially invariant. Some of the phenomena and relationships studied by economists are also largely invariant. Others are not so constant, or at any rate their constant components are embedded in so many others that it is often difficult to discern the presence and extent of uniformities. Again, concepts and distinctions widely used by economists—or even regarded as basic—are imprecise, arbitrary, and shifting, and their real-life equivalents difficult to pin down: primary, secondary, and tertiary activity, or manufacturing and service activity; voluntary and involuntary unemployment; developed and underdeveloped countries; final and intermediate goods (a distinction that is critical for the definition of income); and many others. This extensive fuzziness of concepts and categories in economics limits informative use of mathematical methods: in mathematics the concepts and relationships, although completely abstract, are more precise and consistent.

For these various reasons, the methods for discerning uniformities, and their extent and limitations, differ considerably between the natural sciences, on the one hand—especially those like physics and chemistry that have been most successfully mathematicized—and social study, including economics on the other hand. Some parts of economics, most obviously development economics, deal with events and sequences the informative study of which needs to incorporate practices from historical scholarship, such as reliance on primary sources, close observation, sustained reflection, the tracing of connections, and others.

These remarks on the differences between the study of nature and the study of society are not intended in the least to endorse the view that in economics, or social study generally, objective reasoning is impossible, which is another matter altogether. As I have written on this issue in a number of publications, I shall not develop it here and simply say that objective reasoning is quite as possible in economics as in the natural sciences.

Mathematical methods often provide an effective facade or screen which covers or conceals empty formalism. They can camouflage disregard of basic propositions or simple evidence in models purporting to serve as basis for policy. Statistics, technical jargon, and sophisticated econometric techniques can also serve as a protective screen. But the use of mathematics is particularly effective because of the language barrier it provides. What we see is an inversion of the familiar Hans Andersen story of the Emperor's New Clothes. Here there *are* new clothes, and at times they are *haute couture.* But all too often there is no emperor within.

The achievements of mathematical economics and of econometric techniques have been secured at a great price. This price is not reflected adequately in the direct resource costs. In the book to which I have referred, Wiener insisted that the adoption of mathematical formulation and econometric methods involves misconceived imitation of the natural sciences; and also that it has enabled economists to remove both themselves and their public from the perception of reality.

The Wider Scene

It is not surprising that indifference to reality is not confined to economics, but is extensive on the wider scene also. This divorce from reality is particularly baffling in view of well-nigh universal literacy in the West and the advances in the transmission of information. It is baffling also in view of the profound advances in science and technology. These latter subjects depend on reasoning which, although necessarily abstract, cannot fly in the face of reality.

Disregard of reality encompasses the refusal to accept the plain evidence of one's senses, neglect of simple connected reasoning, and the inability to recognize simple inconsistencies. What is behind all this?

Attempts to explain people's opinions always involve conjecture. Arguments can be assessed conclusively on the basis of logic or evidence. But why people accept or canvass them cannot be determined so confidently. In certain contexts some dominant influences are discernible. Many influences themselves represent a disregard of reality and also promote it; as in so many social situations, the process and the outcome are intertwined, even inseparable.

There are some who argue that there is nothing perplexing about conduct and opinions in evident conflict with reality, since they reflect no more than the promotion of self-interest. In this scheme of things apparently paradoxical and anomalous ideas and modes of conduct emerge from the operation of special interest groups or coalitions, including politicians, public servants, academics, and sections of the electorate. This factor can be significant.

Yet the operation of special interest groups cannot account for some conspicuous anomalies. Thus it can explain neither the hostility to the West in major international organizations nor the supine conduct of the West in them. Some of these organizations existed in embryonic form before World War II: the League of Nations in Geneva and the International Institute of Agriculture in Rome were precursors of today's UN and FAO. But their stances differed radically from what goes on there now. Moreover, the West supports lavishly and treats with deference African rulers who consistently vilify it. Such a stance by the West would have been unthinkable in the 1930s. These rulers have no votes in the West, nor do they advertise much in the media.

Amputation of the Time Perspective

Confusion between advancement of knowledge and promotion of policy undoubtedly contributes to indifference to reality. This influence is certainly important in economics. That this is so is suggested by the profusion of transgressions against reality in those parts of the subject close to policy, such as development economics, the economics of Soviet-type planning, labor economics, the economics of poverty, and the economics of market failure. Some practitioners acknowledge the pursuit of political objectives; they also urge that in any event in social study objective reasoning is impossible. I may mention an experience of mine. On several occasions when my lectures criticized the notion of the vicious circle of poverty, members of the audience said that, whatever the validity of my criticisms, the notion was invaluable in the advocacy of foreign aid.

Much contemporary discourse is also afflicted by ignorance of the past and neglect of the time dimension in cultural and social phenomena. Sir Ernst Gombrich has termed this phenomenon the amputation of the time dimension from our culture. It has vitiated discourse in much of contemporary economics including, for example, mainstream development economics and the discussion of domestic and international income differences. In these and other parts of economics we cannot understand the situation we observe unless we know how it has arisen. For instance, the low income compared with the West in many LDCs with substantial exports of cash crops has often been adduced to support the contention that external contacts and the production of cash crops are not effective for economic progress, or indeed inhibit it. In fact, many cash-crop exporting countries have progressed very rapidly over the last century or less. But how can we expect societies, which in the late nineteenth century were still extremely backward, or even barbarous, to reach, within a few decades, the level of societies with many centuries, or even millennia, of economic development behind them? Another example is provided by changes in the distribution of income within a country. A higher degree of inequality may result, say, from a greater reduction in mortality among the poor (which would represent an improvement in their condition) or from the imposition of a regressive tax regime.

The factors behind the debilitating lack of the time perspective and neglect of evidently pertinent background include the speed of social and technical change and the multiplicity of messages reaching people, often about distant events. Very rapid and discontinuous social and technical change can unnerve and even unhinge people. There is only so much change that people can absorb as individuals, families, or societies. By disrupting sustained observation, these influences inhibit both connected thinking and the poise provided by background and time perspective.

Again, any inclination to equate the methods of natural science with those of the social sciences conduces to the downgrading or neglect of antecedents and processes. Whilst antecedents and processes are largely irrelevant in chemistry and physics, and wholly irrelevant in mathematics, they are critical for the understanding of social phenomena. The signal achievements of natural sciences and the pervasive results of their applications encourage habits of thought in social sciences based on misleading analogies between the two realms of study.

Whatever the factors behind them—and the list proposed here is both tentative and incomplete—lack of knowledge of the past and neglect of the time perspective are evident in much contemporary discourse. The resulting loss of collective memory has also opened the way for the manipulation and rewriting of history.

Collective Guilt

The widespread or at any rate widely articulated feeling of guilt in the West is a significant influence behind some of the novel and baffling manifestations of the contemporary disregard of reality or even its denial. It helps to explain such matters as the acceptance of unfounded notions about Western responsibility for Third World backwardness and of the allegedly damaging effects of commercial contacts between the West and LDCs; the spineless conduct of the West toward African despots with negligible external power and resources, and the readiness of the West to support them in spite of their hostility to the West and in the face sometimes of inhuman domestic policies; and also the readiness of the West to finance international organizations that serve as forums for the embarrassment and undermining of the West. The guilt feeling in the West is reflected, for example, in the hostility toward South Africa. Whatever one may think of the conduct of the rulers there, they certainly treat their subjects no more harshly than various black rulers. As is well known, many people from black Africa are anxious to migrate to South Africa. The rulers of South Africa are singled out for special obloquy because they are white. Were they any color other than white, their conduct would arouse little or no comment in the West.

Again, the readiness to give aid to Asian and African rulers without questioning their policies reflects the same influence. Guilt-ridden people hope to assuage their feelings simply by giving away money (especially taxpayers' money) without questioning the results: what matters is to give away money, not what results from this process.

Although some elements of guilt feeling are part of the Judaeo-Christian tradition, guilt today is novel. Materially, the West has never had it so good, nor ever felt so bad about it. One reason for this is probably the failure of material prosperity to bring about the contentment and happiness so widely expected from it. Guilt has contributed to the confusion between the merits of charity in helping the less fortunate and the notion that income differences as such are reprehensible results of oppression and exploitation. These differences are commonly referred to as inequalities or even as inequities. The confusion has been encouraged by an eagerness of churchmen to see themselves not as spiritual leaders but as social welfare workers or political activists.

Moreover, many influential opinion formers, including teachers, clerics, and people in the media, have come to dislike Western society, or even to hate it. They are apt both to harbor and to provoke feelings of guilt.

A major factor behind the emergence of contemporary collective guilt has been presumably the erosion of personal responsibility under the impact of social determinism. Participation in collective guilt has taken the place of individual responsibility. External forces are held responsible for personal misconduct and personal misfortune. And if we are all guilty, then no individual is.

Guilt feeling in Western societies has promoted indifference to reality, a loss of poise, and a loss of confidence. Loss of continuity and the amputation of the time perspective reinforce these effects of collective guilt. Kenneth Clark wrote that he was not sure what were all the necessary ingredients for civilization but he was sure that confidence and continuity were indispensable. Both have been seriously eroded in recent decades.

Misuse of Language

In recent decades many thoughtful people have commented on the misuse of language, both in public discourse and in education. Disregard of reality promotes erosion of language, which promotes further disregard of reality. Language is to a culture or a society what money is to an economy; their erosion leads to a disintegration. Misuse of language covers the shifting interpretation of concepts such as socialism, equality, growth, monopoly, and many others. At times misuse of language is even acknowledged. If a country is officially designated as democratic or as a people's republic, we know that it is one in which people have no say in the government. Another category of examples is the treatment of countries and other collectivities as if they were single decision-making entities, or entities within which all the people have identical interests, experiences, and conditions. The aggregation of two-thirds of mankind as the Third World is a conspicuous example.

The growth of specialization, including long periods of specialized training, inhibits the exercise of critical faculty outside a narrow range and engenders disregard of reality in much academic and public discourse. This disregard is also facilitated by an understandable and rational reluctance of people to exercise their critical faculties in matters which affect them but about which they feel they can do little or nothing.

The vast expansion of information in recent decades may have been critical in the widespread atrophy of reflection. People, including academics, are expected to absorb so much information and technique that all too often they have little time, inclination, and capacity left for reflection and observation, even for simple assessment of the information reaching them.

The decline of traditional religious belief may also have conduced to a disregard of reality. This explanation could be appealing both to believers and to skeptics. Traditional religious belief provides a unified, coherent world view, the erosion of which enfeebles connected thinking. Conversely, it can be argued that the decline of religious belief diffuses the credulity of mankind over wide and more diverse areas. The speed of the decline reinforces such effects.

In this section and its three predecessors I have suggested some of the forces and influences behind the contemporary disregard of reality. I must remind the reader, however, that such suggestions are necessarily somewhat speculative. This is especially true of reflections on the varied and complex forces behind the Zeitgeist.

Need to Restate the Obvious

What has happened to us in the West for us to be so ready to fly in the face of reality and to reject the evidence of our senses? What makes us lose our poise and self-respect? It is as if amidst unprecedented prosperity and scientific achievement, inexplicable malevolent forces had undermined our mental and moral faculties.

The extensive and baffling indifference to reality matters greatly. Among other results, it has undermined standards in parts of economics, in other social studies, and in wider areas of ostensibly serious discourse. It is reversion to barbarism. Ortega y Gasset wrote that the absence of standards is the essence of barbarism. It is because this condition prevails in parts of economics alongside its great achievements of recent decades that I am now so baffled by the present state of the subject.

The tendency to disregard simple realities has undermined the poise, self-assurance, and stance of the West in the international arena. It has also underpinned the uncritical acceptance of ideas and policies damaging to the West, and much more so to the peoples of the Third World. This is not surprising. Polities and societies bent on disregarding reality must be vulnerable to adversity and also to threats from within and without.

Such concerns highlight the perceptiveness of two observations by authors widely separated in time and very different in general outlook. Their observations make a fitting conclusion to this essay. Pascal wrote in the seventeenth century: "Let us labour at trying to think clearly: herein lies the source of moral conduct" [Travaillons donc à penser bien: voilà le principe de la morale]. And in our own time George Orwell wrote: "We have sunk to such a depth that the restatement of the obvious has become the first duty of intelligent men."

PART II

ECONOMIC GROWTH

The Real Free Lunch: Markets and Private Property

Milton Friedman

I am delighted to be here on the occasion of the opening of the Cato headquarters. It is a beautiful building and a real tribute to the intellectual influence of Ed Crane and his associates.

I have sometimes been associated with the aphorism "There's no such thing as a free lunch," which I did not invent. I wish more attention were paid to one that I did invent, and that I think is particularly appropriate in this city, "Nobody spends somebody else's money as carefully as he spends his own." But all aphorisms are half-truths. One of our favorite family pursuits on long drives is to try to find the opposites of aphorisms. For example, "History never repeats itself," but "There's nothing new under the sun." Or "Look before you leap," but "He who hesitates is lost." The opposite of "There's no such thing as a free lunch" is clearly "The best things in life are free."

And in the real economic world, there *is* a free lunch, an extraordinary free lunch, and that free lunch is free markets and private property. Why is it that on one side of an arbitrary line there was East Germany and on the other side there was West Germany with such a different level of prosperity? It was because West Germany had a system of largely free, private markets—a free lunch. The same free lunch explains the difference between Hong Kong and mainland China, and the prosperity of the United States and Great Britain. These free lunches have been the product of a set of invisible institutions that, as F. A. Hayek emphasized, are a product of human action but not of human intention.

Milton Friedman is a senior research fellow at the Hoover Institution and the 1976 Nobel laureate in economics. This article is based on his remarks at the banquet celebrating the opening of the Cato Institute's new building on May 6, 1993.
Cato Policy Report, July/August 1993

At the moment, we in the United States have available to us, if we will take it, something that is about as close to a free lunch as you can have. After the fall of communism, everybody in the world agreed that socialism was a failure. Everybody in the world, more or less, agreed that capitalism was a success. The funny thing is that every capitalist country in the world apparently concluded that therefore what the West needed was more socialism. That's obviously absurd, so let's look at the opportunity we now have to get a nearly free lunch. President Clinton has said that what we need is widespread sacrifice and concentrated benefits. What we really need is exactly the opposite. What we need and what we can have—what is the nearest thing to a free lunch—is widespread benefits and concentrated sacrifice. It's not a wholly free lunch, but it's close.

Free Lunches in the Budget

Let me give a few examples. The Rural Electrification Administration was established to bring electricity to farms in the 1930s, when about 80 percent of the farms did not have electricity. When 100 percent of the farms had electricity, the REA shifted to telephone service. Now 100 percent of the farms have telephone service, but the REA goes merrily along. Suppose we abolish the REA, which is just making low-interest loans to concentrated interests, mostly electric and telephone companies. The people of the United States would be better off; they'd save a lot of money that could be used for tax reductions. Who would be hurt? A handful of people who have been getting government subsidies at the expense of the rest of the population. I call that pretty nearly a free lunch.

Another example illustrates Parkinson's law in agriculture. In 1945 there were 10 million people, either family or hired workers, employed on farms, and the Department of Agriculture had 80,000 employees. In 1992 there were 3 million people employed on farms, and the Department of Agriculture had 122,000 employees.

Nearly every item in the federal budget offers a similar opportunity. The Clinton people will tell you that all of those things are in the budget because people want the goodies but are just too stingy to pay for them. That's utter nonsense. The people don't want those goodies. Suppose you put to the American people a simple proposition about sugar: We can set things up so that the sugar you buy is produced primarily from beets and cane grown on American farms or so the sugar in addition comes without limit from El Salvador or the Philippines or somewhere else. If we restrict you to home-grown sugar, it will be two or three times as expensive as if we include sugar from abroad. Which do you really think voters would choose? The people don't want to pay higher prices. A small group of special interests, which reaps concentrated benefits, wants them to, and that is why sugar in the United States costs several times the world price. The people were never consulted. We are not governed by the people; that's a myth carried over from Abraham Lincoln's day. We don't have government of the people, by the people, for the people. We have government of the people, by the bureaucrats, for the bureaucrats.

Consider another myth. President Clinton says he's the agent of change. That is false. He gets away with saying that because of the tendency to refer to the 12 Reagan-Bush years as if they were one period. They weren't. We had Reaganomics, then Bushonomics, and now we have Clintonomics. Reaganomics had four simple principles: lower marginal tax rates, less regulation, restrained government spending, noninflationary monetary policy. Though Reagan did not achieve all of his goals, he made good progress. Bush's policy was exactly the reverse of Reaganomics: higher tax rates, more regulation, more government spending. What is Clinton's policy? Higher tax rates, more regulation, more government spending. Clintonomics is a continuation of Bushonomics, and we know what the results of reversing Reaganomics were.

Economic and Political Markets

On a more fundamental level, our present problems, both economic and noneconomic, arise mainly from the drastic change that has occurred during the past six decades in the relative importance of two different markets for determining who gets what, when, where, and how. Those markets are the economic market operating under the incentive of profit and the political market operating under the incentive of power. In my lifetime the relative importance of the economic market has declined in terms of the fraction of the country's resources that it is able to use. And the importance of the political, or government, market has greatly expanded. We have been starving the market that has been working and feeding the market that has been failing. That's essentially the story of the past 60 years.

We Americans are far wealthier today than we were 60 years ago. But we are less free. And we are less secure. When I graduated from high school in 1928, total government spending at all levels in the United States was a little over 10 percent of the national income. Two-thirds of that spending was state and local. Federal government spending was about 3 percent of the national income, or roughly what it had been since the Constitution was adopted a century and a half earlier, except for periods of major war. Half of federal spending was for the army and the navy. State and local government spending was something like 7 to 9 percent, and half of that was for schools and roads. Today, total government spending at all levels is 43 percent of the national income, and two-thirds of that is federal, one-third state and local. The federal portion is 30 percent of national income, or about 10 times what it was in 1928.

That figure understates the fraction of resources being absorbed by the political market. In addition to its own spending, the government mandates that all of us make a great many expenditures, something it never used to do. Mandated spending ranges from the requirement that you pay for anti-pollution devices on your automobiles, to the Clean Air Bill, to the Aid for Disability Act; you can go down the line. Essentially, the private economy has become an agent of the federal government. Everybody in this room was working for the federal government about a month ago filling out income tax returns. Why shouldn't you have been paid for being tax collectors for the federal government? So I would estimate that at least 50 percent of the total productive resources of our nation are now being organized through the political market. In that very important sense, we are more than half socialist.

So much for input, what about output? Consider the private market first. There has been an absolutely tremendous increase in our living standards, due almost entirely to the private market. In 1928 radio was in its early stages, television was a futuristic dream, airplanes were all propeller driven, a trip to New York from where my family lived 20 miles away in New Jersey was a great event. Truly, a revolution has occurred in our material standard of living. And that revolution has occurred almost entirely through the private economic market. Government's contribution was essential but not costly. Its contribution, which it's not making nearly as well as it did at an earlier time, was to protect private property rights and to provide a mechanism for adjudicating disputes. But the overwhelming bulk of the revolution in our standard of living came through the private market.

Whereas the private market has produced a higher standard of living, the expanded government market has produced mainly problems. The contrast is sharp. Both Rose and I came from families with incomes that by today's standards would be well below the so-called poverty line. We both went to government schools, and we both thought we got a good education. Today the children of families that have incomes corresponding to what we had then have a much harder time getting a decent education. As children, we were able to walk to school; in fact, we could walk in the streets without fear almost everywhere. In the depth of the Depression, when the number of truly disadvantaged people in great trouble was far larger than it is today, there was nothing like the current concern over personal safety, and there were few panhandlers littering the streets. What you had on the street were people trying to sell apples. There was a sense of self-reliance that, if it hasn't disappeared, is much less prevalent.

In 1938 you could even find an apartment to rent in New York City. After we got married and moved to New York, we looked in the apartments-available column in the newspaper, chose half a dozen we wanted to look at, did so, and rented one. People used to give up their apartments in the spring, go away for the summer, and come back in the autumn to find new apartments. It was called the moving season. In New York today, the best way to find an apartment is probably to keep track of the obituary columns. What's produced that difference? Why is New York housing a disaster today? Why does the South Bronx look like parts of Bosnia that have been bombed? Not because of the private market, obviously, but because of rent control.

Government Causes Social Problems

Despite the current rhetoric, our real problems are not economic. I am inclined to say that our real problems are not economic despite the best efforts of government to make them so. I want to cite one figure. In 1946 government assumed responsibility for producing full employment with the Full Employment Act. In the years since then, unemployment has averaged 5.7 percent. In the years from 1900 to 1929 when government made no pretense of being responsible for employment, unemployment averaged 4.6 percent. So, our unemployment problem too is largely government created. Nonetheless, the economic problems are not the real ones.

Our major problems are social—deteriorating education, lawlessness and crime, homelessness, the collapse of family values, the crisis in medical care, teenage pregnancies. Every one of these problems has been either produced or exacerbated by the well-intentioned efforts of government. It's easy to document two things: that we've been transferring resources from the private market to the government market and that the private market works and the government market doesn't.

It's far harder to understand why supposedly intelligent, well-intentioned people have produced these results. One reason, as we all know, that is certainly part of the answer is the power of special interests. But I believe that a more fundamental answer has to do with the difference between the self-interest of individuals when they are engaged in the private market and the self-interest of individuals when they are engaged in the political market. If you're engaged in a venture in the private market and it begins to fail, the only way you can keep it going is to dig into your own pocket. So you have a strong incentive to shut it down. On the other hand, if you start exactly the same enterprise in the government sector, with exactly the same prospects for failure, and it begins to fail, you have a much better alternative. You can say that your project or program should really have been undertaken on a bigger scale; and you don't have to dig into your own pocket, you have a much deeper pocket into which to dig, that of the taxpayer. In perfectly good conscience you can try to persuade, and typically succeed in persuading, not the taxpayer, but the congressmen, that yours is really a good project and that all it needs is a little more money. And so, to coin another aphorism, if a private venture fails, it's closed down. If a government venture fails, it's expanded.

Institutional Changes

We sometimes think the solution to our problems is to elect the right people to Congress. I believe that's false, that if a random sample of the people in this room were to replace the 435 people in the

House and the 100 people in the Senate, the results would be much the same. With few exceptions, the people in Congress are decent people who want to do good. They're not deliberately engaging in activities that they know will do harm. They are simply immersed in an environment in which all the pressures are in one direction, to spend more money.

Recent studies demonstrate that most of the pressure for more spending comes from the government itself. It's a self-generating monstrosity. In my opinion, the only way we can change it is by changing the incentives under which the people in government operate. If you want people to act differently, you have to make it in their own self-interest to do so. As Armen Alchan always says, there's one thing you can count on everybody in the world to do, and that's to put his self-interest above yours.

I have no magic formula for changing the self-interest of bureaucrats and members of Congress. Constitutional amendments to limit taxes and spending, to rule out monetary manipulation, and to inhibit market distortions would be fine, but we're not going to get them. The only viable thing on the national horizon is the term-limits movement. A six-year term limit for representatives would not change their basic nature, but it would change drastically the kinds of people who would seek election to Congress and the incentives under which they would operate. I believe that those of us who are interested in trying to reverse the allocation of our resources, to shift more and more to the private market and less and less to the government market, must disabuse ourselves of the notion that all we need to do is elect the right people. At one point we thought electing the right president would do it. We did and it didn't. We have to turn our attention to changing the incentives under which people operate. The movement for term limits is one way of doing that; it's an excellent idea, and it's making real progress. There have to be other movements as well.

Some changes are being made on the state level. Wherever you have initiative, that is, popular referendum, there is an opportunity to change. I don't believe in pure democracy; nobody believes in pure democracy. Nobody believes that it's appropriate to kill 49 percent of the population even if 51 percent of the people vote to do so. But we do believe in giving everybody the opportunity to use his own resources as effectively as he can to promote his own values as

61

long as he doesn't interfere with anybody else. And on the whole, experience has shown that the public at large, through the initiative process, is much more attuned to that objective than are the people they elect to the legislature. So I believe that the referendum process has to be exploited. In California we have been working very hard on an initiative to allow parental choice of schools. Effective parental choice will be on the ballot this fall. Maybe we won't win it, but we've got to keep trying.

We've got to keeping trying to change the way Americans think about the role of government. Cato does that by, among other things, documenting in detail the harmful effects of government policies that I've swept over in broad generalities. The American public is being taken to the cleaners. As the people come to understand what is going on, the intellectual climate will change, and we may be able to initiate institutional changes that will establish appropriate incentives for the people who control the government purse strings and so large a part of our lives.

The Soft Infrastructure of a Market Economy

William A. Niskanen

A Western economist's first visit to a socialist nation is an eye-opening experience. One's first impressions are rather like those from visiting the poorer regions of our own economies—most visibly the lower levels of creature comforts, health, and environmental conditions. It would be a mistake, however, to explain the differences between the market and socialist economies in terms of the conditions that explain the differences over time or among regions in the productivity and average income within a market economy.

An economist studying a market economy, for example, is most likely to focus on the differences in human skills, private and public investment, and natural resources, and the incremental or small differences in government policy. We are less likely to study the basic institutions of a market economy, because they have changed only gradually over time and are common across the nation. Indeed, our standard graduate training in economics hardly mentions these institutions, and few economists have more than a shallow understanding of their importance.

The most important differences between the market and socialist economies, however, are the less-visible or quantifiable differences in these basic institutions. I am not a specialist in the socialist economies, so my understanding of the Soviet economy is necessarily secondhand. For the past several years, however, the inchoate reforms in the socialist economies and my own brief visits to several other socialist

William A. Niskanen is chairman of the Cato Institute. This paper is based on remarks presented at the Cato Institute's conference, "Transition to Freedom: The New Soviet Challenge," Moscow, September 10–14, 1990.

Cato Journal, Vol. 11, No. 2 (Fall 1991)

economies have led me to reflect on the basic institutions, or "soft infrastructure," of a market economy. The present paper gives me an opportunity to share my reflections in a systematic way.

The Legal System

One of the three basic institutions of a market economy is the legal system. Specifically, a market economy is dependent on a comprehensive commercial code and a system of commercial courts to adjudicate disputes. A modern commercial code includes the laws bearing on property, contracts, torts, and those laws specific to the several major types of business enterprises. For this system to be fully effective, property rights should be

- *exclusive*—to provide clear title for the authority to use or sell specific rights;
- *alienable* (sellable)—to permit market exchanges of specific rights;
- *partitionable* (separable)—to permit the separation of a specific right from a package of rights; and
- *extensive* (universal)—to permit market exchanges of all valuable resources, a necessary condition to avoid the abuse of "common pool" resources that is characteristic of environmental problems.

In effect, the political economy of a nation is defined by the nature and distribution of these rights. The distinctive principle of a market economy is that any *change* in the distribution of rights must have the consent of *all* those who own the affected rights.

An American economist is reluctant to conclude that any nation might have too few lawyers. Our army of lawyers is about as large as the U.S. Army and is almost as dangerous. The socialist economies, however, clearly need to extend and refine their commercial codes. The following examples might be helpful.

Although most property in a socialist economy is nominally owned by the state, it is often not clear whether the workers, the local manager, some party official, or the relevant minister has the authority to sell the property and who is to receive the proceeds. This ambiguity has already created cases in which two firms have purchased the same property from different officials, with no clear process for adjudicating the title dispute. The important but necessarily complex process of privatization will be undermined if the general population perceives the initial distribution from the sales to be unfair. A strong assertion of clear title by the state may be the necessary, but somewhat ironic, first step to effective privatization.

In some cases, rights have been granted to farmers or cooperatives to use property but not to sell it. This situation generally leads to inadequate maintenance of the property, most visibly demonstrated by the Yugoslav experience. In other cases, rights have been granted as a package but without the authority to sell specific rights to others. This condition leads to an underutilization of those specific rights that the owner is less qualified to use. In all nations, the most egregious environmental offenders are state firms, primarily because governments have exempted these firms from legal suits or from the regulations that apply to other firms.

A closer look at the Soviet economy would surely produce more examples. My main point is that many of the apparent problems of the socialist economies could be reduced by extending and refining their commercial codes. The Soviet Union should not try to copy the Western commercial codes; the U.S. code, specifically, is too complex and involves too much litigation. Nevertheless, there is a rare opportunity to learn from both our successes and problems. President Gorbachev has pledged to restore the rule of law in the Soviet Union. That task will not be complete until it is extended to the full range of economic rights and relations.

The Accounting System

The second basic institution of a market economy is the accounting system. Specifically, a market economy is dependent on the broad use of a common set of financial accounting rules and an independent system to audit financial reports. The two common reports are a balance sheet (a statement of the value of a firm's assets and liabilities at the end of the prior period) and an income statement (a record of the receipts and expenditures during the period). These reports, with additional internal information, are used by a firm's directors and managers to determine the costs and profits on specific products and the financial performance of component divisions. More important, these reports are critical to a bank or other firm that is considering a loan to or investment in the firm. The accounting rules and auditing systems have evolved over the many years and are not perfect, but one cannot imagine a market economy without a similar set of financial records.

My conversations with Western entrepreneurs who have considered joint ventures with socialist firms, however, indicate that the accounts of these firms are almost worthless, either for internal management or external monitoring. In most of the socialist nations, the accounts of state firms are designed and maintained to provide the insatiable data demands of the state planning system. Most of these data bear on physical flows and are of little use to estimate the costs or profits of individual products or the financial status of the firm, even if the input and output prices were closer to market rates. Indeed, I am informed that the balance sheets of many state firms do not include a measure of net worth. At an earlier, more innocent, time, computers were expected to solve the massive data processing problems of a socialist economy. The problems of a socialist economy, however, are not from the lack of data; indeed, socialist economies are drowning in data. The problem is that these data convey so little relevant information.

One of the major advantages of a market economy is that it minimizes the necessary data flow, since prices convey most of the information necessary to coordinate economic activity among firms and with consumers. A financial accounting system, in turn, provides the information necessary for firm managers to respond correctly to the market prices of inputs and outputs. A major program to train accountants and develop modern financial accounts would be among the highest return investments in the Soviet economy.

Cultural Attitudes

The third basic institution of a market economy is the set of cultural attitudes. Again, this institution is one that Western economists take as given and, as a consequence, have often not understood its importance. The German liberal Wilhelm Ropke may have best expressed the importance of a specific set of cultural attitudes in concluding that

> An intensive and extensive economic exchange cannot exist or last very long without a minimum of natural trust, confidence in the stability and reliability of the legal-institutional framework (including money), contractual loyalty, honesty, fair play, professional honor and that pride which makes us consider it unworthy of us to cheat, to bribe, or to misuse the authority of the State for egoistic purposes.

In turn, the single condition that most distinguishes a modern market economy from an oriental bazaar is the mutual desire for continued relations. I learned this lesson late. As chief economist of the Ford Motor Company, I was surprised to learn that Ford made billions of dollars of purchases a year from regular suppliers over the telephone with only the skeleton of a contract and with few contract disputes. The mutual desire for continued relations was what enforced the performance of both parties in each transaction. At any time that either party expected to end the relation or expected the other party to end the relation, moreover, the primary remaining discipline on the immediate transaction was the value of the firm's reputation with other parties, not the protection of the formal contract. Only when Ford made a major purchase without the expectation of a future relation was the contract extensive and often disputed. The cultural attitudes that contribute to this "evolution of cooperation" are subtle but simple: a mutual commitment to *exchange* (rather than threat) as the primary means to coordinate economic activity, the self-restraint to leave something on the table for the other party in each transaction, and the use of the authority of the state only to discipline gross or repeated breaches of contract.

Ropke was most perceptive about the requisite cultural attitudes for a market economy. But he did not develop on those attitudes that would prevent or destroy a market economy. The one attitude most incompatible with a market economy is a profound and pervasive sense of envy. A society can survive pervasive egoism; indeed a market economy relies on it. A market economy, however, cannot survive the leveling instinct, the concern that your neighbor or former schoolmate might be doing better than you are. One should not be surprised that all of the major religious traditions regard envy, covetousness, or resentment as a major sin. Envy is a human condition, but it is most destructive of social organization. Envy, combined with the erosion of the constitutional limits on the powers of government, has progressively weakened the Western market economies. And envy may prevent the development of stable market economies in some of the current socialist nations. I am disturbed to hear of old Russian folktales in which the peasants prayed, not for a good harvest or a fecund herd, but for their neighbor's barn to burn or for their neighbor's goats to die. As Ropke observed, it is important not to "misuse the authority of the State for egoistic purposes." It is also important not to misuse the powers of government as an instrument of envy.

Conclusion

In summary, the three basic institutions—the requisite soft infra-structure—of a market economy are the legal system, the accounting system, and the cultural attitudes. I have purposefully avoided a ranking of the importance of these three institutions. In combination, these institutions are rather like a three-legged stool, in that any one short or weak leg seriously reduces the stability of the stool. Individual and state investment in these three institutions is far more important than the other elements of a radical perestroika; indeed, these three institutions are requisite to the success of the other measures.

The Causes of Economic Growth

Reuven Brenner

Politicians and economists promise growth, prosperity, and higher standards of living. What do they mean by those terms? Is there some objective measure by which to judge whether people in a particular society, or in the world, expect technological and political innovations (including fiscal ones) to be beneficial and lead to the creation of more wealth? How can we be sure that a financial innovation, a change in company strategy, or a change in government policy makes a society better or worse?

The answer is that changes in the total market value of firms (the market value of debt and equity) in a society added to the market value of its government's outstanding obligations would be the best estimate to use in making such judgments—once financial markets are deep and transparent. When this sum increases, it means that the society's ability to generate revenues and pay back debt—whether private or public—has increased. And the contrary: when this sum drops (measured in terms of a relatively stable unit, rather than a particular currency), people signal that either their government or companies' management is making and persisting with erroneous decisions. The reason is simple: Developed, relatively unhindered financial markets prevent persistence of mistakes. By so doing, they quickly redirect the use of capital and ensure that savings and capital are deployed more effectively.

When the aforementioned sum diminishes, where does the wealth go? That depends. The smaller the ability of capital and people to move, the more their diminished value can be viewed as a perma-

Reuven Brenner, the author of *Labyrinths of Prosperity* and other books, holds the Repap Chair at the Faculty of Management at McGill University in Montreal and is an associate at the DUXX Graduate School of Business in Monterrey, Mexico.

Cato Policy Report, May/June 1998

69

nent loss. Those things that are expected to be solid—the effort and ingenuity of people—melt into thin air. More mistakes can be expected, and their effects can be expected to last longer. The decrease thus reflects diminished expectations of generating future revenues (since every mistake is a cost). Generating future revenues is what "growth" and the ability to pay back debt mean. When capital and people move, though, the wealth that disappears in one country reappears in others.

There are few better examples to illustrate those points than the wealth created by the various diaspora of history—Armenians, Chinese, Huguenots, and Jews—as well as the poor emigrants from Europe, who built the newer continents. (Few of the rich left Europe.) The emigrants were driven out of their homelands by politics and regulations. Let us briefly look at how the movement of the most gifted and energetic of those people led to many of the world's economic "miracles."

Facts behind Miracles

The Cinderella stories of poor or impoverished societies suddenly leapfrogging others have provoked admiration, envy, and intense discussions about why the outdone stumbled, and the humbler rose. The riches of oil-producing Middle Eastern countries did not provoke such discussions because those countries fit the "finding treasure" pattern. But how do societies do it when they not only lack any particular natural resources but even suffer from disasters? Can other countries emulate them and achieve similar high growth rates?

The miracle of 17th-century Europe was neither Spain nor Portugal—both of which fit the "finding treasure" mold—but below-sea-level Amsterdam and Holland, whose riches were created despite natural obstacles. Later there was West Germany, rising miraculously from the ashes of World War II. There were some Asian miracles that deserve our attention, such as those of Hong Kong and Singapore. And there was the almost forgotten example of Scotland, which teaches a particular lesson.

What's common to all those miracles? The Dutch were the first European republic, both tolerant toward all religions (when the rest of Europe was still severely discriminating against many) and with sound rights to property, which opened opportunities for relatively unhindered trade and financial innovation.

But it would be misleading to say that "the Dutch" did it. The openness of the new republic attracted to Amsterdam well-connected and educated immigrant merchants and moneymen (bankers from northern Italy); Jews and Huguenots, discriminated against elsewhere in Europe, were prominent among them. They helped turn Amsterdam into the financial and trading center of the 17th-century world. It had the world's first stock market, where French, Venetians, Florentines, and Genoese, as well as Germans, Poles, Hungarians, Spaniards, Russians, Turks, Armenians, and Hindus traded not only in stocks but also in sophisticated derivatives.

Much capital active in Amsterdam was foreign owned, or owned by Amsterdammers of foreign birth. There was "globalization" during the 17th century, even if nobody bothered to use the term. The difference between then and now, of course, is largely the speed of information flows. Max Weber didn't bother to look at migratory patterns when he came up with his speculation that somehow religion—the Protestant ethic—had much to do with Amsterdam's spectacular success. Although Weber's idea has been quoted frequently enough to pass for fact, it wasn't true in Amsterdam or in any other prosperous trading cities or states. Educated and ambitious trading immigrants, with networks around the world, turned 17th-century Amsterdam into a "miracle." And the same factors have been behind other miracles as well.

The histories of Hamburg, Hong Kong, Singapore, Taiwan, and West Germany have much in common with Amsterdam's, but shared religion is not a factor. In each of those places, the state provided an umbrella of law and order, exacted relatively low taxes, and gave people a stake in what the business society was doing—thereby attracting immigrants and entrepreneurs from around the world.

Sir Stamford Raffles designed Singapore as a port at the beginning of the 19th century, and backed it with an administrative and legal system and an educational system that was open to the whole multiracial population. Trade and security brought prosperity to the penniless immigrants from Indonesia and, in particular, China. Taiwan (after the 17th century), Singapore, and Hong Kong offered immigrants opportunities denied them in China, which was dominated at first by warlords and a status-conscious bureaucracy and later by a communist bureaucracy. Hong Kong benefited from waves of immigrants from China, in particular from the inflow of Shanghai merchants and financiers when Mao Zedong "liberated" China in 1949—much as Amsterdam rose to prominence when merchants and financiers fled the Iberian peninsula in earlier centuries, when the Huguenots fled France, and when Jews fled from many parts of Europe.

Hong Kong's textile and shipping industries were initiated by immigrants from Shanghai. Those people also established a network of merchants, traders, moneymen, and manufacturers—as Jewish, Italian, Armenian, Parsee, and other immigrant groups did throughout history in various parts of the world.

The Marshall Plan

The post–World War II West German miracle fits this pattern too, though in popular memory its success is associated with the Marshall Plan. The impact of that aid has been greatly exaggerated. Historians and economists (subsidized by governments) are very good at creating and perpetuating myths. At times the myths are about nationalism, falsely suggesting that economic miracles have been due to the genius of people living within arbitrary national borders. At times they are about the extremely beneficial roles of foreign aid. Both types of myth conveniently justify increasing the power placed in the hands of government.

Economists have estimated that, from 1948 to 1950, Marshall Plan aid was between 5 and 10 percent of European gross national product, although those numbers are dubious. European statistics from that period vastly underestimate national incomes because of extensive black markets due to price regulation and confiscatory taxation. There were, after all, no miracles in Europe after World War I, when loans and aid to Europe were also estimated to amount to roughly 5 percent of its GNP. True, the world moved toward lower tariffs after World War II, which it did not after World War I. The correct inference would seem to be that miracles are linked with lowered tariffs rather than foreign aid.

So what fueled the West German miracle? From 1945 to 1961, West Germany accepted 12 million immigrants, for the most part well trained. About 9 million were Germans from Poland and Czechoslovakia. Others fled East Germany's communist paradise. Although the movement of that human capital did not appear on the books at the time, its importance can be inferred from the significantly higher ratio of working persons to total population in West Germany than in other countries in the 1950s and 1960s: 50 percent in Germany vs. 45 percent in France, 40 percent in the United Kingdom, 42 percent in the United States, and 36 percent in Canada. And when the European inflow stopped, new waves of skilled young employees arrived from Mediterranean lands. In other words, the West German miracle was due, not to foreign aid, but to the same features that brought about earlier and later miracles elsewhere: migration of skilled people and significantly lower tax rates.

The Scottish Miracle

The Scottish lesson, rarely mentioned in history books, shows what else can be behind economic miracles. Scotland in 1750 was a very poor country. The land was of poor quality, and illiterate people engaged in near-subsistence agriculture; there were no navigable rivers; barren mountains and rocky hills hindered communications. The main export at the time was processed tobacco. Yet, less than a century later, Scotland stood with England at the forefront of the world's industrial nations; its standard of living was the same as England's, whereas in 1750 it had been considerably lower. How did the Scots do it?

The Union of 1707 made Scotland part of England. It came under England's system of taxes, laws, and currency and was allowed access to English markets. The union also abolished the Scottish parliament, leaving Scotland without a distinct administration until 1885. That turned out to be the biggest blessing (reminding one of Hong Kong's later success under distant British rule), as it prevented the banking system and financial markets from becoming an instrument of government finance. The result was a financial market that developed in response to the demands of the private economy.

By 1810 there were 40 independent banks. The orthodoxy of the times held that banks should lend only if the loans were backed by the security of goods in transit or in process, and for no more than 90 days. In contrast, the Scottish banks were free to lend for unspecified periods of time with no tangible securities. The credits of Scottish banks thus became the precursors of junk bonds.

Bills of exchange, the main assets of banks in other countries at the time, were the least important for Scottish banks. The largest volume of loans was made to manufacturers and merchants who received credit backed only by their own signatures with two or more people as sureties. The banks flourished with tiny reserves and made irregular financial reports.

The Scottish financial historian A. W. Kerr captures the specific feature of the country's financial markets: "The comparative immunity from legislative interference which characterizes banking in Scotland until the year 1844 has been an unmistakable blessing to the country, and has saved the banks from those vexatious and unnecessary distinctions and restrictions which have hampered and distorted English banking. In Scotland, banking was permitted to develop as the country advanced in wealth and in intelligence. Nay, it was even enabled to lead the nation on the path of prosperity, and to evolve, from practical experience, a natural and healthy system of banking, which would have been impossible under close state control similar to that followed in other countries." The country showed how, starting from scratch, to become prosperous quickly through trade and finance, unhindered by tariffs but covered by a reliable English political and legal umbrella. (Adam Smith was a Scotsman, you know.)

Contrast Scotland in that period with France, where a great majority of requests for charters for financial institutions were rejected until 1857. Only a severe depression that year led to the liberalization of procedures. Yet even in 1870, banking services in France were not what they had been in Scotland at the beginning of the century, and regulations denied small industrialists access to credit.

Scotland stands out, not only for its unique banking system, but also for the emphasis it put on education. In a piece titled "The Output of Scientists in Scotland," R. H. Robertson presents the relevant statistics. The output of "outstanding Scottish scientists" was at its height between 1800 and 1850 and diminished rapidly after 1870. The reason? The most brilliant Scots migrated—and there was no more Scottish miracle.

Scotland's relative decline in the 20th century has been correlated with the increasing assimilation of Scottish education and banking practices to those of England (the assimilation of banking starting slowly in 1845). If a large fraction of a region's most energetic and brightest people are allowed to migrate, and the access to credit of those who remain is constrained, what can one expect but decline?

There are other lessons to be drawn from the Scottish case. Savings were certainly not a precondition for the prosperity of the Scots. They did not have any to speak of. Nor did they receive foreign aid. But once opportunities were open and financial markets developed relatively unhindered, not only did the Scots save, but their savings were put to good use. In Scotland savings moved to private enterprises, whereas in England and elsewhere they went to governments. No state interference was needed to encourage the Scottish entrepreneurial spirit. In contrast to the previously mentioned miracles, there was no large-scale movement of talent from around the world to Scotland. However, the miracle did end with the emigration of Scottish talent, more regulated financial markets, and higher taxes.

What Are the Lessons?

Human creative sparks are always there, probably randomly distributed around the world. Prosperity, though, is due not to new ideas but to the commercialization of new ideas. And the incentives to commercialize ideas depend on taxation and access to financial markets.

The great advantages of private financial markets are that they decentralize decision-making and prevent persistent mistakes. Thus, when small-scale enterprises meet financial tests, they expand. If they fail, the loss to society is much smaller than it is in the case of failed grandiose government-sponsored projects—which frequently are not allowed to fail.

Continued spending on such projects is justified by a large army of government-sponsored economists, the priesthood of our times, who never fail to come up with half-baked theories of market failures to be remedied by smart, altruistic government regulators and bureaucrats. The result of this myth creation is that good money is thrown after bad.

Economists in the future may estimate exactly how much of the spectacular performance of the U.S. economy since World War II can be attributed to the large movement to America of extremely skilled, ambitious, well-connected people from around the world, a world that until 10 years ago was hostile to initiative and hope. Then we will know how much the transfer of that unmeasured human capital helped cover for many costly and mistaken U.S. government policies. What should be clear from the historical evidence is that when and if the rest of the world retains its talented people, the United States will no longer be able to count on attracting them to cover its costly mistakes.

Governments have a number of options for increasing growth rates. One is to offer a package of taxes and benefits that would attract more talent and capital from abroad. Because such policy may discourage growth elsewhere, it could lead to retaliations. A better alternative would be to encourage more domestic entrepreneurship. That can be done by lowering both income and capital gains taxes, which would rapidly both increase the sums of money people would be ready to invest as venture capital and speed up the redirection of funds toward financing entrepreneurial ventures. Both effects would lead to greater efficiencies—squeezing out mistakes (and thus costs) that prevent higher growth rates.

How best do we put numerical values on wealth creation? Certainly not by government statistics that reflect mismeasured, backward-looking aggregates. The most reliable measure is instead the significant changes in the value of market securitizations—measured in a relatively stable unit of account, gold, rather than a floating paper unit. That is because the opinions of a wide variety of people who back their opinions with money have proven to be a better predictor of where things are heading than are the opinions of all those who do not.

Changes in the aforementioned value are not a perfect indicator of things to come. Nothing is. But they are a better and more reliable measure of wealth creation than are the alternatives. The one important caveat is that financial markets must have the proper depth. That is, security markets must be able to reflect expectations about the policies of government and the central bank, whose laws, policies, and regulations affect the management of companies. When there are few sources of information in a society, or if information is controlled and the players' hands are tied, the stock exchanges will not fulfill their roles. Without proper depth, they will become decapitalized.

Societies that, for political reasons, put impediments in the way of information—as China did when Xinhua, the state-run central news agency, set restrictions on all aspects of Dow Jones's business in the country—will see the same wild fluctuations on their stock exchanges that New York's exchange saw a century ago, before the Dow Jones newsletter and the innovation of annual reports. When that happens, neither security markets nor official statistics will tell us much about what is happening to growth and wealth creation. Remember: on paper, countries were growing wonderfully under communism, but those of us who grew up under communism all knew that political statistics about growth were all one great lie.

The Pseudoscience of Macroeconomics

Though the pseudoscience of macroeconomics was a myth and not a lie, it left in its wake devastating wreckage, unpleasant surprises, and a confusion of confusions. Why did it become a myth? The emphasis on national aggregates hid the reality that in one country things that people wanted were being measured, whereas elsewhere things that the rulers and the establishment wanted were being measured. The fact that behind the aggregate counting there was, initially, a strong assumption that the relation between governments and citizens is, as in a private transaction, based on an exchange of services, was soon forgotten. The macroeconomic models, summarizing the working of the economy in a few simple-minded equations, have led to the same predictions whether "production" and "output" refer to something disastrous or something positive.

Since employment by governments and governments' "output" have been added, respectively, to employment and to whatever was produced in the nongovernment sector—and since there are good reasons, although not macroeconomic ones, for governments to intervene at times to do constructive things—it is no wonder that government expenditures were found to create both jobs and output. By using those numbers unquestioned, economists transformed, with the help of extensive government subsidies to bureaus of statistics and to academics, a self-serving political idea into a neutral-sounding "scientific" debate about numbers and statistical methods, keeping political institutions out of sight. Macroeconomics thus became a nonthreatening theory that could be taught at many universities around the world.

The students became teachers and continued to try to understand the myth of macroeconomics and the illusion of comprehensible national aggregates. By the time some of them noticed that the emperor had no clothes, they may have faced the dilemma of the astronomer Kepler, who, although not believing in astrology, wrote treatises about it because the monarchs paid for them.

Economists have had either to do as he did and disguise their true beliefs or to drop out of the "scientific" enterprise. The mediocre economists have stayed and sustained the enterprise unquestioningly, writing most of the "scientific output," checking it, publishing it, and insisting that everyone should go through channels controlled by them. That is how false ideas have always been turned into "science."

To conclude, the broadest historical evidence suggests that prosperity would be hindered less if governments just created the institutions that make it possible for entrepreneurship and financial markets to flourish. We can be confident that the idea that governments can frequently do more than that is a consequence of government-subsidized myth creation.

PART III

THE WELFARE STATE

Deregulating the Poor

Joan Kennedy Taylor

Is it possible for us to have a society that takes care of everyone and yet, at the same time, is free? Are the elements of coercion that creep in against both donor and donee (in every society that has tried to be comprehensive about social services) organically related to the attempt? Is compassion for the poor inextricably linked to coercion? Sadly that has often been the case throughout American history.

From Poor Law to Great Society

How have past generations of Americans tried to care for the poor? Essentially with variations on a tradition that was, like most of our basic legal-cultural traditions, imported from England.

In feudal society, one was born into a complicated system of privileges and obligations that organized society into a hierarchy within which each level performed duties owed to and received protection from the next higher level. The indigent were legally attached to their birthplaces and cared for by noble or church. The dissolution of feudalism left charity to the church poor box, and later the expropriation of the monasteries during the Reformation secularized it. Gradually, charitable contributions became obligatory and were collected and administered by local officials.

These officials were to see to it that the funds they collected were not wasted. As early as 1349, the Ordinance of Labourers had required that every British subject "not living in merchandize, nor exercising any craft, nor having of his own whereof he may live" be

Joan Kennedy Taylor is the author of *Reclaiming the Mainstream: Individualist Feminism Rediscovered.*

Beyond the Status Quo: Policy Proposals for America, ed. David Boaz and Edward H. Crane (Cato Institute, 1985)

compelled to work at such wages as "were accustomed to be given in the places where he oweth to serve," or be imprisoned. In 1531 an Act of Parliament provided for the registration of those unable to work, who would then be authorized to beg. "As for those who sought alms without authorization, the penalty was whipping till the blood ran." With the passage of the Elizabethan Poor Law in 1601, a tax—the "poor rate"—was assessed to care for paupers, while at the same time justices of the peace were required to put paupers to work.

Basically then, the idea embodied in the Elizabethan Poor Law was that the poor were attached to their communities of residence, where they were required to work if they could. If they could not, they would be cared for in some minimal way—but the community could set stringent requirements in return for such care. One requirement became popular and was established by law in England in 1723: the poorhouse, in which the indigent had to live and work in order to receive aid. These ideas were transferred to the American colonies by the British settlers, both in the institutions transplanted directly from England and in the British common law, which became the fundamental legal underpinning of all the original colonies and was either assumed or adopted by new states (with the exception of Louisiana) as they were formed and added to the Union.

For the poor in a small community, a poorhouse (or poor farm, as it was often called in rural areas) was not always available. To cite a 1983 study of nineteenth-century rural poor relief in Massachusetts:

> By 1655, each town took responsibility for its own poor and had authority to forbid entrance to strangers. Towns often quarreled over vagrants and who was responsible for them. In the cities and large towns, almshouses or poor farms were established as early as 1660 in Boston and 1702 in Hatfield, a large and prosperous rural town . . . in Western Massachusetts. However, most small communities continued the established practice of auctioning off the poor to the lowest bidder at town meeting, usually once or twice a year, and the town would then pay the citizen-bidder to keep a pauper or two at home.

This "bidding out the poor," as it was called, was a system with great potential for cruelty—paupers were literally sold at auction to the lowest bidder, that is, to the person who required the least amount of taxpayer contribution to feed, house, and clothe a pauper for the indicated period. In return, of course, the bidder had the right to the pauper's labor. Orphans were often apprenticed in a similar fashion.

Although the bidding out of paupers and the apprenticing of orphans continued to be practiced in some localities, poorhouses continued to spread. By the time of the Great Depression, according to Frances Fox Piven and Richard Cloward, "the main legal arrangement for the care of the destitute was incarceration in almshouses or workhouses."

The establishment of poorhouses didn't lessen the incidence of poverty. After the Civil War, cities suddenly expanded as a result of migration from rural areas and the flocking of immigrants to the United States to seek their fortunes. Cities were centers of jobs in manufacturing, which, low-paying and wretched as they were, were preferable to either the exigencies of rural life or the conditions of starvation and repression in Europe. But the new urbanites were poor. One writer recounts that in the late nineteenth century, in New York, Chicago, San Francisco, Detroit, and Cleveland, "three-fourths of the population were immigrants or the children of immigrants. Many of the immigrants came from impoverished rural communities, and most of them came to find better jobs and make more money." Not all succeeded.

Still, most Americans at the time assumed that the poor could overcome poverty with enough effort. The majority of the immigrants who came to seek their fortunes did indeed see their children rise out of the poverty they experienced. Thus, they too felt that those who spent entire lives in destitution did so for lack of enterprise, or were "intemperate" or even criminal. This idea persisted almost unquestioned, except by a few reformers, despite severe business cycles and depressions, until the worldwide calamity of the Great Depression with its massive unemployment—and the coincidental droughts that produced the Dust Bowl—shook it to its roots.

With the election of Franklin Delano Roosevelt that fall, the way was paved for the New Deal measures that initiated the contemporary welfare state. But by today's standards the welfare state of the thirties was modest. It was generally assumed that the dole was demoralizing and that the solution to the problem of poverty would be social insurance—social security—rather than welfare. The assistance instituted by the New Deal was a four-part system of general relief (still funded primarily by state and local governments); public jobs (federally supported under the Work Projects Administration); federal assistance for the blind, the elderly, and dependent children; and social insurance, which included unemployment insurance.

83

With the coming of World War II, prosperity and full employment returned to the economy. But the social insurance programs were, along with AFDC, retained, as well as the idea that help for the dependent was ultimately a federal responsibility. The seeds of the welfare state and the welfare bureaucracy had been sown.

Victims of the War on Poverty?

The story after World War II is more familiar to most of us. A period of self-congratulation at having put poverty behind us (the fifties) was succeeded by a period of soul searching that rediscovered poverty and then initiated the Great Society programs to put an end to it once and for all.

Today in the eighties, after billions of dollars have been spent on the poor, we are realizing that our inner cities are in worse shape than they were before. We now have a multigenerational dependency on welfare that seems to be forming an almost unreachable underclass; and we find that the ranks of the unemployable, certainly among poor blacks, seem to be swelling. It would be bad enough if all that money had gone to create a New Class of poverty bureaucrats, leaving the problems of the poor untouched. The reality seems to be even worse.

The question we are now confronting is this: What invisible hand, what combination of forces, is responsible for these unintended results of the War on Poverty that Lyndon Johnson announced in 1964? Pieces of the answer have been presented by various social critics, most of them conservative. The short answer, which seems uncompassionate and even unreasonable to liberals, is that the welfare system provides an incentive for people to give up and be dependent. Liberal critics reply with some plausibility that the unreformed welfare system is harsh, unfeeling, intrusive, niggardly, and demeaning. In a rich society like ours, they charge, the basic necessities of life should be available to all as a matter of right. Many agree with the conclusions of Frances Fox Piven and Richard Cloward in their very influential book, *Regulating the Poor*, that welfare systems have always been instituted to control the poor. The purpose of welfare and relief in the past, write Piven and Cloward, was never to help the poor, but rather to defuse discontent and potential rebellion. Another purpose was to enforce work by setting up such unpleasant conditions for relief that they would be all but unacceptable. A proper society would provide for all its members.

But in 1984 there appeared *Losing Ground: American Social Policy, 1950–1980,* a book by Charles Murray, a professional evaluator of social programs with seven years' experience at the nonprofit American Institutes for Research. In this work Murray presents a comprehensive and persuasive case for the view that we have indeed, with the best will in the world, created a welfare system in which incentives have been disastrously undercut.

The book sets forth the thesis that the social policies implemented in the Great Society programs and thereafter have been wrong in two ways. First, they have not worked, that is, they have not attained their stated goals. Second, they have been morally wrong, victimizing precisely those people who least deserve it and can least afford it—those of the poor who are struggling to be self-sufficient and perhaps even to better their lot.

Why did these policies fail? The reason is simple: because of their assumption that the purpose of welfare is the eradication of poverty, rather than the care of the destitute who have no other recourse. This well-intentioned and even visionary goal set forces in motion that not only changed the economic incentive structure that had previously encouraged the poor to better themselves (mainly, as the author points out, through negative incentives to avoid the consequences of learning nothing in school or being unwilling to seek and hold a job), but also altered status relationships among the poor.

Up until this century most Americans were poor or had grown up in poor households. "Forty-two percent of the population lived on farms in 1900, and most of them were cash poor." Considering also that "as many as 40 percent of wage earners were poor by the standards of the day in 1900," one can see that, although we have always had a social policy of care for the helpless and destitute in this country, ending poverty as such could only be, until relatively recently, an unthought of and unthinkable goal of social programs.

Instead, there were important distinctions among the poor. Murray points out that farmers, though poor, were proud of their status as the backbone of the nation.

A person might work hard and be poor; that was the way of the world. Poverty had nothing to do with dignity. A person might be out of a job once in a while because of hard times. That too was the way of the world, and a temporary situation. But a person who was chronically unable to hold onto a job, who neglected children and spouse, was a bum and a no good, consigned to the lowest circle of status.

Paradoxically, as economic growth pulled more and more people out of poverty, the goal of eradicating *all* poverty began to seem possible. All we had to do was change what were seen as the inequities of the system. Welfare must be cleansed of its stigma, said the reformers; half of the people eligible for help were not applying for it. The system was broadened to cover the working poor, and recipients were told that help was theirs by right. Thus the differences of dignity and pride between the working poor who stressed not taking charity and those who did take it were erased by these and similar government policies (pertaining not only to welfare, but to crime and education) aimed at helping all the poor and holding them blameless for their condition.

But if the delinquent is not to blame for his delinquency, then the youngster who holds a menial job while going to school does not deserve praise, either—in fact, he's a chump. By making all the poor, whether working or nonworking, eligible for welfare supplements, food stamps, and Medicaid, the previous stigma associated with welfare was indeed removed (as the reformers intended). At the same time, however, status was withdrawn from the working poor family and, what is more, from the behaviors that engender escape from poverty—all the difficult investments of time, energy, work, and penny-pinching in the hope of a far-distant payoff that are almost impossible to make without both faith that they will pay off and encouragement, praise, admiration along the way.

Instead, the reformed policies insisted on treating the poor as if they were a homogeneous group. In fact, they made it useful to behave in counterproductive ways—to be delinquent, addicted, or unemployed—in which cases one got help and special programs tailored to ensure success. By contrast, "the ambitious and hardworking students were passed along with A's and with the teacher's gratitude for not contributing to the discipline problem, but without an education that enabled them to compete in a good university."

We are just beginning to realize how profoundly these social programs have failed, especially in the case of inner-city blacks. Blacks who have been part of the middle class and older blacks whose work norms were formed before the welfare programs came into effect have prospered with the decline of official racism and segregation. But more and more young, poor blacks have dropped out of the labor force and have had illegitimate children in ever increasing numbers, thus sealing themselves into a borderline existence.

The overwhelming impact of Murray's data may, unfortunately, distract attention from his overall purpose. This purpose is not just to show that the particular programs whose effects he is analyzing have been misconceived; it is to show why there is generally an inverse relationship between the goals of social programs and their effects. There are, he suggests, three general laws that will frustrate the goals of social programs in a democracy:

> # 1. The Law of Imperfect Selection. Any objective rule that defines eligibility for a social transfer program will irrationally exclude some persons.
> # 2. The Law of Unintended Rewards. Any social transfer increases the net value of being in the condition that prompted the transfer.
> # 3. The Law of Net Harm. The less likely it is that the unwanted behavior will change voluntarily, the more likely it is that a program to induce change will cause net harm.

These laws should be the subject of a book in themselves. One can see that all three imply a constant growth in the number of people covered by a program, independent of both population growth and the condition of the economy. The Law of Imperfect Selection leads to a constant redefinition of the rules in order to include those who have been identified as irrationally excluded. The Law of Unintended Rewards means that the target population broadens as people find it either more rewarding or less punitive to be in the specified condition. The Law of Net Harm finds that the more tenacious the undesired behavior, the more likely that a program will be powerful enough to induce it, but not powerful enough to change it.

If one couples the tendency of automatic growth with the understanding that the effects of the programs are unjust—and that what is actually involved is nonmonetary transfers of "safety, education, justice, status" from the working poor to the irresponsible poor—one can see that a proper social policy is advocated neither by present-day Democrats nor their Republican counterparts. More of the same, as the Democrats propose, clearly will not suffice if "the same" is unfair. On the other hand, keeping our present programs and merely slowing them down will not change things enough to provide real alternatives to those trapped in the present set of disincentives to economic self-sufficiency.

The Paradox of Coerced Good Intentions

But the conclusion that many poverty experts come to when contemplating the growth of the underclass is that morality requires us to do even more in the way of government programs. In his introduction to the fourth edition of *The Affluent Society* in 1984, economist John Kenneth Galbraith devotes himself to an analysis of how society is growing heartless as people become more affluent, thus seemingly equating compassion with the support of more government transfer programs.

Galbraith is one of the most influential advocates of the view that the very structure of our economy requires some people to be poor. Poverty, according to this view, cannot be cured by economic growth, but must be attacked either by radical changes in our economic structure or by redistributive social programs. The general argument of such structuralists as Galbraith goes something like this: (1) industrial society leaves people at the bottom who cannot better themselves; (2) since industrial society is based on self-interest (competition is a war), the poor will continue to suffer unless the government does something about it; (3) even coercion is better than this sort of suffering.

A good example of the coercion routinely advocated today is the suggested solution to the plight of the homeless visible on the streets of our largest cities. Many of these people have obviously been released from mental institutions under court rulings that those not dangerous to themselves or others may not be confined against their will. There is a mounting feeling, however, especially when such people endanger health by insisting on staying out-of-doors in cold weather, that they should be involuntarily committed to mental institutions or hospitals once more.

Even more commonplace than advocating the coercion of the objects of charity is the idea that charity itself must be coerced. Economist Barbara R. Bergmann's 1981 article in the *New York Times*, "Charity Needs Coercion," set forth a number of arguments for replacing voluntary philanthropy with government programs and drew a fiery response from a number of executives of charitable organizations. A year earlier, Samuel Brittan had argued a similar point in the British magazine *Encounter*:

> The libertarians are not necessarily lacking in personal compassion, but their system is. Redistribution in any democratic society depends on altruism or solidarity on the part of the more fortunate citizens. But

whether one thinks of the relief of poverty or (more ambitiously) of income redistribution, personal charity is not enough—for reasons of economic logic. Redistribution is, like defense, a "public good." This means that there is little incentive for the individual to provide it. I might be—indeed would be—willing to pay a voluntary contribution to transfer some of my income to the poor as part of a compact with millions of others. But it would not be rational for me to do so, to the same extent, on my own. The benefit to the income of the poor would be negligible, and the loss of my own income and welfare substantial.

The history of caring for the destitute is threaded with varying amounts of coercion for all concerned. But any coercion, even for a seemingly good cause, is troubling in a society supposedly based on rights. The question inevitably arises: Since people who are free to make choices may make bad or improvident choices (as well as anti-social choices), is it in fact possible to have at the same time a society that provides for all its citizens and a society that is free?

Feudal society stated the intention to care for all its members, but was limited by its poverty. When the centralized power of feudal society declined and poverty persisted, it seemed to some that the freedom gained by the poor came only at a great price.

The distinguished economic historian and British Labour Party theorist, R. H. Tawney, noted in his famous account of the separation of religion and economic thought, *Religion and the Rise of Capitalism*, that "Bishop Berkeley, with the conditions of Ireland before his eyes, suggested that 'sturdy beggars should . . . be seized and made slaves to the public for a certain term of years.'" Tawney considered this early nineteenth-century suggestion a sign of the deterioration of religious morality that occurred in the transition from a feudal to an industrial society. Shocking as it sounds, however, there is little practical difference between that suggestion and the English workhouse system as it existed for some time after Berkeley's day. This is how a later nineteenth-century writer, Edmund Ruffin, described it:

> The pauper ceases to be a free agent in any respect. If at work far from the place of his birth, (in England,) he is remanded and transported to his own or native parish, there to obtain support. If either this forced exile from his long previous place of residence and labor, or other reasons of expediency require it, husband and wife, and parents and children, are separated, and severally disposed of at the will of the overseers of the poor. The able-bodied laborer, who at his agricultural or other work can earn but six shillings a week, and cannot support his family for less

than ten, may, indeed, obtain the deficient four shillings from the parish. But to do so, he is subject to be forced to take any service that the authorities may direct. And as the employer receives the pauper laborer against his will, and only because he thereby pays so much of his share of the poor-tax, he not only has the pauper as an involuntary slave, but he has not even the inducement of self-interest to treat the pauper slave well, or to care to preserve his health or life. The death of the pauper laborer is no loss to his temporary employer, and is a clear gain to the parish.

Other critics of early capitalism have decried the replacement of feudal-religious society, which stressed charity and brotherhood, with the labor competition of early industrialism. But not all of them felt, as R. H. Tawney did, that slavery suffered in the comparison. In an early work on sociology, nineteenth-century American writer George Fitzhugh (1806–1881) defended what he saw as the only logical alternative to the chaos he found in Northern cities.

The competition among laborers to get employment begets an intestine war, more destructive than the war from above. There is but one remedy for this evil, so inherent in free society, and that is, to identify the interests of the weak and the strong, the poor and the rich. Domestic Slavery does this far better than any other institution. Feudalism only answered the purpose in so far as Feudalism retained the features of slavery. To it (slavery) Greece and Rome, Egypt and Judea, and all the other distinguished States of antiquity, were indebted for their great prosperity and high civilization.

Mr. Fitzhugh defended the system of slavery as an institution that allowed different races to relate, and he also recommended its extension to the workers in the Northern states and in other countries, especially those where want was widespread.

A half million died of hunger in one year in Ireland—they died because in the eye of the law they were the equals, and liberty had made them the enemies, of their landlords and employers. Had they been vassals or serfs, they would have been beloved, cherished and taken care of by those same landlords and employers. Slaves never die of hunger, scarcely ever feel want.

In other words, said the defenders of slavery, if what you are concerned about is the care and security of those of the working class who cannot work, we know a system that makes better provision for the young and the old than does the growing industrial system.

Slaves may not be free, but where is the freedom of the inhabitant of the workhouse? To the extent that the feudal-medieval-Elizabethan view of society was that of an organic whole out of which one could not fall, it retained many elements of coercion from the social organization that preceded feudalism—slavery.

The point is, it is hard to devise a system in which people are coercively linked together economically that does not have at least some elements of slavery in it. This applies even in our seemingly enlightened age. Rules are made to ensure the orderly distribution of benefits, and then gradually these rules become more stringent. Government funding often starts out under the guise of filling the needs of citizens. These needs progress to the status of economic "rights." Then it is discovered that the so-called rights entail obligations that the funded citizen owes society in return.

We have seen this happen with welfare in contemporary America. First we were told that the community—that is, the government—has a moral obligation to feed and shelter the destitute. Then we were told that all the poor have a right to receive funds that will maintain them on a level with the economic standards of the rest of the community. And then, as it became apparent that there was a budget crunch, the government's fundamental obligation revealed itself as not so fundamental after all. We discovered that welfare recipients could be required to work for the government—even, in many instances, to replace public sector union workers at jobs paying well below the legal minimum wage.

One can see that such an argument leads to the slippery slope of a more and more coercive society and, ultimately, to the kind of totalitarian planning that solves the problems of poverty and crime by regulating the lives of all citizens. If charity is not only a good thing to do voluntarily, but is such a good thing that the government must enforce it—first through escalating taxation, next through forced service, and finally through a planning of safeguards and activities so thorough that no one can fall through the safety net—the secure society becomes indistinguishable from the slave society. In such a case perhaps we need to reassess our assumptions about charity and welfare.

One of the reasons for this slippery slope of coercion in charity is the fact that government *is* coercion. Because it exists to enforce rules, the more that the various operations of society become government operations, the more coercion will rule our lives. What we all want in this country is a compassionate society that will restore the progress toward the elimination of poverty that we were making in the first two-thirds of this century—liberals and conservatives can agree on that. But the compassionate society is the personal society, not the bureaucratized and regulated society. Americans used to be very nosy about the poor: they used to call on them, lecture them, be missionaries to them, bring them food, and establish community schools that poor children were expected to attend. That a surprising number of people still do the equivalent was shown by a Gallup poll in 1981 that found that 31 percent of all Americans volunteer their services on a regular basis. But much of what used to be done by individuals and associations has been delegated to the bureaucracy. Private charitable organizations have been preempted by welfare and have turned to other areas—they no longer visit poor homes.

One should remember that, for all the rhetoric of social service indulged in by supporters of government programs, the incentives for bureaucrats do not reward efficient delivery of services. Rather, bureaucrats are rewarded for expanding the size of their organization. Not only does more spending mean more appropriations, but, as C. Northcote Parkinson pointed out in *Parkinson's Law,* a larger staff of subordinates means a step up in rank and an increase in salary. Bureaucrats are also rewarded for postponing decisions and going through channels. To paraphrase Parkinson again, the bureaucrat says no not because he is mean, but because if he said yes he might be asked to explain his enthusiasm.

Steps toward a More Compassionate Society

If, then, we are faced with the very real possibility that government welfare programs are working in a direction opposite to that intended; if, as Charles Murray is persuasively arguing, almost any other replacement programs would similarly make worse the conditions they were designed to ameliorate; if the history of welfare reveals a universal tension between perfect security and freedom, with the balance always tipping toward coercion as programs become more expansive; and if governments are inherently inefficient economically—if all this, then what alternatives are left? What concrete steps can we take to restore a more personal, compassionate society?

One thing we can do immediately as a matter of government policy is to revise our tax code so that we no longer collect taxes from families below the official poverty level. It makes no sense at all for us to be taking with one hand and giving benefits with the other. If it is government policy to help these people, the least we can do is not take from them what little money they have.

Economists such as Walter Williams have detailed how such government policies as minimum wage and licensing laws make it harder for the poor to better themselves. Williams has documented the fact that in 1948, before minimum wage laws became widespread, "black youths aged 16 to 17 experienced less unemployment than their white counterparts." The laws restricting pushcarts and peddlers—to say nothing of the laws requiring complex examinations or licensing fees for such occupations as barber, carpenter, or taxi driver—put a disproportionate burden on the poor. We are driving economic opportunity from our inner-cities with our tax policies and economic regulations and, again, we are victimizing the most productive, most responsible, and most ambitious of the poor.

Charles Murray points out that "American society is very good at reinforcing the investment of an individual in himself," but that we no longer allow such mechanisms to work for the poor. "I begin," he writes,

> with the proposition that it is within our resources to do enormous good for some people quickly. We have available to us a program that would convert a large proportion of the younger generation of hardcore unemployed into steady workers making a living wage. The same program would drastically reduce births to single teenage girls. It would reverse the trendline in the breakup of poor families. It would measurably increase the upward socioeconomic mobility of poor families. These improvements would affect some millions of persons. . . . A wide variety of persuasive evidence from our own culture and around the world, from experimental data and longitudinal studies, from theory and practice, suggest that the program would achieve such results.
>
> The proposed program . . . consists of scrapping the entire federal welfare and income-support structure for working-aged persons, including AFDC, Medicaid, Food Stamps, Unemployment Insurance, Worker's Compensation, subsidized housing, disability insurance, and the rest. It would leave the working-aged person with no recourse whatsoever except the job market, family members, friends, and public or private locally funded services.

What would happen if we did as Murray suggests? Murray points out that one of the main reasons we do not is that we, the voters, want to think of ourselves as trying to provide for the needs of everyone. Disbanding the present system would clearly help many people immediately, but it would also leave some in distress. Unfortunately, we cannot specify exactly what options would arise in a free society if the current government-regulated welfare system were abandoned. We can be sure that there would still be family ties, many kinds of associations (Tocqueville said that the genius of America was its formation of associations to get various things done), and a wider range of optional decisions. But we can also be sure that problems would be solved in ways we cannot now foresee.

Social Security: Has the Crisis Passed?

Carolyn L. Weaver

In 1977 it was announced that the Social Security program had "unexpectedly" accrued a deficit of $4.3 trillion, triggering the widely held belief that there existed a "crisis" in Social Security. Elimination of this deficit would, it was suggested, require massive tax increases. Payroll tax rates projected in 1972 to peak at 11.9% early in the twenty-first century were projected only three years later to reach nearly 30% by the year 2050. To this state of affairs, past Secretary of the Treasury William Simon was prompted to say, "The future prospects of the system as we know it are grim."

According to the "official" perspective, which saw the crisis as essentially financial, the 1977 Amendments should put the claims of impending bankruptcy to rest and mark the passing of the crisis. The indexing provision that overresponded to inflation was modified, and tax rate and taxable earnings schedules were adjusted upward so that projected deficits as a percent of taxable payrolls were slashed from 8% to 1.46%. In the words of the Acting Commissioner of Social Security, the system is, once again, "sound and will remain so." For President Carter, these "tremendous achievements" represent the most important amendments to the law since the program's inception in 1935.

From an actuarial perspective, of course, an average deficit of 1.46% of taxable payrolls is still quite substantial. Even with the 1977 Amendments, which entailed the largest peacetime tax increase in U.S. history, it is anticipated that the average deficit for the OASDHI system will rise from $800 million in 1980 to $1.7 trillion in 2025, and reach $7 trillion in 2050, when expenditures are projected to reach 24% of tax-

Carolyn L. Weaver is director of social security and pension studies at the American Enterprise Institute.
Cato Policy Report, January 1979

able payrolls. The annual tax payment (employee plus employer) for individuals earning more than the taxable maximum is scheduled to rise from $2,140 in 1978 to $4,580 in 1983, reaching $6,550 in 1988. When the college students of today retire, moreover, people who are working at that time will be expected to saddle themselves with 24% tax rates to finance Social Security alone. How can it be said that the financial crisis in Social Security is behind us, particularly when it is remembered that the cost projections used by Congress to expand the program in 1972, just prior to the onset of the "fiscal crisis," actually projected that the system was *overfinanced?* Some wariness in embracing the "official" view about Social Security seems prudent.

Politics and the Social Security Crisis

But is the Social Security crisis simply financial in nature? Do the fundamental sources of this crisis lie in such recent and "unexpected" problems as double-indexing, cyclical recessions, and declining fertility rates? Long before any of these problems materialized, the cost of Social Security grew at an increasingly rapid rate. From a limited-objective, old-age insurance program designed to distribute monthly benefits to retired workers, Social Security grew in just 43 years to encompass four compulsory social insurance programs—old-age, survivors, disability, and hospital insurance—distributing monthly benefits on a pay-as-we-go basis to more than twenty beneficiary categories. Between 1940 and 1977, the number of beneficiaries grew from 222,000 to 33 million who, on average, now receive a monthly cash benefit of nearly $200. While this expansion took place, the combined employee-employer tax rate rose from 2% paid by 35 million taxpayers to 11.7% paid by more than 100 million taxpayers, and the real maximum individual tax payment grew by more than 600%. Social Security has become the largest domestic government program in the United States, spending nearly $100 billion a year.

Since Social Security has developed within a political rather than a market setting, perhaps the crisis in Social Security is at base political rather than financial. Perhaps the current financial difficulties are just visible expressions of what is essentially an evolving political crisis. Accordingly, the historical evolution of Social Security may simply be the natural outgrowth of institutional weaknesses embedded in the early program, so that truly effective reform will require excision of these central weaknesses. To examine this alternative perspective, some details of the evolution of Social Security must first be presented.

As enacted in 1935, the Social Security program consisted of only one compulsory federal program, old-age insurance, which appeared to be simple and relatively narrow in scope, possessing some attributes of private insurance. There was only one beneficiary category, the eligible retired worker. Monthly benefits, which ranged from $10 to $85, were to be paid to worker-taxpayers only, and were to be directly related to their earnings. Coverage was limited to 60% of the civilian work force and was generally concentrated in lower-income occupations. Finally, the system was intended to be fully funded, with tax rates rising from 2% to a maximum combined rate of only 6%.

Similar to private insurance, benefit tables had been designed to ensure that every worker received at least what he had paid in taxes (employee's share only) plus interest, and, importantly, that all workers with the same earnings histories were entitled to exactly the same monthly benefits. While the benefit formula tended slightly to favor workers with lower incomes, the program was primarily designed to supplement private sources of retirement income in a "systematic and safe" way, while relegating the relief of old-age poverty to the newly created old-age pension (means-tested) program.

These features of the original Act provided a set of institutional constraints on the size of the program and its redistributive potential. There was little ability to finance program expansion by postponing tax costs to future generations, because funding would ultimately require each generation to fully meet the tax obligation implied by its future benefit promises. Moreover, by restricting compulsory tax and benefit coverage to lower-paid workers, by placing a ceiling on taxable earnings (initially set at $3,000), and by restricting benefits to worker-taxpayers only, the ability to employ the program as a means of redistributing income between beneficiaries was quite limited.

Major Flaws in the Act

Nonetheless, the original law contained two serious flaws. First, the new Social Security Act created an apparatus through which coalitions of voters could potentially vote for transfers to themselves to be made good by claims on other workers' incomes. Since any "rights" bestowed under the Act were statutory rather than contractual, the political process could be used as effectively to rescind them as it had been used to bestow them. The likelihood that political demands for income transfers would emerge was enhanced by a confounding of the objectives of the old-age insurance program with those of the old-age welfare program. The original benefit formula, which was weighted downward to benefit the near-elderly, was at the same time weighted toward lower-income workers. In effect, these workers would be provided benefits as a "right" under the earnings-related insurance program, even though they had not fully contributed to their cost. This precedent would certainly encourage the growth of demands for larger unearned benefits as a matter of "right" or "social adequacy," thereby obscuring further the relation between a person's benefits and tax payments.

Second, the Act simply removed broadscale old-age insurance from the traditional realm of voluntary, private sector activity and, in so doing, took an important step toward monopolizing the provision of old-age insurance. The introduction of the compulsory old-age insurance program compelled purchase from a single supplier, the federal government. By eliminating voluntary patronage flows among insurance carriers as an indicator of social value, this step sharply curtailed the information- and efficiency-generating forces of competition. Moreover, any inherent advantages of private companies in providing insurance to the poor and near-elderly were destroyed by the introduction of redistributive features into the benefit formula.

This initial granting of monopoly power to the public supplier, along with the consequent stifling of competing sources of information, ultimately led to a disproportionate weighting of the interests of social insurance advocates and bureaucratic suppliers. These advocates, who had invested heavily in amassing political support for the original bill, were installed in the newly created bureaucracy, where they evaluated the bureau's performance, disseminated information, and drafted legislation. They were in the position of determining not only which issues would be studied internally and which results would be communicated, but also which ones would not. By controlling the production of information relevant for political decisions, Social Security bureaucrats were in a position to use their influence to expand the size and scope of the program.

And this they did. Only four years after the enactment of the original law, and before any monthly retirement benefits had been paid, the new bureaucracy and its carefully selected "citizens' advisory council" engineered a radical redirection of the program. The 1939 Amendments eliminated the fund for a pay-as-we-go system, abandoned individual equity for the goal of social adequacy, and legislated large windfall gains to most workers who would retire in the early years of the program.

Two of the changes enacted in 1939 would prove crucial to the program's future course: changes in the distribution of benefits, and changes in the means of financing. First, modification of the benefit formula and the introduction of benefits for survivors and dependents tilted the pattern of returns not only more in favor of lower-income workers and early retirees, but also in favor of workers with survivors and dependents. In so doing, the distribution of benefits was made to differ increasingly from the distribution that would have arisen in a competitive setting, thus buttressing the monopoly position of the bureau and eliminating the individual equity benchmark as a means of evaluating future changes.

Full Funding Rejected

Second, the intention of building up a funded system was rejected in favor of a pay-as-we-go system of finance, a decision of monumental importance. Under a funded system, each retiring generation would have earned a market rate of return on its tax payments. By requiring that assets ultimately be maintained sufficient to finance all accruing liabilities, this would have been accomplished without imposing burdens on, or making decisions for, future generations. Under the new pay-as-we-go system, on the other hand, benefits would not be financed from accumulated reserves. Instead, benefits paid to the currently retired would be financed by taxes imposed on the currently productive. Rather than being determined by the productivity of investment within the market process, therefore, the rate of return on Social Security payments would come to be determined after 1939 by the relatively unconstrained operation of majority rule.

This change in method of finance would have a dramatic impact on the incentive for beneficiary groups to lobby for program expansion. Under a funded system, beneficiaries would have been able to increase their benefits only by saving more during their working years through the imposition of higher taxes on themselves. Under a pay-as-we-go system, however, beneficiaries would be able to acquire higher benefits by imposing higher taxes on those currently working. Such windfall gains could also be captured by simply expanding the number of people forced to pay the tax.

These types of pressures on the new pay-as-we-go system could only intensify as the proportion of elderly in the voting population increased and as politicians became more responsive to their demands. At the same time, the incentive and ability of taxpayers to monitor the ensuing growth and evolution of the program would be dulled by the broad dispersion and misunderstood incidence of tax costs, and by the Social Security Administration's monopoly on information, particularly with regard to such issues as the actuarial status of the program and the rates of return payable in the distant future. As a result, the interests of beneficiary groups, politicians, and bureaucrats would become increasingly coincidental and, moreover, an increasingly dominant force in shaping the evolution of the new system.

The ultimate power of these groups to determine the future course of the program would derive from the ability of a pay-as-we-go system to make current decisions binding on future generations. Regardless of how high the tax rates or how large the gratuitous transfers to current beneficiaries might become, the system, and therefore benefit payments, would not be able to be terminated or even curtailed once under way without imposing uncompensated losses on all those persons who had paid taxes up until that time. Incredibly, this massive institutional restructuring of incentives and constraints that took place in 1939 was, at the same time, obscured by the formal introduction of insurance terminology (insurance, fund, contributions, trustees) into the Social Security law and into the vocabulary of the Social Security bureaucracy. Could such a system have been characterized by anything short of fiscal irresponsibility?

Expansion and Redistribution

In the years that followed, the redistributive potential of the pay-as-we-go system was achieved. New beneficiary categories were introduced and eligibility requirements were reduced, thus increasing the proportion of beneficiaries whose tax contributions were well outweighed by their redistributed gains and whose livelihoods had historically fallen within the auspices of old-age welfare. Repeated increases in the ceiling on taxable earnings during the 1960s and 1970s raised the maximum individual tax payment from $288 to $2,141. Expansion of compulsory coverage to nine out of ten workers during the 1950s increased the number of claims on the system while helping to finance an 875% increase in real expenditures over the decade. In other words, each of the program's three originally defined objectives—benefits to worker-taxpayers only, limited coverage, and full funding—was abandoned as the institutional constraints implied by those objectives were eroded by the political process.

Today, currently retired couples enjoy real rates of return well in excess of a market rate, replacement rates of roughly 66%, and annual benefits of up to $8,415, at the same time that the system rapidly approaches a "mature" state. A mature state refers, of course, to the time when these transitional financial gains have been fully captured by beneficiaries through prior, unsustainable rates of increase in the taxable wage base. As population growth declines, the real return on Social Security tax payments—which is determined by the rate of growth of the taxable wage base—must then fall, approaching the rate of growth of labor productivity, or roughly 2%. Taking into account the redistributive elements of the benefit formula, this real return for future retirees will be even lower for higher-income earners.

Toward Meaningful Reform

The prospects for reform of Social Security will be determined, to an important extent, by the views that are generally held on the program's history and current operation. As the foregoing discussion reveals, there are at least two quite distinct views of the crisis in Social Security and, consequently, two possible futures for the system. For those who maintain the view that the crisis is basically financial in nature, simply eliminating long-run imbalances in fiscal accounts—through marginal adjustments to tax rates, taxable earnings, benefit schedules, or eligibility requirements—will imply an elimination of the "crisis." For them, moreover, "reform" of the system will simply constitute an expansion of the program, perhaps to yet uninsured risks, while maintaining balance in fiscal accounts.

The types of proposals generated by the proponents of this view fail, of course, to recognize the possibility that the crisis in Social Security is political in nature and that the same set of institutions being marginally adjusted are those that are coercing a growing proportion of young workers to abide by a program that is making them increasingly worse off than they would have been in its absence. Moreover, their proposals fail to recognize that the system has created a loss even larger than that attributable to the visibly rising proportion of one's income devoted to Social Security. By transferring resources from those planning for retirement to those already retired, the system transfers resources from savers to spenders, thus ultimately depressing the nation's capital stock and wealth, and reducing the well-being of everyone. Since there is no real saving and, therefore, no real investment of tax receipts under the current system, the choice of a pay-as-we-go system has implied the sacrifice of an opportunity to enjoy a real return on savings, as determined by the productivity of capital, of roughly 12%. Estimates by Martin Feldstein in 1975 suggest that this loss is hardly inconsequential, having translated into a reduction in Gross National Product of potentially $285 billion. In short, to view the crisis as essentially financial in nature is to fail to recognize that the losses associated with young workers forgoing the opportunity to invest in private markets and the losses associated with this never-achieved wealth both fundamentally derive from the loss of choice in 1935.

To view the crisis, instead, as essentially political in nature and as having evolved predictably from institutional weaknesses in the early program, points to the clear need for truly radical reform of the system. Reform, from this perspective, implies the introduction of choice, voluntarism, and competition into the provision of Social Security as the only effective constraints on the future course of the program.

But how can choice be reintroduced into Social Security? At this point, of course, simply permitting individuals the choice between Social Security and private insurance cannot be done without defaulting on promises already made. By nature of a pay-as-we-go system, all current beneficiaries, and many workers who have already paid taxes into the system, would be made worse off by such a change. As young and higher-income workers left the system in search of better private investments, the tax base would be eroded, and benefit payments curtailed. Simply put, a pay-as-we-go system cannot survive in a competitive setting.

A Program for Transition

How, then, can the transition to choice and competition be made without threatening the continuation of outstanding benefit promises? One possibility is to accumulate a funded system of Social Security and, in so doing, place the public supplier on a more equal footing with private insurers. Since under a funded system there is no significant relationship between the total number of participants and individual benefit levels, the accumulation of a fund would assure all those who wished to remain under the public system that their benefit payments would be met even if the number of younger workers subject to the tax declined. Once funded, therefore, the need would be eliminated to coerce others to remain in the system simply as a means of protecting one's own expected income.

While the problems of financing the huge unfunded liability in the transition to a funded system cannot be ignored, the various means that might be chosen seem to be, at least at this time, of considerably less importance than an understanding of their likely impact on the future of Social Security. In an institutional environment in which people are permitted free choice between the public suppliers and competing private suppliers of retirement income, each worker-taxpayer could be assured—even without contractual agreement—that the return on his payments to Social Security would be no less favorable than in the market. By eliminating the potential for discriminatory income redistribution, the funded system with competitors would, therefore, introduce a lower bound on returns which, being determined by the productivity of investment in the economy, would well exceed the return ultimately payable under the pay-as-we-go system. In addition, the type of information on alternative price-output bundles that would be generated automatically by voluntary patronage flows between competing suppliers of old-age insurance would serve as an effective means of monitoring both private and public suppliers alike.

That this suggestion constitutes a truly radical reform proposal today only attests to the extent to which Social Security has been redirected since its inception in 1935, and the extent to which the initial choice of bureaucratic supply has tended to put, in the words of Hayek, a "straitjacket on evolution." In 1935, an amendment that was offered to the original Social Security Act to permit individuals free choice between the new public program and private suppliers actually won majority approval in the Senate and went on to stalemate the Congressional conference committee. The failure to reconsider such "radical" reform of Social Security in the 1970s may well mean the acceptance of "the ineluctable lesson of recent events that Social Security can no longer be a positive sum game where everybody wins and nobody loses."

The Success of Chile's Privatized Social Security

José Piñera

It's an honor for me to share with you some of the experiences we have had in Chile with our new private pension system. I would like to comment on how the new system works, how we were able to make the transition from the old system to the new one, and what have been the main economic, social, and political consequences of the new system. I will not explain the shortcomings of the old pay-as-you-go system in Chile. Those shortcomings are very well known because that is the system that is failing all over the world.

In Chile we accomplished a revolutionary reform. We knew that cosmetic changes—increasing the retirement age, increasing taxes—would not be enough. We understood that the pay-as-you-go system had a fundamental flaw, one rooted in a false conception of how human beings behave. That flaw was lack of a link between what people put into their pension program and what they take out. In a government system, contributions and benefits are unrelated because they are defined politically, by the power of pressure groups.

So we decided to go in the other direction, to link benefits to contributions. The money that a worker pays into the system goes into an account that is owned by the worker. We called the idea a "capitalization scheme."

We decided that the minimum contribution should be 10 percent of wages. But workers may contribute up to 20 percent. The money contributed is deducted from the worker's taxable income. The money is invested by a private institution, and the returns are un-

José Piñera, who as Chile's minister of labor privatized the state pension system, is president of the International Center for Pension Reform and co-chairman of the Cato Institute's Project on Social Security Privatization.

Cato Policy Report, July/August 1995

taxed. By the time a worker reaches retirement age—65 for men, 60 for women—a sizable sum of capital has accumulated in the account. At retirement the worker transforms that lump sum into an annuity with an insurance company. He can shop among different insurance companies to find the plan that best suits his personal and family situation. (He pays taxes when the money is withdrawn but usually at a lower rate than he would have paid when he was working.)

As I said, a worker can contribute more than 10 percent if he wants a higher pension or if he wants to retire early. Individuals have different preferences: some want to work until they are 85; others want to go fishing at 55, or 50, or 45, if they can. The uniform pay-as-you-go social security system does not recognize differences in individual preferences. In my country, those differences had led to pressure on the congress to legislate different retirement ages for different groups. As a result, we had a discriminatory retirement-age system. Blue-collar workers could retire at 65; white-collar workers could retire more or less at 55; bank employees could retire after 25 years of work; and the most powerful group of all, those who make the laws, the congressmen, were able to retire after 15 years of work.

Under our new system, you don't have to pressure anyone. If you want to retire at 55, you go to one of the pension-fund companies and sit in front of a user-friendly computer. It asks you at what age you want to retire. You answer 55. The computer then does some calculations and says that you must contribute 12.1 percent of your income to carry out your plan. You then go back to your employer and instruct him to deduct the appropriate amount. Workers thus translate their personal preferences into tailored pension plans. If a worker's pension savings are not enough at the legal retirement age, the government makes up the difference from general tax revenue.

The system is managed by competitive private companies called AFPs (from the Spanish for pension fund administrators). Each AFP operates the equivalent of a mutual fund that invests in stocks, bonds, and government debt. The AFP is separate from the mutual fund; so if the AFP goes bankrupt, the assets of the mutual fund—that is, workers' investments—are not affected. The regulatory board takes over the fund and asks the workers to change to another AFP. Not a dime of the workers' money is touched in the process. Workers are free to change from one AFP to another. That creates competition among the companies to provide a higher return on investment and better customer service, or to charge lower commissions.

The AFP market opened on May 1, 1981, which is Labor Day in Chile and most of the world. It was supposed to open May 4, but I made a last-minute change to May 1. When my colleagues asked why, I explained that May 1 had always been celebrated all over the world as a day of class confrontation, when workers fight employers as if their interests were completely divergent. But in a free-market economy, their interests are convergent. "Let's begin this system on May 1," I said, "so that in the future, Labor Day can be celebrated as a day when workers freed themselves from the state and moved to a privately managed capitalization system." That's what we did.

Today we have 20 AFPs. In 14 years no AFP has gone bankrupt. Workers have not lost a dime. Of course, we created a regulatory body that, along with the central bank, set some investment diversification rules. Funds cannot invest more than x percent in government bonds, y percent in private companies' debentures, or z percent in common stocks. Nor can more than a specified amount be in the stock of any given company, and all companies in which funds are invested must have credit ratings above a given level.

We set up such transitional rules with a bias for safety because our plan was to be radical (even revolutionary) in approach but conservative and prudent in execution. We trust the private sector, but we are not naive. We knew that there were companies that might invest in derivatives and lose a lot of money. We didn't want the pension funds investing workers' money in derivatives in Singapore. If the system had failed in the first years, we would never have been able to try it again. So we set strict rules 14 years ago, but we are relaxing those rules. For example, only three years ago we began to allow the funds to invest abroad, which they weren't allowed to do initially, because Chilean institutions had no experience in investing abroad. The day will come when the rules will be much more flexible.

Let me say something about the transition to the new system. We began by assuring every retired worker that the state would guarantee his pension; he had absolutely nothing to fear from the change. Pension reform should not damage those who have contributed all their lives. If that takes a constitutional amendment, so be it.

Second, the workers already in the workforce, who had contributed to the state system, were given the option of staying in the system even though we thought its future was problematic. Those who moved to the new system received what we call a "recognition bond," which acknowledges their contributions to the old system. When those workers retire, the government will cash the bonds.

New workers have to go into the new private system because the old system is bankrupt. Thus, the old system will inevitably die on the day that the last person who entered that system passes away. On that day the government will have no pension system whatsoever. The private system is not a complementary system; it is a replacement that we believe is more efficient.

The real transition cost of the system is the money the government ceases to obtain from the workers who moved to the new system, because the government is committed to pay the pensions of the people already retired and of those who will retire in the future. That transition cost can be calculated. In Chile it was around 3 percent of gross national product. How we financed it is another story. It will be done differently in each country. Suffice it to say that even though governments have enormous pension liabilities, they also have enormous assets. In Chile we had state-owned enterprises. In America I understand that the federal government owns a third of the land. I don't know why the government owns land, and I don't know the value. Nor am I saying that you should sell the land tomorrow. What I am saying is that when you consider privatizing Social Security, you must look at assets as well as liabilities. I am sure that the U.S. government has gigantic assets. Are they more or less than the liabilities of the Social Security system? I don't know, but the Cato project on privatizing Social Security will study that. In Chile we calculated the real balance sheet and, knowing there were enough assets, financed the transition without raising tax rates, generating inflation, or pressuring interest rates upward. In the last several years we have had a fiscal surplus of 1 to 2 percent of GNP.

The main goal and consequence of the pension reform is to improve the lot of workers during their old age. As I will explain, the reform has a lot of side effects: savings, growth, capital markets. But we should never forget that the reform was enacted to assure workers decent pensions so that they can enjoy their old age in tranquility. That goal has been met already. After 14 years and because of compound interest, the system is paying old-age pensions that are 40 to 50 percent higher than those paid under the old system. (In the case of disability and survivor pensions, another privatized insurance, pensions are 70 to 100 percent higher than under the old system.) We are extremely happy.

But there have been other enormous effects. A second—and, to me, extremely important—one is that the new system reduces what can be called the payroll tax on labor. The social security contribution was seen by workers and employers as basically a tax on the use of labor; and a tax on the use of labor reduces employment. But a contribution to an individual's pension account is not seen as a tax on the use of labor. Unemployment in Chile is less than 5 percent. And that is without disguised unemployment in the federal government. We are approaching what could be called full employment in Chile. That's very different from a country like Spain, with a socialist government for the last 12 years, that has an unemployment rate of 24 percent and a youth unemployment rate of 40 percent.

Chile's private pension system has been the main factor in increasing the savings rate to the level of an Asian tiger. Our rate is 26 percent of GNP, compared to about 15 percent in Latin America. The Asian tigers are at 30 percent. The dramatic increase in the savings rate is the main reason that Chile is not suffering from the so-called tequila effect that plagues Mexico. We do not depend on short-run capital flows because we have an enormous pool of internal savings to finance our investment strategies. Chile will grow by about 6 percent of GNP this year, the year of the "tequila effect." The stock exchange has gone down by only 1 or 2 percent and will be higher at the end of the year. Chile has been isolated from short-run capital movement because its development is basically rooted in a high savings rate.

Pension reform has contributed strongly to an increase in the rate of economic growth. Before the 1970s Chile had a real growth rate of 3.5 percent. For the last 10 years we have been growing at the rate of 7 percent, double our historic rate. That is the most powerful means of eliminating poverty because growth increases employment and wages. Several experts have attributed the doubling of the growth rate to the private pension system.

Finally, the private pension system has had a very important political and cultural consequence. Ninety percent of Chile's workers chose to move into the new system. They moved faster than Germans going from East to West after the fall of the Berlin Wall. Those workers freely decided to abandon the state system, even though some of the trade-union leaders and the old political class advised against it. But workers are able to make wise decisions on matters close to their lives, such as pensions, education, and health. That's why I believe so much in their freedom to choose.

Every Chilean worker knows that he is the owner of an individual pension account. We have calculated that the typical Chilean worker's main asset is not his small house or his used car but the capital in his pension account. The Chilean worker is an owner, a capitalist. There is no more powerful way to stabilize a free-market economy and to get the support of the workers than to link them directly to the benefits of the market economy. When Chile grows at 7 percent or when the stock market doubles—as it has done in the last three years—Chilean workers benefit directly, not only through higher wages, not only through more employment, but through additional capital in their individual pension accounts.

Private pensions are undoubtedly creating cultural change. When workers feel that they own a fraction of a country, not through the party bosses, not through a politburo (like the Russians thought), but through ownership of part of the financial assets of the country, they are much more attached to the free market, a free society, and democracy.

By taking politicians out of the social security business we have done them a great favor because they can now focus on what they should do: stop crime, run a good justice system, manage foreign affairs—the real duties of a government. By removing the government from social security, we have accomplished the biggest privatization in Chilean history—someone even called it, paraphrasing Saddam Hussein, the mother of all privatizations, because it has allowed us to go on to privatize the energy and telecommunications companies.

That has been our experience. Of course, there have been some mistakes. There are some things that should be improved. There is no perfect reform. With time and experience, I know I would do some things differently. But on the whole, I can tell you that it has been a success beyond all our dreams.

Ending Welfare as We Know It

Michael Tanner

Detailing the failures of the current welfare system and proposed liberal and conservative reforms is easy. However, critics of welfare have an obligation to go beyond attacking the system to provide an effective, compassionate alternative.

The first step is to recognize that the 1996 welfare reform legislation falls far short of what is needed to fix the system. Welfare cannot be reformed. Instead, we should eliminate the entire social welfare system for individuals able to work. That means eliminating not just Aid to Families with Dependent Children (AFDC) but also food stamps, subsidized housing, and all the rest. Individuals unwilling to support themselves through the job market should have to fall back on the resources of family, church, community, or private charity.

As both a practical matter and a question of fairness, no child currently on welfare should be thrown off. However, a date should be set (for symbolic reasons, I like nine months and one day from now), after which no one new would be allowed into the welfare system. As we have already seen, there are two distinct populations of welfare recipients. Those who currently use the system as a temporary safety net will be out of the system relatively soon. Immediately ending their eligibility would have only a minor impact on the system but would risk flooding the job market and private charities without allowing for a transition.

We have seen that there are serious problems with expecting hardcore, long-term welfare recipients to be able to find sufficient employment to support themselves and their families. When we established the incentives of the current system, we may have made a Faustian bargain with those recipients. Now it may be too late to change the

Michael Tanner is director of health and welfare studies at the Cato Institute.
Michael Tanner, *The End of Welfare* (Cato Institute, 1996)

rules of the game. We should do whatever we can to move those people out of the system but recognize that success may be limited. It is far more important to prevent anyone new from becoming trapped in the system. That will be possible only if the trap is no longer there.

What would happen to the poor if welfare were eliminated? First, without the incentives of the welfare state, fewer people would be poor. For one thing, there would probably be far fewer children born into poverty. We have seen that the availability of welfare leads to an increase in out-of-wedlock births and that giving birth out of wedlock leads to poverty. If welfare were eliminated, the number of out-of-wedlock births would almost certainly decline. How much is a matter of conjecture. Some social scientists suggest as little as 15 to 20 percent; others say as much as 50 percent. Whatever the number, it would be smaller.

In addition, some poor women who did still bear children out of wedlock would put the children up for adoption. The civil society should encourage that by eliminating the present regulatory and bureaucratic barriers to adoption. Other unmarried women who gave birth would not be able to afford to live independently; they would choose to live with their families or with their boyfriends. Some might even choose to marry the fathers of their children.

Poor people would also be more likely to go to work, starting to climb the ladder that will lead out of poverty. A General Accounting Office report on women who lost their welfare benefits after the Reagan administration tightened eligibility requirements in 1981 found that, on average, the women increased the number of hours they worked and their hourly wage and had a significantly higher overall earned income. Two years after losing their eligibility, a significant minority of the women (43 percent in Boston, for example) had incomes as high as or higher than they did while receiving benefits.

Similarly, in 1991 Michigan abolished its General Assistance program, which provided cash assistance for poor adults without children. Two years later, a survey for the University of Michigan found that 36.7 percent of those people were working in the month before the survey. Of those with at least a high school education, 45.6 percent were working. Two-thirds of former General Assistance recipients, regardless of education, had held a job at some point during the two years before the survey.

It is important to recognize that job opportunities do exist for individuals willing to accept them. That can be seen in the experience of unskilled immigrants who enter this country with disadvantages at least as significant as those of welfare recipients. Many have less schooling than the average welfare recipient and many cannot even speak English. Yet the vast majority finds jobs, and most eventually prosper.

Of course, it may be necessary for people to move where the jobs are. In some ways, the availability of welfare disrupts normal labor migration patterns by allowing people to remain in areas with low employment. If welfare had been in place at the beginning of the century, the great migration of black sharecroppers and farm workers from southern farms to northern factories would never have taken place.

People forced to rely on themselves will find a variety of ways to get out of poverty. Richard Vedder and Lowell Gallaway of the University of Ohio examined the movement of poor individuals out of poverty. They found that 18.3 percent of poor people receiving welfare moved out of poverty within one year. However, 45 percent of poor people who did not receive welfare were able to escape poverty.

Even many liberals understand that without welfare many poor people would find other options. As Gary Burtless of the Brookings Institution says, "My guess is that if welfare recipients realize their benefits are going to stop . . . it will cause them to search much, much harder for alternatives."

Of course, many people will still need help. As the Bible says, "The poor always you will have with you." The civil society will not turn its back on those people. Instead, they will be helped through a newly invigorated system of private charity.

Replacing Welfare with Private Charity

Private efforts have been much more successful than the federal government's failed attempt at charity. America is the most generous nation on earth. Americans already contribute more than $125 billion annually to charity. In fact, more than 85 percent of all adult Americans make some charitable contribution each year. In addition, about half of all American adults perform volunteer work; more than 20 billion hours were worked in 1991. The dollar value of that volunteer work was more than $176 billion. Volunteer work and cash donations combined bring American charitable contributions to more than $300 billion per year, not including the countless dollars and time given informally to family members, neighbors, and others outside the formal charity system.

Private charities have been more successful than government welfare for several reasons. First, private charities are able to individualize their approach to the circumstances of poor people in ways that governments can never do. Government regulations must be designed to treat all similarly situated recipients alike. Glenn C. Loury of Boston University explains the difference between welfare and private charities on that point. "Because citizens have due process rights which cannot be fully abrogated . . . public judgments must be made in a manner that can be defended after the fact, sometimes even in court." The result is that most government programs rely on the simple provision of cash or other goods and services without any attempt to differentiate between the needs of recipients.

Take, for example, the case of a poor person who has a job offer. But she can't get to the job because her car battery is dead. A government welfare program can do nothing but tell her to wait two weeks until her welfare check arrives. Of course, by that time the job will be gone. A private charity can simply go out and buy a car battery (or even jump-start the dead battery).

The sheer size of government programs works against individualization. As one welfare case worker lamented, "With 125 cases it's hard to remember that they're all human beings. Sometimes they're just a number." Bureaucracy is a major factor in government welfare programs. For example, a report on welfare in Illinois found procedures requiring "nine forms to process an address change, at least six forms to add or delete a member of a household, and a minimum of six forms to report a change in earnings or employment." All that for just one program.

In her excellent book *Tyranny of Kindness*, Theresa Funiciello, a former welfare mother, describes the dehumanizing world of the government welfare system—a system in which regulations and bureaucracy rule all else. It is a system in which illiterate homeless people with mental illnesses are handed 17-page forms to fill out, women nine months pregnant are told to verify their pregnancies, a woman who was raped is told she is ineligible for benefits because she can't list the baby's father on the required form. It is a world totally unable to adjust to the slightest deviation from the bureaucratic norm.

In addition to being better able to target individual needs, private charities are much better able to target assistance to those who really need help. Because eligibility requirements for government welfare programs are arbitrary and cannot be changed to fit individual circumstances, many people in genuine need do not receive assistance, while benefits often go to people who do not really need them. More than 40 percent of all families living below the poverty level receive no government assistance. Yet more than half of the families receiving means-tested benefits are not poor. Thus, a student may receive food stamps, while a homeless man with no mailing address goes without. Private charities are not bound by such bureaucratic restrictions.

Private charity also has a better record of actually delivering aid to recipients. Surprisingly little of the money being spent on federal and state social welfare programs actually reaches recipients. In 1965, 70 cents of every dollar spent by the government to fight poverty went directly to poor people. Today, 70 cents of every dollar goes, not to poor people, but to government bureaucrats and others who serve the poor. Few private charities have the bureaucratic overhead and inefficiency of government programs.

Second, in general, private charity is much more likely to be targeted to short-term emergency assistance than to long-term dependence. Thus, private charity provides a safety net, not a way of life.

Moreover, private charities may demand that the poor change their behavior in exchange for assistance. For example, a private charity may reduce or withhold benefits if a recipient does not stop using alcohol or drugs, look for a job, or avoid pregnancy. Private charities are much more likely than government programs to offer counseling and one-on-one follow-up rather than simply provide a check.

By the same token, because of the separation of church and state, government welfare programs are not able to support programs that promote religious values as a way out of poverty. Yet church and other religious charities have a history of success in dealing with the problems that often lead to poverty.

Finally, and perhaps most important, private charity requires a different attitude on the part of both recipients and donors. For recipients, private charity is not an entitlement but a gift carrying reciprocal obligations. As Father Robert Sirico of the Acton Institute describes it, "An impersonal check given without any expectations for responsible behavior leads to a damaged sense of self-worth. The

115

beauty of local [private charitable] efforts to help the needy is that . . . they make the individual receiving the aid realize that he must work to live up to the expectations of those helping him out."

Private charity demands that donors become directly involved. Former Yale University political science professor James Payne notes how little citizen involvement there is in government charity:

> We know now that in most cases of government policy making, decisions are not made according to the democratic ideal of control by ordinary citizens. Policy is made by elites, through special interest politics, bureaucratic pressures, and legislative manipulations. Insiders decide what happens, shaping the outcome according to their own preferences and their political pull. The citizens are simply bystanders.

Private charity, in contrast, is based on "having individuals vote with their own time, money, and energy."

There is no compassion in spending someone else's money—even for a good cause. True compassion means giving of yourself. As historian and social commentator Gertrude Himmelfarb puts it, "Compassion is a moral sentiment, not a political principle." Welfare allows individuals to escape their obligation to be truly charitable. As Robert Thompson of the University of Pennsylvania said a century ago, government charity is a "rough contrivance to lift from the social conscience a burden that should not be either lifted or lightened in that way."

That is the essence of the civil society. When George Washington contrasted government to civil society in his farewell address, warning that "government is not reason, it is not eloquence—it is force," he was making an important distinction. Government relies on force and coercion to achieve its objectives, including charity. In contrast, the civil society relies on persuasion—reason and eloquence—to motivate voluntary giving. In the civil society people give because they are committed to helping, because they believe in what they are doing.

Thus private charity is ennobling of everyone involved, both those who give and those who receive. Government welfare is ennobling of no one. Alexis de Tocqueville recognized that 150 years ago. Calling for the abolition of public relief, Tocqueville lauded private charity for establishing a "moral tie" between giver and receiver. In contrast, impersonal government relief destroys any sense of morality. The donor (read taxpayer) resents his involuntary contribution, while the recipient feels no gratitude for what he receives and inevitably believes that what he receives is insufficient.

Perhaps the entire question of government welfare versus private charity was best summed up by Pope John Paul II in his recent encyclical *Centesimus Annus*.

> By intervening directly and depriving society of its responsibility, the welfare state leads to a loss of human energies and an inordinate increase in public agencies, which are dominated more by bureaucratic ways of thinking than by concern for serving their clients, and which are accompanied by an enormous increase in spending. In fact, it would appear that needs are best understood and satisfied by people who are closest to them and who act as neighbors to those in need. It should be added that certain kinds of demands often call for a response which is not material but which is capable of perceiving the deeper human need.

Better yet, consider this simple thought experiment: If you had $10,000 available that you wanted to use to help the poor, would you give it to the government to help fund welfare or would you donate it to the private charity of your choice?

Big Charity and Big Government

Interestingly, some of the biggest critics of replacing welfare with private charity are some of the country's biggest charitable organizations. Their attitude has been summed up by Brian O'Connell, president of Independent Sector, an organization that represents most of the large charitable groups. "We lose our perspective on the voluntary sector and society when we exaggerate the importance of private philanthropy and volunteer organizations, particularly when we put them ahead of our responsibility to democratic government."

At first, such an attitude seems surprising for organizations that should be cheerleading for private charity. But a closer look shows that large charitable foundations are no longer private charities; they have become virtual arms of the government.

Most large nationwide charities now derive most of their income, not from private donations, but from government itself. For example, federal, state, and local governments provide nearly two-thirds of the funding Catholic Charities USA uses to operate its nearly 1,400 programs. The Jewish Board of Family and Children Services receives 75 percent of its funding from the government. Many other prominent charities receive similar levels of government funding.

A recent newspaper investigative report described those organizations as "transformed from charitable groups run essentially on private donations into government vendors—big businesses wielding jobs and amassing clout to further their own agendas."

Not only does government provide most of the funding for those organizations, but in terms of their bureaucratic structure and lack of accountability, they frequently resemble government agencies. Writing for the Philanthropy Roundtable, Payne compares large, bureaucratic charities with small, community-based organizations. According to Payne, the large organizations are generally managed and directed by a class of permanent, professional social workers. That is the final result of the professionalization of social work that began in the early part of the century.

Payne says that the big charities "are best understood as commercial charities, entities that rely on mass-marketing techniques to sell a charitable concept to distant, rather uninformed donors." As a result, there is little or no direct donor supervision and a lack of volunteers in supervisory roles. In contrast, Payne notes,

> In the task-oriented local voluntary organizations, those who supply cash and labor are well-informed about its problem-solving activities. The group is run by an inner core of several dozen volunteers who carry out operational duties. They are the managers and policy makers of the group. If the organization has paid employees, the active volunteers work with them, and are in a position to observe and evaluate their performances. Beyond this core group, the organization has several hundred less active supporters, individuals who occasionally volunteer, and who also provide financial support.

Like government, big charities have become an instrument of the elites. Professional social workers prescribe the correct policies. Direct citizen involvement is unneeded and unwanted.

That situation produces three results. First, an increasing amount of the charitable dollar is eaten up by bureaucratic overhead and salaries. Less and less reaches the poor. Before his conviction for embezzling funds from the organization, William Aramony of the United Way had a salary of $390,000, a $4.4 million pension, an apartment in New York paid for by the charity, and a personal chauffeur and car. His successor earns $195,000 plus benefits.

Second, the organizations become more and more distant from the poor they serve. The United Way, for example, does not even operate anti-poverty programs of its own. It simply collects funds and then farms them out to other organizations, such as the National Council of Churches and the Council of Jewish Federations, that, in turn, farm the money out to other agencies.

Third, it becomes extremely important for the organizations to protect their flow of money from the government. As Kimberly Dennis, executive director of the Philanthropy Roundtable, complains, the big foundations "have been more interested in expanding government's responsibilities than in strengthening private institutions to address social concerns."

Many charities actually maintain lobbyists on Capitol Hill to seek more of the taxpayers' money. Private donors may be surprised to find that their contributions go, not to help the poor, but to influence votes in Washington.

Private Charity in Action

The type of charity that will make a difference in the civil society will not be the large bureaucratic monsters described above. Rather, it will be local, individually based operations, capable of close interaction between donors and recipients. For example, the Center for the Homeless in South Bend, Indiana, provided shelter for approximately 2,500 homeless men, women, and families in 1994. Its three dormitory rooms hold beds for 72 men and 20 women. In addition, there are 13 apartments for families with children.

Throughout the center, the approach is one of "tough love." As Louis Nanni, the center's executive director, explains, "I realized that providing free food, material goods, and a place to sleep was not enough. In fact, simply doing that would be counterproductive. Unconditional handouts would sustain bad habits and allow people to put off facing their real problems."

When homeless people decide to stay at the center, they are presented with a set of strict rules that must be read and signed. The rules are reviewed in daily orientation sessions. All guests receiving income (either government benefits or wages) must save at least 75 percent of it after deducting obligations such as child support. Alcohol and drugs are strictly forbidden, and guests may be randomly tested for their use.

A case manager works individually with each homeless person to develop a plan to address his or her problems and work toward self-sufficiency, whether that involves job search, education, literacy classes, or drug and alcohol therapy. Peer monitoring and mentorship programs assist the person to complete his or her program.

The shelter's goal is to provide not just a temporary roof and food but self-sufficiency, which Nanni defines as "having the knowledge, discipline, and skills necessary to secure one's own shelter, maintain a healthy livelihood, and establish the relationships necessary to flourish personally and in a community."

Another private charity assisting the homeless is the St. Martin de Porres House of Hope in Chicago. The program is run by Sister Connie Driscoll, who specializes in helping homeless women. Women staying at the shelter are required to be drug free. Those who don't work must perform chores around the shelter. Sister Connie describes the program's philosophy: "Giving people a bag of food and a pat on the head is not the answer anymore. Once people stop thinking of help as a right, they'll understand they have to work."

The shelter is not a big-budget charity. It spends less than $7 per person per day, compared to an average of more than $22 per person per day in government-funded homeless shelters. Yet it has a phenomenal success rate. Fewer than 6 percent of women who go through its program end up back on the street.

Kid-Care, Inc., provides food to poor children in inner-city Houston. Operating as a sort of "meals on wheels" for children, Kid-Care delivers nearly 20,000 meals per month to more than 300 needy families. When there are extra funds, Kid-Care also provides shoes and clothing. Kid-Care workers are nearly all volunteers, and the operation spends more than 80 percent of its budget directly on food.

Kid-Care demands that the people it helps be taking steps to help themselves. As the organization's founder, Carol Doe Porter, says, "Kid-Care is not an entitlement. It's a privilege. I'll withdraw in an instant if you're a user or abuser. Instead of giving a hand-out, we should be giving a hand up."

One of the most successful private charities in Washington, D.C., is the Gospel Mission, which has been operating since 1906. The mission operates a homeless shelter for 150 men, a soup kitchen and food bank, and a drug treatment center. The mission operates on the principle that no one should receive something for nothing. Therefore, the homeless must pay $3 a night or agree to perform one hour of work around the mission in exchange for their lodging.

The mission tries to address the full range of its clients' needs, providing not only food and shelter but also education classes, job placement assistance, and spiritual advice. Recipients must demonstrate their desire to improve their lives.

"Sometimes we have to put a time limit on a guy, " says Rev. John Woods, the mission's director. "I had one guy tell me, `Reverend, the best thing you ever did for me was kick me out.' He was using the mission for a crutch. Compassion is lifting people out of the gutter, not getting down there with them and sympathizing. These people need responsibility."

The Gospel Mission has had extraordinary success at helping its clients put their lives together and return to mainstream society. For example, nearly two-thirds of the addicts completing its drug treatment program remain drug free. By comparison, a government-run drug treatment center just three blocks away has only a 10 percent success rate yet spends nearly 20 times as much per client.

In Grand Rapids, Michigan, an organization called Faith, Inc., provides job training to the homeless and others without jobs. Faith, Inc., operates a small assembly and packaging operation to provide its clients with training and work skills. As clients gain skills, they are subcontracted to other area firms for a fee. Counseling and education are also provided. Eventually, clients are assisted in finding full-time jobs with outside companies. About 50 percent of those who enter the program eventually complete it and find employment. The program has been so successful that it has become self-financing and even earns a small profit.

A similar approach is used by St. Paul's Community Baptist Church in one of the most poverty-stricken sections of Brooklyn. The church has purchased a number of small businesses that it uses to provide jobs for neighborhood poor people. If people are willing to work—and only if they are willing to work—St. Paul's will help them get a job at one of the church-run enterprises.

The church has also purchased and refurbished a number of houses and is offering them to poor families for mortgages as low as $400 per month. Still, the poor are always required to pay at least something. As the church's pastor, Rev. Johnny Ray Youngblood, explains, St. Paul's philosophy is, "Never do unto others what they can do for themselves."

All across America tens of thousands of small local charities like those are achieving real results in helping the poor. Those charities will form the vanguard of the civil society's fight against poverty.

Will There Be Enough Charity?

Those who oppose replacing welfare with private charity often argue that there will not be enough charitable giving to make up for the loss of government benefits. That criticism is based on some serious misunderstandings. First, it assumes that existing government programs would simply be transferred intact to private charity. All that would change would be the funding source. But the government programs have failed. Why would private charities want to replicate them? All the charities described above have far smaller budgets and operate far more efficiently than do their government counterparts.

Second, it assumes that private charity would have to care for the same number of poor as the government does today. However, as discussed above, without the incentives of today's welfare system there would actually be fewer people requiring assistance.

Finally, there is every reason to assume that charitable giving will increase in the absence of welfare. As we have already seen, welfare crowds out private charitable giving. A number of studies have demonstrated that "displacement effect." Giving, which had been rising steadily throughout the 1950s and early 1960s, declined dramatically in the wake of the Great Society. In the 1980s, as the rise in welfare spending began to flatten out, the public was deluged with media stories warning of cutbacks in government programs (although, as we have seen, such cutbacks were more in the minds of the public and the media than in reality). The public responded by increasing private giving.

It is important to note that only a portion of all private charitable giving goes to social welfare programs. Although overall charitable giving increased, donations to social welfare programs increased even more. For example, in the wake of the Great Society, the proportion of philanthropic giving devoted to social welfare declined from 15 percent to 6 percent. Following the pattern of overall giving, during the Reagan years social welfare giving increased, peaking at 11.6 percent of total giving in 1985. Following the Reagan years, as people again became convinced that government programs would take care of the poor, the proportion of charity dedicated to such purposes again declined, reaching 9.9 percent in 1993.

That is a natural reaction. If people believe that their contributions are not needed to help the poor, they will contribute instead to the symphony or the Friends of the Earth. When convinced that their contributions are needed, they give more to the poor.

That is not a new phenomenon. There is evidence from Frederic Almy's study of outdoor relief in the 1890s that private giving increased as government programs decreased and decreased as government programs grew more generous, leaving the overall amount of charity in society (both public and private) relatively constant. If government welfare disappears, there is no reason to believe that Americans will not respond, as they have in the past, with increased giving.

If worst-case scenarios do come true, and private charities initially lack sufficient funds, there are ways for the government to spur charitable giving. One method, strongly promoted by the National Center for Policy Analysis, would be to provide taxpayers with a dollar-for-dollar tax credit for private charitable contributions. That is to say, if an individual gives a dollar to charity, he should be able to reduce his tax liability by a dollar. Since current federal welfare spending is equivalent to 41 percent of the revenues generated from personal income taxes (for all major means-tested programs), the credit could be capped at 41 percent of tax liability.

Such an approach is not perfect. It is a coercive method of financing charity, but it does give individuals greater control over where their charitable dollar goes, and it puts day-to-day operation of charity in private hands. Unlike government grants to private charitable organizations, there are no strings attached or other government controls. Nor does government decide which charities are worthy of funding.

That is quite different, it should be pointed out, from proposals by some conservatives, such as Sen. Dan Coats (R-Ind.), to provide federal government grants to the type of small private charitable organizations described above. Allowing the federal government to get involved in funding local charities risks destroying exactly what makes those charities so effective. In a very brief time they would be transformed into smaller clones of the large, national government-dependent charities. Richard Cornuelle, founder of the Center for Independent Action, a private charitable organization, warned about the dangers of a Coats-style approach 30 years ago in *Reclaiming the American Dream*.

> Those who are succeeding with the poor, helping them climb out of poverty—like the Y.M.C.A., Urban League, community welfare councils—are independent institutions. It seems logical then to subsidize the independent institutions. And, just as logically, that is how to kill them. You can almost see the work slow down and the "co-ordination" begin, the substitutions of administrators for workers. And then the paper blizzard. The tragedy is that the final effect of the poverty program may be to destroy the agencies which could eliminate poverty.

Therefore, any direct government subsidy of private charity should be avoided. But that is not what is envisioned by a tax credit. Under the National Center for Policy Analysis approach, individuals are contributing their own funds to the charity of their—not the government's—choice. Government policy simply serves as an encouragement for them to do so. As an interim measure, that would certainly be preferable to the current welfare system.

Conclusion

Welfare has failed and cannot be reformed. It is time to end it. In its place, the civil society would rely on a reinvigorated network of private charity.

An enormous amount of evidence and experience shows that private charities are far more effective than government welfare programs. While welfare provides incentives for counterproductive behavior, private charities can use their aid to encourage self-sufficiency, self-improvement, and independence. Private charities can individualize their approaches and target the specific problems that are holding people in poverty. They are also much better at targeting assistance to those who need it most and at getting the most benefit out of every dollar.

Most important, private charity is given out of a true sense of compassion, which forms a moral bond between giver and receiver. Private charity enriches the lives of everyone involved and helps to nurture the true tendrils of community.

Eliminating welfare does not mean turning our backs on the poor. It does mean finding a more effective and compassionate way to help them.

Preschool in the Nanny State

Darcy Olsen

Make no mistake: The push for universal preschool is on. Already the state of Georgia offers free preschool to every 4-year-old, and New York is phasing in a statewide system. Legislators in California, Massachusetts, and New Jersey are itching to follow suit. If Al Gore is elected president in 2000, this state-by-state expansion could be preempted by a federal mandate. As the vice president recently told a Denver audience, "If you elect me president, I will make high-quality preschool available to every child."

Naturally, public officials hedge when asked whether preschool should be mandatory. But supporters call it a "necessity" for every child, a clear indication that calls for compulsory attendance loom in the shadows. Vermont legislator Bill Suchmann, for example, who introduced a bill to study the cost of compulsory preschool, denies that he advocates compulsory attendance—but says only compulsion can guarantee "equal educational opportunity."

The theory is that putting kids on the "right track" will get them to the "right destination." Gore explains, "The right kind of start—through quality preschool—can lead to higher IQs, higher reading and achievement levels, higher graduation rates, and greater success in the workplace." Yet, after hundreds of experimental preschool intervention programs over more than thirty years, there is no evidence that preschool is the cure-all Gore describes.

Supporters of universal preschool, like the church leaders who dismissed the Copernican theory of the solar system, prefer their convictions to the evidence. They invariably point to the Perry Preschool Project to show that preschool confers lasting benefits on kids. That

Darcy Olsen, former director of education and child policy at the Cato Institute, is now executive director of the Goldwater Institute.
Weekly Standard, August 9, 1999

1960s project tracked 123 children deemed "at-risk" through age 27. Half of them attended preschool as 3- and 4-year-olds, the other half didn't. According to the research team, "Program participation had positive effects on adult crime, earnings, wealth, welfare dependence, and commitment to marriage." The Perry research team seized on these results to produce the oft-cited "fact" that preschool provides "taxpayers a return on investment of $7.16 on the dollar."

It wasn't long before independent peer reviewers uncovered sizable sampling and methodological flaws in the Perry study. For example, preschool participants, but not the control group, had to have a parent at home during the day, which might have inflated the Perry findings. More important, in three decades the Perry results have never been replicated. Undeterred, both the California Department of Education and the New York State Board of Regents recently relied on the spurious cost-benefit analysis of the Perry Preschool Project to garner support for their universal preschool legislation.

Preschool proponents also shrug off inconvenient findings from Head Start, the federally funded preschool program for low-income children. Like universal preschool, Head Start is largely public-school-based, serves 3- and 4-year-olds, and espouses the mission of "school readiness." As the nation's largest and oldest preschool program, Head Start is filled with lessons for educators.

The most comprehensive synthesis of Head Start impact studies to date was published in 1985 by the Department of Health and Human Services. It showed that by the time children enter the second grade, any cognitive, social, and emotional gains by Head Start children have vanished. By second grade, that is, the achievement test scores, IQs, achievement-motivation scores, self-esteem, and social behavior scores of Head Start students are indistinguishable from those of their demographically comparable peers. The net gain to children and taxpayers is zero.

The first line of defense for Head Start proponents is to complain that the program has had too little money and too little time. But it has spent $35 billion over 34 years, which ought to be enough money and time to create a successful program if that were possible.

The second line of defense is to blame public schools. Head Start defenders claim that the benefits of preschool would be sustained if public schools shaped up. But there is no evidence to support this theory. And even if there were, there is little reason to think that the public schools will rise to the task.

Take Goals 2000, the plan hatched by President Bush and the nation's governors in 1990. One goal was for American schools to rank first internationally in math and science. The most recent findings of the Third International Mathematics and Science Study place U.S. twelfth graders 19th out of 21 countries in math and 16th out of 21 countries in science. Another goal was safe classrooms. A joint report of the National Center for Education Statistics and Bureau of Justice Statistics published in 1998 shows that more than half the nation's public schools experienced serious crimes in the past few years. Maybe the public schools, too, just "need more time."

The most common line of defense is simply to deny the facts, although a few educators have been willing to be honest. Consider the views of child-development scholar Edward Zigler, a founder of Head Start and director of Yale University's Bush Center in Child Development and Social Policy. As far back as 1987, when educators were debating the merits of universal preschool, he warned, "This is not the first time universal preschool education has been proposed. . . . [In the past], as now, the arguments in favor of preschool education were that it would reduce school failure, lower dropout rates, increase test scores, and produce a generation of more competent high school graduates. . . . Preschool education will achieve none of these results."

What Zigler recognized is that a child's academic performance and personal growth turn on a lot more than preschool.

Factors such as genetics, family, neighborhood, and life experiences from birth onward easily outweigh the influence of preschool. Preschools may teach children how to count, follow directions, and get along; Zigler himself favors universal preschool as a means to achieve school readiness. But preschool alone confers no lasting advantage. To put all children on an equal footing would require genetic engineering, surrogate parents, and for many kids, homes away from home.

In any case, the desirability of universal preschool should not hinge only on whether preschool works. Even more basic is the moral question of whether the government should entrench itself still further in the schooling of children. On this question, Al Gore and his allies are swimming against a powerful tide—witness the grass-roots movement sweeping through the states, offering charter schools, home-schooling, multi-million-dollar private scholar-

127

ship funds, vouchers, and tax credits. Parents are working to loosen the government's grip on K-12 education, even as the vice president is seeking to extend that hold to preschoolers. The most effective education reforms of the 1990s have featured decentralization, greater parental involvement, and private alternatives—while universal preschool is a throwback to the era of "government knows best."

PART IV

THE REGULATORY STATE

The High Cost of Government Regulation

Yale Brozen

Productivity growth in the United States since 1973 has dropped to one-third the previous, postwar growth rate. Among leading industrial nations, only England has done as poorly as the United States. Regulation is a major factor in that sad record. We are suffering from both a rapid expansion in the *scope* of government regulation and increased regulation within *each* of the regulated fields. Regulation, particularly in health, safety, and environment, accounts for almost half of the decline in productivity growth and for about one percentage point in the rate of rising costs.

The Proper Scope and Stringency of Regulation

There are three general principles defining the proper scope of regulation. First, where the costs of an action or lack of action fall on the decision maker, *no* regulation is needed. This is the case in which economists say that "all costs are internalized." If the buyer of an automobile does not order and use injury-minimizing devices, it is he who suffers from that decision when he has an accident in which his injuries are greater than they would have been had he bought and used protective hardware. There is no need for regulating the design of automobiles to require air bags or seat belts, since only the automobile user suffers any costs from their absence. (This sort of regulation is analogous to requiring people to wear heavy down parkas outdoors when the temperature is below 32 degrees.) Similarly, employers bear the cost of accidents in their plants, and there is no need to regulate plant safety.

Yale Brozen (1918–1998) was a professor of business economics at the University of Chicago and an adjunct fellow of the American Enterprise Institute.
Cato Policy Report, May 1979

The second principle is a corollary of the first. If costs are *not* internalized—that is, if some of the costs of an activity are paid by others who do not benefit from the activity—then regulation is needed. Automobile emissions affect people who get no benefit from the transportation services provided by the emitting automobiles. In theory, at least, there are two ways of getting pollution reduced to the right amount. Either the citizenry could offer payments to automobile users to reduce their contribution to pollution, or automobile users could offer payments to the citizenry for the right to pollute. The result either way is that automobile users face pecuniary consequences when they pollute. But the costs we impose on others cannot always be "internalized" this way. A system of payment such as the one just suggested would be very cumbersome. Regulation is a more efficient approach in this case, although a tax on emissions varied according to the ambient conditions in the region in which the auto is used would be far more efficient.

The third principle is that when we do regulate, we should recognize that as the stringency of regulation increases, we will incur progressively greater costs and gain progressively lower benefits. We *can* get more of a good thing than it is worth having. It was worth cutting down on auto emission—up to a point. It has been estimated that the first $4 billion of annual outlay on auto emission control produced about $5 billion of benefits. But we will be requiring automobile users to spend $11 billion annually for emission controls (in capital costs for hardware, maintenance costs, and extra fuel consumption) by 1985. For the additional $7 billion of expenditure, we will be getting, at the most, less than an additional billion dollars in benefits. That is a waste of capital and an inefficient use of our resources.

Incidentally, to say that there is a cost of $7 billion for $1 billion of benefits is not to put a price on health. This is not a callous calculation of the sort Scrooge would make. It simply says that we could get $7 billion worth of improved health by spending that $7 billion on health in more effective ways. As it stands, we are giving up $7 billion of things we value (including things that make us healthier) if we insist on going to the 1985 standards for auto emissions nationwide to get $1 billion worth of benefits. That is a very bad bargain!

Counterproductive Regulation

For a great many types of regulation, it is not a question of getting too much of a good thing. From many of our regulatory activities, we are getting *no* benefits. That happens to be the case with auto safety regulation. It surprised me to learn from a carefully done study that the multi-billion-dollar expenditure required by auto safety regulation (approximately $28 billion to date) has produced no improvement in safety. I expected at least part of the cost to be recovered.

In some cases, in fact, we are getting less of what is desired than we would if we eliminated the regulations. The Food and Drug Administration's regulation of drug safety and efficacy is a case in point. The 1962 amendments to the Food, Drug, and Cosmetics Act required the FDA to pass on the efficacy of all new ethical pharmaceuticals before allowing them on the market. Also, the amendments gave the FDA additional powers to regulate drug research. As a consequence, the cost of getting a new chemical on the market is four times greater than it would otherwise be—rising to $54 million. This has cut the annual number of new drug introductions by two-thirds. The result is, paradoxical as it may seem, that the drugs on the market are more dangerous than they would be if we had never responded to the thalidomide tragedy in Europe by amending U.S. drug laws in 1962. Because it has become so difficult and costly to get FDA approval of new drugs, we have not introduced new, safe drugs to replace some of our old, dangerous drugs, although some of those new drugs have been available abroad for years. We have had to go on using dangerous drugs for many illnesses because we lack safe replacements. The productivity of pharmaceutical research and development departments has been cut by 75 percent as a result of FDA regulation. No offsetting benefits exist to justify accepting this decline.

In the case of one new safe drug that was a replacement for an old dangerous drug, a pharmacologist has estimated that just the additional delay in getting the drug on the market as a result of the FDA's powers under the 1962 amendments caused 3,000 needless deaths. If a three-year *delay* for one drug caused that many deaths, think of the number of deaths caused by the fact that a dozen drugs a year are never invented because so much of our research resources are consumed trying to clear the FDA regulatory requirements for efficacy.

The ironical footnote to the new efficacy requirement is that the incidence of ineffective drugs has not been reduced a particle. Of course, why anyone would expect it to be reduced is a mystery in itself. After all, ineffective drugs are costly to produce and market, and they don't sell well enough to be profitable. There never was an incentive to market ineffective drugs, and the only reason any appeared is that they were mistakes. The FDA draws the same mistaken conclusions from research data that manufacturers do when manufacturers make a mistake. No one intentionally markets an ineffective drug. There were few marketed before efficacy regulation began and the incidence has remained unchanged since regulation began in 1962. It is time to repeal the 1962 amendments.

The Occupational Safety and Health Act is largely redundant and, perhaps, counterproductive. The evidence of its counterproductivity is not as clear as in the case of the 1962 drug amendments simply because no careful study has been done. A few data strongly suggest what the relative weights of costs and benefits might be. The number of lost work man-days per year due to injuries has increased from 53.3 per 100 workers in 1973 to 54.6 in 1974 to 56.2 in 1975 to 60.5 in 1976 to 61.6 in 1977. OSHA does not seem to have done much for safety at work. Of course, there was little reason to expect an improvement in safety. Employers were already motivated to do well. Let me explain.

First, let us recognize that there is a cost to providing safety. To provide a totally safe set of working circumstances would require infinite cost, which would mean that no potential employer could ever hire anyone if this were what the law required. If a totally safe job is impossible to provide, just how safe should the workplace be?

Recognizing that the greater the amount of safety, the more costly it is to provide a job and produce the goods people desire— hence fewer jobs and less goods—where does the socially responsible employer compromise between more safety and more jobs and goods?

Some argue that we need OSHA because the profit-seeking employer will avoid all outlays for safety in his desire to maximize profits. They believe that the employer will increase his profits by using less costly, less safe machinery, unless restrained by a sense of responsibility or by OSHA. In the absence of OSHA, wouldn't profits be made at the expense of a high injury rate for employees?

To put the answer in its most ludicrous form, let us take the complaint by Eula Bingham, the head of the Occupational Safety and Health Administration, about the recent Supreme Court ruling that an employer can, if he wishes, refuse entry to an OSHA inspector who does not have a search warrant. She said that in the case of a gas leak, a whole factory could blow up in the time that it took OSHA to get a warrant. "It seems never to have occurred to her that factory owners don't want their plants blown up, or their workers either, and are likely to find and eliminate such dangers before OSHA's inspectors can."

Perhaps we can safely leave it to employers to try to avoid gas leaks in the interest of preserving their property. But can we safely leave it to employers to avoid other kinds of injuries to their employees?

Before answering this question, let us recognize that there are gains to be had from engaging in risky behavior. I drove to Rockford recently from Chicago at 55 miles an hour. My risk of injury or death would have been less if I had driven at 40 miles an hour, or still less if I had cut my speed to 20 miles per hour. But driving at 55, I save time. I was willing to take the extra risk in order to get that return.

We can improve safety but the question is, "How much safety are we willing to pay for?" I don't drive at 90 because the extra time saved is not worth the extra risk. And I don't drive at 20 because the extra safety is not worth the price in time.

Similarly, employers can offer safer workplaces if their employees are willing to work at a less productive pace and accept the lower wage rate that would result from the reduced productivity. What employers find is that workers prefer higher wage rates to reduced risk (up to a point). Put another way, employers offering riskier jobs find that, to attract workers, they have to pay higher wage rates for any given skill than do employers offering less risky positions. When the wage is high enough, employees prefer risky jobs to those less risky. What we find is that an employer offering jobs where the fatality rate is three per thousand per year must pay about $500,000 more wages annually to a thousand workers to attract a work force than if he installs programs that reduce the fatality rate to two per thousand per year. If the fatality rate can be reduced to two per thousand workers at an annual cost of $400,000, the employer will spend that amount since he will save $500,000 in wage costs. He is motivated to improve the safety of his plant by the profit motive. This provides employees with what they prefer—lower risk at a sacrifice in wages which is worth it to them.

Now suppose that with an additional annual expenditure of $1 million, the employer can further reduce the fatality rate to one per thousand workers. If the saving in wage *and* accident costs is less that $1 million, the employer will not make the expenditure. He would make it if his 1,000 employees would take a $1 million reduction in wages. They are willing to take a $500,000 reduction, but not a $1 million reduction. Should OSHA force him to make the outlay?

Unless we want to take the paternalistic or elitist attitude that we should force people to do what we regard as good for them regardless of what they want, then the action of the profit-maximizing employer is what his employees prefer. In this case, they would rather have the higher wage that can and will be paid than a reduction in the fatality risk to one per thousand. If OSHA forces the expenditure of the extra million dollars on safety, workers will get risk reduction of a specific type worth only $500,000 to them. As buyers, they will be getting $1 million less product, or $1 million less risk reduction in the alternative uses to which these resources could be applied. They will suffer a net loss of $500,000 in their welfare as they view their own preferences. In effect, we will have told workers what they are allowed to buy with their incomes or in what areas risks are to be minimized.

If we force employers to use resources to buy mandatory safety for their employees, the net result may be less safety rather than more. First, let us recognize that mandatory standards have forced employers to make outlays that buy less safety than those outlays would have bought if businesses were free to choose the safety programs they prefer. Second, the lower wage rates resulting from mandated uses of capital means employees may not have the means to buy safety equipment for their homes. Since the evidence available "suggests that the hours spent at work are safer than the hours spent at home," it would seem that more may be done for safety by improving off-work safety than by further reducing risks on the job. By taking a riskier job at the higher wage paid for riskier jobs, employees can then afford smoke alarms, nonslip tread and handrails for stairways, fire extinguishers, safer tools for use in their gardens, etc., which will do more for their safety than additional expenditures by their employers. Add to this the fact that the record of mandatory standards, such as those imposed by OSHA and the Coal Mine Safety Act, demonstrates no detectable improvement in safety, despite the large expenditure caused by these activities. Evidently employers find it profitable to provide as much safety as any socially responsible government would force them to provide. OSHA, by all evidence, is causing large costs with no benefits—and even with negative benefits.

Automobile Design Regulations

I could go on with an endless list of unnecessary regulations—unnecessary in the sense that either costs are already all internalized and no regulation is needed or in the sense of going far beyond the point of diminishing returns. I must mention one more set of regulations—a set that suffers from both defects.

The requirement that auto manufacturers downsize their cars in order to attain a fleet average of 27.5 miles per gallon fails to recognize that auto buyers are already motivated to buy fuel-economizing cars to the extent that it is worthwhile to do so. Second, it fails to recognize that the mandatory expenditure of billions to satisfy this arbitrary goal is draining capital from uses where it could do more to economize energy than it can do by saving gasoline. A few more dry process kilns for producing phosphates or cement would save more energy and would be a more productive use of capital than the same funds spent on downsizing, but the fertilizer and cement industry rate of conversion to the dry process is being slowed by the scarcity of capital aggravated by investment being diverted to increasing fleet mileage. Third, it fails to recognize that the lightweight materials that have to be used to reduce the weights of automobiles will be more petroleum- and energy-intensive than the heavy materials for which these substitute, thus offsetting the gasoline saving. Fourth, it fails to recognize that getting rid of uneconomic regulations such as the five mile an hour bumper, which increases accident repair costs, and the mandated safety equipment, which provides no safety, could save energy. This path to saving energy has no cost—it would actually save cost with no loss in benefits—whereas the mandated path to fuel saving has large costs. Also, getting rid of standards for emission regulation could save about 5 percent of the petroleum required to produce gasoline with a negligible loss in benefits and a further large saving in capital. The petroleum refining companies would not have to use the available capital to add the extra refining facilities necessary to produce lead-free gasoline. They would then have the capital to install the desulphurization units that would enable us to use the abundant high sulphur crudes in place of the scarce low sulphur crudes. That would end the threat of a petroleum shortage.

Conclusion

If we abolish some of our old line agencies engaging in economic regulation, such as the ICC, the CAB, and the FMC, transfer all anti-pollution responsibilities from the EPA to the Department of Justice, and abolish the NHTSA, OSHA, Mine Safety Bureau of the Department of Interior, CPSC, SEC, and the various state hospital certification agencies, and repeal the powers given to the FDA by the 1962 amendments, reasonable estimates suggest that consumer benefits would amount to over $50 billion. In addition, productivity would rise more rapidly and add $20 billion a year increments to total output which, in five years, would increase annual national income by $100 billion. Elimination of these regulations would free capital to produce more of the benefits intended and leave more to increase productivity and moderate rising prices in many areas.

Enviro-Capitalism vs. Environmental Statism

Terry L. Anderson and Donald L. Leal

It may be true that "we are all environmentalists now," as Michael Kellogg claimed in his article "After Environmentalism," but it is not true that you have to accept command and control to be an environmentalist. Nonetheless, for mainstream environmentalists the litmus test of "greenness" is the acceptance of more government to achieve environmental ends. They typically call for more environmental regulation and more government ownership of land, ad nauseam. But the message from free-market environmentalism is that more government is not necessary to improve environmental quality and may even be inimical to that end.

Those who wave the banner of environmental statism cling to the notion that the stick is better than the carrot when it comes to the rights of private property owners. They ignore the enormous growth over the last decade in recreational markets, especially for fee hunting and fishing, that have led landowners such as International Paper Company, a major industrial industrial forest owner, to nurture its environmental assets. Instead, their first line of defense against landowners always seems to be regulation. No wonder private landowners see endangered species and wetlands as liabilities instead of valuable assets. Not surprisingly, ranchers in northwest Montana, for the sake of their own financial survival, say in private that the remedy for grizzly bears or wolves on their property is "to shoot, shovel, and shut up." Meanwhile, the clamor goes on for more restrictive legislation, more lawsuits, more government intrusion.

Management of Yellowstone National Park, the crown jewel of our park system, demonstrates governmental control of amenities has

Terry L. Anderson and Donald L. Leal are scholars at the Political Economy Research Center.
Regulation, 1994 No. 2

run amok. Independent scientists provide strong evidence that the park's policy of letting nature regulate park wildlife has thrown the ecology of the park into a tailspin. Aspen and willow are being devoured by populations of hungry elk that exceed carrying capacity. Beaver, a species dependent on aspen and willow, has all but disappeared from the park. Add to that Yellowstone's "enlightened" fire management policy that supplanted 70 years of fire suppression and an enormous buildup in fuels with an incredible "let it burn" policy. It was only a matter of time before fires like those in 1988 burned over half the park's pristine forests. Today, Yellowstone's managers still fumble with their dual mission of protecting park assets and providing the public with carte blanche access. Meanwhile, throngs of people that visit the park trample paths along pristine streams, crowd the deteriorating highways, and continually come into conflict with wildlife. Similar, if not worse, problems throughout the national park system have been aptly described by park officials as "greenlock." In short, the record of political control of natural resources and the environment has not been stellar, to say the least.

In light of the many failures, we must ask why so many environmentalists consider policies based on command and control to be the litmus test for greenness. Our answer is that only those coercive powers allow environmentalists to remain pure in a fantasy land of zero costs where others bear the costs of purity. Put this in the context of oil development in pristine areas such as the Arctic National Wildlife Refuge. True environmentalists "just say no." No oil is worth desecration of the environment; "costing the environment" is irrelevant because it implies a willingness to make tradeoffs.

Trading off some environmental disturbance for oil revenues even if those revenues can be used for other environmental causes is not pure enough. This explains why many members of the National Audubon Society are not proud of the fact that the Society condones oil and gas development on some of its private preserves while opposing development on federal lands.

One exception to total command and control that recently has gained acceptance in the environmental community is market-based solutions such as tradeable pollution permits. Those are accorded at least a light shade of green from mainstream environmentalists because they still "let the government steer." But market-based solutions really have little to do with markets; they are simply ways of making command and control more efficient. Such market-based solutions have been advocated for some time by economists pointing out that those solutions improve efficiency. Under a system of tradeable permits, a party holding a permit will have an incentive to reduce his pollution and sell the permit if he can do so at a profit. That will reduce the cost of meeting pollution standards by encouraging those with the lowest cost of reducing pollution to do so.

Unlike a market, however, the level of pollution is not determined by willing buyers and willing sellers, but by command and control. A market for pollution would have the polluter paying the receptor in a voluntary transaction. If the polluter is willing to pay the receptor more than the cost the receptor bears, more effluent will be emitted. That requires a system of well-specified property rights and a system of common-law torts that forces a polluter to pay for any damages he generates. Market-based solutions, on the other hand, establish the level of pollution through a political process with little if any compensation paid to those who receive the pollution. It is true that market-based solutions can make the process of meeting governmentally imposed pollution allowances more efficient, and free-market environmentalists applaud such efficiency gains. But there should be no mistaking the fact that the process of determining the level of pollution ought to be a market process.

The alternative to environmental statism is free-market environmentalism. As Kellogg notes, free-market environmentalism seems "like an oxymoron" but only because it does not depend on the coercive hand of government to steer the boat. Instead, free-market environmentalism depends on property rights and the law of contracts and torts, wherein willing buyers and sellers determine the course through their bargaining over the exchange of property rights. In the context of free-market environmentalism, pollution is not pollution as long as those who receive the byproducts are compensated for taking on what is unwanted by others. Hence the sign on the garbage truck that reads, "It may be garbage to you, but it's our bread and butter."

Free-market environmentalism is based on two premises, the first of which is that free markets provide the higher incomes that in turn increase the demand for environmental quality. Few would deny that the demand for environmental quality has increased dramatically in the past 25 years, and there is growing consensus that the cause of that increased demand is rising incomes. New studies show that the relationship between per capita income and environmental quality follows a "J-curve" pattern. At very low levels of income, environmental quality may be high because no effluent is produced. As incomes rise above some minimum, pollutants increase and the environment deteriorates. But then at per capita incomes of approximately $5,000 per year, environmental quality begins to become a luxury good. Above that income level, estimates by Don Coursey of Washington University in St. Louis show that for every 10 percent increase in income there is a 30 to 50 percent increase in the demand for environmental quality. We may all be environmentalists now, but the cause is not a born-again experience at Walden Pond; it is increasing wealth generated by free markets that has given us the wherewithal to afford environmental luxuries.

The second bulwark of free-market environmentalism is that markets for environmental amenities provide incentives for individuals to treat the environment as an asset rather than a liability. Kellogg acknowledges that there may be something to free-market environmentalism in that " the market can take us almost anywhere we want to go." But this misses the basic problem that the free-market environmentalism paradigm confronts: where do we want to go? Coercive environmentalists claim to know where we ought to go and use the powers of government to get us there. For them there is never enough wilderness, species should not go extinct, and pollution should not exist. That asserted, why not use command and control?

Free-market environmentalists make no claims that they know what ought to be done. That will be determined by human action revealed in voluntary transactions where prices provide incentives for willing buyers and sellers to cooperate to achieve their mutual ends. In Kellogg's words, "If someone wants to buy Yosemite and put up condos . . . , then condos there will be." Free-market environmentalists have no trouble with this conclusion, which is not to say that they necessarily prefer condos over a pristine Yosemite Valley. (Of course, a pristine valley is not what we now have under command and control so it may be that even condos would be more pristine than the overcrowding under bureaucratic management.) Free-market environmentalists would say that if they cannot outbid the condo lovers for whatever uses they want, then preferences, constrained by budgets, have been revealed.

142

Here two criticisms usually are forthcoming, one raised by Kellogg and one not. The one not raised has to do with wealth distribution. Since the rich have more wealth than the poor, they will outbid the poor, it is said, in a market system. But the fact is that the rich do not always prevail. Rich people may prefer fancy cars like the Lexus over the Geo, but the latter gets produced. Indeed, Henry Ford got rich by producing for the masses, not for the elite, wealthy market. If environmental quality is demanded by lower- and middle-income consumers, suppliers will get rich supplying it. Of course, if that is not what people actually want (as opposed to what coercive environmentalists believe they should want), the market will "fail." Moreover, distributional problems as they relate to the environment are no different than with food. If there are poor people, it is surely better to give them money and let them decide whether they want wilderness areas or water parks. If they choose the latter, free-market environmentalists have no worry. Coercive environmentalists, however, generally conclude that they have the wrong preferences.

The second criticism of letting voluntary transactions determine what environmental goods will be produced is that "some things simply should not be reduced to monetary terms. Some things are, or should be, sacred." Here the true colors of the coercive environmentalists shine through. Knowing what is sacred, they have no qualms coercing those without the correct vision into doing what is right. In the vernacular of coercive environmentalists, the environment has "intrinsic value," which Kellogg defines as "a value that is independent of the choices of particular individuals and, hence, transcends market considerations." What he really means is that intrinsic (substitute sacred, spiritual, godliness) values are infinite and therefore cannot be traded off against other values or uses. They are the trump card. Not surprisingly then, "free-market environmentalism, in its purest form, cannot" take intrinsic values into account.

Kellogg's solution is to have "a public debate in which the intrinsic value of nature can be considered by society as a whole, not simply bartered away in the private dealings of individuals." Here again sleight of hand makes everything seem fine. Who is this "society," and what is the process whereby society decides? Free-market environmentalism recognizes that society simply is a subterfuge term for political solutions fraught with at least as much failure as the "private dealing of individuals."

The Clinton administration's Timber Summit, in which the "public" voiced its intrinsic value for spotted owls and the government listened, exemplifies the political approach called for by Kellogg. In the end, seven-plus million acres of prime timber land have been removed from timber production, costing thousands of jobs in the Northwest and a proposal for a "workfare" program for misplaced workers. It was brute politics in which the environmentalists beat out the timber producers. At least the debate over alternative approaches to producing environmental amenities will be more honest if we recognize that coercive environmentalism substitutes politics with all of its shortcomings for freedom, however imperfect.

Kellogg believes that the Achilles heel of free-market environmentalism is that voluntary transactions require property rights and that those property rights must come from the government. Here again he misses a crucial point regarding the evolution of property rights, namely that they can and do evolve through the private law of contracts and torts. Examples of the evolution of property rights through customs and private law abound in the American West. Mineral rights and water rights, for example, evolved in the mining camps and irrigation regions long before government bureaucrats established their presences in the territories or state capitals. Such property rights still form the basis for water marketing. Throughout the western states, a system of prior appropriation water rights very different from the eastern riparian tradition allows parties to move water to high-valued uses while protecting against third-party impairment. Unfortunately, many public laws such as those prohibiting the sale of water to instream amenity uses have gotten in the way of market transactions. Returning to the establishment of property rights through common-law process would help solve the property rights problems Kellogg worries about.

As Roger Meiners and Bruce Yandle document in their book *Taking the Environment Seriously*, the historical record shows that property rights can and do evolve through the common law and that those common rules did protect individuals against pollution and other environmental externalities. Government officials seldom recognize the need for property rights. Indeed, much of this evolution took place in an era when technology was for less sophisticated and when information about the potential harms from pollution was more costly to obtain. True, enforcement may require governmental coercion, but such enforcement is a far cry from the methodical creation and redistribution of property rights based on transaction costs suggested by Kellogg and falsely attributed to Nobel Laureate Ronald Coase.

Free-market environmentalism recognizes that it is enviro-capitalists who discover the market potential of defining rights to environmental amenities, and capitalize on their discoveries by establishing property rights. For example, The Nature Conservancy recently tried to purchase and retire grazing rights on federal lands in New Mexico. Though the government may have created the grazing right on the public domain, it was the entrepreneurship of the Conservancy that attempted to create a new stick in the bundle of rights. Interestingly, an administrative law judge for the Department of the Interior disallowed the voluntary transaction designed to achieve an environmental end.

While working as a biologist for International Paper, environmental entrepreneur Tom Bourland also carved out new sticks in the bundle of property rights. By enforcing against trespass, marketing hunting rights, and renting land for recreation, Bourland was able to turn environmental amenities into assets that the company had an incentive to preserve. The list of enviro-capitalists is growing as the value of environmental amenities increases and is bounded only by the imagination of entrepreneurs.

Free-market environmentalism challenges the status quo by offering a way of "rethinking the way we think" about environmental problems. Most of us accept that food, housing, and the production of other basic necessities are best left to the marketplace. Why not the environment? Even environmental problems offer profit niches to the environmental entrepreneur who can define and enforce property rights. Political solutions may be called for in cases where the costs of establishing property rights are presently insurmountable, but there is no reason to begin with the premise that only command and control can produce environmental quality. To the contrary, free-market environmentalism points out that it is often "bureaucracy versus the environment" and that political solutions become so entrenched that they often stand in the way of innovative market solutions. Overcoming the mindset of environmental statism is no small task because this has been the dominant paradigm for environmental policy formulation for nearly a century. Moving beyond the status quo will require forming new coalitions and abandoning the anti-market mind-set.

This has happened with water allocation because fiscal conservatives and environmentalists have found a common ground. Federal involvement in massive water projects designed to make the desert bloom like a rose seldom pass cost-benefit muster and generally wreak environmental havoc. Because of this, progress has been made in removing water allocation from the political agenda and turning it over to market forces. Even in the case of enhancing stream flows for environmental purposes, there is growing evidence that markets can outperform politics.

"We are all environmentalists now" because we in the United States and other wealthy Western countries can afford to demand (as opposed to command) environmental quality. The basic premises of free-market environmentalism are 1) that environmental quality comes with increased wealth and 2) that free markets provide the incentive structure for increasing wealth and for producing environmental amenities. If coercive environmentalists with their elitist agendas continue to dominate environmental policy, the likelihood is that we will eventually have less wealth and fewer amenities. Of the three alternatives reviewed by Kellogg, only free-market environmentalism offers the prospect of more wealth, more amenities, and more freedom, the scarcest resource of all.

Federal Deposit Insurance Source of S&L Crisis

Catherine England

Politicians, the media, and the general public finally are waking up to the existence of a longstanding crisis in the savings and loan industry. Current losses, estimated at $125 billion, are now large enough to capture attention, even in Washington. Unfortunately, most of the political rhetoric and news analyses concerning the savings and loan crisis have focused on the wrong issues. The partial deregulation of the industry that took place in 1982 did not cause the fiasco. Nor is funding the cleanup the most important issue with which Congress should wrestle in the next few months.

Since President Bush's plan for resolving the thrift industry problem was announced, it has served as the starting point for many news discussions. The plan is also a useful example of how the debate over structural reform of the industry is being directed onto a road that offers little promise of arriving at a permanent solution to the fiasco.

The Bush proposal for addressing the savings and loan industry crisis offers a plan for funding the cleanup and suggests reforms that President Bush argues will prevent similar problems in the future.

The Bush Plan

Briefly, the president expects that dealing with the insolvent S&Ls will cost $90 billion plus interest. If the Bush plan is adopted, the money necessary to pay insured depositors in decapitalized institutions would come from newly issued 30-year bonds. Taxpayers

Catherine England was director of regulatory studies at the Cato Institute and is now visiting assistant professor at the Institute of Graduate and Professional Business Studies, George Mason University.
Cato Policy Report, March/April 1989

would be responsible for at least half of the interest, and thrift industry resources would be tapped to pay the remaining interest and repay the principal. The promise that industry resources will absorb a large portion of the costs allows most of the funding requirements to be kept off the federal budget (at least for now), thus minimizing the impact on the reported deficit. The total cost of the 30-year package could easily reach $200 billion when interest is included.

President Bush also has resolved to provide tougher regulation. The administration's proposal would give the Justice Department an additional $50 million to beef up its program to prosecute depository managers suspected of fraud or malfeasance. In addition, the Federal Savings and Loan Insurance Corporation (FSLIC) would be separated from the Federal Home Loan Bank Board and placed under the supervision of the Federal Deposit Insurance Corporation (FDIC), though the funds of the two agencies would remain separate. The administrative structure of the Federal Home Loan Bank System would also be changed. The three-member board would be eliminated, and the system's chairman would serve in the Treasury Department just as the comptroller of the currency, the overseer of nationally chartered banks, is housed within Treasury. The suggested reforms seek to recast the thrift industry regulatory structure into a mold more like that of the banking industry. It is widely believed that bank regulators have been significantly more successful at controlling industry risk than have S&L supervisors.

Most news stories have focused on funding the cleanup, and the proposal does have several flaws. The administration's assumptions about the future performance of the economy and expected growth in the thrift industry undoubtedly are overly optimistic. If insolvent institutions have suffered greater losses than are now recognized, if additional institutions require aid, or if the economy or the industry does not perform as well as the Bush administration's projections, the ultimate costs will climb higher than $200 billion, and taxpayers will be forced to shoulder a much larger share of the burden than currently expected.

While criticism is deserved, however, the details of funding the cleanup are not critically important. The economy has already suffered the losses and misallocations caused by the thrift industry fiasco. Consequently, even recognizing the full costs of the cleanup on-budget should have no serious implications for the broader economy, even though the reported deficit would increase. The important question is how to avoid repeating the crisis.

President Bush and his advisers apparently believe that the massive thrift industry losses resulted from a failure to adequately police the industry. That conclusion is true only in a superficial sense. The shovels used by S&L managers and owners and federal authorities to dig this $200 billion hole were overregulation and federal deposit insurance.

The Victims of Government Involvement

The industry first encountered difficulties because the federal government required S&Ls to provide long-term, fixed-rate mortgages funded with short-term deposits. Then interest rates began to rise in the late 1970s. Housing sales slumped just when S&Ls needed to turn over their portfolios more rapidly. Meanwhile, savers removed their money from $5\frac{1}{4}$ percent accounts and put it in money market mutual funds. Thrift institutions found their costs rising rapidly while their income remained stagnant. During 1981, some 85 percent of the industry reported operating losses, and capital at many institutions was rapidly absorbed.

Because institutions throughout the industry experienced simultaneous difficulties, the Federal Home Loan Bank Board and the FSLIC were unable to respond. While the regulators asked for more resources, the industry lobbied against additional funding and urged Congress to give undercapitalized thrifts an opportunity to outgrow their problems. Thus, capital standards were lowered, accounting trickery was encouraged, and insolvent institutions were allowed to continue operating.

Congress did make half-hearted attempts in 1980 and 1982 to address the regulation-induced problems of the thrift industry. The deregulation of interest rates paid on deposits was begun in 1980 so that S&Ls (and banks) could retain their deposit customers. In 1982 thrifts also were given broader powers enabling them to reduce their dependence on fixed-rate mortgages. Unfortunately, these deregulatory steps, though necessary, were taken without dealing with the already decapitalized institutions and, even more importantly, without addressing the incentive problems created by federal deposit insurance.

The Two "Levels" of Mistakes

Most analysts now recognize that forbearance (i.e., the decision to allow hundreds of S&Ls to continue operating without capital) was a serious mistake. Managers and owners with none of their own funds at stake sought investment opportunities promising high returns as they attempted to recoup past losses. But greater promised returns also involved larger risks, and most institutions that were managed with an eye toward finding a big payoff suffered large losses instead.

The failure to close decapitalized thrifts constitutes only the first level of mistake, however. While politically motivated forbearance now has been roundly condemned, the policy that supported forbearance has received less attention. Without federal deposit insurance, there would have been no opportunity for conditions within the thrift industry to deteriorate as they did.

The Incentive Problems Created by Federal Deposit Insurance

In the wake of the Great Depression, Congress sought to encourage people to put their money in healthy banks and leave it there. The introduction of federal deposit insurance was an element in the congressional response to the economic crisis. Since their founding, the federal deposit insurance agencies have attempted to avoid even inconveniencing depositors in bankrupt institutions, much less imposing significant losses on them.

Most failures are handled through arranged mergers over weekends so that disruption is minimized. In many cases all depositors are protected, particularly when large institutions are involved. Deposit insurance also focuses on individual accounts, providing virtually unlimited coverage for depositors willing to place their funds in several institutions. And if there is a delay in distributing the funds of a failed bank or thrift, the federal insurers guarantee accrued interest as well as principal.

In fact, the federal government has been too accommodating. Its policies have created an environment in which most depositors have no reason to concern themselves about the management practices or reputations of those depository managers to whom they entrust their money.

So managers of insolvent institutions, as well as those simply inclined to take more risks, easily outbid more conservative banks and

S&Ls for funds. Individuals who place deposits of less than $100,000 bear none of the risk themselves, and many focus solely on return. As a result, money is flowing to the worst-managed institutions in the country. Extensive federal deposit guarantees, coupled with the policy of capital forbearance, have acted as a magnet for frauds, just as deposit insurance has supported bad managers. Without discipline from the depositors who fund these operations, the burden of supervising the practices of S&L managers falls almost entirely on federal regulators. As Gerald P. O'Driscoll, Jr., an economist with the Federal Reserve Bank of Dallas, has observed, "It is no accident that federal deposit insurance and the modern federal regulatory system were created by the same act. The incentives established by the insurance system necessitated the regulatory framework."

But that brings us full circle. It was government-sponsored regulation that first led to the extensive problems of the thrift industry. Obviously, the federal government simply cannot substitute for market oversight in controlling risk.

The Failings of Government Oversight

In the first place, government-sponsored rules and regulations are by their nature inflexible. The federal government could not have anticipated the high interest rates of the late 1970s and early 1980s; even if it had, appropriate legislative and regulatory responses probably would not have survived the inevitable political challenges. Nor can new rules and guidelines be written today that foresee the economic or technological changes that will make them obsolete in the future. As a result, every regulatory scheme can carry within it the seeds of widespread industry difficulties.

Secondly, the federal regulatory agencies will never have the personnel nor the financial resources to effectively regulate a financial system as large and diverse as ours. Adequate oversight requires not only having interested parties who are in a position to monitor managerial behavior on a regular basis, but also an environment in which the attention of depository managers is focused on making decisions that emphasize financial stability and health first.

Finally, the problems created by federal deposit guarantees are just as real for banks as for thrift institutions. The current system is generating instability throughout the financial structure. With the thrift industry teetering over the abyss and the banking industry on a similar path, it is time to address the problems created by federal deposit insurance.

Reforming the Federal Deposit Insurance System

To return the U.S. financial industry to long-term stability, depositor dependence on federal deposit guarantees must be reduced and eventually eliminated. When depositors can no longer rely on the federal government (i.e., their fellow taxpayers) to protect their interests in the event of a depository failure, then managers and stockholders of financial institutions will have to change the way they do business. To attract and retain accounts, bankers will need first to convince their customers of the financial health and stability of their institutions.

To signal their financial strength, successful depository institutions would hold more equity capital than many have today. Banks and S&Ls would develop more extensive secondary markets for common types of loans so they could increase the liquidity of their portfolios. In addition, portfolios would be better diversified to reduce the risk associated with overdependence on sector-specific loans. Healthy institutions would no longer seek to hide behind vague and misleading accounting rules, but would increase their use of market-value accounting to inform their depositors of continued financial strength. Stronger institutions would also encourage the development of rating services providing reliable, third-party information to potential customers about depository strength. Finally and most importantly, before making investment and lending decisions, depository managers would consider the impact of potential problems on future depositor confidence.

These changes would represent a radical departure from the way business is done today at many institutions. Since 1934, the federal government gradually has assumed from bank and thrift managers more and more of the responsibility for reassuring depositors. This has freed depository managers and stockholders to pursue other goals. Increased returns and institutional growth have replaced financial strength as the primary objective of many depository decisionmakers.

This shift in the focus of the deposit-taking industry is responsible for many of the problems facing the financial markets today. In addition to the speculative investments made by many thrifts, the LDC debt problem and the absence of sufficient capital at many banks, to name just two examples, can be laid largely at the door of federal deposit insurance.

The failure to understand how substantially the market would differ in the absence of federal deposit insurance is the source of many misunderstandings. Unfortunately, these misunderstandings have made their way into a report released recently by the FDIC.

In its report, *Deposit Insurance for the Nineties,* the FDIC talks about the need to develop "an appropriate balance between depositor discipline and financial stability." Later this view is made more specific when the FDIC concludes that "the trade-off between stability and depositor discipline must be weighed heavily in favor of stability."

But as explained herein, there is no tradeoff between stability and the market-sponsored discipline that would arise if explicit and implicit government guarantees were removed. In fact, quite the opposite is true. Only the market can muster the resources and create the environment that will lead managers and stockholders to pursue financial strength and stability as their first priority. As the financial markets increase in complexity and as money is transferred around the world in milliseconds, only the market can control the risktaking of depository managers.

Conclusion

The savings and loan fiasco has revealed a structural flaw in our system for supervising depository institutions. Unfortunately, most analysts and observers have misinterpreted recent events or are choosing to ignore the true source of the problem. Without federal deposit guarantees to distort the market for deposits, no amount of politically sponsored forbearance or lax supervision could have created a crisis of the current magnitude.

The existing system rewards speculative behavior at the expense of more prudent management. It has encouraged funds to run to, rather than away from, the worst-managed, most-indebted institutions in the country. And while the banking industry's regulatory structure is currently viewed as a model operation, its performance is praiseworthy only in relation to the thrift industry fiasco. Banks face similar incentives for excessive risktaking, and cracks in the bank regulatory and deposit insurance systems remain unnoticed only because attention is focused elsewhere.

Taxpayers, who will ultimately pay most of the thrift industry's cleanup costs, should receive something more for their contribution than a reshuffling of the government's organizational charts and empty promises of "tougher regulation." Taxpayers deserve substantive reforms that address existing flaws in a way that will eliminate the possibility of future crises. Federal deposit insurance is a source of disease that eventually will cause the U.S. financial system to stumble and collapse. It is time to set in motion reform of the federal deposit insurance system. It is time to begin eliminating depositors' and bankers' dependence on federal guarantees.

Parasite Economy Latches onto New Host

David Boaz

Perhaps the biggest success story of the American economy in the past decade is the Microsoft Corp., which made a profit of $2.2 billion in fiscal 1996. Founder Bill Gates and many other millionaires in Redmond, Washington, got rich the only way you can in a free market: by producing something other people wanted. A lot of brilliant people worked long hours producing computer software that millions of people chose to buy, in the midst of a highly competitive market that offered lots of other options.

But in our modern politicized economy—which Jonathan Rauch called the "parasite economy" in his book *Demosclerosis*—no good deed goes unpunished for long. For many years all those brilliant minds at Microsoft and all the money they earned were devoted to making products that would help people. Then the federal government noticed that Microsoft was just too good and was helping its customers just too much. It launched a Federal Trade Commission investigation, later compounded by a Justice Department investigation, of whether Microsoft "has monopolized or has attempted to monopolize" markets for personal computer software and peripherals. Microsoft gave in and agreed to restrictions on its contracting and pricing policies in order to avoid long and costly litigation. That wasn't enough for the government—or for some of Microsoft's competitors—who went on to launch more antitrust investigations.

The issue today isn't whether Microsoft is or was in fact a monopolist, though the facts shed a lot of doubt on that claim.

What concerns me here is how the government lured Microsoft into the political sector of the economy. For more than a decade the company went about its business, developing software, selling it to

David Boaz is executive vice president of the Cato Institute and author of *Libertarianism: A Primer.*

Cato Policy Report, November/December 1996

customers, and innocently making money. Then in 1995, after repeated assaults by the Justice Department's Antitrust Division, not to mention its growing encounters with immigration, tax, trade, and other regulations, Microsoft broke down and started playing the Washington game—entirely defensively, it appears.

As early as 1990 it had employed the Washington office of Preston Gates Ellis & Rouvelas Meeds, a Seattle law firm that includes Bill Gates's father, as its chief outside counsel in Washington. In 1995 the company opened its own Washington office, headed by Jack Krumholtz, a Washington lawyer. It also hired the lobbying firm Downey, Chandler, headed by two former congressmen, and the public relations firm Bozell Sawyer Miller Group. It worked on policy issues through several trade associations. (It also, I might note, for the first time made contributions to the Cato Institute, the Center for Democracy and Technology, and other think tanks and public interest groups.)

There's no evidence that Microsoft has done anything more than try to protect itself from depredation by the federal government. The tragedy is that the most important factor in America's economic future—in raising everyone's standard of living—is not land, or money, or computers; it's human talent. And some portion of the human talent at one of America's most dynamic companies is now being diverted from productive activity to protecting the company from political predation, motivated by envy, lust for power, or simply the desire to win in the political arena what you can't win in the economic arena. The parasite economy has sucked another productive enterprise into its destructive maw. And while Microsoft's lobbying and public affairs efforts are entirely defensive at present, will Microsoft someday perhaps be tempted to use its newfound political assets to gain something in Washington that it can't win in the marketplace?

The slowdown of the American economy over the past few decades can be blamed in large measure on just this process—the expansion of the parasite economy into the productive economy. As Rauch points out, the number of corporations with Washington offices increased 10-fold between 1961 and 1982. *Congressional Quarterly* reports show that the number of people lobbying in Washington at least doubled and may have tripled between the mid-1970s and the mid-1980s. The number of lawyers per million Americans stayed the same from 1870 to 1970, then more than doubled by 1990.

Of course, all this investment in Washington reflected Willie Sutton's observation about robbing banks: "That's where the money is." The federal budget has grown inexorably over the past 60 years or so. Even if you don't want to get a piece of that budget, the long arm of the government reaches out to affect you. The number of pages in the *Federal Register*, where new regulations are printed, doubled between 1957 and 1967, tripled between 1970 and 1975, and remains at some 60,000 a year. No wonder so many corporations have opened Washington offices.

Microsoft's new presence in Washington is entirely understandable, but it is a tragic symbol of the diversion of America's productive resources into the unproductive world of political predation and the struggle to resist it.

PART V

A WORLD IN TRANSITION

Fear and Loathing in the Soviet Union

Edward H. Crane

It has always struck me as ironic that so many conservatives view libertarians as being "soft on communism"—particularly with regard to the Soviet Union. For it is arguable that the political system in the Soviet Union has more in common with contemporary American conservatism than with libertarianism. Nationalism, government enforced morality, and use of state-run schools to mold young people into "proper" citizens are just a few examples where libertarians find themselves on the opposite side of the fence from conservatives and the Soviets.

All of which is to say that, communism and libertarianism being in essence ideological opposites, it should come as no surprise that my recent visit to the Soviet Union left me with a distinctly negative impression of that society. It is one thing, however, to understand that central economic planning cannot work and that totalitarianism is inconsistent with the nature of human beings. It is quite another thing to experience it in all its glory, albeit briefly, as I did last September.

My week in the Soviet Union came about when three libertarian friends and I decided to extend our trip to Stockholm (where we were attending a Mont Pelerin Society meeting) by taking a boat to Helsinki and a train from there to Leningrad. One doesn't, of course, just up and go to Russia. All this was preceded by getting approval from various governments to allow us to travel to and from the countries involved. Obtaining the Russian visa was the major hurdle, and once that was achieved we all prepared for our adventure by reading Hedrick Smith's excellent book, *The Russians*. In it Smith describes an incredibly backward and oppressive society. As it turned out, he greatly understated the case.

Edward H. Crane is president of the Cato Institute.
Update, January and February 1982

The first thing you notice when you get on the Russian-run train to Leningrad is an almost overwhelming stench. It is an odor that seems to permeate every building and everybody in the Soviet Union. The phrase "the unwashed masses" is not a mere cliche in Russia. As with so many elements of our visit, you had to be there to believe it.

The train ride itself—along the very route Lenin took on his triumphant return to Petrograd—took on the trappings of a grade-B World War II movie. Clacking along tracks greatly in need of repair (Ayn could have warned us), huddled in two tiny "deluxe" cabins and trying to converse without breathing the foul air, we determined the best course of action would be to open a bottle of Stolichnaya and prepare for whatever lay ahead. It was a strategy we would frequently employ.

When we reached the Finnish-Soviet border, the train groaned to a halt and a half dozen Soviet military thugs clamored on board and began checking everyone's papers. Their modus operandi was almost comical as they threw open doors, slammed them shut, ordered us to "stand!" or "sit!" and vigorously searched our luggage, all the while eyeing us suspiciously as though the next suitcase they opened would contain arms and ammunition or, worse, a copy of *The Russians.* Two of us had brought along our copies of the book, and when my colleague's was confiscated and mine was not, my friends accused me of collaborating with the enemy. One of them even suggested the incident probably reflected the Soviets' appreciation of my years as publisher of *Inquiry* magazine.

We had been informed prior to the trip that the KGB would likely assign an agent to us on the train to find out, among other things, why we would be visiting the USSR. (It was a question, we were to discover, with considerable merit.) Sure enough, fifteen minutes into the trip a Swede, who claimed to be going to Leningrad to visit his Russian wife, befriended us. One by one he would ingratiate himself with us and we would cheerfully answer his laundry list of questions. Surprisingly, our new friend was unaware of the dominant role played by the Libertarian Party in American politics. Perhaps he related all of this to his "wife" whom he greeted at the Leningrad train station with a formal handshake.

Leningrad is a sprawling city that appears little changed from what it must have been like in the 19th century. There are virtually no new buildings (for reasons of "historical preservation," we were told) other than some sagging highrise apartments on the outskirts of the city. Not only has nothing new been built since Leningrad was Petrograd, nothing has been repaired there either. Everything in the USSR, in fact, seems to be in a state of chronic disrepair. I have seen socialism up close and it doesn't work.

We were provided with an Intourist guide and a car and driver. The driver raced through the streets of Leningrad with reckless abandon, which created little concern on our part since it appeared that we had the only car in the city. Indeed, such a curiosity was our beat-up limo (which looked something like a 1954 Packard) that whenever it came to a stop crowds of people would gather around it to peer in the windows with awestruck faces. But cars are not the only item in short supply in the Soviet Union.

What we are talking about here is definitely *not* a consumer-oriented society. The largest department store in Leningrad—some two square city blocks wide and two stories high—was virtually empty. Hundreds of people milled around dozens of compartments within the store simply because they had nothing better to do. There was, you see, nothing on the shelves. Occasionally there would be a display of, say, shoelaces or rubber boots, but really not much else. An "electronics" department displayed a few radios and what appeared to be vacuum-tube televisions. They were not for sale but you could order one if you had the rubles.

Socialist Economics

A word about rubles. The Soviets, in an almost childlike way, have set the official exchange rate at .8 ruble per dollar. That way a ruble is absolutely more valuable than a dollar, see? Except for the fact that one could readily unload a dollar for four rubles in the black market. Because our merry group wore clothes that were neither frayed nor frumpy we were easily spotted as visitors and not inmates. On numerous occasions people would sidle up to us, disclaim employment by the KGB, and ask to exchange their rubles for our dollars. Other than a surreptitious purchase of a jar of black market caviar, however, we avoided numerous opportunities to commit crimes against the state.

The Soviet Union is a backward nation with no rational division of labor, no price system, and a command economy that clearly doesn't work. There is hardly any food to eat—even in the "best" hotels. Potatoes, cucumbers, and bread were in reasonable supply, but what little meat there was turned out to be inedible. We hear reports in the U.S. from business groups from time to time pointing out how much greater our GNP is than Russia's or how many more hours a Russian peasant has to work in order to buy what his American counterpart does. But that kind of analysis rather leaves the impression that if a Soviet worker was industrious and saved money, then one day, per- haps at a later stage in life than in the U.S., but one day, he could have a decent standard of living. The truth is that there is no way for So- viet workers to have a decent living. The appearances are that peo- ple have to work hard just to survive, and that the economy is in a perpetual state of stagnant decline.

But if it is hard to describe the economic wasteland of Russia to someone who hasn't been there, it is even harder to describe what their totalitarian system has done to the human spirit of 260 million people. It isn't just the drabness and grayness one sees everywhere. Or the rudeness and surliness one encounters so often. It's that you virtually never see people laughing, smiling or just seeming to enjoy themselves. People seem to walk slightly bent over, their eyes always averted from a stranger. There is an overwhelming sense of oppres- sion and depression. It is no wonder that alcoholism is a major prob- lem in the Soviet Union.

When we occasionally had opportunities to talk to people in parks or on the street, there was a phrase that kept recurring. We'd ask them if they had ever been outside the USSR, if they would ever own a car, if they could switch jobs if they wanted. The answer, with a shrug of the shoulders, was often an emotionless "It's impossible." Whereas in our society one frequently encounters a sense of outrage at injustice or a determination to achieve a goal against all odds, in the Soviet Union one just shrugs. It's impossible.

Ideology in Russia is on the wane. The bright young university graduates who guided us around Leningrad and Moscow sounded like robots when speaking of Lenin and the Revolution. They never asked us what life was like in the United States. They couldn't an- swer the simplest criticism of socialism without employing some Leninist cliche. One got the distinct impression that they didn't really believe what they were saying. There are no billboards or signs in Russia other than massive banners with giant red letters proclaiming the glories of the revolution in general and Lenin in particular. Our guides seemed embarrassed to read them to us. In the few places one could purchase books there was nothing but the works of Marx and Engels. (One comedian in our group kept pestering our guides with a deadpan, "Why aren't there any books by Stalin in the stores?") The "non-official" people we talked to, however, never discussed ideology or attempted to defend socialism. Their political concerns seem to center on U.S. militarism, and they were pleasantly surprised to find that our group shared those concerns. Our rejoinders regarding Afghanistan and Poland were met with only mild resistance. One young man told us that he'd willingly defend his homeland but that "I don't want to die in Poland."

I was surprised to find tremendous reverence for the Czars and Czarist Russia among the people. If Nicholas was criticized it was because he was "too weak." Numerous palaces and museums damaged in World War II are being painstakingly (if clumsily) restored at tremendous cost to an economy that can ill afford it. It is as though the Soviets feel the artistic and architectural achievements of eighteenth and nineteenth century Russia dwarf any post-revolutionary accomplishments. That does, indeed, seem to be the case.

Our flight from Leningrad to Moscow on an Aeroflot jet was an experience none of us would ever want to repeat. We arrived at the airport early and went to the "food" counter in a section that looked down on the massive ground floor where passengers stood in long lines. About two dozen pigeons shared the area with a few people, flying from table to table and generally doing the things that pigeons do. No one seemed to mind. We had to walk a quarter of a mile out on the runway to board our plane, on which we sat for an hour waiting for it to fill up (very efficient that way, you see). I do not recommend sitting in a plane (knees to chest—efficiency again) crowded with 200 teeming Russians and lacking air conditioning and oxygen. It seems impossible, I suppose, but you *can* hold your breath for three hours. A greasy-haired naval officer in the seat ahead of me slept with his head on the shoulder of a nervous citizen next to him throughout the flight while a flock of contented flies circled above.

When we landed in Moscow, we waited for our luggage with our fellow passengers for about an hour. I, having gulped some air and happy to be alive, was entertaining our troupe with my famous quarter trick. The dour-faced Russians looked at us incredulously as we laughed and joked about the airport. Soldiers (who are everywhere) scowled. The reason for the delay in getting our luggage was evident when it arrived with clothing sticking out of the sides—everyone's having been searched.

Moscow looks more like a modern city than Leningrad. There are more cars and some tall office buildings. But the food and product shortage had been, in good communist style, generously shared with this city as well. Women still swept the streets with bound-twig brooms. Everything was still gray and depressing. One of our group lost his papers, reported it to the hotel authorities, and was subjected to a two-hour interrogation in a padded room decorated only by a large picture of Brezhnev in full military garb. We celebrated his release with another bottle of Stolichnaya.

We stayed at what was billed as one of the premier hotels in Moscow: the Hotel Intourist. Architecturally, it combined all of the worst of schlock 1950s design. In the lobby a "gift" shop offered dozens of pins, buttons, medals, busts and photos in honor of the gangsters past and present who rule the Soviet Union. Since you can't exchange rubles back into dollars when you leave the USSR, I purchased several handsome red lapel buttons bearing a likeness of Lenin (who else?) with the last of my rubles.

By the time of our departure to London we felt as though we were escaping the country. The oppressiveness of a police state is something that affects even a short-term visitor very quickly. At the Moscow airport one of us discovered that the restrooms had no toilet paper. To get some one must track down a surly female custodian who then grudgingly issues a few sheets from a roll on a broom. If toilet paper were in the restrooms, we were told, it would be stolen by locals as it, like everything else, is in short supply.

There was a spontaneous cheer that went up when our British Airways pilot informed us we were leaving Soviet air space.

From a libertarian standpoint, my visit to the Soviet Union served to reinforce the wisdom and necessity of a non-interventionist military and foreign policy for the U.S. War is quite literally the only thing that could "save" the USSR. It is a society that appears to be crumbling from within. If we can avoid confrontation with the Soviets over the next twenty years, their system should collapse of its own bureaucratic weight. It is a society in deeper trouble than the much-publicized Polish situation. In my view, if the cracks that are appearing in the Eastern bloc nations reach the USSR, they will spread rapidly throughout the country. We were exposed only to the ethnic Russian minority that controls their society. If it represents fertile ground for revolution—and it does—think how the rest of the USSR would react to an opportunity for change.

The Soviet Union is not just an oppressive nation. It is a *weak* society. One is left with a sense of pity rather than fear. People survive at a subsistence level, beaten down by their oppressors and generally unaware of how people live on the outside. The fear that we should have is that the "leaders" in the U.S. will precipitate an incident that could trigger World War III. For it is time this corrupt and failing Soviet system cease being an excuse for building our military-industrial complex.

Someone in our group suggested it would be interesting if there were a "Sovietland" section at Disneyland so that Americans could see what society is really like there. The problem, we agreed, was that, with all the propaganda spewed forth from those with a vested interest in the arms race, no one would believe it. In a sense, Americans are as ignorant of what life is like in the USSR as the Soviets are of life here. And that is dangerous.

I wish more political activists on both the left and the right could spend a few days in the Soviet Union. Leftists could see firsthand how thoroughly corrupt and unworkable socialism is. Conservatives could see how absurd it is to view the Soviet system as a threat to the West or attractive to the Third World. Peace and free trade. That is the answer to the Soviet "threat."

The Strikes in Poland: Workers against the Workers' State

Don Lavoie

For the third time in as many decades of Communist Party rule in Poland, nationwide strikes have forced the government to replace its leadership and yield to sweeping popular demands for liberalization. The workers have once again wearied of submitting complaint letters to the faceless bureaucrats of the Central Council of Trade Unions and have demanded—and at least temporarily won—independent unions with the officially recognized right to strike, as well as the relaxation of censorship, substantial economic reforms, and generous wage settlements.

On July 1, 1980 Premier Edward Babiuch had decided to raise meat prices, and this policy was confirmed on August 12 in an announcement by the Party's national secretary, Jerzy Lukaszewicz. The next day, over 50,000 workers at the giant Lenin Shipyard in Gdansk went on strike and took over the yard. Although the action was touched off by the meat-price hike, it had been brewing for months and reflected a deep-seated resentment of general economic and political conditions in Poland.

Initially, the Party's First Secretary, Edward Gierek, struggled to confine the rebellion to the Lenin Shipyard and negotiate on narrowly restricted issues. Four days into the strike, the workers at the shipyard overruled the wage settlement agreed to by their own strike committee and extended their demands in a 16-point list of grievances that fundamentally challenged the communist system. The strike quickly spread to other cities and over 250 factories, and the list of demands grew longer and more bold. On August 20 Gierek

Don Lavoie (1951–2002) was David H. & Charles G. Koch Professor of Economics at the George Mason University School of Public Policy.
Cato Policy Report, November/December 1980

168

had 14 leading dissident intellectuals arrested for supporting the strike. He tried to suppress news coverage of the strike and refused to negotiate with the newly created "integrated strike committees," which were, he said, composed of "antisocialist elements." The head of the legal trade unions, Jan Szydlak, tried to circumvent the rebellious strike committees by meeting with more conciliatory workers and stated confidently that "the authorities do not intend to give up their power or to share it with anyone else."

Submissive workers were, however, increasingly hard to find. Energized by the Gdansk strikes, workers throughout the country were joined by dissident intellectuals in supporting the rebellion. By August 22 the powerful Polish Roman Catholic Church had given its moderate endorsement to the strike, and Gierek had begun referring to "mistakes" that had been made by his regime.

Eleven days into the strike, with the entire economy at a standstill, Gierek tried to forestall further unrest by announcing a major shake-up of the Party leadership, dismissing many hardliners such as Szydlak and Babiuch, and replacing them with moderates. But strike leader Lech Walesa described Gierek's personnel changes as "patching up holes" and scoffed at Gierek's solemn promises that free elections would be conducted within the old unions.

Finally, on the last day of August, the beleaguered Gierek regime ended the 17-day strike by agreeing to the workers' demands, including the unprecedented official sanction of an independent, self-governing trade union with the right to strike, a concession the *Washington Post* reported as having been "unthinkable" only a week before. In addition, the strikers won the release of 28 dissidents and obtained substantive concessions on government censorship and economic reform, largely intended to decentralize the economy and make the production of consumer goods a greater priority. The only points on which the strike committee seemed to yield were vague and symbolic: acceptance of "the leading role" of the Party and "the principle of nationalized means of production."

Yet hardly had this startling agreement been signed than 200,000 Silesian coal miners walked off the job. This strike was quickly settled by an explicit extension of the Gdansk agreement to the whole country. At its height the strike had involved almost 400,000 workers at hundreds of factories and several coal mines. By early September the forces of liberalization had increased their power, and in the wake of the strike settlement rights were being demanded at all levels by almost everyone, from students and artists to Party members.

Finally, on the excuse of bad health, Edward Gierek himself was removed from power and replaced by the little known *apparatchik,* Stanislaw Kania. A former head of the secret police, Kania is not expected to permit the dilution of the Party's monopoly of power to proceed very far or for very long, but his initial moves have been largely conciliatory. He seems intent upon riding out the crisis by appearing more liberal than Gierek, whom he is accusing of having had too much power.

Meanwhile, membership in the new trade unions continued to accelerate throughout September, and, as if to demonstrate that they meant business, the new unions called a one-hour work stoppage on September 29 to protest the government's failure to meet wage demands and to allow them access to the national press. The next day the unions issued a statement that if the "warning strike" did not bring concrete results by October 20, another general strike would be considered.

It is unlikely that the Polish workers are going to be persuaded by the verbal assurances of the new Kania leadership. The same Gierek who is today an object of vilification for his cynical use of state power rose to popularity ten years ago by opposing the policies of his predecessor, Wladyslaw Gomulka. In 1968 Gomulka had crushed a student revolt in his own country and had enthusiastically supported the Russian invasion and occupation of Czechoslovakia. But his repressive policies went too far in December 1970, when his troops shot into crowds of striking Gdansk workers, killing more than a hundred. Yet this tyrant had come to power in 1956 because of his image as a liberal reformer who had been imprisoned by *his* tyrannical predecessor, the hardline Stalinist Boleslaw Bierut. Given this history of Polish leadership, we can expect the Poles to be suspicious of Kania's newfound role as advocate of democracy and liberalism.

This is not to say that Gomulka and Gierek were always and unambiguously tyrannical or that Kania is likely to be now. Each leader ushered in a period of genuine liberalization, both politically and economically, the impact of which greatly improved the cultural and economic life of the people. Ironically, it is precisely by *relaxing* its tremendous power that the government has been able to win enough of the confidence of the masses it needs to *regain* that power. The pattern has been a couple of years of hopeful reform followed by a gradual erosion of liberty until the conditions of economic rigidity and political intolerance have worsened enough to lead to another cycle of revolt, government concessions, and liberalization.

As *New York Times* journalist John Darnton put it, "To resigned and cynical Polish intellectuals, the society seemed so full of contradictions that disorders appeared inevitable and even cyclical, like the economic depressions Marxists insist will dog the West."

Since the first Stalinist-style six-year plan was launched thirty years ago, the Polish leadership has been trying to steer a precarious course between obedience to its central planning ideology and deliverance to the people of at least some of the promises of that ideology. Conforming to the ideology of Russian-style central planning entails the continuation of unworkable economic policies that are certain to provoke further strikes, while economic concessions to the strikers are sure to undermine the last vestiges of ideological justification for the Communist Party's control over the Polish economy.

The roots of the most recent rebellion can be found in the failure of the theory and practice of the Soviet-style central planning that the Poles have endured since World War II.

The Myth of Central Planning Theory

The Soviet model of "central planning" is itself a hybrid, born of the conflict between Marxist theory and Russian reality. The origins of central planning ideology in Poland, as in all of eastern Europe, can be traced to Karl Marx, although its day-to-day operation bears little resemblance to the notion of "conscious planning" Marx described. Marx condemned the market for being an undesigned result of the contention among private owners for profit and argued for a system in which producers can take direct and conscious control over production and deliberately *design* the direction of social evolution. In place of the "anarchic" ordering mechanism enforced by the "law of value" in which errors are discovered *after* investments are made, Marx wanted production processes that were designed in advance *in toto* and ordered by fitting all economic decisions into a unified central plan.

Despite his blindness to the impracticability of this scheme of central planning, Marx has to be credited with the virtue of consistency.

Market institutions reflect the competition for profits that serves as a social ordering mechanism guiding capitalist production. If all production is to be *consciously* planned, such spontaneous, unplannable institutions as market prices and even money must be eradicated. One could no more consciously plan a price system than one could plan a football game. By its very nature a price system (or a sporting match) is a rivalrous process, its outcome the result of the clash of separate and mutually inconsistent plans.

The competitive struggle for profit in which some market participants outbid others for resources is an inherently unplannable process. The structure of relative prices that emerges from this competition among private owners depends on the pulling and tugging of contending and conflicting plans. In a sporting match it is the contention itself that is valued, but in an economy it is the prices that result from the struggle that are needed. The information contained in the price system enables competing entrepreneurs to engage in technologically sophisticated methods of production and satisfy the ever-changing demands of consumers.

The notion of a centrally planned economy, then, implies the absence of all market relations and money prices, as Marx understood. What Marx did *not* realize is that an economy organized in such a way precludes the advanced and complex technological production processes of modern society. As the Austrian economists Ludwig von Mises and Friedrich Hayek have explained, there is no substitute for the price information that is continuously generated by a competitive market economy. Lenin's attempt to abolish the price system was an unmitigated disaster, and the idea has been almost completely abandoned by contemporary socialists, to whom prices and money are indispensable. The prevailing schemes of "central planning" are now less theoretically consistent but also less obviously catastrophic amalgams of planning and market institutions.

If it is true that a football match cannot be consciously planned in advance and still *be* a football match, the facade of planning can still be preserved. One can publish a football plan that says a touchdown will be scored by team A in the first period, watch the game, and then revise the "plan" after the first quarter to read that a field goal be kicked by team B instead. By the end of the game the continuously revised "plan" will have been fulfilled to the last detail.

Similarly, as Paul Craig Roberts has demonstrated, socialist planners gather last year's production statistics from each plant, add a percentage increase, and publish this as next year's "plan." When economic forces reveal this plan to be unachievable, revisions are passed back up the hierarchy to the central office and are incorporated into revised "plans." The much vaunted "scientific" plan that is supposed to guide all of production is actually derived from decentralized market-guided decisions made previous to its design and continuously revised throughout its implementation, on the basis of changing market considerations, until the plan period is over and the newly revised plan has been miraculously "achieved." This is not Marx's conscious, rational, ex ante guiding of production processes by the central planners but more like the ex post guiding of plan making by realized production processes. In practice, socialist production is at least as "anarchic" as capitalism.

The "common" ownership of the means of production is effectively undermined by the fact that plant managers separately compute profit/loss accounts, bid against one another for resources, and are offered material incentives in lieu of profits. This bidding process is extremely cumbersome, and the lack of open-market institutions and secure property titles seriously hinders the efficient operation of the socialist price system, but a clumsy kind of competition nonetheless takes place and must be permitted to operate for the prices used in accounting to have any meaning.

The Chaos of Central Planning Practice

Although one could not replace the competition of football players with a script without destroying the game, one could significantly *interfere* with the competitive process that constitutes the essence of a sporting match without completely ruining it. One could, for example, periodically introduce ad hoc rule changes and point redistributions without entirely destroying the contest. Of course, one would in such a case not be planning the football game, since its outcome is still the spontaneous consequence of decentralized decisions; one would merely be obstructing it.

If a Soviet-style economy is not genuinely planned in the sense dictated by Marx's theory, this is most definitely *not* to say that the economy is unaffected by the activities of the central planning bureau. A

173

considerable measure of chaos is introduced into the competitive process by the daily interferences of "planners" with the decisions of producers. A planning bureau is, after all, a bureaucracy. To justify its existence mountains of paperwork have to be generated, red tape has to obstruct the introduction of the slightest changes in routine, and, in general, getting anything done through official channels takes endless maneuvering, if not outright bribery. The socialist system works somewhat like a capitalist price system in extreme slow motion. Price changes eventually lead to revisions in production processes, but only at so slow a pace that the revision is likely to be obsolete by the time it is enacted. The pricing of certain items, such as meat, can have serious political consequences, and these items are often subsidized to placate consumers, using general state revenues. (These revenues are drying up as Poland's economy now reports negative growth while it shoulders the weight of a $20 billion debt to the West. Most of this money was used to finance a crash industrialization program, which seems to have failed.)

The interference of the planners with production often takes bizarre forms, particularly in the promulgation of numerous mutually contradictory production "targets" that plant managers are supposed to fulfill in addition to avoiding a monetary loss. Thus the planners would set a target for so many linear meters of cloth, thereby encouraging textile manufacturers to narrow the width of the product. A target specified in terms of the "total value" of production encourages enterprises to use the costliest materials, and produce, for example, pointlessly ornate dishes. The planners' reaction to this result—making a target index for "cost reduction"—in turn leads to the production of goods so badly made as to be worthless. Planning indices to reduce personnel or to ration the use of capital have led to similar absurdities. The profusion of indices, among which simple profit-and-loss considerations are only one, and not always the most important one, so seriously and so evidently hampers any rational production activity that the official rationale for the central plan as the ordering mechanism of the economy is not taken seriously by the workers or management.

So unwieldy is production under a central plan that recourse is regularly taken to thriving black and gray markets, where forms, indices, and prying bureaucrats can be circumvented in favor of straightforward if only semi-legal transactions. Indeed it seems that the useful production that does get accomplished occurs more in spite of, rather than because of, the activities of the busy central planning offices.

The gross inefficiencies of the attempts by socialist governments to control production have been serious enough to be acknowledged by even some of the most eager advocates of the Soviet model. Apologists such as Maurice Dobb have contended that this inefficiency is insignificant in the long run because the great virtue of central planning is its capacity to promote *growth*. A bit of microeconomic efficiency must be sacrificed today, but the benefits of the high rate of growth will surely outweigh this cost in a few years.

Yet it is probably here, in the sphere of new investment for economic growth, that the most serious economic flaw of central planning lies. Lacking legitimate markets for stocks and bonds, such economies have no rational mechanism to guide the flow of new investment toward more valuable avenues of production. Little genuine innovation occurs in the bureaucratic atmosphere, and a great proportion of investment is poorly integrated with the existing capital structure and therefore largely wasted. The bulk of resources has been diverted from the direct or indirect satisfaction of consumer demand and has gone instead to the satisfaction of the demands of the Communist Party elite for impressive macroeconomic "growth" statistics. By pushing out record numbers of tons of steel, the authorities can impress gullible Western macroeconomists with meaningless aggregate growth rates while promising the populace future abundance when the current investment yields its rich rewards.

Although the annual growth rate of gross industrial production was measured at 16.2% in Poland from 1951–1955, during its most intense period of rigid planning, very little beneficial impact of this industrialization program on the real standard of living of the Poles, then or since, can be attributed to that growth rate. Only the relaxation of this planning in the late fifties started to contribute to the real incomes of Polish workers, which still lag far behind those of the West.

About the only catastrophic policy of the Soviet model that the Poles have managed to escape is the collectivization of agriculture. Despite the fact that state-directed investment has been almost exclusively funneled into heavy industry at the expense of agriculture, the foodstuffs that Poland exports are primarily produced by private landowners.

Probably the most irritating consequence of the central planning system, in Poland and elsewhere, has been what is often called "the problem of supply." People have to stand in long lines for hours for virtually everything, and the waiting lists for more substantial purchases are measured in years (four for a car in Poland). But worse than the sight of a long line in front of a store is the absence of one: In a country that boasts of being the eleventh largest industrial power in the world, the average family frequently has to do without meat, bread, milk, or whatever else happens to be unavailable. As one Warsaw resident put it, "What good are all the cars, automatic washers, new coal mines, copper smelters, and shipyards if I cannot find a pair of shoelaces or have to stand in three one-hour lines to buy a roll of toilet paper?"

It may be difficult for a Westerner to comprehend the extent of this problem. We too have had to wait in line for a driver's license or to cash a check or, recently, to get some gas. But when shortages are as prevalent as they are in Poland, the queues are not an inconvenience, they are a heavy daily burden (disproportionately carried by women, incidentally) borne by the common people year after year and unavoidable for any but the Party elite, who have special shops. Indeed, the supply problem more than any other single factor is probably responsible for the angry rebellion of the Polish workers. A Gdansk striker expressed the intense frustration that has been felt in every socialist country when he screamed, "You know why I'm here? Because I have to stand in line for four hours for a tiny piece of meat that's disgusting to look at." Imagine the liberation East European refugees must experience when they first walk down the aisle of an American supermarket!

Perhaps even worse than the tremendous waste caused by the central planning system has been its political consequences. In place of the relatively civilized and peaceful rivalry for profits in the competitive marketplace is the brute-force rivalry among technocrats for a leading position in the central planning apparatus. Power is vested in the bureaucrats who enlist the aid of Party contacts or the secret police. Purges such as the one going on now in Poland periodically eliminate some factions and propel others to temporary leadership. In the recent shakeups, for example, Kania's political position has been consolidated by the aid of a certain Mieczyslaw Moczar, who has been unearthing scandal about Kania's rivals. Moczar had made an unsuccessful but well-organized bid for power himself in 1967 by launching an anti-Semitic smear campaign against his rivals (Gomulka's wife was Jewish). This kind of thuggish power politics is standard fare in socialist countries, and it surely makes the capitalist struggle for profits that Marx so condemned a pretty innocuous-sounding activity.

The political implications of the attempt to control the economic life of an entire nation by the state should not require much in-depth analysis. It is evident that when the government legally "owns" everything it is in a position to crush its opposition. With no independent court system the populace is at the mercy of the police state. Indeed, what is amazing about Poland is the extent to which underground organizations such as Nowa publishers have succeeded, despite all of the efforts of the state, in disseminating *samizdat* literature (for example, the reproduction of 10,000 copies of Tadeuz Konwicki's full-length novel, *Small Apocalypse*).

Toward an Alternative Economic System

This, then, is the central planning system with which the Polish workers are so justifiably angered. They are saying, in no uncertain terms, that they no longer believe in the promises of a future communist paradise, that they want a freer, more decentralized, more responsive economy—and they want it now. This has not been expressed in explicit free-market terminology yet, nor could it be in the shadow of Soviet tanks, but the consequences of the reforms already conceded to the courageous strikers could put Poland, and help put all of eastern Europe, on an accelerated path toward a free society.

Yet this is precisely what neither the Polish nor the Soviet Communist Party leaders can let happen. How far they will let their power deteriorate before cracking down is impossible to guess, but the extreme dangers of the attempts toward liberalization are understood by all participants. The one consequence nobody wants, least of all perhaps the Soviets themselves, is the desperate solution of sending in troops. The memory of Czechoslovakia haunts every discussion of the current crisis in Poland.

How this volatile situation will develop is uncertain, but one thing is clear: If the Soviets try to squelch "the Polish August" by force, they will encounter far more dogged resistance than they faced twelve years ago in Czechoslovakia. In virtually every respect the Poles are less likely to succumb easily to Russian dominance. The Slovaks had had a historical admiration for the Russians prior to the invasion, whereas the Poles have a long tradition of hatred for them. The Czechs and Slovaks had no single national heritage before 1918, and the union was never a very happy one, but Poland's population is outspokenly nationalistic, 98% Polish, and 90% Roman Catholic, with a rich cultural heritage extending centuries into the past. During "the Polish October" in 1956 when Poland and Hungary were both basking in newly won post-Stalinist reforms, it was Hungary that the Soviets chose to invade to make its imperialist point, and with good reason.

Furthermore, Poland today is probably less susceptible to a crackdown than ever before in its Communist history. All its previous social upheavals had been prompted and carried out either by the workers or the intellectuals and students, but never *both*. However, following Gierek's arrests and dismissals of workers who participated in the September 1976 price-increase riots, leading intellectuals founded the Committee for the Defense of the Workers and for the first time made effective organizational common cause with less privileged ordinary citizens. Since 1978 this organization, now called the Social Self-Defense Committee, has become by far the most significant human rights organization in eastern Europe, collecting and distributing thousands of dollars to victims of the state, publicizing cases of police brutality and torture, and issuing its own *samizdat* bulletins on show trials and the imprisonment of dissidents and strikers. The unity of all sectors of the Polish human rights movement was evident throughout the August strikes, when the intellectuals' support for the workers was immediate and effective.

Lastly, given their own domestic and international problems, the Soviets will be extremely reluctant to resort to military options. They too, after all, are trying to salvage the unworkable central planning system. At home the regime faces an increasingly influential dissident movement of its own, despite recent KGB campaigns—complete with five-year repression plans and arrest targets—to eliminate dissent. The Soviet consumer is beginning to demand some economic reform, and protests against the war in Afghanistan have spread. That war has already tightened the U.S.-China military alliance and cost the Soviets much of what was left of its support in the

Third World. With 45 divisions committed to the Chinese border and a hundred thousand troops fighting a protracted guerrilla war with the Afghans, the last thing Brezhnev wants is another military front.

The Polish strikes are an indication of the failure of the idea of central planning, and that idea is being increasingly discredited throughout the world, whatever the Soviets or the Kania regime try to do to save it. The centrally planned economy works only to the extent that the plan is consciously circumvented, ignored, or adjusted to decentralized production decisions. It has failed badly enough and long enough for its ideological justifications to be no longer credible, and without ideological support it is a program without a future.

The Polish underground is preparing the way for both the burial of the central planning ideology and the rise of an alternative ideology of freedom. Plans are now underway by the Nowa publishers to print volume one of Solzhenitsyn's *Gulag Archipelago,* which should accomplish the first task, as well as political tracts by none other than Friedrich Hayek, which should go a long way toward accomplishing the second.

Let a Billion Flowers Bloom

George Gilder

We're on the threshold of a new economic era that will be a great benefit for China, because China almost entirely missed the last economic era. If the incomes of the Chinese people in China had grown just one-third as fast in the past 40 years as the incomes of Chinese in other countries, China today would be the world's largest economy and the global economy would be 25 percent bigger than it is.

Today's new economic era is the age of information. Forget oil, gold, land—forget all those material things; the single greatest untapped natural resource in the world is the Chinese people. Sometimes other people treat the Chinese people as if they're mouths, but the Chinese people are minds. And the crucial issue of the next 25 years, when the information economy will increase its importance across the world, is whether the minds of the Chinese people are emancipated.

This new era involves a new technology—the microchip. The substance of a microchip is the silicon in sand. What matters is the content, the idea, the design, the function of the device. What this new technology means for China is that one of Chairman Mao's great dreams can now come true: power to the people. Twenty-five years ago, Chairman Mao launched a program of steel mills in every backyard. This was very stupid. Steel mills require huge economies of scale and thousands of regimented workers to produce efficiently. However, the new chip technology is based on economies of microscale. The smaller each device on the chip, the more powerful the chip. Not only can a single workstation create value in the new economy greater than that created by a huge steel mill, a workstation can

George Gilder is chairman of Gilder Publishing LLC. These remarks were presented at the Cato Institute conference, "Economic Reform in China," in Shanghai in September 1988.

Cato Policy Report, November/December 1988

also transmit more value around the world in microseconds than a fleet of supertankers can transport in months.

To fulfill Mao's dream of industrial power distributed to the people, however, we must give up his other dream of central planning of an economy. The law of the microcosm—the law of the microchip—is that the power of individual workstations always grows much faster than the power of large computer systems. The long dream of socialists that the computer will allow you to plan the economy has been confounded at the heart of the computer itself. The power of the chip always grows faster than the power of the larger system.

The previous technology of the industrial era to some extent favored control—control over natural resources, control over territory, control over tax systems; governments could increase national power by increasing their control. On the other hand the new technology favors freedom. Mao said, "Let a hundred flowers bloom." This statement showed his incomparable misunderstanding of the powers of the Chinese people. The rule of capitalism is "Let a billion flowers bloom."

I believe what will happen is an efflorescence of entrepreneurship in China that will make China the richest economy in the world over the next 25 years. How do I know this? Because everywhere else in the world the Chinese people are in the forefront of the information age. In the United States, thousands of crucial companies have been launched by Chinese entrepreneurs. And now there are very favorable signs within China itself. For example, one of the fastest-growing computer firms on the face of the earth is Stone Computer, started by Won Runan. In just four years this company outproduced all the government computer companies in China. Today on a street in Beijing there are 170 high-technology companies, and 1,000 more such companies are applying for licenses. They should get those licenses very fast. Let a billion flowers bloom.

Prospects for Peaceful Change in South Africa

Helen Suzman

I'm very impressed that Americans continue to be concerned about South Africa, considering all the other problems that you have to contend with—the deficit, the failed coup in Panama, the aftermath of Hurricane Hugo, the HUD scandal, Cuban refugees, difficulties in your inner cities, and, of course, Jackie Mason's comments about David Dinkins. I would have thought that you would be occupied with your own affairs. But no, you are still interested in South Africa, and I'm genuinely pleased about that. I believe that it is absolutely essential that the most powerful democracy in the world, with human rights as its basic value, use its influence to safeguard those rights everywhere.

South Africa has undoubtedly breached human rights, but it is by no means the only country to have done so. Race discrimination is practiced everywhere—in the United States, in England, and in all other democratic countries. Indeed, there are many countries where race discrimination, in practice, is even worse than in South Africa. South Africa's unenviable position as the pariah of the Western world is, of course, due to its being the only country that has established race discrimination by statute.

I've had the dubious privilege of serving in the South African Parliament for 36 of the 40 years that race discrimination has been on the statute book. I've seen the National party, which has now been in power for more than 40 years, place on the statute book legislation to enforce racial separation in every facet of life. In the area of eco-

Helen Suzman was a member of the South African Parliament from 1953 to 1989. This article is based on her remarks as the Cato Institute's sixth Distinguished Lecturer in October 1989.
Cato Policy Report, March/April 1990

nomics, there was the Job Reservation Act, which reserved all skilled work for white people and did not recognize black or racially mixed trade unions. There were statutes that prohibited marriage across the color line. (Americans shouldn't be too smug about that, because a Mississippi statute that prohibited interracial marriage was only recently abolished. Of course, nobody had been prosecuted for many years, but nevertheless, the act was still on the statute book.)

Sociopolitical entrenchment of racial separation was brought about by a law that prohibited racially mixed political parties. The Separate Amenities Act gave to local governments the power to require that people use public amenities on a racially separate and unequal basis. And the Group Areas Act laid down that people could occupy or own land only in the area set aside for their particular ethnic group.

Politically, blacks were taken off the common roll, in the one province where they enjoyed voting rights, in 1936, before the present regime came to power. So-called colored people, people of mixed race, lost their common-roll franchise in the mid-1950s and lost their separate-roll franchise in the 1960s.

Educationally, the races were always segregated, even before the present government came to power. And I might point out that white children are segregated as well if they go to the state schools. Afrikaans-speaking children go to the Afrikaans schools, and English-speaking children go to the English schools. Private schools, however, are integrated. Many of the private schools, in fact practically all of them, have not only English and Afrikaner students but students of other races as well.

All those factors have been in play for years and, as I said, have given South Africa the status of a pariah nation. I had a ringside seat from which to watch those laws come onto the statute book and spent all my time opposing them.

Pari passu came the erosion of the rule of law. The denial of habeas corpus effectively destroyed due process. On the statute book in South Africa are laws that allow the minister of justice and the minister of law and order to indefinitely detain people in solitary confinement without trial. And that, to my mind, is one of the most oppressive aspects of the entire regime. Whenever legislation is passed without the approval of the people to whom it applies, due process will not be sufficient to maintain law and order, and the government will therefore assume additional, oppressive powers.

That has been the case in South Africa, which has lurched from crisis to crisis over the years—from Sharpeville in 1960 to Soweto in 1976 to the sporadic outbreaks of unrest in the townships, in Johannesburg, in Cape Town, and in Pretoria. In 1984 a new constitution was accepted by the white electorate. That constitution set up a tricameral system, which is still in effect, under which votes were set aside on separate rolls for the colored people, for the Indian people, and for the white people. No provision was made for the votes of the black people, so 72 percent of the population were denied the franchise by the new constitution.

The violence that broke out in 1984 in the Vaal Triangle (Johannesburg, Pretoria, and the industrial area of Vereeniging) has continued ever since and has resulted in a declared state of emergency, as a consequence of which 30,000 to 40,000 people have been detained—some just for a matter of days, others for months, and a few for years. That situation, which still obtains, means that we have strict censorship of the press, which is not allowed to report any unrest-related incidents without permission; it has of course resulted too in the banning of most protest meetings. Such is the present state of affairs in South Africa, and such are the circumstances under which the general election of September 6, 1989, took place.

To be fair, I should point out that during the past 10 years, under the leadership of prime minister and state president P. W. Botha, unaffectionately known as the Great Crocodile, many changes have taken place in South Africa. Some are considered cosmetic, such as the desegregation of sports, hotels, theaters, cinemas, and public places such as post offices and beaches. The Prohibition of Mixed Marriages Act has finally been abolished, along with the section of the Immorality Act that prohibited sex across the color line outside of marriage.

I must say I've had some wry moments in Parliament watching laws that I opposed when they came onto the statute book being repealed 10, 15, or 20 years later, and I can remember that when I moved to get those laws repealed, I was told that I didn't understand the mores of South Africa. Well, the mores apparently changed; the laws were taken off the statute book, and the heavens did not fall.

There have been more significant reforms as well, such as the repeal of the Job Reservation Act and the legal recognition of black and mixed-race trade unions, a very important future weapon for the black resistance movement and the blacks' attempt to attain equality. Powers of collective bargaining have now been given to the black trade unions. Blacks have been accepted at last as permanent residents of the urban areas. And most important of all, what I consider perhaps the most offensive laws on the statute book, the pass laws and influx control, which restricted the mobility of black South African citizens and prevented their moving from a rural area to an urban area or from one urban area to another, were abolished in 1986. Those were the laws that resulted in the arrest of thousands of black people every year for not having the correct permits in what were known as their "passes."

I used to ask many questions in Parliament—indeed, I consider it an important task of parliamentarians to extract as much information as possible from ministers in Parliament. One of the questions I asked was how many people had been arrested under the pass laws in the last two years before they were abolished. I was told that half a million people had been arrested. When that question was put, one of the National party members said to me bitterly, "Your questions embarrass South Africa." And I said to him, "It's not my questions that embarrass South Africa; it's your answers."

Repeal of the pass laws was not cosmetic. They were in fact very real restrictions on the development of the black economy and on the efforts of blacks to climb the economic ladder in South Africa. The government did not receive much recognition from blacks when it repealed those laws, because, understandably, blacks were not very grateful for the repeal of laws that should never have been enacted in the first instance.

Nor did the government receive much recognition from the rest of the world. Integration of sports, for instance, has not led to South Africa's readmission to the Olympic games or any other international sporting events. A cabinet minister said to me, sadly, in Parliament one day, "Our main problem is that we are confronted with a moving target. Whatever we do doesn't seem to be enough. We are constantly being asked to do more." And I said, "Well, of course you're being asked to do more. You should abolish all the remaining laws of racial discrimination."

I should mention that the laws that have been changed have been changed because of both economic factors and the steady escalation of black resistance within South Africa. The changes in the laws were not the consequences of sanctions, as some people claim. The changes took place between 1979 and June 1986. The U.S. Comprehensive Antiapartheid Act was enacted in November 1986, after those laws had been abolished. I'm not trying to say that international pressures do not play a part. Of course they do. They have an effect on the thinking of white politicians, and certainly they've had an effect on the integration of sports and in other areas where the political power structure itself is not affected.

Nevertheless, I must emphasize that economic factors within South Africa have been the main forces behind the changes that have already taken place. Job reservation disappeared because there just were not enough whites to do the skilled work. The pass laws and influx control disappeared because they could no longer be implemented, given the massive urbanization that resulted from poverty in rural areas and job opportunities in urban areas.

De facto residential integration, despite the Group Areas Act, has taken place in some white suburbs because of the acute shortage of housing in the black urban areas, and the passage of the Free Settlement Areas Act in 1988 gave de jure recognition to some of the racially mixed areas. The shortage of housing has also given rise to vast squatter camps at the outskirts of metropolitan areas all over the country. An estimated 7 million black people are now living in squatter camps.

All the factors I have mentioned have played a part in precipitating South Africa into the throes of a "silent revolution," in the telling phrase of John Kane-Berman, the director of the South African Institute of Race Relations. According to his estimate, by the year 2000 blacks will outnumber whites in South African cities by 3 to 1. Another factor is the increased number of blacks who are benefiting from secondary and tertiary education. Kane-Berman says that by the year 2000, 7 of every 10 matriculants in South Africa will be black. That's a very significant figure. It also makes South Africa very different from the rest of Africa.

Already 40 percent of South Africa's university students are black. The leading so-called white universities, such as Witwatersrand and Cape Town, have a student body that is about 25 percent nonwhite. That is a very important increase in the number of educated and trained black people, and it has led to middle management's becoming increasingly black in South Africa. Naturally, that has had a considerable impact on income distribution and consumer spending.

Blacks' share of disposable income is rising all the time. The importance of black consumers is increasingly being brought to the attention of white South African businessmen. Just recently there were boycotts in two towns that had tried to reintroduce the segregation of public facilities. Those towns found themselves practically bankrupt because the entire black population refused to buy in them and went to nearby towns to make purchases.

Black entrepreneurship has taken off in a truly remarkable fashion. Black taxi services, for example, have been competing very successfully with established transport companies. The informal sector has played a very important role by reducing black unemployment, which is a result of the low economic growth rate, which is due to the shortage of investment capital, which is, in turn, due to sanctions and disinvestment.

I don't want to leave the impression that apartheid has disappeared from the landscape in South Africa. It has not. As long as such laws as the Population Registration Act, which requires that every child born in South Africa be registered in a racial category, the Group Areas Act, the Separate Amenities Act, and the Land Act remain on the statute book, apartheid will remain alive and well. Most important, as long as black South Africans cannot vote for members of Parliament, who pass the laws that govern their lives, white domination will remain intact.

On September 6, 1989, the National party, under a new state president, F. W. de Klerk, was returned to power. Although it lost 17 seats to the Conservative party and 13 seats to the Liberal Democratic party, it nevertheless came to power with a 27-seat majority, and it has been able to govern without forging alliances with either of the other parties.

During the electoral period the Mass Democratic Movement emerged as a symbol of solidarity between the disenfranchised and the people who sympathized with them. When its members took to the streets just after the election, the police were not sent in with their tear gas, their birdshot, and their quirts. That, I think, is a significant change.

Another significant change is that for the first time a National party leader has claimed that he has a mandate for reform. De Klerk has said that he has a 70 percent mandate for reform. Now, he only got 50 percent of the vote, so quite obviously he has included the 20 percent who voted for the Democratic party.

De Klerk has not told us how he is going to use that mandate. He has to clarify exactly what he intends to do to realize his goal, which he said was "a new South Africa, a totally changed South Africa, a South Africa which has rid itself of the antagonism of the past, a South Africa free of domination or oppression in any form." Those are laudable sentiments, but what are they going to mean?

The five-year plan released by the National party during the election campaign says nothing about which laws are to be repealed. The plan reiterates the party's adherence to the concept of the protection of racial interests, although it defines that concept less rigidly and provides for greater freedom of association.

The government has said that it may introduce a bill of rights—something desperately needed in South Africa—and that it favors holding a conference, a great *indaba* at which representatives of all the racial groups would be present, to negotiate the political accommodation of black people within the parliamentary structure. Such an assembly is absolutely essential if we are to have a new South Africa with a new goal and without oppression or domination. But whether de Klerk will include the African National Congress and other banned organizations in the *indaba*, whether he will soon release Nelson Mandela and the other political prisoners, whether he will lift the state of emergency—all of which black leaders have cited as preconditions for their coming to the negotiating table—we do not yet know. My crystal ball is cloudy, but I think it's obvious that both sides will have to make concessions if negotiations are to have any hope of success; otherwise the *indaba* is going to be stillborn.

I think de Klerk intends to try to restore South Africa's credibility in the Western world. I hope he'll get a move on, for I have no doubt that the patience of the Western nations is wearing thin. But I am convinced that sanctions and the threat of further punitive actions notwithstanding, de Klerk will not hand over power to the black majority. He was not elected to do so. However, he will explore every means of bringing blacks into the parliamentary system that falls short of threatening white domination, and he will make incremental changes. I believe he will allow many laws simply to erode by nonprosecution; possibly the Group Areas Act will go that way. Certainly the Separate Amenities Act is already going, and the Johannesburg City Council, which is controlled by the National party, has desegregated all public facilities.

Another important postelection development is that the government is now negotiating with the people's representatives in the urban townships, the leaders of civic associations, whom it had always refused to recognize. It is no longer insisting on negotiating with the people elected under local government ordinances.

I firmly believe that sanctions and disinvestment are ultimately counter-productive. They may result in different political thinking and changes in the political structure, but if they also wreck the economy of South Africa, every South African, white or black, will be hurt. There is no point in inheriting a wasteland. If disinvestment continues and comprehensive sanctions are imposed, South Africa will lose its export markets, and there will be widespread unemployment, mainly among the black population.

I'm not impressed by the argument that blacks are already suffering so much that a little more suffering will do no harm. Remember, South Africa has no social security safety net—no dole and no food stamps—so to be unemployed there is a dire experience. Every political candidate in the United States tells voters that he's going to create jobs in his jurisdiction. Does anyone really think that black South Africans' views on employment are different? They also need and want jobs. They also fear unemployment.

If one could say with certainty that sanctions and disinvestment would, in one swift blow, bring down the regime and dismantle apartheid and that the whole economic setup would be reestablished, there might be some sense to them. But change won't come that way. Instead the economy will erode as unemployment increases and growth ceases altogether, and half a million young blacks will enter the labor market every year to find that there are no jobs.

The result of sanctions and disinvestment is not going to be a sudden conversion to a nonracial democracy in a prosperous South Africa. It is going to be a gradual descent into poverty for everybody, and that means more oppression—it means more money diverted from education and training to the military and the police. In other words, there will be a long, drawn-out confrontation between a government backed by the military and the police and a popular mass movement that must turn to IRA-type violence. That is not a desirable scenario for South Africa.

Some years ago there was a nationwide survey on blacks' attitudes toward sanctions in South Africa. Sixty percent of the respondents were opposed to sanctions if job losses would be sustained. When the question about job losses was omitted, a far greater percentage favored sanctions. A recent Gallup poll—financed by the Chamber of Mines, which, of course, made it suspect to a lot of people—confirmed that blacks do not support sanctions if, as is inevitable, job losses would result. The percentage of respondents opposed to sanctions increased to 67 percent when it was stipulated that many people would lose their jobs, and over 70 percent opposed sanctions if their own jobs would be jeopardized. Those polls, I think, belie such statements as "Blacks don't care if they lose their jobs."

Please don't misunderstand me. I totally understand the moral outrage that so many people feel about apartheid. After all, I think I can claim to have fought apartheid longer in Parliament than anyone else in South Africa. I just don't believe that punitive measures that would wreck the economy and reduce the country to chaos would improve the situation. I must also admit that the many black leaders who support sanctions, including Archbishop Desmond Tutu, say that the onus is on those who oppose sanctions to propose another method of dismantling apartheid. Well, the method I propose is the long-term economic development of South Africa, which would draw blacks into the skilled occupations. Such development can occur only in an expanding economy.

The front-line states also say that they want sanctions, but anything that affects the South African economy affects the economy of the front-line states, for the whole of southern Africa is one economic unit. All the front-line states depend on South Africa for electricity, transportation, and jobs. Unfortunately, they seem to have the mistaken impression that the West—America, Britain, and mainly West Germany—will pick up the tab to make good any damage suffered.

What can Americans do? I know it upsets Americans no end to be told that there's a limit to what they can do, but there *is* a limit, and the solution to South Africa's problems is going to be found by the South African people—*all* the South African people.

In the meantime, countries that have freedom and human rights as their basic values must continue to use all diplomatic channels to protest long and loud against the miserable practices of apartheid and employ all positive means to speed their demise. Those means include the valuable social responsibility programs that many Western firms have initiated to educate and train blacks for the postapartheid society that must evolve. When disinvesting firms go, very often their social responsibility programs go too, to the detriment of the country as a whole.

Western nations must assist in the development of strong black trade unions, which can then use their economic muscle to redress inequalities that go beyond the workplace. Power takes many forms, and South African blacks are slowly but surely accumulating economic power as they're drawn into the national economy not only in ever-increasing numbers but at rising levels of skill. Economic muscle can be used, as has been shown in every industrializing country, to redress imbalances in wealth, privilege, and power. I don't believe that South Africa will be the exception. I do believe that we have to create a favorable climate for nonracial negotiations, that the ANC and the other banned organizations must participate in those negotiations, and that Nelson Mandela must participate as well.

Finally, I want to say that notwithstanding all the flagrant injustices of the apartheid system—the miserable laws and the glaring inequality between black and white standards of living—all South Africans are not right-wing whites or radical blacks. South Africa is home to fine, creative people of all races, most of whom are determined to remain there, strive to end all discriminatory practices, and be part of a democratic postapartheid society. People of all races who want the same things—peaceful progress, a decent standard of living, a good education for their children, proper housing—should form the majority that runs postapartheid South African society.

Transition in the East: Democracy and Market

Peter Bauer

In the transition in the East, the distinction between democracy and the market system is crucial. However, in current discourse on Eastern reform, political democracy and the market system are largely equated, seen as two sides of a coin. Multiparty democracy under universal suffrage (democracy for short) is regarded as a precondition or corollary of a free society and of a market system.

Democracy and the market may indeed both be deemed desirable. But to equate them diverts attention from basic distinctions and acute difficulties and dilemmas facing the reformists. The practice may also inhibit the establishment and successful operation of both.

Mass democracy is plainly neither necessary nor sufficient for a market system. For instance, the freest market economy in the contemporary world is Hong Kong, which is not a democracy. Early 19th-century Britain had a market economy but extremely restricted suffrage. Nor is democracy sufficient for a free market. In the late 1940s and early 1950s, Britain was certainly a democracy, but the economy was extensively government controlled. In Chile, the elected Marxist Allende government had to be replaced by an authoritarian regime before the economy could be liberalized. Thus, democracy is neither necessary nor sufficient for a market system. Whether democracy promotes or inhibits the market depends on governmental policies.

Peter Bauer is Emeritus Professor of Economics at the London School of Economics and Political Science and a fellow of the British Academy. This article is a slightly amended version of comments he made at a regional meeting of the Mont Pèlerin Society in Prague, November 1991, on papers presented by Václav Klaus and Michael Novak.

Cato Policy Report, March/April 1992

The merits of major components of political freedom, such as universal suffrage, free expression of opinion, rule of law, and freedom of association, depend on how the political system is operated. Thus, freedom of association, much emphasized by Michael Novak, often enables people to restrict severely the opportunities of others who may be much poorer. And Prohibition in the United States, spearheaded by the Women's Christian Temperance Union (a voluntary association), was introduced under universal suffrage and under the rule of law.

James Buchanan, Allan Meltzer, Gordon Tullock, and others have shown that universal suffrage can lead to persistently increasing government. Thus, the practice of treating democracy and the market system as two sides of a coin obscures fundamental distinctions. Moreover, in current discourse primary emphasis is on democracy rather than on the market. The reverse, however, would seem more appropriate for two reasons. First, most people consider the freedom of the market—such as choice in employment, movement between places and jobs, and setting up businesses—of greater moment than the extent of suffrage and freedom of political speech. Second, historical experience suggests, though the evidence is not conclusive, that democracy is more likely to grow out of the market than the market out of democracy.

There are some major benefits of democracy. First, it reduces dependence on a single ruler or party. Second, it serves as a safety valve because discontent, even strongly felt discontent, can be registered by voting without recourse to physical force. Third, in the modern world, it confers legitimacy on the government. Election by some kind of popular, and not obviously rigged, vote is often seen both within a country and abroad as giving a government legitimacy, which enhances its effectiveness.

Limiting Government

It is generally agreed that a market system is required both for personal freedom and for economic improvement, especially improvement of general living standards. The market system, in turn, requires a government that performs certain necessary tasks but refrains from direct control of economic life beyond the taxation required for its basic tasks. The list of those tasks is familiar if not universally agreed on: public security, which means protection of life and property, including the definition and enforcement of property rights; maintenance of the value of money; management of external relations in the interests of the population; provision or supervision of basic education, public health, and transport; and assistance to those in need (perhaps by income support schemes) who cannot help themselves and are not helped by others. Effective performance of those tasks would stretch the human and financial resources of Eastern governments. It is notable that those functions do not normally imply direct control over people's lives and activities. They, therefore, do not set up the tensions and conflicts often engendered by such control.

What matters for a market system, and therefore for personal freedom and economic advance, is not how a government originates but what it does. What matters in this context is not elected government but limited government. Whatever its origins, a government is most likely to promote personal freedom and economic advance when it effectively performs a specific range of tasks without directly controlling economic life. It is a paradox that many modern governments cannot or will not perform those basic tasks, including public security, while simultaneously they intervene, or try to intervene, extensively, in economic life. They are often bloated without being firm.

In the East, limited government, notably absence of extensive state economic intervention, implies substantial depoliticization of life. The establishment of limited and stable post-communist government requires drastic measures, as proposed by Vaclav Klaus. There are major obstacles, however, in the way of far-reaching reform. They derive from two sources: extremely powerful hostile interests and widespread apprehension about the effects of reform, closely linked with unfamiliarity with the market.

The reformists have to rely on existing personnel in the public services, including the military, the police, the civil service, the public utilities, and the state enterprises, most of whom oppose dismantling the command economy. They try to stir up popular discontent and fear and to deny supplies to the private sector or to activities controlled by the reformists. As U.S. Sen. Strom Thurmond (R-S.C.) has said, "You cannot get a hog to butcher itself."

In the East, many people fear the results of reforms, such as steep rises in prices and rents, the withdrawal or reduction of health services, and unemployment following closure of inviable enterprises. Various other legacies of communist rule add to the difficulties of the reformists. Under the command economy, people did not look for jobs but were directed into them. Production was divorced from the value of output, which was measured by the cost of inputs, which was unrelated to economic cost. Many people, therefore, find it difficult to face the opportunities, risks, and rewards of the market.

Communist rule has given a new lease on life to the ancient misconception that the incomes of relatively prosperous people, especially foreigners or members of distinct groups, have been extracted from others, notably the poor, rather than produced by themselves or with their resources. Under the command economy, the incomes of the prosperous were indeed all too often extracted from others. And many of the beneficiaries are still well placed to remain or become prosperous. Such ideas and circumstances add to the difficulties of the reformists.

The drastic measures required to dismantle a comprehensive command economy are unpopular and difficult. The government may need some sort of popular mandate before it can proceed with them. Even if such measures are introduced by presidential or ministerial decree, a government can claim a mandate if it was elected through reasonably extensive suffrage. In that sense, democracy may be helpful or necessary for dismantling the command economy.

Democracy May Inhibit the Market

On the other hand, effective ongoing functioning of the market is often inhibited by certain widely prevalent tendencies in mass democracies. Forces are at work that promote extensive government intervention through taxation, government spending, lax monetary and fiscal policies, and also intervention to placate special interest groups in both the public and the private sector.

Buchanan and Tullock have shown, in truly seminal writings, how the operation of special interest groups and coalitions (including coalitions between bureaucrats and legislators) brings about such results. Allan Meltzer has cogently argued that redistributive taxation and state spending to benefit the majority of the electorate—that is, recipients of the median income or less—persistently increase the role of government.

The factors analyzed by Buchanan, Tullock, and Meltzer are not mutually exclusive. They tend to reinforce each other. They are likely to lead to an ever-increasing role of government in mass democracies unless held in check by strong tradition against government intervention or by special constitutional provisions, designed to tame democracy (to borrow from Hayek). They may also be checked if their consequences patently damage the majority of the electorate, represented in this context by the median income recipient.

In the East, those factors are likely to operate forcibly. Ethnic and cultural diversity, which extends into small regions, multiplies special groups and coalitions. The market system and its institutions are less developed or deep-rooted than in the West. Although there is currently much revulsion against a totalitarian system, state intervention in economic life is traditionally more readily accepted than in Britain or the United States. Again, the ancient misconception that the incomes of relatively prosperous people have been taken from others is widespread and firmly held.

Redistributive taxation and large-scale government spending in post-communist countries are likely to be encouraged by the influence of statists and dirigistes on official contacts between the West and the post-communist governments, especially on the administration and allocation of the official subsidies known as aid (including technical assistance, soft loans, and guaranteed bank lending). International organizations such as the European Commission, the World Bank, and the European Bank for Reconstruction and Development (which in reality are political institutions and not banks) are in the forefront of the advocacy and administration of those subsidies. Much of their personnel is indifferent or outright hostile to the market system and to voluntary decisions generally, though they may pay lip service to both. The influence of the personnel, especially over the long term, is likely to favor more official spending and redistributive taxation, and generally government economic intervention.

Thus, the extensive and lasting depoliticization of economic life required for a successful market system is likely to be difficult in the East under mass democracy. Yet failure to achieve it will prove even more harmful than in the West. Extensive state economic control engenders tension and conflict, especially in the heterogeneous societies of the East. Resources, energy, and attention are diverted from productive economic activity to concern with the outcome of political struggles and administrative decisions. Such politicization of economic life is damaging to economic performance, and at times it provokes civil strife.

The wide ethnic and cultural diversity in the East means that economic controls can lead to extensive and costly fragmentation of those economies. Centrifugal forces can be set up, at least until opposition is suppressed. Unless reined in, those forces under mass democracy will impede the operation of the market and thereby improvement in living standards.

Traditional Societies

I should like now to turn briefly to two subsidiary matters. Novak made a comparison between the traditional and the free societies. Is the comparison helpful? It is rather like classifying a pack of cards into red suits and kings. Traditional societies are often free societies. People may freely accept a hierarchical and differentiated society. Governments of traditional societies are often limited. And neither the government nor the nobility needs to have the power in traditional societies to coerce people or to reduce them to dependency, let alone to serfdom. Novak refers to the Austro-Hungarian Empire (the Dual Monarchy) and mentions that dukes, counts, knights, and petty officials were people to whom the population was subject. But neither the monarchs nor the nobility had absolute powers. In Britain (and elsewhere) there also are dukes, earls, and knights. People are occasionally referred to as Her Majesty's subjects. But that does not mean that Britain is less free than the United States. In many ways people in the Dual Monarchy were freer than they are in the United States. When Novak's forebears migrated from Slovakia to the United States, they did not need passports. People could move freely between places and jobs, were free to set up businesses, to come and go, to drink, and to take money in and out of the country. And petty officials with coercive power are ubiquitous in today's democracies.

Following Mises and Hayek, Klaus writes that the indicators of success under economic planning were irrational. His statement is true if the aim of planning is to improve economic welfare, especially general living standards. But the process and its success indicators can be quite rational if the purpose is to keep the rulers in power, whether the Communist party or African despots. Then, the policies make sense. So do the success indicators, because they impress supporters and sycophants abroad, and may impress or terrorize people at home. The policies and the rulers may eventually collapse. But such policies have kept African despots in power for decades, and the Communist party of the Soviet Union ruled the country for more than 70 years. It is thus somewhat misleading to call central planning irrational. The policies usually suit the purposes of the rulers. The term irrational also suggests that outside observers, especially academics, are better qualified than are seasoned politicians to assess what best serves the interests of the rulers.

Depoliticizing Economic Life

The West can influence developments in the East. The preceding discussion suggests that such influence should be targeted primarily to the promotion of the market. For instance, official aid—that is, subsidies in cash or kind, including technical assistance, soft loans, and government-guaranteed bank credits—if provided at all, should go to the governments that are politically committed to the market system. If the governments change their course, the subsidies should be withdrawn. Aid should be administered and allocated by people who are themselves market oriented. In reality, all too many people in charge of those programs are indifferent or antipathetic to the market, even though they pay lip service to it.

Finally, reduction of Western trade barriers would do far more to promote the market in the East than would official subsidies. Getting rid of such obstacles, however, requires the depoliticization of economic life—something that democratic politicians who respond to special interest pressures and those in charge of international organizations have little incentive to do. The problem, then, is to place constitutional limits on democratic rule in order to cultivate a private market system in which individuals are free to pursue their own interests and at the same time to revitalize national economies.

The Communist Road to Self-Enslavement

Karl R. Popper

No theoretician contributed as much to the downfall of commu-nism—or socialism—as did Friedrich August von Hayek. He did so nowhere more forcefully than in his small book *The Road to Serfdom*, first published in 1944, when the end of the Second World War was in sight. He followed it up with many excellent works—books as well as articles. The most important of these were *The Constitution of Liberty*, published in 1960, and the three volumes of *Law, Legislation and Liberty*, published between 1973 and 1979. When he was 89, he published, supported by W. W. Bartley, a most successful book, *The Fatal Conceit* (1989). These books form an extraordinary series of scholarly works that, at the same time, are hammer blows against to-talitarianism. They contributed much to the fall of Khrushchev's Berlin Wall and of Stalin's Iron Curtain.

But Hayek did not confine himself to writing these politically so amazingly powerful works. Although a great scholar and distin-guished gentleman, rather reserved in his way of living, thinking, and teaching, and averse to taking political action, he founded, shortly af-ter the Second World War, the Mont Pèlerin Society. Its function was to provide a balance to the countless intellectuals who opted for so-cialism. Hayek felt that more had to be done than writing papers and books. So he founded a society of scholars and practical economists who were opposed to the fashionable socialist trend of the majority of

Sir Karl Popper (1902–1994) was professor of logic and scientific method at the London School of Economics and the author of many books, including *The Open Soci-ety and Its Enemies*. These remarks, subtitled "How the Communist Slave-Owners En-slaved Their Brains and Thereby Themselves," were delivered for Sir Karl at the an-nual meeting of the American Economic Association, New Orleans, January 4, 1992. Copyright 1992 by Karl Popper.

Cato Policy Report, May/June 1992

intellectuals who believed in a socialist future. The society was founded in Switzerland in 1947 on Mont Pèlerin, on the southern shores of Lake Geneva. I had the honor of being invited by Hayek to be one of the founder-members. Among the surviving founders are Milton Friedman and Aaron Director. This society still exists; and for many years it has exerted a considerable influence within the ranks of the intellectuals, especially the economists. Its first and perhaps greatest achievement was, I feel, to encourage those who were fighting the then overwhelming authority of John Maynard Keynes and his school. However, not being an economist myself, I am probably not competent to assess the historical influence of the Mont Pèlerin Society. This is a task—I think an important task—for future historians of economic doctrines and economic policies. Yet having been for many years a member of the London School of Economics, I could experience the growing undermining of leftist teaching which, in the first few years after the war, had been immensely powerful.

Justice demands that I point out that the movement, started by Hayek with his book *The Road to Serfdom*, had an important forerunner. I am alluding to Hayek's teacher, Ludwig von Mises, whom I first met early in 1935 in Vienna, owing to his interest in my first book. I met Hayek about six months later in London. It was Mises who advanced the first and fundamental modern criticism of socialism: that modern industry is based on a free market, and that socialism, and especially "social planning," was incompatible with a free-market economy and consequently bound to fail. ("Socialist planning" was in those days the most thrilling new slogan in intellectual circles.) This thesis of Ludwig von Mises was, as everyone can see today, of fundamental importance. Hayek was convinced—perhaps even converted; for he told me that he, like myself, was once in the days of his youth inclined towards socialism, and if my memory does not deceive me, he has said so somewhere in his published works. It is well to remember that Hayek was among the first to take over this immensely important thesis of Mises, that he greatly developed it, and that he added to it a most important second thesis—an answer to the problem: what will happen if a powerful government attempts to institute a socialist economy, that is, "socialist planning"? The answer was: this can be done only by force, by terror, by political enslavement. This second almost equally important thesis is, so far as I know, due to Hayek; and just as the earlier thesis of Lud-

200

wig von Mises was at once accepted by Hayek, so Hayek's thesis was almost at once accepted by Mises.

I must say again that I am neither an economist nor an historian of economic doctrines: the historical remarks just made may perhaps turn out not to be correct when all the historical documents, especially letters, have been examined. However, it may be of interest that things appeared this way to someone who, though not an economist, was not altogether an outsider.

Ludwig von Mises was, after Hayek, of course the most important founder-member of the Mont Pèlerin Society. I was always very conscious of Mises' absolutely fundamental contribution, and I admired him greatly. I wish to emphasize this point since both he and I were aware of a strong opposition between our views in the field of the theory of knowledge and methodology. I think that Mises saw in me a dangerous opponent—perhaps one who had robbed him of the complete agreement of his greatest pupil, Hayek. Mises' methodology was, to put it briefly, subjectivist, and led him to claim absolutely certain truth for the principles of economic science. My methodology was objectivist, and led to the view that science is fallible and grows by the method of self-criticism and self-correction; or, to put it more elaborately, by the method of conjecture and attempted refutation. I respected Mises, who was much older, far too much to begin a confrontation with him. He often talked to me, but he never went beyond allusions of dissent: he never really opened a discussion by direct criticism. Like myself, he appreciated that there was some common ground, and he knew that I had accepted his most fundamental theorems and that I greatly admired him for these. But he made it clear, by hints, that I was a dangerous person—although I never criticized his views even to Hayek; and I would even now not wish to do so. However, I have by now mentioned to several people the fact of my disagreement, without entering into critical arguments. So much about those distant days.

An Empire Ruled by Lies

I now wish to go one step beyond those days and to formulate the thesis of this paper. It is this.

The demise of the Soviet Union can be perhaps explained, in the last instance, by economic collapse due to the absence of a free mar-

ket; that is to say, by what I have called the first theorem due to
Mises. But I think that the second theorem, the enslavement theorem
due to Hayek, is even more important for understanding what has
happened—and is still happening—in the former Soviet Empire. For
this theorem has a most important corollary or appendix. It may be
formulated as follows:

The road to serfdom leads to the disappearance of free and rational discussion; or, if you prefer, of the free market in ideas. But this
has the most devastating effect on everybody, the so-called leaders
included. It leads to a society in which empty verbiage rules the day;
verbiage consisting very largely of lies issued by the leaders mainly
for no purpose other than self-confirmation and self-glorification.
But this marks the end of their ability to think. They themselves become the slaves of their lies, like everybody else. It is also the end of
their ability to rule. They disappear, even as despots.

Of course, these are also, partly, matters of individual personal tal-
ents. But I suggest that they are mainly dependent upon the temporal length of the enslavement. The acceptance of lies as the universal
intellectual currency drives out truth—just as bad money drives out
good money.

Gorbachev was the first general secretary of the Communist Party
of the Soviet Union to pay several personal visits to the West. I think
it improbable that he understood much on his first or second visit.
But he liked his reception and came again and again. And then he noticed something. I do not mean that the West was rich and that the
U.S. worker was vastly better off than the Soviet worker. I mean that
he noticed that the Soviet Empire was "not a normal country," as indeed he put it himself when he said that he hoped to make Soviet
Russia "a normal country." He somehow noticed, probably subcon-
sciously, that his own empire was suffering from a kind of suppressed mental disease; as indeed it was, together with all its leaders.
It was the rule of lies.

The loss of freedom through the constant fear of terror is, indeed,
a terrible thing that deprives those who live under such circumstances of a part of their humanity: of their intellectual responsibility
and also of part of their moral responsibility. First, they cannot
protest where they should; then, they cannot help where they ought
to help—not even their friends. Under Stalin, this affected everybody, even those highest in the hierarchy. All realistic and genuine

thinking, all non-lying thinking, at least within the hierarchy, concentrated on personal survival. A picture of this—not a very open one—was painted in Khrushchev's mammoth speech (released by the U.S. Department of State on June 4, 1956) ending with: "Long live the victorious banner of our party—Leninism. (*Tumultuous prolonged applause ending in ovation. All rise.*)"

But as we all know, Khrushchev was soon—not too soon—overthrown by the party bureaucracy; and his departure helped to accelerate the intellectual decline of the Communist Party hierarchy, within the Empire as well as outside it. In spite of the compulsory teaching of a highly complex Marxist-Leninist ideology, including a philosophy called "Dialectical Materialism," all that remained of this theory was the following historical dogma (I am quoting from *Khrushchev Remembers*): "The liquidation of the capitalist system is the crucial question in the development of society."

Destroying Capitalism—and the World

Economists often describe our Western societies as "capitalist societies," meaning by "capitalist" a society in which people can freely buy and sell houses, land, and shares; and, if they like, can risk their savings on the stock exchange. But they forget that the term "capitalism" has become a popular term through Marx and Marxism, and that in the Marxist terminology it means something else. In Marxian language and theory, capitalism is a social system that enslaves all human beings by holding them in its claws—not only the workers but also the capitalists: they all are forced by its mechanisms to do, not what they want, but what they must do, what they are compelled to do. Capitalism is interpreted as an economic mechanism that has the most terrible and inescapable consequences: increasing misery for the workers and proletarianization for the majority of the capitalists. In the struggle of competition, "one capitalist kills many others," writes Marx. Capital becomes concentrated in very few hands—a few very wealthy people are faced by a vast mass of miserable starving proletarians. That is how Marx visualizes capitalism.

Quite obviously, this "capitalism" never existed. It was a delusion—no more, no less. Yet indeed, such delusions have influenced humankind throughout its history.

The great task of the Marxist party, of Marxist policy, was to kill, or to liquidate, this delusionary social system. Khrushchev got a chance to do it. The chance was Andrei Sakharov's Big Bomb.

Sakharov was then 39 years old, and he had spent many years, and had had several half-failures, on the construction of a nuclear bomb which would be far more powerful than any American bomb. In the autumn of 1961 he succeeded: a test of his big bomb was positive. The bomb was, as he writes, "several thousand times more powerful than the bomb dropped on Hiroshima." Only consider what this means: Hiroshima was before the bombing a city of more than 340,000 inhabitants. Does "several thousand times more powerful" mean that a densely built up district of 340 million or more could be devastated by one bomb? Far more than there are inhabitants in the United States? Probably not: there are nowhere in the world such districts. At any rate, any existing densely built up district in the world can be completely devastated by one such bomb.

It appears that, when Khrushchev heard about the successful testing of Sakharov's Big Bomb, he was in Bulgaria. He writes in *Khrushchev Remembers* (1971): "It was during my visit to Bulgaria that I had the idea of installing missiles with nuclear warheads in Cuba without letting the United States find out that they were there until it was too late to do anything about them." It was a mad idea. At the time when he had to transport them back, 38 missiles had been delivered, each equivalent to "several thousand" Hiroshima bombs. Assume that "several" means merely three: this would mean 114,000 Hiroshima bombs. Fortunately, they were not yet ready. Khrushchev says, of course: "When we put our ballistic missiles into Cuba, we had no desire to start a war." I believe him: his desire was not a war but the unexpected delivery of 150,000 Hiroshima bombs in one blow; for about 12 more missiles and warheads were on the way. He writes: "I don't think that America had ever faced such a real threat of destruction as at that moment."

I agree. Indeed, it was the most dangerous threat to mankind in human history so far. Khrushchev could have destroyed America with one blow. But in spite of the deadly wounds received, the U.S. rockets would have flown too; Russia would have been destroyed also, and the consequences, especially of the radiation, would have destroyed mankind.

But Khrushchev lost; and the United States quite rightly armed. The race was lost by the Soviet Union, and Sheverdnadze showed the white flag. In this situation, Hungary permitted the exodus of the young East Germans. Obviously, the situation made it impossible for Gorbachev to interfere. So came the East German collapse, and everything else followed.

All this, because it was the task of Marxism to liquidate a nonexistent capitalist hell. One can well say that Marxism dropped into an intellectual black hole—into an absolute zero of fiction.

We should take it as a warning of what an ideology can achieve. Obviously, the danger is not yet over. It will need intellectual responsibility to see us through.

The Rule of Law

As far as the republics of the former Soviet Union are concerned, no amount of economic planning by the state (insofar as the state exists) can help. The help they need is not to come from the economists, not even from Hayek the economist. It can only come from Hayek the political philosopher.

No state can have the duty to build up a working economic system. But every state has the duty to build up a rule of law. This we can learn from Hayek. There was no rule of law in the Soviet Union, and there still is no rule of law: neither are there laws that are acceptable and workable, nor acceptable judges; there are only traces of party rule and of judges beholden to the party. As long as that is the case, there is no difference between legality and criminality. Now the rule of law must be built up from scratch. For without the rule of law, freedom is impossible; and without the rule of law, a free market is equally impossible.

It is this side of Hayek's work that is most urgently needed in the former Soviet Union.

China's Quiet Property Rights Revolution

Douglas Wu

"Privatization" is still a taboo word in the official Chinese media, but the emergence of a growing private sector has been one of the most dramatic phenomena in China since Deng Xiaoping instituted his economic reform two decades ago.

As more of China's state-owned enterprises become insolvent under pressure of increasing market competition, the private sector is becoming more important than ever before; it is providing goods and services, creating jobs, and generating government revenues. There is widespread consensus among economists in China and abroad that this process will continue, and that not even the Chinese Communist Party can reverse it.

The key to China's changing economy is the privatization that has been unfolding in the rural areas, partly because privatization originated in the countryside and partly because the problems associated with rural privatization are some of the greatest challenges that Chinese leaders face.

Background: 1949 to 1966

Before the Communists took power in 1949, China was basically an agricultural society in which farmland was owned by the rich. The sale and purchase of farmland were permitted and protected by the Nationalist government, which was in power from 1911 to 1949. The land reform of 1949–51 deprived the landowners of their land and distributed it among the peasants—tenants who had little or no land of their own. At the same time, the landowners were politically

Douglas Wu, a senior contract administrator for Globecom Systems Inc., is a native Chinese who worked for a major Chinese financial institution for 16 years.
Cato Policy Report, November/December 2000

ruined: they were declared to be the lowest social class in China; they lost all their political rights and were treated like prisoners on probation. The new regime intended thus to secure the support of peasants and to legitimize its ruthless crushing of any opposition.

That not only gave peasants land but also enhanced their social status. Before long, however, their euphoria was replaced by the new concern that some of them were becoming rich while others remained poor or became even poorer. Obsessed with the traditional Chinese belief that inequality was worse than destitution and convinced by Marxist doctrine that private ownership of the means of production was the root of all social evils, the government under Mao Ze-dong did away with land reform by forcing Chinese peasants to organize themselves into millions of production units (known as collectives) and to pool their land and other significant means of production. Every member of a collective became a part owner of the pool and as such was entitled to a share of the collective's harvests.

Under the new arrangement, individual peasants no longer possessed any means of production, and no collective member could do anything about his or her share of the pool, which was indivisible.

In the urban areas the Communist government assigned a job to every adult who was able to work and provided workers with all job-related benefits: salary, medical care, housing, and a pension at government-stipulated rates. But China was very poor and had a rural population of nearly 500 million, so the government assumed no such responsibility in the rural areas. To stick to its principle of "no private ownership of means of production" and to be realistic, the government threw the burden onto collectives and made it an unwritten law that each infant born to a member of a collective automatically became a member of the collective entitled to the benefits that the collective would provide. Whether the collective was able to provide any benefit at all, however, would depend on such factors as natural endowments, climate, and the efforts of the collective members.

By unwritten law, the government was not the owner of the collective and, therefore, had nothing to do with maintaining the income level of collective members. The government might reduce agricultural taxes to avoid starvation, but nothing more was to be expected in most cases.

Mao was pleased with the new arrangement, which some of his followers extolled as his "great contribution to the Marxist theory of public ownership." According to orthodox Marxism, to eliminate private ownership of the means of production, the state must take responsibility for organizing production and looking after all the workers. Under the new arrangement, private ownership of the means of production was effectively eliminated, but the government had no direct responsibility for either production or peasants' welfare.

Contrary to government propaganda, the new arrangement was unpopular in the countryside from day one. Being a part owner of a collective didn't arouse much enthusiasm in practical Chinese peasants, whose dream had always been to farm a piece of land they could call their own. The peasants also felt that the new arrangement had rendered them inferior to urban residents, whose welfare was provided for under the government budget while theirs was at the mercy of the weather or the quality of the land.

Nevertheless, the peasants did not offer any open opposition to the new arrangement. What they did instead, because every collective member got more or less the same share of the harvests, regardless of differences in individual contributions, was to shirk and to be very careful to do no more than others did. Consequently, agricultural productivity was low and the resultant food shortages haunted the government.

The government tried to inject a spirit of collectivism into the peasants' minds, without much success. To diminish the threat that starving peasants might rebel—almost the exclusive cause of political upheavals in China's 5,000-year history—the government reluctantly agreed that a small piece of the collective land could be used by each farming household to plant crops of its own choice and that the harvest from that land could be retained by the household. (Those small pieces of land became known as private reserved land.)

To justify its policy change, the government emphasized that the private land could not be more than a small fraction of the collective land and that peasants should not be allowed to farm their private land until they had finished their daily work for the collective. Despite those restrictions, the new policy brought wealth and life to China's countryside. The enthusiasm with which Chinese peasants worked their private land and the resultant high productivity were in such sharp contrast with what was happening on the collective land that the official Chinese media frequently complained that, "if we fail to do a good job of educating peasants properly so as to free them from selfishness and narrow-mindedness, capitalism will prevail in China."

Although the private reserved land policy saved Chinese peasants from starvation after 1963, most of the country's farmland was still in collective hands, and the time peasants were permitted to work on their private land was very limited. Meanwhile, the government's persistent efforts to re-educate peasants failed to show positive results. Consequently, the low productivity of the agricultural sector remained a big headache for the government at a time when the population was doubling. There seemed never to be enough to eat, so food had to be rationed again and again in urban areas. Despite the fact that people had been working hard under Communist rule for nearly 30 years, their standard of living had not improved much.

At last, complaints against the government policy were voiced, disenchantment with Mao's ideology grew, and people began to dream of better lives, not just empty promises. Mao perceived all such developments as evidence that some of his fellow Communist leaders were trying to undo his accomplishments. He couldn't tolerate such subversive efforts. The Cultural Revolution was instituted in 1966 with a view to sweeping away all that was in Mao's way.

Cultural Revolution and Economic Reform

The Cultural Revolution dominated China for 10 years, during which millions of Chinese families were plunged into tragedy and the economy was pushed to the verge of collapse. The actual effects of that catastrophe were to tear to pieces Mao's mystique (which had been the pillar of his rule), to expose fully the fatal diseases inherent in China's Soviet-style social and economic structures, and to lead the Chinese to seek different solutions to their problems.

Mao's death in 1976 presented China with a chance to break with its past. The Chinese elite led by Deng seized that chance, terminated the Cultural Revolution immediately, and after about a year launched "economic reform," the original aim of which was to raise the people's living standards by liberating the economy from the fetters of the Soviet model and by introducing market mechanisms to solve some of China's economic problems.

The economic reform started in the countryside, the chronic low productivity of which made it increasingly difficult for China to feed its 1 billion people. Thanks to the experience with the private reserved land, Deng and his followers were pretty sure that Chinese peasants would be able to create economic wonders if and only if they were given back what had belonged to them and allowed to farm their own land. The leaders knew that the reform would not cause any loss to or require any new investments from the government, as the government was not the owner of the collectives. The solution was simple and straightforward. But before anything could be done to implement it, the reformists, while insisting that the system of collective land ownership was not being dismantled, had to develop a "socialist" theory by which peasants could effectively reclaim their land. In the years right after the Cultural Revolution, although most people were convinced of the inefficiency of the state sector, their support for "socialist" ideals was not diminished. Their fear of private ownership was deep-rooted. Without justification by a theory that sounded definitely "socialist," any reform would be viewed as an attempt to deviate from the right path and thus could not succeed.

Fortunately, there existed in the West the practice of leasing, which the reformists found readily usable. They lost no time in transforming it into a set of policies (later known as the household responsibility system) aimed at launching the Chinese countryside into a new production system that would solve the problem of food shortage once and for all. Under the household responsibility system,

- the collective remained the owner of the collective land and other means of production used by collective members; therefore, the system was still "socialist";
- if so desired by collective members, however, the collective land and other means of production could be leased to any household in the collective;
- the quantity of the object to be leased to each household could not exceed the quantity that the lessee had contributed to the collective at the time of its formation almost 30 years earlier;
- the terms of leases might be as long as 50 years;
- during the term of a lease, the lessee did not need to pay any rent to the collective but had to pay taxes to the government in proportion to the quantity of the object leased; and

- the object so leased could be re-leased among collective members during the term of the original lease, subject to the consent of the collective.

The household responsibility system spread through the countryside almost overnight. The peasants seized their chance with such vigor that soon all the collective belongings fell into private hands and the collectives existed in name only. That unexpected development embarrassed the reformists for a while but was soon forgotten because "economic wonders" were appearing in the countryside. Virtually free from any interference from either the collective or the government, the Chinese peasants devoted their hearts and souls to the land under their control and made every effort to provide whatever consumers were demanding. Very soon, bumper harvests led to flourishing peasants' markets, where nearly every kind of food that can be grown in China was in abundant supply. Food shortage became a problem of the past, and the government found itself called upon to address a new issue: food oversupply.

The whole nation benefited so much from what the peasants were doing that the virtual disappearance of the collectives aroused little political opposition. Deng drew some important insights from that. In later years, whenever he intended to introduce a new "reform policy" that might give rise to a new ideological battle in the Communist Party, Deng would launch the policy first and let it become popular with ordinary folks before his opponents could block the policy.

With increasing productivity, greater purchasing power, and accumulated capital, some of the peasants gave up farming and started their own industrial enterprises (known as township enterprises). By the early 1980s, thanks to the success of the economic reform, the official attitude toward private ownership of the means of production had changed substantially. As a result, the township enterprises were granted formal status as part of a legitimate private sector, the existence and growth of which, according to the official line, are not ideal but are necessary to the country's efforts to "lift itself to a higher level of a truly socialist society."

The past two decades have seen great changes in China's countryside: virtually all means of production have been shifted from the state to the private sector, and efficient markets for agricultural products and equipment have been created. Given that some 80 percent of China's population live in the rural areas, nearly all the rural economy is effectively in private hands, and most of the working adults in the countryside are employed by the private sector, it is difficult to accept the official claim that "socialism" is still dominating China's countryside.

Under the household responsibility system, peasants were permitted to re-lease their land to others. As a result, a market for farmland has been in active operation since the early 1980s. However, it is a market for which the government has failed to provide any clear guidance. More often than not, there is no written contract for land re-leasing. Even if there is one, it is not legally enforceable, because, in accordance with the official rule, any land releasing must have the prior consent of the collective, which is long gone in most cases. Nevertheless, the government is unwilling to officially admit this fact, as such admission would be equivalent to saying that China's countryside is no longer "socialist." However, the government has neither the intention nor the resources to change the status quo, so peasants are the de facto owners of the land under their control and, as such, are buying and selling land as they wish. One can anticipate that the peasants will feel frustrated when they have problems involving their re-leased land and cannot go to the government for justice.

The Present Challenge

Although the Chinese government has been fully convinced of the effectiveness of privatization in solving the country's economic problems and has implemented privatization bit by bit whenever politically feasible, it still has great difficulties in officially accepting it. There are two main reasons for this dilemma. First, nobody doubts that China has gone a long way in transforming itself into a market economy. But people still fear the social conflict that Karl Marx warned would be the result of private ownership of the means of production. Under such circumstances, any open advocacy of privatization is likely to be very unpopular with the majority of the population until they have been fully convinced in theory that Marx's analysis is outdated and that privatization, if properly structured and implemented, can bring economic benefits to most people without causing social conflict.

The second (and perhaps more important) reason is that, if the government lifted the taboo on privatization now, it might well encourage people to demand an end to the one-party system, which is far easier than privatization to justify under orthodox Marxist theory. So, any official pronouncement about privatization would be likely to lead to a review of the mandate to rule, something the Chinese leaders are not yet ready to face.

What has happened in China's countryside during the past two decades can be characterized as de facto privatization, in the sense that the process has resulted in virtually all of the means of production of the agricultural sector being transferred to private hands.

At the same time, it is definitely different from the privatization we have seen in other countries. Although the transfer has involved nearly 1 billion people, it has not caused any changes in the government's financial accounts. (Under the new arrangement, the government did not acquire either the collectives or any of their property. As a result, when the peasants reclaimed what had belonged to them, the government did not lose anything.) Indeed, privatization cost the government nothing and brought it large tax revenues.

The Chinese peasants still have a long way to go before they have proper legislation and institutions for protecting their legitimate property rights. Nevertheless, what has taken place in China's countryside is one of the largest and most successful privatizations the world has witnessed.

Why Socialism Collapsed in Eastern Europe

Tom G. Palmer

Why now? Why has Eastern Europe's liberation happened in just the past year? Why not 10 years ago, or 25, if socialism was such a tremendous failure? Let me suggest several reasons.

Above all the other reasons is a sort of meta-reason, the Gorbachev factor. Gorbachev is no classical liberal; in fact, the origins of perestroika were immensely anti-liberal. Perestroika was an attempt to revive socialism, beginning with the law on unearned income, which was an attempt to smash the few elements of a free market there were in the Soviet Union, and a reduction of vodka production, which caused a massive sugar shortage as the Russians began making moonshine. But finally, it seems, Gorbachev and his advisers have figured out that you need market forces to make an economy work. They are now in the process of learning that you cannot have a market without property rights.

Gorbachev did not just decide to be a nice guy—to let Eastern Europe go and to allow people to speak freely. Instead, there was a realization that there was a very deep crisis in communism. In the case of Central and Eastern Europe, the empire was simply too expensive to maintain, and a kind of political decision was made—Moscow had to let those countries go. It could no longer afford to maintain the empire. Consequently, restraints were loosened and the communist leaders in Central Europe were told that they would get no further support from Soviet tanks and soldiers. The Czechs had a bit of good luck in that the major events of the Czechoslovakian revolution took place when Presidents Bush and Gorbachev were meeting in the

Tom G. Palmer is a senior fellow at the Cato Institute.
Cato Policy Report, September/October 1990

Mediterranean; the story is that Gorbachev didn't want to have a bloodbath on his hands during his meeting with Bush, so the word was sent to Prague to lay off.

Several factors combined to force the Gorbachev leadership to let Eastern Europe go. The first was exhaustion of the capital stock. The capital accumulated over hundreds, indeed thousands, of years has been used up. Through the 1960s and the 1970s there was near unanimity among Western economists that the rate of growth in Soviet-style economies was not only positive but higher than in Western Europe or the United States. Clearly, a positive rate of growth, over a period of 40 years or so, should produce wealth, but it didn't. The mistake that was made, and pointed out by a few economists such as G. Warren Nutter, was to measure capital investment, the amount of inputs, not wealth creation. That was a big mistake. It led to what the Hungarian philosopher Michael Polanyi, a great critic of communism, called "conspicuous production"—production for the sake of production. Steel was produced to make a factory to make more steel to make more factories, but the whole process never produced any real consumer goods. It did not translate into an increase in the standard of living. And, indeed, it was often politically motivated.

The industrial proletariat was to be the new universal class, which would subsume all other classes and resolve all previous conflicts among them, according to the Marxian system. So the communists had to create an industrial proletariat, even where there had been almost none. In Romania, for example, during the forced industrialization that followed the Second World War, almost all the horses were killed because, after all, in a modern society no one would need them anymore; everyone would have a tractor. Well, the tractors were never produced, so people began to breed horses in secret. Today horses are the most common means of transportation in the countryside.

Instead of growing, the capital stock of socialist countries has been declining. They've been consuming it. Most of the textile mills in eastern Czechoslovakia were built before the First World War. They still operate with the original machinery. In East Germany, many of the buildings seem not to have been painted since 1945. In some cases, no one even painted over the old and faded Nazi slogans on the walls. In the Soviet Union, there are chemical factories built 110 years ago that are still producing the same chemicals in the same way. It is a general principle that under socialism no factory is ever closed.

The capital stock inherited from previous generations has been largely worn out, and there are real declines in the standards of living of many East European countries. Those declines would have taken place sooner had it not been for the enormous amount of Western capital that was pumped in by the International Monetary Fund, the World Bank, and other international lending institutions and used largely to finance current consumption.

A second factor that led to the revolutions of 1989 was the difficulty of controlling information. I mean not just political news but also the kind of information about how people live in other countries that you get from watching Western movies. The VCR and the Walkman have had a tremendous impact on life in socialist countries. Radio Free Europe was certainly important, especially in countries such as Romania that didn't have much access to VCRs, but Radio Free Europe could always be discounted as propaganda. In other countries, principally Poland and Hungary but also the Soviet Union, there was a massive influx of electronic devices. Initially, the state tried to control or outlaw them because it knew how subversive they could be. But their suppression was simply impossible.

Western movies show people a picture of Western life—a very funny and distorted picture, but still a view of Western clothes, homes, and the like. When we watch movies, that kind of information just washes over us, but to people of a different society it can be very revealing. In Moscow last fall, for example, the Swedish movie *Fanny and Alexander* was showing, and a scene of a Christmas banquet had a big impact on viewers. There is a long table with wonderful food on it, and the camera begins at one end and very slowly, lovingly goes down the table, showing us turkeys, sauces, vegetables, and all sorts of fantastic things. At that point, the Soviet audiences stood up and applauded. Perhaps the silent heroes in the revolutions of 1989 were Sony and Mitsubishi and others who keep making more powerful and fantastic devices that convey more information in smaller packages at lower cost.

A third cause of the revolutions was virtual ecological collapse in many of the countries of Central and Eastern Europe. Many Western ecologists have argued for years that the causes of pollution are property rights and capitalism. That is an interesting hypothesis, and it is subject to an empirical test. Let us find an economy with no private property and no capitalism. The theory says that there should be no pollution or, at least, less pollution. But in fact, where there are no private property rights or capital markets, pollution is a nightmare. Some places in the Soviet Union have infant mortality rates that are higher than the rate in Burkina Faso, the poorest nation in Africa. Silesia in Poland has one of the highest rates of birth defects in the world.

The ecological movement that has arisen in socialist states quite naturally is supported by people who want to defend their homes and their children against being poisoned. And that has had several effects. One is simply the growth of political movements, which in some cases have been very important. In Bulgaria, the first public demonstrations against the regime were called by Ecoglasnot, an ecological movement. A major realization of the movement is that not only does the ruling class not have the people's interests at heart, but central planning is to blame for a lot of their problems. When the order comes from the Central Planning Bureau to produce so much cotton, the head of a collective farm will do anything to meet the dictated quota for this year. Next year can take care of itself. If the way to meet the quota this year is to pour herbicide on the earth or exhaust the soil, that is what he does. In economic terms, there is no residual claimant, no one who profits if the capital value of the resource is maximized. Among intellectuals and academics there is a growing discussion of the value of property rights in solving environmental problems.

The final cause of the revolutions was the virtual collapse of socialist ideology and of the legitimacy of the ruling class. Mere power is usually not enough to sustain a tyrannical regime; in most cases there also has to be, on the parts of both the ruled and the rulers, some sense that the ruling class has the right to rule, that it has moral legitimacy. In the Soviet Union, the rulers claimed to act on behalf of the proletariat. Of course, their primary motivation was power and privilege, but an important additional element was their own sense of legitimacy. The rulers thought that they were morally justified, that they were acting in the interests of the working class, so it was reasonable to ask the people for just a few more sacrifices. I don't think anyone really believes that anymore, but the people accepted the illusion for a very long time.

217

That illusion is gone for two reasons: One, according to Ibn Khaldun, a historian of the Islamic world, it takes about two generations for fanatical ideas to lose their steam. It has been about that long since communism was imposed on most of Eastern and Central Europe; in the Soviet Union, it has been longer, but we have to take into account the shot in the arm that Soviet communism got from the Great Patriotic War against fascism. Two, it is typically the ruling class that travels outside the country, and the communist rulers have been to a large extent demoralized by the experience. Rich and powerful people travel to America or Germany and realize that their standard of living is lower than that of the average industrial worker in a Western country. So the ruling class has been more demoralized, in a sense, than the average person, who has never seen the West. The rulers still want to hold on to power, but they have lost the sense of their right to rule.

The socialist ideology promised equality, fraternity, and prosperity. Did it keep its promise? Did it deliver equality? The answer is no. Many people in the West will say, although they say it less often now, "Well, yes, of course they wait in lines in Poland or the Soviet Union, but they have a sense of solidarity; they are more equal; there is less income disparity." That's nonsense. If you compare the standard of living of the average citizen of East Germany, the richest of the fraternal nations of the socialist camp, with that of the party members who lived in Wandlitz, the neighborhood of the party elite, you find incredible disparities of income—but until recently they were kept secret. Similarly, if you look at the 22 palaces of the Ceausescu family in Romania, or the sports complexes in Bulgaria that were only for members of the Zhivkov family, or the dachas of the Soviet party elite, you find more inequality than in the market societies of the West.

The second promise of socialism was fraternity: everyone would live together as one big, happy family. But in fact, the fight over a shrinking economic pie generates a lot more hostility than is found in a system with property rights and market exchange. Often after waiting in line for hours for a bar of soap, clothing, shoes, and so on, would-be consumers in Moscow get to the front of the line only to have the window closed on them and be told, "Go away; we have no more." Among the first things one sometimes hears is grumbling about the "goddamn Jews"—they are the ones who get all the goods—or the Armenians, or the Azerbaijanis, or whomever. Communism was supposed to subsume such malicious forms of nationalism, but it clearly failed.

And the third promise, prosperity? Socialism not only did not produce prosperity, it produced mass poverty.

So socialism is virtually gone as an ideology. Two other ideologies are emerging to replace it. First, nationalism, which takes two forms: very broadly, there are malignant nationalism and benign nationalism. Malignant nationalism, or chauvinism, is the desire to impose your culture, your religion, your language on another group. And, unfortunately, we see a lot of that in the countries of Central and Eastern Europe. There is another kind of nationalism, however, that has been very important: the desire not to be ruled by foreigners, which is quite understandable and consistent with liberal principles. Overall, I found in Central Europe very little hatred of Russians per se. Central Europeans just want the Russians to go home and leave them alone.

The other ideology is liberalism, in many cases aligned with the benign form of nationalism and, indeed, in explicit opposition to chauvinism. The one name that you hear more than any other throughout Central and Eastern Europe is Friedrich Hayek. Underground, or *samizdat*, editions and rare English copies of *The Road to Serfdom* are widely read.

It should be no surprise that that influential and powerful book was written by a Central European, who spoke to his readers' condition most forcefully. Marx had failed. He had predicted something that didn't happen. Hayek predicted something that did: that the effort to implement socialism would lead to tyranny and serfdom. And he offered an alternative—liberty, a market economy, prosperity, and the rule of law.

Now, having gone through a kind of exercise in political economy, I'd like to mention a historical thesis that might explain some of the most recent occurrences. I'm borrowing this from a Hungarian scholar, Istvan Bibo, who propounded a thesis about the three parts of Europe: Western, East-Central, and Eastern. According to Bibo, East-Central Europe is more or less the region east of the Elbe. Western Europe is identified with Roman or common law and the emergence of civil society from "little circles of liberty"—associations, groups, neighborhoods, clubs, farms, markets, cities, and so on—

from which political authority flowed upward in a limited way. Eastern Europe is identified with the Byzantine and Ottoman systems in which the state was at the top and enforced its will downward.

The big difference between Eastern and Western Europe is the relative separation of church and state in the West, where it came to be recognized that the empire had secular authority and the church spiritual authority. They were separate forms of authority that even had separate court systems. Under the Byzantine system, the emperor remained the head of the church, so such a separation never took place. Also, because of its feudal inheritance and German folk law, political authority in the West broke up much earlier than it did in the East.

The countries of Western Europe are fairly obvious—Britain, Germany, Switzerland, France, and so on. Eastern Europe can largely be identified by the sway of the Orthodox church. Hungarian political scientist Laszlo Urban has pointed out that liberal parties have done well recently outside the areas long dominated by the Orthodox church. Liberal parties have not done so well in Russia, Romania, Bulgaria, and Serbia. The division even cuts across a country in the case of Yugoslavia where Catholic Slovenia and Croatia identify with the Roman West but Serbia is Orthodox and less liberal. The mixed countries, or Central Europe, include Poland, Lithuania, to some extent Czechoslovakia, Hungary, and perhaps the Ukraine and Belorussia. Throughout their tempestuous history, those countries have been dominated or influenced by both the East and the West. Hungary was under Ottoman rule for quite a long time. Big pieces of Poland were once part of the Russian empire.

Thus there may be cultural factors that will make the transition to freedom easier for those countries than for the Eastern European countries. As Bibo points out, political developments that took place in Western Europe—liberation of the serfs and so on—usually hit East-Central Europe about 200 years later and took even longer to reach Eastern Europe. With our help and with the growth of technology, we could accelerate that process, but the liberals in those countries have a harder job.

One of the reasons that I am so excited about what is happening in Central and Eastern Europe is that I see a very real chance that in the next 10 to 20 years an intellectual and political culture that is more liberal than the one we now have in Western Europe or North America will develop in those countries. I don't mean necessarily a more liberal system; we must remember that Central and Eastern Europe are starting from a different base. The seeds of liberal intellectual and political ideas that have been planted there may sprout; produce mighty trees; and, if we are lucky, drop seeds back into our societies to reinfuse us with the spirit of liberty.

Systemic Change: The Delicate Mixture of Intentions and Spontaneity

Václav Klaus

The Transformation Process

In this paper I shall not present a more or less standard and descriptive summary of the current stage of the transformation process in my country and elsewhere in Central and Eastern Europe. I find it appropriate to defend the achieved results because, in spite of all existing problems, this historic transformation process has been—in principle—successful. Nevertheless, it is our task to understand more deeply the fascinating social mechanism that makes such a process possible and to describe the delicate interplay of the political, social and economic factors at work.

My theoretical background and my practical experience tell me that systemic change—and that is what we have been undergoing while dismantling communism in our countries—is an evolutionary process and not an exercise in applied economics or political science. It is based on a very complicated mixture of planned and unplanned, of intended and unintended events, or, to put it differently, on a mixture of intentions and spontaneity. By participating in such a process we have opened another chapter in the never completed book devoted to the study of the relative role of human action and human design in the history of mankind, the book devoted to the study of the relative role of human action and human design in the history of mankind, the book devoted to the study of "made orders" and "catalaxies"—to use well-known Hayekian terms. I hope we can add something to that study. We may confirm that successful transformation is not the result of detailed reform blueprints in the hands of omnipotent reform politicians. Rather, success depends on the unconstrained activity of human be-

Václav Klaus, then prime minister of the Czech Republic, is now president of the Czech Parliament.

Cato Journal, Vol. 14, No. 2 (Fall 1994)

ings together with "modest constructivism" in selecting foundational rules and in shaping transformation policy.

I believe that a negative stance toward an ambitious constructivism and toward all forms of regulation of free citizens is one of the basic revelations of truth for all of us. We have learned that this idea is as relevant for the explanation of changes inside an existing system as it is for the transition from one social system to another. Again and again those of us transforming countries have to caution against attempts to follow scientifically prepared sequencing rules to restructure and construct political, social, and economic institutions.

Our ability to control social events is restricted and no masterminding of reform (or transition) measures is possible. I stress this impossibility because traditionally we have been *a priori* against all forms of political constructivism and social engineering. In addition, we have learned from experience that they are unrealizable in practice. Assisting in the creation of a new social order means, we have to implement liberalization and deregulation measures (which is a more or less passive contribution). However, we also have to devise and enact new rules that define certain abstract features of the new order (which is a more active contribution). Ultimately, we have to accept the existence of an evolutionary, spontaneous process, which establishes new political, social, and economic arrangements.

The question is whether and how the various mechanisms should interact and how the spontaneous side of the process can be supplemented by reason, by intended measures aimed at avoiding chaos and heavy transformation costs. In raising this question I definitely do not want to defend utopian social constructivism. Rather, I want to focus on intentional organized measures that may shorten the transformation process and diminish transformation costs.

Systemic change, which usually starts unexpectedly in a sudden burst of popular discontent, is a complicated mixture of intentions and spontaneity. It seems to me that the transformation process moves through three basic stages and that each stage has a spontaneous and an intentional side.

The First Stage

The Spontaneous Side

The whole process starts with the collapse of old institutions and rules. They are either swept away or made inefficient. To achieve that result in the late days of communism was relatively simple and the forthcoming danger was not the possibility of turning back; it was instead the initiation of a vicious circle of half measures and of truncated evolutionary changes, leading to no improvement either in the moral or in the efficiency properties of the new order. This moment represents the first crucial transformation danger. The two potential alternatives are, on the one hand, a long chaotic process and, on the other hand, a more or less controlled and fast formation of a new, coherent system.

Politically, the ruling communist party ceases to govern (and sometimes even to exist). A simple and a very favorable political situation—a temporary nationwide unity—is achieved. This unity, however, exists only in a negative sense (i.e., it is against the old system).

A very unique and an unrepeatable psychological euphoria prevails. There is a widespread readiness to actively participate in reversing the past, in getting rid of old, unpopular institutions and even in "belt tightening." This moment is suitable for fast implementation of various painful measures.

Economically, central planning (I use this term with some reluctance because nothing like the textbook case of central planning ever existed in our country) disappears practically overnight and with it the old, extremely inefficient, but nevertheless coordinating economic mechanism. Implicit markets, which are very weak and heavily constrained, start to function. However, with no formal deregulation, with no price liberalization, and with no widespread implementation of explicit property rights, markets are prevented from performing their functions efficiently. To create real markets, somebody has to react and to implement a coherent set of system-changing measures.

The Intentional Side

As for the political system, we understood that no direct measures against the communist party are necessary or even helpful. It is sufficient to liberalize the political environment, i.e., to secure free entry for newly emerging political parties. As a result, the basically unreformed communist party remains a political entity, unimportant and in opposition; whereas if the original communist party is forbidden, the communists in renamed parties succeed in controlling parliament afterwards—as in Poland or Hungary nowadays.

224

New political parties, which are spontaneously created, begin to formulate positive visions of the future and try to explain them to the citizenry. This represents the only way of transforming the national unity (and consensus) from a negative to a positive one.

In the economic sphere, the termination of the existing economic paternalism—as a radical, bold, but "nonconstructive" measure—is crucial. Swift elimination of subsidies of all kinds, which brings about a dramatic upward shift in prices, must be done without hesitation. Later on it becomes difficult or impossible to do that, because the newly formed pressure groups successfully try to block it. The authorities have to resist pleas for "constructive" supplementary measures, for helping firms in trouble by picking future winners and losers. Such a dramatic move changes the whole climate of the country—practically, it changes the system—because goods, services, and all kinds of economic assets suddenly acquire their true values. In this process there is no room for any form of gradualism, and this specific measure must be done in a "shock therapy" manner. The result, then, is the emergence of a totally different way of thinking, which is exactly what is necessary for breaking old behavior and habits. There is no alternative to that. No "teaching" can lead to a new behavior; it can be achieved only as a result of sheer necessity.

Together with the elimination of subsidies, macroeconomic stabilization, as a precondition for liberalization and deregulation of markets, must be initiated. After decades of grave economic disequilibria both at the macro as well as at the micro level, fiscal and monetary policies must be very restrictive. Otherwise, rapid inflation starts to dominate the economic and social peace. A budget surplus (or, at least, a balanced budget) and a very cautious monetary policy (slower rate of growth of money supply than of nominal GDP) are unavoidable. Public finances must be, on the contrary, fully independent. Without such preparatory steps, price and foreign trade liberalization measures represent an irresponsible move that solves nothing, aggravates existing economic difficulties, and makes other reform measures impossible to implement.

Liberalization steps cannot wait. Opening of domestic markets (by means of price liberalization) and of foreign markets (by means of foreign trade liberalization) must follow these steps. Without liberalization, economic agents cannot behave rationally, government cannot step out of economic intervention, and a new coordinating mechanism cannot be efficient. Liberalization should be accompanied by an internal convertibility of the currency. Our experience tells us that, for a small open economy, it is extremely helpful that the exchange rate be fixed, thereby becoming the nominal anchor of the whole economy and the only fixed variable in the system. (Alternative nominal anchors are less reliable and more difficult to maintain.)

To summarize, the main tasks for the first stage include political liberalization, elimination of old subsidies, fiscal and monetary stabilization policies, independence of the central bank, a balanced budget, and liberalization of prices and foreign trade.

The Second Stage

Spontaneous Reaction to the Liberalization and Deregulation Stage

The expectations of the citizens are enormous, yet positive, tangible results are not to be seen. After decades of zero inflation, zero unemployment, slow, distorted, but undeniable economic growth, relatively simple and undemanding life, the non-zero transformation costs must be paid. Inflation and unemployment appear (their magnitude depends, however, on the success or failure of previous reform steps) and a dramatic decline of GDP and of living standards becomes inevitable. It is difficult to explain to the public that we are not going through an economic crisis or recession caused by macroeconomic mismanagement, but through a healthy transformation shakeout of nonviable economic activities.

As a result of the high and unpleasant transformation costs, the former euphoria evaporates. The nationwide unity (mostly in a negative sense) is lost and the scene is gradually dominated by conflicting positive visions of the future. This conflict results in an enormous degree of political atomization and increasing political instability.

The pressure groups that are formed begin to misuse the existing institutional vacuum, the weak markets, and the various gaps and holes in the rapidly changing legislation and in the initiated privatization process (especially during the spontaneous privatization of state firms in the moment of their privatization agony). Wealth and income disparities grow, markets remain imperfect, and privatization revolutionizes the whole social structure.

At that moment comes the second turning point: either adherence to the original transformation strategy and the consequent positive overcoming of the situation or chaos and a vicious circle of half measures and concessions to pressure groups with the inevitable loss of "the whole."

Intentional Fixing Up

 The rules of the new order should be stabilized, new legislation should redefine the rules of the game. The politicians should resist the temptation to rule by means of laws instead of making laws solely for defining the rules of the game.

Macroeconomic stabilization must continue. There is absolutely no room for expansionary monetary policy or for fiscal activism. Disinflation must go further and a fixed exchange rate should be maintained.

New market distortions need not be created, residual deregulation of all prices, the elimination of remaining subsidies, and an aggressive fight against all forms of protectionism should not decelerate. No concessions to vocal pressure groups should be made.

New private firms spontaneously emerge but organized privatization, based on a mixture of standard and nonstandard methods, still represents the core of the intentional part of stage two. Privatization of the whole country has a different scope, style, and meaning than privatization in a country where it is only a marginal activity. Countrywide privatization must be fast, it must discover new owners, it should not attempt to maximize state privatization revenues, and it should not be confused with restructuring (and modernization) of individual firms.

Politicians must offer clear rules and be accountable. No false promises should be made. There must be an ongoing effort to explain the role of privatization with the objective of maintaining or even strengthening the fragile political consensus. Without broad support, the transformation process cannot continue.

Standard political parties (instead of civic initiatives, national fronts, and civic forums) start to prevail. The extreme political atomization is slowly transformed into a normal political structure with only a handful of ideologically well-defined political parties (with standard names).

Reasonable social policy—concentrated on helping those who really need it—must accompany the above-mentioned political and economic changes. Wrongly targeted, extremely costly welfare programs should be avoided—a social "spotlight" approach should replace the social "sun" approach. Social policy must be done with due respect to those social groups that are the short-term losers of the transformation process.

Rewards should be reconciled with performance—both individually and nationally. At the individual level, wages (and other forms of income) should temporarily lag behind productivity; at the national level, the exchange rate (dramatically devalued before foreign trade liberalization) must temporarily stay below purchasing power parity. Those two principles represent the basis of my recently formulated "hypothesis of two transformation cushions." Weak markets and newly born private owners need such a cushion for some time; the higher the speed of transformation, the thinner the cushion. To achieve that task, indirect methods (restrictive macroeconomic policies) together with the resistance to the excessive trade union demands are more important than direct measures (wage regulation).

To summarize, privatization is what distinguishes the first and second stages; it must be accompanied by continuing macroeconomic stabilization and by the rationalization of social policy.

The Third Stage

If the fixing up suggested in the previous section is successful, a stage that may be called the *early post-transformation stage* is reached. The extraordinary, temporary, constructive role of the state is over; it should start to play—once again—a standard, more or less passive, nonconstructive role.

The country in this early post-transformation stage is, of course, characterized by weak economic and political markets and structures. Their deepening and widening, something that cannot be directly done by the state, is the main challenge. The government must only try to eliminate all the barriers to political and economic freedoms before the Schumpeterian heroes finally take over the stage and the standard evolutionary process begins. The Czech Republic has reached this early post-transformation stage. Of course, the dangers and pitfalls inherent in this stage need our close attention and scrutiny as much as the previous stages of the transformation process did.

Private Education Emerges in China

Ma Lei

In the mid-1980s, Wenzhou, a coastal community of nearly 7 million people, was one of the first regions in China to experiment with market reforms. Since that time, private enterprise—and the region as a whole—has flourished.

In 1993 the gross industrial output of Wenzhou was approximately 34 billion RMB, making it one of the wealthiest regions in China. State-owned enterprises accounted for only 3 billion of that total output, or less than 10 percent. In contrast, private enterprises—of which there are more than 10,000—were responsible for approximately 18 billion, more than half the total. Businesses owned jointly by the private and the public sectors accounted for the rest.

The development of the private sector has fundamentally changed the way residents of Wenzhou look at the world. Traditionally, Chinese peasants lived by the motto, "facing the earth with the back toward the sky." They were tied to their land. Where they were born was, almost always, where they would work and where they would die. Their options were limited in the extreme. In comparison, a child born in Wenzhou now has an endless number of choices. He can decide to work the land or work for an industrial firm or even start his own business. Market forces have broadened the horizons of Wenzhou residents and educated them to the ways of the world. They have learned that in a market economy entrepreneurs frequently fail. But they have also learned that risk taking, when combined with foresight and hard work, can pro-

Ma Lei teaches at the Center for American Studies at Fudan University in Shanghai and participated in the Cato Institute's June 1997 conference, "China as a Global Economic Power: Market Reforms in the New Millennium," in Shanghai.

Cato Policy Report, March/April 1998

duce significant rewards—a fact that many business owners in Wenzhou appreciate.

Most important, the people of Wenzhou realize that on the market all is harmonious—that one earns his living not through coercion or brute force but by serving others. That realization has produced a climate in which private industry and private organizations—including private schools—can thrive.

From Mao's earliest days in power to less than a decade ago, education in China was controlled entirely by the state. All children were educated in government schools; private schools were prohibited by law. However, education is now just one of many goods offered privately—and there are plenty of buyers.

In Wenzhou, more than half of the 600 million RMB spent on education comes from the private sector. That's a claim that few, if any, communities in the United States can make. Private schools—like Yu Ying Middle School, which has an annual operating budget of approximately 5 million RMB—frequently enjoy greater financial support than their public counterparts and often offer a wider range of classes and substantially better teaching. An increasing number of parents have recognized the superior quality of private institutions and have opted for private schools for their children. There are more than 2,300 privately run kindergarten classes in Wenzhou, in which more than 90 percent of all children of kindergarten age are enrolled. In addition, there are 21 private high schools, which educate about a quarter of the total high school student population. And half of all vocational students attend one of Wenzhou's 36 private vocational institutions.

While many of the private schools in Wenzhou are nonprofit—with their operating deficits covered by donations from individuals and organizations that realize the importance of independent education—there are a growing number of for-profit schools, as well. Soon, business will be the main investor in education in Wenzhou.

Numerous regions in China are following Wenzhou's lead. For example, in Shanghai more than 100 private schools are in operation, educating approximately 60,000 students. And as the market economy continues to develop—and as Beijing realizes that private schools can help ease the government's financial burdens—one can expect that number to grow.

China, once a stagnant and inward-looking country, is becoming increasingly cosmopolitan—thanks in no small part to the introduction of market forces. The people of Wenzhou have found that, if left to their own devices, human beings will provide whatever is desired by their fellows—including education—and that the world can be much larger than the farm on which you were born.

China's Future: Market Socialism or Market Taoism?

James A. Dorn

China's goal of building a "socialist market economy" is a grand illusion. The market and its supporting institutions, notably private property and the rule of law, cannot be grafted onto socialism. Markets are based on voluntary exchange; socialism destroys the spontaneous nature of markets and substitutes government control for individual responsibility. Market socialism, even with "Chinese characteristics," is an unnatural and artificial system which, like the Yugoslav experiment with workers' management, is destined to fail. Without widespread private property, economic decisions—especially investment decisions—will continue to be political decisions and be subject to the corrupting influence of government power.

China's state-owned enterprises (SOEs) and banks do not need partial reform; they need to be divorced from the state and subjected to the full force of market competition. Turning to the half-measure of market socialism will only prolong the costs of transition to a real market system and continue to politicize economic life. What China needs are free private markets, not regulated socialist markets. Privatization of SOEs would create real owners who were responsible for their firms' performance and had an incentive to maximize profits by hiring efficient managers and producing what consumers wanted.

The absence of a hard budget constraint for SOEs means that bankruptcy is a hollow threat for most of China's 305,000 state enter-

James A. Dorn is vice president for academic affairs at the Cato Institute and professor of economics at Towson University.
Cato Journal, Vol. 18, No. 1 (Spring/Summer 1998)

prises. And the absence of that threat means SOEs have little incentive to change their inefficient ways. As a result, 50 percent of China's 118,000 state industrial enterprises reported net losses in 1996.

Although China's leaders have been willing to sell off smaller SOEs, they have not embraced the idea of large-scale privatization, for obvious political reasons. Selling off all SOEs would relieve China's massive headache due to the financial drain on the state budget of having to subsidize SOEs, but it would also jeopardize the authority of the Chinese Communist Party. With socialism being the dominant ideology in China, there remain serious obstacles to fostering the market component of market socialism. Turning SOEs into "public" corporations, with the state retaining a controlling interest and restricting the marketability of shares, may be appealing at first sight, but on closer examination can never replicate real markets. As economist G. Warren Nutter noted 30 years ago when he examined the theoretical case for market socialism. "Markets without divisible and transferable property rights are a sheer illusion. There can be no competitive behavior, real or simulated, without dispersed power and responsibility." That is why he called the idea of market socialism "a grand illusion."

To "revitalize" SOEs, China has begun to establish large, state-run holding companies, called "state asset operating companies," which are supposed to substitute for real capital markets. In this setup, the state retains majority ownership, restricts the transferability of "shares," and limits the restructuring process to what is politically acceptable. Thus, politics, not the market, prevails. That approach to SOE reform is akin to the experiment with *perestroika* in the former Soviet Union: it is a pseudo-reform that tries to dress SOEs in market garb but never really changes the underlying ownership structure from state to private property. Commenting on the Soviet effort to revitalize state enterprises, Alexander Tsypko wrote,

> It took us five wasted years of perestroika to understand that, essentially, the revitalization of Stalinist socialism is impossible; there is no third way between modern civilization and socialism as it is. The market cannot be combined with . . . public ownership of the means of production. A return to the market is impossible . . . without broadbased privatization.

The same criticism applies to China's experiment with market socialism.

China's state-owned enterprises cannot be revitalized; they have a terminal disease that is eating up China's scarce capital. In 1996, for the first time since 1949, state enterprises as a whole suffered a net loss. SOEs absorb more than 50 percent of state investment funds, employ 66 percent of the urban workforce, but produce less than 30 percent of total output. China's leaders should have the courage to go beyond the policy of "grasping the big enterprises and giving a free hand to the small ones" (*zhua da fang xiao*). All SOEs should be candidates for privatization. Making large SOEs the "pillars" of the national economy by "corporatizing" them, with the government holding all or most of the stock, is a recipe for disaster. That would be market socialism in spades.

From Market Socialism to Market Taoism

China need not be confined to the ideological cage of market socialism by fear of copying Western traditions of market liberalism. The way of the market is universal. The free-market economy is, as Václav Havel has so elegantly stated, "the only natural economy, the only kind that makes sense, the only one that can lead to prosperity, because it is the only one that reflects the nature of life itself." Since 1978, market liberalization has substantially increased the standard of living of millions of Chinese, and a recent poll showed that many Chinese now believe that "private property is sacred. Today more than 22 million entrepreneurs in China are members of the National Association of Private Entrepreneurs.

The climate is ripe for further market liberalization in China. At the Communist Party's 15th Congress, in September 1997, President Jiang Zemin stood firmly behind Deng Xiaoping's economic reforms and favored turning SOEs into joint-stock companies. And, at the National People's Congress, in March 1998, Premier Li Peng stated, "The incompatibilities of government institutions to the development of a socialist market economy have become increasingly apparent." As long as China confines itself to creating a socialist market economy and restricts economic liberties, the future path of China's market economy will remain unclear.

In considering what steps to take next, China's leaders should look to their own ancient culture and rediscover the principle of spontaneous order—the central principle of a true market system.

In the *Tao Te Ching*, written more than 2,000 years before *The Wealth of Nations*, Lao Tzu instructed the sage (ruler) to adopt the principle of noninterference as the best way to achieve happiness and prosperity:

> Administer the empire by engaging in no activity.
> The more taboos and prohibitions there are in the world,
> The poorer the people will be.
> The more laws and orders are made prominent,
> The more thieves and robbers there will be.
> Therefore, the sage [ruler] says:
> I take no action and the people of themselves are transformed.
> I engage in no activity and the people of themselves become prosperous.

From a public-choice perspective, the foregoing passage implies that the more the state intervenes in everyday life, the more rent seeking and corruption there will be. Alternatively, if people are left alone to pursue their own happiness, a spontaneous market order will arise and allow people to create prosperity for themselves and their country. Like Lao Tzu, China's leaders should realize that corruption stems not from freedom but from freedom being overly constrained by government. As Nobel laureate economist Gary Becker stated, "Markets grow up spontaneously, they are not organized by governments, they grow on their own. If individuals are given freedom, they will help to develop markets for products that one cannot imagine in advance."

Just as the principle of spontaneous order is central to economic liberalism, the principle of *wu wei* ("nonaction") is fundamental to Taoism. Rulers rule best when they rule least; that is, when they take "no unnatural action." When government is limited, it can help cultivate an environment in which individuals can pursue happiness and practice virtue (*te*). Thus, Lao Tzu writes, "No action is undertaken, and yet nothing is left undone. An empire is often brought to order by having no activity."

Like water, the market is resilient and will seek its natural course—a course that will be smoother, the wider the path the market can take and the firmer the institutional banks that contain it. The challenge for China is to widen the *free* market and provide the institutional infrastructure necessary to support *private* markets. The solution is to discard market socialism and make the transition to "market Taoism." Or, as Gao Shangquan, vice minister of the State Commission for Restructuring the Economy, recently stated, the challenge is to throw SOEs "into the sea of the market economy."

Breaking the Planning Mentality

If China wishes to continue its rapid economic growth into the next century and end corruption, it must strive for institutions that are consistent with free-market principles and the rule of law. The Soviet system failed because it disregarded reality—namely, the reality that the way of the market, not the plan, is most consistent with human nature and, thus, with individual rights to life, liberty, and property. Soviet-style planning destroyed the institutions of property and contract that underpin the free private market and created a rigid economic system that finally collapsed of its own weight. What Soviet citizens witnessed during *perestroika* and *glasnost* was "not the organic revitalization of socialism but the withering away of forcibly imposed economic and political structures." Today, China is also witnessing the "withering away" of the state-controlled economy, but its "political structures" still await fundamental reform.

Ultimately, economic and political reform are inseparable. To depoliticize economic life, China needs constitutional change and new thinking (*xin si wei*). Chinese scholar Jixuan Hu writes, "By setting up a minimum group of constraints and letting human creativity work freely, we can create a better society without having to design it in detail. That is not a new idea, it is the idea of law, the idea of a constitution." To accept that idea, however, means to understand and accept the notion of spontaneous order and the principle of nonintervention (*wu wei*) as the basis for economic, social, and political life.

China's leaders and people can turn to the writings of Lao Tzu for guidance. According to noted Chinese philosopher Wing-Tsit Chan, the *Lao Tzu*

> strongly opposes oppressive government. The philosophy of the *Lao Tzu* is not for the hermit, but for the sage-ruler, who does not desert the world but rules it with noninterference. Taoism is therefore not a philosophy of withdrawal. Man is to follow Nature but in doing so he is not eliminated; instead, his nature is fulfilled.

"Lao Tzu Thought," not "Mao Zedong Thought," is the beacon for China's future as a free and prosperous nation. Deng Xiaoping implicitly recognized Lao Tzu's way of thinking when he said in 1987,

> Our greatest success—and it is one we had by no means anticipated—
> has been the emergence of a large number of enterprises run by villages
> and townships. They were like a new force that just came into being
> spontaneously. . . . If the Central Committee made any contribution in
> this respect, it was only by laying down the correct policy of invigorat-
> ing the domestic economy. The fact that this policy has had such a fa-
> vorable result shows that we made a good decision. But this result was
> not anything that I or any of the other comrades had foreseen; it just
> came out of the blue.

Although China can return to its own vision of freedom by embracing and extending Lao Tzu's thought, the idea of "market Taoism" can be enhanced by a deeper understanding of classical liberal
economic thought and a study of free-market institutions and public
choice. In breaking the planning mentality, therefore, China can
learn both from its own culture and from the West.

The Tao of Adam Smith

In 1776, Adam Smith argued that, if "all systems either of preference or of restraint" were "completely taken away," a "simple system of natural liberty" would evolve "of its own accord." Each individual would then be "left perfectly free to pursue his own interest
his own way, and to bring both his industry and capital into competition with those of any other man, or group of men," provided "he
does not violate the laws of justice."

In Smith's system of natural liberty, the government would no
longer have the obligation of overseeing "the industry of private
people, and of directing it towards the employments most suitable to
the interest of the society"—an obligation "for the proper performance of which no human wisdom or knowledge could ever be sufficient."

Government would not disappear under Smith's market-liberal
regime, but it would be narrowly limited to three major functions: (1)
"the duty of protecting the society from the violence and invasion of
other independent societies"; (2) "the duty of protecting, as far as
possible, every member of society from the injustice or oppression of
every other member of it"; and (3) "the duty of erecting and maintaining certain public works and certain public institutions."

In the private free-market system advocated by Smith, people get rich by serving others. Thus, the system of natural liberty has both a moral foundation and a practical outcome. Private property and free markets make people responsible and responsive. By allowing individuals the freedom to discover their comparative advantage and to trade, market liberalism has produced great wealth wherever it has been tried. There is no better example than Hong Kong.

The chief architect behind the Hong Kong economic miracle was Sir John Cowperthwaite, a Scot who admired the work of Adam Smith and other classical liberals. As Hong Kong's financial secretary from 1961 to 1971, he constantly challenged attempts to increase the power and scope of government in Hong Kong. Like Smith, he believed that free private markets would keep people alert to new opportunities by quickly penalizing mistakes and rewarding success in the use of society's scarce resources. Sir John understood that no system is perfect but that, of all known economic systems, the market price system, with its automatic feedback mechanism, has performed the best:

> In the long run, the aggregate of decisions of individual businessmen, exercising individual judgment in a free economy, even if often mistaken, is less likely to do harm than the centralized decisions of a government, and certainly the harm is likely to be counteracted faster.

The idea that people have a natural tendency to make themselves better off if left alone to pursue their own interests, and the notion that a laissez-faire system will be harmonious if government safeguards persons and property, are the foundation of the West's vision of a market-liberal order, but they are also inherent in the ancient Chinese Taoist vision of a self-regulating order—an order we might properly call "market Taoism."

The Taoist system of natural liberty, like Smith's, is both moral and practical; moral because it is based on virtue and practical because it leads to prosperity. The Chinese puzzle is to discard market socialism and institute market Taoism by shrinking the size of the state and expanding the size of the market—and, in the process, to give rebirth to China's civil society.

Market Taoism and China's Civil Society

China's transition from central planning to a market-oriented system since 1978 has been bumpy, but China is moving ahead. Market liberalization has opened China to the outside world, increased opportunities in the nonstate sector, generated new ideas, and energized civil society. That China's civil society has benefited from the end of communal farming, the expansion of foreign trade, and the increased competition from nonstate enterprises should be no surprise. The more economic activity occurs outside the state sector, the more freedom individuals have to pursue their own happiness and lead their own lives. The demand for economic freedom cannot long be separated from the demand for other freedoms.

The market and its supporting institutions follow both formal and informal rules. The informal rules of conduct that underlie the free market, however, are entirely different from the obedience-driven rules of behavior under central planning. Zhang Shuguang, an economist at the Unirule Institute in Beijing, one of China's first private think tanks, writes,

> Mandatory economy and market economy belong to entirely different ideologies and different ethics. . . . Planned economy is based upon some idea of ideal society and beautiful imagination, but compulsory implementation has been its only means of realization. In such a system, [the] individual is but a screw in a machine, which is the state, and loses all its originality and creativeness. The basic ethics required in such a system is obedience. In the market system, which is a result of continuous development of equal exchange and division of labor, the fundamental logic is free choice and equal status of individuals. The corresponding ethics in [the] market system is mutual respect, mutual benefit, and mutual credit.

Understanding those differences is the first step in China's long-march to market Taoism.

Although China has yet to accept the rule of law, a legal system is emerging and property rights are beginning to be respected. Informal codes of business behavior are being adopted to better serve consumers and to improve the efficiency of exchange. The opening of the legal system is important because it paves the way for the transition from "rule by law" to "rule of law." Marcus Brauchli of the *Wall Street Journal* writes,

> The state's steel-clad monopoly on the legal process, which makes the courts just another arm of government, is corroding. China's economic liberalization . . . has spawned a parallel legal reform that raises the prospect of rule of, not merely by, law.

Princeton University professor Minxin Pei argues that the gradual development of China's legal system toward affording greater protection for persons and property, the growing independence and educational levels of members of the National People's Congress, and the recent experiments with self-government at the grassroots level will help transform China into a more open and democratic society. He points to the upward mobility of ordinary people, occasioned by the deepening of market reform, and to the positive impact of China's open-door policy on political norms. In his view, public opinion and knowledge of Western liberal traditions, such as the rule of law, "have set implicit limits on the state's use of power."

People are beginning to use the court system to contest government actions that affect their newly won economic liberties. According to Pei, "The number of lawsuits filed by citizens against government officials and agencies for infringements of their civil and property rights has risen sharply, and an official report reveals that citizens have won about 20 percent of these cases."

Anyone who has visited China's booming coastal areas and new urban centers, such as Shishi in the province of Fujian, can see first-hand the transformation of economic life that is occurring every day in China and witness the regeneration of civil society.

China has a long way to go, but denying China most-favored nation trading status or imposing sanctions on China with the hope of advancing human rights, as some in the U.S. Congress have threatened to do, would be a costly mistake. It would isolate China and play into the hands of hard-liners who are critical of market liberalization thereby undermining the prospects for further reform. The best way to advance human rights in China is not to close China off from the civilizing influence of trade, but to continue to open China to the outside world. That will be a slow process, no doubt, but the progress made since 1978 should not be underestimated.

In the coastal community of Wenzhou, for example, there are now more than 10,000 private enterprises, and life is vastly different and freer than before liberalization. According to Ma Lei:

> The development of the private sector has fundamentally changed the way residents of Wenzhou look at the world. Traditionally, Chinese peasants lived by the motto, "facing the earth with the back toward the sky." They were tied to their land. Where they were born was, almost always, where they would work and where they would die. Their op-

tions were limited in the extreme. In comparison, a child born in Wenzhou now has an endless number of choices. He can decide to work the land or work for an industrial firm or even start his own business. Market forces have broadened the horizons of Wenzhou residents and educated them to the ways of the world. They have learned that in a market economy entrepreneurs frequently fail. But they have also learned that risk taking, when combined with foresight and hard work, can produce significant rewards—a fact that many business owners in Wenzhou appreciate.

Most important, the people of Wenzhou realize that on the market all is harmonious—that one earns his living not through coercion or brute force but by serving others. That realization has produced a climate in which private industry and private organizations—including private schools—can thrive.

The Path to China's Future

In the long run, market socialism, like central planning, is bound to fail because it is contrary to human nature. For more than 70 years, various forms of socialism were tried in the Soviet Union—with no success. Why should market socialism succeed in China? Adding an adjective to socialism—even if it is "market"—will not cure the institutional inconsistencies in China. As Soviet dissident Vladimir Bukovsky wrote in *To Choose Freedom,*

> Those of us who have lived under socialism exhibit the once bitten, twice shy syndrome. Perhaps Western socialism is in fact different and will produce different results. . . . The truth of the matter is that the various ideas that seem fresh and innovative to Western specialists have already been tested in the USSR. And if some of those experiments were eventually repudiated, it was not because socialism has been perverted in the USSR, . . . but because these innovations proved to be utterly unfit for real life. A cruel experiment half a century long has failed to alter human nature.

The "fatal conceit" inherent in the Soviet vision was to think that government planners could run an economy like a machine and achieve long-run prosperity. Although China has recognized the error of central planning and has introduced a market system, that system is still half-baked. The question is: Will China move all the way to market liberalism or remain mired in market socialism? Will China jump into the sea of private enterprise or remain suspended in a trancelike state under the illusion that market socialism will solve its problems?

In considering that question, China's leaders would do well to heed the advice of Nien Cheng—who, like many in China, suffered the grave injustices of the Cultural Revolution. She writes,

China is faced with the choice between socialism and a market system; a mixed system is doomed to failure. The obstacles to China's development can be removed only if China goes all the way toward a private market system with constitutional protection for both economic and civil liberties. China's crisis is a crisis of confidence; the people are in a half-awakened state of mind. The old regime has lost its legitimacy but a new regime has not emerged to fill the vacuum, and there has been no clear commitment to the path of markets and freedom of choice.

To regain consciousness and emerge from the semi-conscious state that now envelops China will take time. But reality requires that China recognize the death of communism. Reality also requires that China embark on throughgoing reform or face the prospect of being left behind in the wake of the liberal revolution that is now sweeping the globe.

China has been willing to experiment with institutional change since 1978 and has made great progress in reducing poverty. Future prosperity, however, will depend on whether China turns away from the artificial path of market socialism and follows the natural path of market liberalism. The market-liberal vision is not new to China; it was inherent in the Taoist doctrine of *wu wei* developed by Lao Tzu and his disciples. China's leaders need only let the Chinese people return to their roots to see the wisdom of letting the spontaneous market process organize economic life, while limiting government to the protection of life, liberty, and property. In that effort, Hong Kong can play an important role by spreading the "tao" of Adam Smith and Sir John Cowperthwaite to all of China—thus allowing the West and the East to meet in one spirit of market Taoism.

PART VI

FOREIGN AFFAIRS

From Republic to Empire:
The Constitution and the Evolution
of U.S. Foreign Policy

Ted Galen Carpenter

The recent congressional hearings investigating the Iran-contra scandal underscore how far the American republic has drifted from the foreign policy moorings established by the Founders. Oliver North, John Poindexter, and other members of the president's staff casually asserted that the executive branch may legitimately circumvent Congress in order to implement foreign policy measures. They justified such conduct on the basis of "the national interest," much as practitioners of amoral Old World realpolitik have done for generations.

Theirs is the language of empire, not a republic based on the principles of limited government and political accountability. Both the foreign policy they advocate and the tactics they employ to execute it are profoundly alien to American traditions.

A prominent feature of the republic during its formative years was the ability of its political leaders to pursue a perceptive and restrained foreign policy. Throughout the Revolutionary War and the decade that followed, a generation of statesmen learned a crucial lesson about international affairs. Although the Founders conceded that temporary alliances with other governments might be necessary when the nation's security was in dire jeopardy, they perceived that such entanglements were generally undesirable.

Alliances, the Founders realized, threatened to involve the new nation in a multitude of complex quarrels, most of which would have little or no bearing on its legitimate security concerns. The

Ted Galen Carpenter is vice president for defense and foreign policy studies at the Cato Institute.
Cato Policy Report, September/October 1987

United States would dissipate its wealth, incur an unhealthy militarization of its society, and even endanger its hard-won independence through a rash involvement in European-dominated power politics. Historian Selig Adler aptly summarized the Founders' policy conclusions as follows: "There seemed to be little sense in jeopardizing the peace of the New World with the ingrained rivalries of the Old. European wars could mean nothing but trouble for America."

There was also a growing conviction during the initial years of independence that America's destiny was to set a powerful example for the rest of the world. Freed from the stifling impediments of a corrupt Old World aristocracy, the United States symbolized an invigorating experiment in limited government and individual liberties. In such an atmosphere Americans could both pursue commercial success and establish ethical standards that oppressed people everywhere would wish to emulate. That unique mission required the United States to remain aloof from foreign, especially European, political and military entanglements. They would not only imperil the nation but compromise its commitment to liberty, thereby undermining the appeal of the American model.

For those reasons, isolationism—or, more accurately, noninterventionism—became the foreign policy foundation of the republic. Advocates of noninterventionism eschewed political and military obligations but welcomed extensive commercial connections. Thomas Jefferson invoked that distinction when he asserted that America's policy should be to seek "peace, commerce, and honest friendship with all nations, entangling alliances with none."

The earliest detailed delineation of a noninterventionist foreign policy, though, is contained in George Washington's Farewell Address. Washington cautioned his fellow citizens against "inveterate antipathies" to certain nations and "passionate attachments" to others. The latter were especially insidious, he warned, "facilitating the illusion of an imaginary common interest" and leading to "participation in the quarrels and wars" of the favored nations "without adequate inducement or justification." Although he acknowledged that the republic might employ "temporary alliances for extraordinary emergencies," Washington clearly favored an aloof approach to world affairs: "The great rule of conduct for us in regard to foreign nations is in extending our commercial relations and to have with them as little *political* connection as possible."

Nonintervention in the Constitution

The nation's commitment to noninterventionism would reach its zenith in the decades following Washington's Farewell Address, but its strength was already evident in several provisions adopted by the Framers when the Constitutional Convention convened in 1787. The structure of the new national government was hardly conducive to the pursuit of imperial ambitions. A critical feature of the Constitution was an emphasis on the dispersal of political power. That attitude was embodied in the principle of federalism, which entailed a division of authority between the states and the central government. A similar principle operated at the national level. Power was divided among three coequal branches, each able to check the excesses of the others.

The power-sharing rationale was also applied to foreign policy responsibilities. Out of concern about problems that had arisen during the confederation era, the Framers made the presidency the repository of authority over the day-to-day conduct of foreign affairs. Moreover, they invested the president with the responsibility of being commander in chief of the nation's armed forces.

But the Framers also granted a significant foreign policy role to the legislative branch. They accorded the Senate the right to "advise and consent" before treaties were effected. Congress as a whole was empowered to authorize the raising of military forces and allocate funds for their operation. That obstacle to an interventionist foreign policy reflected the Framers' profound distrust of standing armies, typified by James Madison's statement in the *Federalist,* no. 41, that even a small army "has its inconveniences. On an extensive scale its consequences may be fatal." Most important, the Framers gave Congress, not the president, the power to declare war. And in the parlance of the times, "declare" meant "authorize" or "begin."

The political system most conducive to an interventionist foreign policy is a powerful, unitary national government that is dominated by an unfettered executive and has considerable taxing and regulatory authority plus the ability to raise and sustain a large military force. The Constitution that emerged from the Philadelphia convention created precisely the opposite type of government. Noninterventionism thus not only was the preferred foreign policy doctrine of most Americans, it was embedded in the nation's political structure.

247

Forgetting the Framers

The United States has since deviated markedly from the intent of the Framers in several areas, but nowhere has the departure been more pronounced than in its foreign affairs. Both the substance of contemporary U.S. foreign policy and the manner in which it is conducted violate virtually every noninterventionist precept established by the revolutionary leaders. The vision they articulated has been transformed beyond recognition, with results that are little short of calamitous.

Today the United States is entangled in multilateral or bilateral arrangements to defend more than 40 nations. They include not only well-known formal agreements such as NATO, the Rio Pact, and the Japanese Defense Treaty but a host of more obscure ones. Moreover, the United States is bound by numerous informal promises of assistance. Its "special relationship" with Israel leaves little doubt that U.S. officials would back that nation in any Middle East conflict, even in the absence of treaty provisions.

The United States has also incurred vague but entirely real obligations as a result of presidential proclamations. The Truman Doctrine, promulgated in 1947, pledged the United States to aid friendly nations in resisting either external aggression or internal "armed minorities." That promise had no discernible geographic limitations, and it has in fact served as the basis for Washington's global policy of striving to contain communism. More recently, the so-called Reagan Doctrine pledged the United States to assist anti-Marxist insurgent forces in several left-wing Third World countries, thereby adding an entirely new dimension to America's already extensive foreign entanglements.

The Costs of Intervention

Adherence to collective security strategies has had a corrosive impact on American lives, values, and institutions. In human terms alone, the cost has been staggering. Since the abandonment of noninterventionism in the early 1940s, nearly 400,000 young Americans have perished in combat. More than 100,000 of them lost their lives in the Korean and Vietnam wars—conflicts whose relationship to U.S. security was obscure at best.

The financial cost of interventionism has been devastating as well. In the past four and a half decades the United States has spent nearly

$4 trillion on the military. Moreover, the bulk of that vast sum has not been spent on homeland defense. Cato senior fellow Earl C. Ravenal has amassed persuasive evidence that throughout the cold war era more than half of America's "defense" budget has been used to subsidize the security of its allies and client states.

Such burdensome military spending offers a graphic contrast to the noninterventionist foreign policy that prevailed during the nation's first century and a half of independence. As historian Bruce Russett noted, even as late as 1939 U.S. military spending barely exceeded 1 percent of the gross national product. Under the interventionist regime the lowest post–World War II level was 3.9 percent, reached in 1947. Since the Vietnam War the military spending level has fluctuated between 5 and 7 percent; it is currently about 6.5 percent.

The opportunity cost of increased militarization should not be ignored. Wealth spent on soldiers and armaments cannot be used for consumer goods or civilian capital investment. The drain is especially debilitating in a rapidly changing global economy that is increasingly dependent on high technology. More than a decade ago Seymour Melman predicted in his seminal work *The Permanent War Economy* that excessive military spending would sap America's economic vitality. More recently Cato adjunct scholar Lloyd J. Dumas, in *The Overburdened Economy*, validated Melman's warning by presenting sobering evidence that significant deterioration had already occurred. The Founders understood that an excessive military establishment threatened the prosperity as well as the liberty of a free people. That lesson apparently has eluded many of their descendants.

The Imperial Presidency

Interventionism has also corroded America's political structure. The most ominous development is the malignant growth of an imperial presidency. A dramatic expansion of executive power that had grave implications for the system of checks and balances coincided with the advent of a global interventionist foreign policy in the early 1940s. During the months prior to Pearl Harbor, Franklin Roosevelt maneuvered a reluctant nation toward war through a series of unilateral actions. Once the United States officially entered the war, he circumvented Congress to an even greater degree. Major decisions reached with Great Britain and the Soviet Union, not only about the conduct of the war but about the postwar settlement, were concluded by executive agreement rather than by treaty; thus, the Senate was excluded from the decision-making process.

Roosevelt's successors duplicated or even exceeded his arrogance. Harry Truman scorned congressional prerogatives by involving the United States in the Korean conflict without even asking for an authorizing resolution, much less a declaration of war. Sen. Robert Taft aptly termed that act "a complete usurpation by the President of authority to use the Armed Forces of this country."

The zenith of the imperial presidency occurred when both Lyndon Johnson and Richard Nixon asserted the right to direct U.S. participation in the Vietnam War without congressional approval. (They even dismissed the Tonkin Gulf resolution as superfluous moral support.) Instead, each president invoked an expansive interpretation of his constitutional authority as commander in chief of the armed forces and spun elaborate theories of "inherent" presidential power.

Congress finally reclaimed some of its foreign policy prerogatives in the early 1970s, thereby restoring at least a semblance of the system of checks and balances that the Founders had envisioned. The War Powers Resolution, restrictions on U.S. foreign aid programs, and provisions for congressional oversight of intelligence agencies curbed the worst abuses of the imperial presidency. That achievement may prove to be transitory, however; the Reagan administration has embarked on a concerted campaign to reinstitute unlimited executive power over foreign affairs. Actions it has taken with respect to Lebanon, Grenada, Libya, Nicaragua, and Iran all suggest a foreign policy formulated in arrogant isolation from Congress and the American people. The constitutional system of checks and balances is still in jeopardy.

It is important to understand that cold warriors do not conceive of an unfettered presidency as an end in itself. Rather, they view it as a powerful, if not indispensable, means to pursue an interventionist foreign policy. The linkage is evident in Secretary of State George Shultz's complaint that post-Vietnam restrictions on "presidential flexibility" have "weakened our country" and caused it to pull back from "global leadership."

During the early years of the cold war Senator Taft and other conservatives condemned presidential usurpation of policymaking power and led an unsuccessful fight to reactivate the system of checks and balances. Contemporary conservatives, however, are among the foremost apologists for an imperial presidency. The editors of the *Wall Street Journal* seem especially enamored of executive supremacy; they have devoted numerous editorials to condemning the War Powers Resolution and asserting that the Founders intended to give the president untrammeled authority over foreign affairs. That revisionist assertion resembles something out of George Orwell's *1984*. Such interventionists would have us believe that the Founders—inheritors of the British Whig tradition, with its distrust of executive power—invested the presidency with unilateral foreign policy authority that not even the British monarchy possessed.

Undermining Our Political Values

An interventionist foreign policy has also eroded fundamental American values. Military conscription has been a prominent, largely accepted feature of our society throughout much of the cold war. The emergence of a national security state during and immediately following World War II led inexorably to a demand for conformity, especially on foreign policy issues. Even such conservative critics of globalism as *Chicago Tribune* publisher Robert McCormick and Senators Taft and Kenneth Wherry were confronted with innuendoes about their patriotism. Liberal and radical critics were routinely subjected to allegations of disloyalty. As the cold war deepened, "loyalty" became a political obsession; it culminated in the outrages against civil liberties committed during the McCarthy era.

Although it might be tempting to dismiss McCarthyism as an unfortunate aberration—a collective hysteria created and exploited by a political demagogue—a review of both earlier and later developments casts doubt on that sanguine conclusion. An intolerance of foreign policy dissenters even more intense than that of the McCarthy period emerged during the First World War, a conflict that, not coincidentally, was the first major departure from America's noninterventionist tradition. Pacifists and other critics of America's involvement were intimidated, assaulted, and imprisoned. Likewise, members of America First and other "isolationist" groups attempting to keep the United States out of the Second World War were repeatedly smeared as "profascist" and harassed by the Roosevelt administration.

Nor did the erosion of civil liberties end with the McCarthy era. Throughout the Vietnam conflict antiwar organizations had to contend with governmental surveillance, infiltration, and disruption. Recently the cynical "politics of loyalty" has reappeared; advocates of interventionism are once again accusing their opponents of being "soft on communism." Former White House communications director Patrick Buchanan made use of that rhetorical ploy when he asserted that a vote on U.S. military aid to the Nicaraguan contras would determine whether members of Congress stood with President Reagan or with "Daniel Ortega and the communists."

Just as interventionism has eroded freedom of expression and other civil liberties at home, it has undermined American values abroad. The credibility of the U.S. commitment to democracy and free enterprise is compromised when Washington endorses and subsidizes "friendly" Third World autocrats. Yet in an effort to line up client states and insulate various regions against Soviet influence, U.S. officials frequently portray such tyrants as members of the free world and contribute economic and military aid to keep them in power. The strong strain of anti-Americanism in the Third World cannot be understood apart from that betrayal of America's heritage.

John Quincy Adams asserted that a grave corruption of fundamental American values would occur if the United States abandoned its commitment to noninterventionism. America, Adams proclaimed, "goes not abroad in search of monsters to destroy." He then issued this prophetic warning:

> She well knows that by once enlisting under other banners than her own . . . she would involve herself beyond the power of extrication, in all the wars of interest and intrigue, of individual avarice, envy, and ambition, which assume the colors and usurp the standard of freedom. The fundamental maxims of her policy would insensibly change from liberty to force. . . . She might become the dictatress of the world. She would be no longer the ruler of her own spirit.

One would be hard-pressed to find a more concise description of America's foreign policy since World War II.

Intervention in the Nuclear Age

The nation's abandonment of noninterventionism not only has had unpalatable consequences, it has been based on faulty premises. Twentieth-century proponents of globalism typically contend that technological developments have rendered an "isolationist" policy obsolete and that peace-loving nations must unite to thwart an aggressor or fall victim to a divide-and-conquer strategy. Alliances and other collective security measures, they claim, are therefore essential.

But reliance on collective security rather than noninterventionist strategies constitutes a dangerous anachronism. At one time it was plausible to argue that allies might help deter an aggressor and thereby preserve peace. But in the thermonuclear era allies are either superfluous or profoundly dangerous. Washington's ménage of associates and clients would be irrelevant in a U.S.-Soviet clash over an issue central to both superpowers. On the other hand, the United States and the Soviet Union might well become embroiled in a nuclear conflagration sparked by a dispute between reckless clients. There is more than a remote possibility that World War III could evolve from conflicts between Israel and Syria, North and South Korea, or Pakistan and India, even if the underlying issues were of marginal relevance to both superpower patrons. In the nuclear age alliances are, in Earl Ravenal's apt phrase, lethal "transmission belts for war."

The Founders charted a noninterventionist course that served the republic well for 150 years. Since abandoning noninterventionism, the United States has drifted into a series of bloody conflicts, undermined its credibility abroad, and suffered grievous domestic consequences. Worst of all, the country has embraced a strategy that menaces rather than enhances its security. A foreign policy based on noninterventionist principles is even more essential today than it was at the dawn of the republic.

The Case for U.S. Strategic Independence

Ted Galen Carpenter

The goal of global stability, which is the guiding principle of President Bush's "new world order," will mean preserving a host of Cold War era security burdens while creating several new ones for the United States. An emphasis on stability has been the underlying theme in the administration's response to numerous situations, including the "tilt" toward the central government in Belgrade during the initial stages of the Yugoslavian crisis and the lack of enthusiasm for secessionist movements in the Soviet Union before the failed August 1991 coup. The same attitude was evident in President Bush's comments after the November 1991 NATO summit in Rome: "The enemy is unpredictability. The friend is stability."

Although global stability might be appealing in the abstract, the costs and risks entailed in achieving that goal are excessive. One of the worst effects is the perpetuation of such obsolete Cold War era military alliances as NATO and the bilateral defense treaties with Japan and the Republic of Korea (ROK). Those commitments are enormously expensive. The NATO commitment alone cost American taxpayers more than $120 billion a year during the latter stages of the Cold War. Even with the scaled-down U.S. troop presence in Europe that the Bush administration projects, the annual price tag will still be approximately $92 billion. Washington's obligation to defend Japan, South Korea, and other East Asian allies costs another $40 billion.

The financial consequences of maintaining such alliances can be measured in another way. The United States currently spends nearly seven times as much on the military as does any other member of the Group of 7 (G-7) industrial powers. Indeed, it spends some 60 per-

Ted Galen Carpenter is vice president for defense and foreign policy studies at the Cato Institute.
Cato Institute Foreign Policy Briefing No. 16, January 16, 1992

cent more than all of the other G-7 countries combined. A nation that faces daunting domestic problems, including a ballooning federal budget deficit, an overtaxed citizenry, and a sluggish economy, can ill-afford that kind of disparity. We must ask whether in a post-Cold War world the United States really has seven times the security interests of Germany—or France, or Britain, or Japan—to defend.

Washington's Cold War era alliances also have the potential to entangle the United States in a host of obscure conflicts that have little relevance to America's legitimate security concerns. The ongoing transformation of NATO from an alliance to deter Soviet aggression against Western Europe into a regional crisis management organization is a case in point. That new mission blurs the boundaries of NATO's traditional theater of operations and threatens to involve the United States in volatile and intractable ethnic conflicts in Eastern Europe and the decaying Soviet empire. The commitment to defend South Korea puts American forces on the front lines of one of the most dangerous areas of the planet—even though the Cold War rationale for assuming such a grave risk has vanished.

It is time to recognize that with the disintegration of the Soviet Union, the mission of America's Cold War alliances has been accomplished. U.S. policymakers must now move to create a new defense strategy that is appropriate for a post-Cold War setting and that does not waste American resources or needlessly risk American lives. We cannot afford to maintain alliances for the sake of having alliances. We now have both the opportunity and the need to adopt a new policy of strategic independence.

The Unattainable Objective of Global Stability

Making global stability the guiding star of U.S. foreign policy in the post-Cold War era is dangerously short-sighted. The immediate future is likely to be extremely turbulent, regardless of what the United States does. Many regions are still dealing with the legacy of the imperial age. Throughout the Balkans, the Middle East, Sub-Saharan Africa, and South Asia, the European imperial powers carved out colonies or established client states without reference to the wishes of the indigenous inhabitants or long-standing linguistic, cultural, and economic patterns. In some cases, ancient enemies were grouped together in a single jurisdiction; in other instances, ancient cultures were arbitrarily divided.

It is hardly surprising that those imposed artificial political settlements are now being challenged. Iraq's attempted annexation of Kuwait, the turmoil in Yugoslavia, and the disintegration of the last multinational empire—the Soviet Union—are all omens of the post-Cold War era. An attempt by Washington to maintain global stability in the face of such deeply rooted trends is doomed to failure.

Advocates of a global stability mission also mistakenly assume that other major international actors will be cooperative junior partners in U.S.-led security efforts. But the belief that Japan and the Western European powers will continue to follow Washington's leadership as they did throughout the Cold War is erroneous. International relations theory (as well as international relations history) would predict the gradual dissolution of Cold War era solidarity now that there is no longer a credible common threat to promote cohesion among allies. U.S. leaders cannot assume that the diplomatic, economic, and military agendas of the other G-7 powers will always coincide with our own—much less that those nations will routinely defer to Washington's policy preferences.

America's Cold War era allies have already begun to pursue increasingly independent political and military policies. The members of the European Community (especially Germany) have rather unceremoniously edged Washington to the diplomatic sidelines in efforts to deal with the Yugoslavian crisis. France and Germany have proposed an expansion of their joint military brigade to approximately 50,000 troops—an action that is clearly the first step toward the creation of an all-European force. Japan—long diffident about playing a leadership role in security matters—surprised most observers by suggesting a security dialogue with the members of the Association of Southeast Asian Nations (ASEAN).

Instead of welcoming such signs of growing self-reliance on the part of other major democratic capitalist powers—or at least adjusting gracefully to the changing realities—U.S. officials have often reacted petulantly. National Security Adviser Brent Scowcroft chastised the members of the European Community for adopting "independent" positions on security issues and then presenting those positions to the United States. Similarly, Secretary of State James A. Baker III criticized the notion of Japanese-ASEAN security cooperation. The Bush administration expended considerable diplomatic capital to thwart French efforts to create a rapid reaction force under the auspices of the European Community rather than NATO and viewed with suspicion the expansion of the Franco-German military brigade.

Such responses are most revealing in light of Washington's long-standing habit of prodding U.S. allies to share security burdens. Apparently, the U.S. concept of burden sharing means only that other great powers should pay for a larger percentage of the costs of policies adopted by Washington, not that they should take greater responsibility for defending their own security interests, much less adopt independent strategies for doing so.

Washington's Obsolete Alliances

Instead of seeking to preserve an expensive system of U.S.-dominated alliances, the United States should view the eclipse of Soviet power as an opportunity to adopt a less pretentious and more cost-effective policy. For the first time in 50 years, there is no powerful challenger, such as Nazi Germany or the Soviet Union, that could pose a grave threat to America's security, nor is there a potential new threat visible on the horizon. That is a watershed development that should fundamentally alter U.S. defense policy.

The post-Cold War world is likely to be a disorderly place, but without a powerful rival to exploit the turmoil most of the conflicts and quarrels will be largely irrelevant to America's own security interests. The United States can, therefore, afford to view them with detachment, intervening only as a balancer of last resort if a conflict cannot be contained by powers in the affected region and is expanding to the point where America's security is threatened.

The vastly changed international system means that Washington's network of Cold War era alliances is an expensive anachronism. It makes little sense to maintain more than 150,000 U.S. troops in Europe to defend Western Europe from a Warsaw Pact that no longer exists. When NATO was established in 1949, the European democracies, still devastated and demoralized by World War II, faced an aggressively expansionist Soviet Union. Today, Western Europe is economically powerful and politically vibrant while the Soviet Union is extinct. Given their economic and military resources, the members of the European Community should certainly be able to defend themselves against any present or future secondary threats.

A similar transformation has occurred in East Asia. When the United States first undertook to defend the security of South Korea in the 1950s, that country was an impoverished, war-torn hulk confronted by a communist North Korean adversary backed by the Soviet Union and China. Today, South Korea is an economic dynamo with twice the population and more than 10 times the gross national product of North Korea. Moreover, North Korea is becoming increasingly isolated as both Beijing and Moscow seek to forge closer political and economic ties with the South. Given such conditions, it is absurd to contend that South Korea cannot build whatever military forces are needed for its security and must, therefore, forever remain a U.S. protectorate.

It is even more difficult to justify keeping Japan a protectorate. Japan has the world's second largest economy as well as one of the most dynamic and technologically sophisticated. Yet Tokyo spends an anemic 1 percent of its GNP on the military while the United States spends more than 5 percent. Given the increasingly fierce competition between American and Japanese firms in a host of international markets, we can ill-afford to burden our economy with excessive military expenditures that enable Japan to save vast sums that it might otherwise have to use to protect its own security.

Other U.S. alliances in East Asia, most notably ANZUS and the bilateral security treaty with the Philippines, are equally obsolete. Even if it once made sense to protect those countries from the Soviet Union or other communist expansionist powers (in the unlikely event that such a threat materialized), that rationale has disappeared. Yet Washington insists on preserving its obligations throughout East Asia.

Instead of viewing the changes in the international system as an opportunity for the United States to shed security burdens and downsize a bloated military budget, U.S. officials search for new missions to justify the perpetuation of old alliances. For example, they insist that NATO and the U.S. troop presence in Europe are needed to prevent instability in Eastern Europe—essentially a scarecrow function. Aside from the question of whether such a mission is worth $92 billion a year, the onset of civil war in Yugoslavia demonstrates that a U.S. military presence has little ability to deter the kind of ethnic conflicts that are likely to plague Eastern Europe in the post-Cold War era.

It would not be in our interest to become involved in such conflicts. Most Americans accepted the costs and risks associated with the NATO commitment during the Cold War. But the rationale for that commitment was the need to prevent an expansionist Soviet Union from gaining control of the population and technological assets of Western Europe and then using that additional strength to pose an increased threat to America's own security. Accepting the risks and costs of a vague mission to preserve an elusive stability in Eastern Europe is another matter entirely. The division of power between Croats and Serbs, the unity or breakup of Czecho-Slovakia, and the treatment of the Hungarian minority in the Transylvanian region of Romania may all be extremely important issues to the parties involved. But such disputes would rarely affect even the European, much less the global, geopolitical balance and are therefore hardly essential to America's security. Taking the risk of becoming entangled in the ancient and intractable ethnic conflicts of Eastern Europe is not merely unnecessary; it would be foreign policy masochism.

The same is true of the U.S. treaty obligation to defend South Korea. In a Cold War context, it was possible to argue that a North Korean attack on the South would pose a threat to America's security because such an attack would in reality be an expansionist probe by a Soviet or Chinese surrogate. That is no longer a plausible scenario. Pyongyang may still harbor aggressive ambitions, but even if it were to launch an attack on the ROK, the resulting conflict would now be a parochial one between the two rival Korean states. It need not and should not have cosmic geostrategic ramifications. In a post-Cold War setting, South Korea is, at most, a peripheral U.S. interest whose defense does not warrant the expenditure of billions of dollars or the risk of thousands of American lives.

There has been considerable discussion recently about the threat posed by North Korea's apparent effort to acquire nuclear weapons. The emergence of North Korea as a nuclear power would be an unsettling development for the entire East Asian region, and Washington should diligently pursue diplomatic initiatives (including enlisting the aid of Beijing and Moscow) to pressure Pyongyang to honor the agreement reached with the ROK to make the Korean peninsula a nuclear-free zone. Nevertheless, even a nuclearized North Korea must not become a justification for indefinitely preserving the U.S.

security commitment to South Korea. Indeed, it should be an additional reason for severing that commitment. The only thing worse than becoming involved in a conflict between states armed with conventional weapons when vital U.S. interests are not at stake is becoming involved in a conflict in which one or more of the combatants have nuclear weapons. It is true that without the U.S. nuclear shield, Seoul might decide to acquire an independent deterrent if the agreement with North Korea eventually unravels. Although such a proliferation of nuclear weapons is not an appealing prospect, it is better than putting the United States at risk in an effort to deter one of the most unpredictable and irrational regimes on the planet.

An Alternative: U.S. Strategic Independence

A new U.S. policy of strategic independence is needed. Strategic independence would have three guiding principles. The first would be a definition of "vital" security interests that is narrower than the vague and casual one used during the Cold War. A vital interest ought to have a direct, immediate, and substantial connection to America's physical survival, political independence, and domestic liberty. The second principle would be an emphasis on U.S. decisionmaking autonomy and flexibility. Washington should avoid alliances, especially those with vague, long-term obligations, since they both limit America's options and can entangle the United States in conflicts that are of little relevance to its own security. They also lock the United States into commitments that may make sense under one set of global conditions but are unnecessary or undesirable when those conditions change. The final principle would be to resist pursuing ambitious international "milieu" goals—especially "stability," which lies at the heart of President Bush's new world order. America would undoubtedly be happier in a world composed entirely of peaceful democratic states, but such a goal is unattainable—or at least it is not attainable at an acceptable level of cost and risk to the United States. Moreover, while such a transformation of the international system might be desirable, it is not essential to America's security.

Strategic independence is not merely another sterile exercise in burden sharing. Washington has tried to get its European and East Asian allies to pay more of the expense of collective defense efforts for the past four decades—without a great deal of success. (The Bush administration's ability to cajole the allies into paying for much of the Persian Gulf operation is an impressive, but probably unique, exception. Even those contributions were obtained only after unprecedented diplomatic browbeating.) If meaningful burden sharing was difficult to attain during the Cold War, when the U.S. defensive shield was of considerable value to allies facing a looming Soviet threat, it is likely to prove even more difficult to attain in a post-Cold War world. The value of Washington's military protection to the allies has depreciated markedly in the past two years, and their willingness to pay more for that protection can be expected to decline as well. For the same reason, the notion that maintaining an extensive U.S. troop presence in Europe and East Asia will give Washington "leverage" on trade and other economic issues is an illusion. The U.S. presence is no longer valuable enough to induce the Europeans or the Japanese to make more than cosmetic concessions.

Instead of embarking on another futile round of burden-sharing campaigns, Washington should adopt a policy of burden shedding. A burden-shedding policy would entail the gradual but complete devolution of responsibility to America's allies for the defense of their respective regions. The process can be completed in an orderly fashion over a five-year period in both Europe and East Asia. Although the exact pace and timing of security devolution should be determined in consultation with the allies, the ultimate result should not be subject to negotiation—much less an allied veto.

Just as strategic independence is not burden sharing, it is also not isolationism. The United States can and should maintain extensive diplomatic, cultural, and economic ties with the rest of the world. Washington must also maintain sizable and capable military forces and be prepared to take decisive action if a serious threat to America's security does emerge. A judicious, albeit aggressive, pruning of security commitments is needed, not the creation of a hermit republic.

The most difficult adjustment for U.S. officials will be to accept other powers' assuming larger roles in regions where America abandons its strategic hegemony. It is predictable that major European powers, acting either collectively through the European Community or individually, will adopt more assertive positions. Similarly, Japan is likely to eventually play a political and military role in East Asia commensurate with its status as an economic great power.

Such changes may be unsettling not only for the United States but for smaller powers in the affected regions. But attempting to preserve U.S. dominance would involve even greater risks. For example, perpetuating a large-scale U.S. military presence in the western Pacific could ultimately create serious frictions in U.S.-Japanese relations. A majority of Japanese favored the American security shield throughout the Cold War because it offered reliable protection from a menacing Soviet Union and spared Japan from spending scarce resources on the military. But with the dissipation of the Soviet threat, it will not be long before many Japanese begin to wonder why such large numbers of American forces remain. Eventually, the suspicion (not entirely unfounded, if one can judge from the comments of some outspoken U.S. military leaders) will grow that they are there to "contain" Japan. That suspicion could poison the entire range of U.S.-Japanese relations. Many Germans are likely to harbor a similar suspicion and feel alienated from the United States once the last Soviet forces leave German territory, if Washington still insists on maintaining a sizable military presence.

A policy of strategic independence is based on a more modest and sustainable security role for the United States and on a realistic assessment of the post-Cold War international system. It takes into account the fundamental changes that have occurred in the world in recent years and seeks to position the United States to benefit from the emerging multipolar political, economic, and military environment.

The new strategy would make it possible to defend America's security interests with a military force of approximately 900,000 active duty personnel—compared with the current force of some 2 million and the force of 1.6 million contemplated by the Pentagon for the mid-1990s. A policy of strategic independence would enable the United States to reduce its military budget from the current $291 billion a year to approximately $125 billion a year (measured in 1991 dollars) over a five-year period. The beneficial economic impact of a "peace dividend" of that magnitude, if returned to the American people in the form of tax reductions, would be enormous.

After those reductions, the United States would still be spending three times as much on the military as any other G-7 member. The reductions seem radical only in the context of the bloated Cold War era military budgets that have come to be considered "normal." But the Cold War is over, and with its passing we must change our ideas of what constitutes normal defense spending. Instead of accepting marginal changes in military budgets that are still largely based on obsolete Cold War assumptions, the American people should insist on the defense policy equivalent of zero-based budgeting. That approach would require the adoption of a coherent defense strategy based on the realities of the post-Cold War international system and a careful assessment of what is actually needed to protect the nation's security. America cannot afford to pursue the mirage of a new world order, nor can it tolerate the continuing hemorrhage of its wealth to subsidize the defense of prosperous allies who are now capable of defending themselves.

Does U.S. Intervention Overseas Breed Terrorism?

Ivan Eland

The terrorist bombings of U.S. embassies in Nairobi, Kenya, and Dar es Salaam, Tanzania, and retaliation by the United States with cruise missile strikes against Afghanistan and Sudan have once again focused international attention on the problem of terrorism. Secretary of State Madeleine Albright noted the importance of the issue to the Clinton administration: "We have said over and over again that [terrorism] is the biggest threat to our country and the world as we enter the 21st century." Many analysts agree with Albright, especially in light of the possibility that terrorists may be able to buy, steal, or develop and produce weapons of mass destruction (nuclear, chemical, or biological weapons).

Considerable attention, both in and out of government, focuses on combating terrorism by deterring and disrupting attacks before they occur or retaliating after the fact. Less attention has been paid to investigating the motives of terrorists or their backers. Charles William Maynes, president of the Eurasia Foundation and former editor of *Foreign Policy*, advocates examining the motives of those who support terrorism in order to lessen their grievances. If more emphasis were placed on exploring why terrorists launch attacks against the United States, innovative policy changes might be made that would reduce the number of such attacks and lower their cost—both in money and in lost lives.

Activist Foreign Policy and Terrorism

The Defense Science Board's 1997 Summer Study Task Force on DoD Responses to Transnational Threats notes a relationship between

Ivan Eland is director of defense policy studies at the Cato Institute.
Cato Institute Foreign Policy Briefing No. 50, December 17, 1998

an activist American foreign policy and terrorism against the United States:

> As part of its global power position, the United States is called upon frequently to respond to international causes and deploy forces around the world. America's position in the world invites attack simply because of its presence. *Historical data show a strong correlation between U.S. involvement in international situations and an increase in terrorist attacks against the United States.* (emphasis added)

In an August 8, 1998, radio address justifying cruise missile attacks on Afghanistan and Sudan in response to terrorist bombings of two U.S. embassies, President Clinton admitted as much but put a positive spin on it with political hyperbole:

> Americans are targets of terrorism in part because we have unique leadership responsibilities in the world, because we act to advance peace and democracy, and because we stand united against terrorism.

Richard Betts, an influential authority on American foreign policy at the Council on Foreign Relations, has written about the connection between U.S. activism overseas and possible attacks on the United States with nuclear, chemical, and biological weapons: "American activism to guarantee international stability is, paradoxically, the prime source of American vulnerability." Elaborating, he notes, "Today, as the only nation acting to police areas outside its own region, the United States makes itself a target for states or groups whose aspirations are frustrated by U.S. power."

Attempts to Obfuscate the Link between U.S. Foreign Policy and Terrorism

There are analysts who try to obfuscate the link between U.S. intervention and terrorism against American targets by arguing that a multitude of factors leads to such attacks. Rep. Frank Wolf (R-Va.), introducing legislation that would establish a national commission on terrorism, argued that "our military, industrial, and commercial presence around the world attracts frustration from many terrorist groups." Other analysts include American "cultural dominance" as a lightning rod for terrorist attacks against the United States.

President Clinton, in a speech to the UN General Assembly, also attempted to diffuse the link between U.S. foreign policy and terrorist incidents:

Because we are blessed to be a wealthy nation with a powerful military and a worldwide presence active in promoting peace and security, we are often a target. We love our country for its dedication to political and religious freedom, to economic opportunity, to respect for the rights of the individual. But we know many people see us as a symbol of a system and values they reject, and often they find it expedient to blame us for problems with deep roots elsewhere.

Curiously, however, later in the same speech, President Clinton seemed to reject the "clash of values" origin of terrorism that he had propounded earlier:

Some people believe that terrorism's principal fault line centers on what they see as an inevitable clash of civilizations. . . . Specifically, many believe there is an inevitable clash between Western civilization and Western values, and Islamic civilizations and values. I believe this view is terribly wrong.

Yet the perception that the United States is targeted because of "what it is" rather than "what it does" endures. Gerald Seib, writing in the *Wall Street Journal*, admits that Islamic militants see the United States as propping up the secular government of Egypt and desecrating the Islamic holy sites by the presence of its troops in Saudi Arabia. At the same time, he observes that Islamic militants also see the United States as a political and cultural enemy, standing for everything they abhor—secularism, debauchery, and liberty. He concludes, "The U.S. is a target not because of something it has or hasn't done, but simply because it exists." Seib's conclusion underestimates the offense caused by propping up undemocratic regimes with dubious human rights records through aid or the presence of troops.

Logic and Empirical Data Support the Link

The logic behind the claim that there are other primary causes for terrorism against the United States needs to be examined. Many other Western nations are wealthy; have an extensive industrial and commercial presence overseas; export their culture along with their products and services; and believe in religious freedom, economic opportunity, and respect for the rights of the individual. Yet those nations— Switzerland and Australia, for example—seem to have much less of a problem with worldwide terrorism than does the United States.

According to the U.S. State Department's *Patterns of Global Terrorism: 1997*, one-third of all terrorist attacks worldwide were perpetrated against U.S. targets. The percentage of terrorism targeted at the United States is very high considering that the United States—unlike nations such as Algeria, Turkey, and the United Kingdom—has no internal civil war or quarrels with its neighbors that spawn terrorism. The major difference between the United States and other wealthy democratic nations is that it is an interventionist superpower. As Betts notes, the United States is the only nation in the world that intervenes regularly outside its own region.

The motives for some terrorist attacks are not easy to discern. They may be protests against U.S. culture or overseas business presence. Two incidents in 1995—the deadly attack by two gunmen on a van from the U.S. consulate in Karachi, Pakistan, and the bombing of a "Dunkin Donuts" in Bogotá, Colombia—could fit into those categories. But with no statement of motives by the terrorists, such attacks could just as easily have been responses to the perceived foreign policies of a global superpower.

Even if some terrorist attacks against the United States are a reaction to "what it is" rather than "what it does," the list of incidents later in this paper shows how many terrorist attacks can be traced back to an interventionist American foreign policy. A conservative approach was taken in cataloging those incidents. To be added to the list, a planned or actual attack first had to be targeted against U.S. citizens, property, or facilities—either at home or abroad. Then there had to be either an indication from the terrorist group that the attack was a response to U.S. foreign policy or strong circumstantial evidence that the location, timing, or target of the attack coincided with a specific U.S. intervention overseas.

Although the Defense Science Board noted a historical correlation between U.S. involvement in international situations and an increase in terrorist attacks against the United States, the board apparently believed the conclusion to be so obvious that it did not publish detailed data to support it. Some analysts apparently remain unconvinced of the relationship. The data in this paper provide the empirical evidence.

Recognizing the Link Is Even More Important Now

The large number of terrorist attacks that have occurred in retaliation for an interventionist American foreign policy implicitly demonstrates that terrorism against U.S. targets could be significantly reduced if the United States adopted a policy of military restraint overseas. That policy change has become even more critical now that ostensibly "weak" terrorists—whether sponsored by states or operating independently—might have both the means and the motive to inflict enormous devastation on the U.S. homeland with weapons of mass destruction.

In the post-Cold War world, rampant U.S. military intervention overseas is no longer needed. A rival superpower no longer exists to threaten vital U.S. interests by taking advantage of "instability" in the world. The overwhelming majority of the conflicts in the post-Cold War world—95 of 101 from 1989 to 1996—involved disputes between parties within states, the outcomes of which are far less likely to be dangerous to U.S. security than are cross-border wars between states. Yet it is those intrastate wars, many of which are volatile ethnic or religious conflicts, that could spawn the terrorist groups that might attack the United States with weapons of mass destruction. Intervention in such conflicts does little to enhance U.S. security, but it may have the opposite, catastrophic, effect.

Betts, referring to the threat of terrorists' using weapons of mass destruction, argues that the "danger is that some angry group that blames the United States for its problems may decide to coerce Americans, or simply exact vengeance, by inflicting devastation on them where they live." He continues:

> If steps to deal with the problem in terms of capabilities are limited, can anything be done to address intentions—the incentives of any foreign power or group to lash out at the United States? There are few answers to this question that do not compromise the fundamental strategic activism and internationalist thrust of U.S. foreign policy over the past half-century. That is because the best way to keep people from believing that the United States is responsible for their problems is to avoid involvement in their conflicts.

If the U.S. government adopted a policy of military restraint overseas, in the long term the number of devastating, and potentially catastrophic, terrorist attacks against the United States—attacks like those described in this paper—could be reduced significantly. Even if some remaining terrorist incidents can be attributed to a hatred of U.S. economic power, individual freedom, or culture, those national attributes are much harder and more costly to alter, and it would be undesirable to do so. It is much easier (and after the Cold War, relatively painless) to change U.S. foreign policy than it is to change the American way of life. In fact, the interventionist foreign policy currently pursued by the United States is an aberration in its history. Adopting a policy of military restraint would return the United States to the traditional foreign policy it pursued for the first century and a half of its existence before the Cold War distorted it. Such a foreign policy is more compatible with the individual freedoms and economic prosperity that define the American way of life.

Highlights of the List of Terrorist Incidents

Terrorism against American targets has changed over time. As the Cold War ended and the influence of Islamic radicalism grew, terrorism by leftist groups in the 1970s and 1980s was eclipsed by terrorism by Muslim fundamentalists in the 1980s and 1990s. As state-sponsored terrorism has declined, independent terrorist groups with loose ties among members have arisen. Finally and most important, terrorists now seem more willing to inflict mass casualties and can more readily obtain the weapons of mass destruction needed to do so.

Attempts at Catastrophic Terrorism

The Defense Science Board commented on the increased capability and willingness of terrorists to inflict mass casualties:

> There is a new and ominous trend to these threats: a proclivity towards much greater levels of violence. Transnational groups have the means, through access to weapons of mass destruction and other instruments of terror and disruption, and the motives to cause great harm to our society. For example, the perpetrators of the World Trade Center bombing and the Tokyo Subway nerve gas attack were aiming for tens of thousands of casualties.

Although the fundamentalist Islamic perpetrators of the World Trade Center bombing in 1993 were unsuccessful at mass slaughter, the mastermind of the plot said he was attempting to kill 250,000 people by collapsing the towers to punish the United States for its policies in the Middle East. (In a follow-on attack, the group planned to blow up buildings and key transportation nodes in New York

City—UN headquarters, a U.S. government building, two tunnels underneath the Hudson River, and the George Washington Bridge—which would have inflicted substantial casualties.)

Plans for another such catastrophic attack on the United States were also uncovered. In a little-noticed incident with potentially catastrophic ramifications, members of the Aum Shinrikyo (Supreme Truth) religious cult—the same group that released poison gas on the Tokyo subway—planned a nerve gas attack at Disneyland when it was most crowded, during a fireworks display. Fortunately, U.S. law enforcement officials, tipped off by Japanese police, apprehended members of the group before they could perpetrate the attack. Aum Shinrikyo believes in a final Armageddon between the United States and Japan near the millennium and that acts of mass terror will hasten it. It is interesting that the cult perceived an allied nation—the United States—as Japan's enemy rather than Japan's regional neighbors that are now or are much more likely to become rivals—for example, China, Russia, and North and South Korea. The U.S. role as a global superpower and the U.S. military presence in Japan most likely had something to do with the group's choice of the United States as a target.

U.S. Military Presence Overseas: Lightning Rod for Terrorism

The U.S. military presence in Lebanon in the early 1980s and in Somalia and Saudi Arabia in the 1990s also spawned terrorist attacks. Beginning in 1979, with the takeover of the U.S. embassy in Tehran, Iranians or Iranian-sponsored groups—such as Hezbollah in Lebanon—perpetrated many terrorist attacks against the United States. Two of the best known incidents were the suicide bombings by Hezbollah of the U.S. embassy and the Marine barracks in Beirut. Those Hezbollah attacks were launched in retaliation for U.S. military support of the Lebanese Christian government against the Muslim militias. The Iranians hated the United States for its long-time support of the shah and resented the U.S. presence in Lebanon.

In Somalia in 1993 the now-infamous Osama bin Laden trained the Somali tribesmen who conducted ambushes of U.S. peacekeeping forces in support of Somali clan leader Mohammed Farah Aideed. The result of the attack was 18 dead U.S. Army Rangers and U.S. withdrawal from Somalia. Osama bin Laden, a Saudi, did not merely object to U.S. intervention in Somalia. His main reason for attacking U.S. targets was the American presence in Saudi Arabia and Washington's support for Israel. Bin Laden was allegedly linked to the 1996 truck bombing of the U.S. military apartment complex, Khobar Towers, in Saudi Arabia that killed 19 U.S. airmen and wounded 515 others. He was also allegedly linked to the simultaneous bombings of U.S. embassies in Kenya and Tanzania in 1998 and other attacks.

Public Wars against Terrorism Have Been Tried Before

President Clinton is not the first president to launch a public war against terrorism. In the summer of 1981 Ronald Reagan began a very public "war" against Moammar Qaddafi, the ruler of Libya, shortly after taking office. Reagan believed that Qaddafi was a Soviet agent and was heavily involved in terrorism against the West. The Reagan administration pursued ways of getting rid of Qaddafi or, failing that, of isolating him politically and economically. (Some analysts assert that Reagan inflated the threat posed by Qaddafi to justify increased defense spending.)

The "war" began with an attempt by the Reagan administration to provoke Qaddafi by entering claimed Libyan territorial waters and air space during war games in the Mediterranean. In August 1981 U.S. jets—to challenge Libya's extension of its territorial waters and air space over the Gulf of Sidra—entered the gulf and shot down two Libyan aircraft that intercepted them. Reagan later accused Qaddafi of aiding the perpetrators of the bombings at the Rome and Vienna airports. In March 1986 Reagan sent a naval armada across the "line of death" that marked Libya's claimed territorial waters in the gulf, and another military altercation ensued. In April 1986 Qaddafi retaliated by sponsoring the bombing of the La Belle disco in West Berlin, which was frequented by U.S. servicemen. (Before 1986 there was little evidence that Qaddafi was targeting Americans. Reagan interpreted Qaddafi's terrorism as anti-American, but Western European nations had been Libya's major target.) The United States retaliated for the La Belle bombing with air strikes against Tripoli and Benghazi that apparently were meant to kill Qaddafi.

Contrary to popular belief, the air strikes did not cause Qaddafi to desist from terrorist acts. In fact, according to the Defense Science Board, over the next several years Qaddafi began a series of secret attacks on American targets in revenge for the air strikes. The most famous attack was the bombing of Pan Am Flight 103 over Lockerbie, Scotland, which killed 270 people (200 of whom were Americans).

Reagan's public war on terrorism may have been effective in helping to garner an increase in U.S. defense spending but not in curbing Qaddafi's terrorist activities. In fact, Qaddafi's secret activities seemed to accelerate in retaliation for Reagan's public military actions.

Assassinations and Attempted Assassinations

Independent or state-sponsored terrorists have attempted to assassinate prominent U.S. citizens in retaliation for perceived American meddling overseas. Sirhan Sirhan, Robert Kennedy's assassin, had grown up on the West Bank and regarded Kennedy as a collaborator with Israel. U.S. support for Israel and Kennedy's role in that policy were implicated in the assassination.

In 1993, 17 Iraqis were arrested trying to infiltrate Kuwait with a large car bomb and were accused of being part of an Iraqi government plot to kill former president Bush on his visit to Kuwait. According to the U.S. government, Saddam Hussein tried to assassinate Bush in retaliation for Bush's direction of the Gulf War (a threat Saddam had made during the war).

[A lengthy list of terrorist attacks directed at the United States and caused by an activist U.S. foreign policy from 1915 to 1998 is omitted for space. It can be found at http://www.cato.org/pubs/fpbriefs/fpb50.pdf.]

Conclusion

All of the examples of terrorist attacks on the United States can be explained as retaliation for U.S. intervention abroad. Empirically validating the connection between an interventionist foreign policy and such attacks is more critical than ever now that terrorists can more readily obtain weapons of mass destruction and seem to be more willing to use them. The extensive number of incidents of terrorism linked to U.S. foreign policy implies that the United States could substantially reduce the chance of catastrophic terrorist attacks if it lowered its military profile overseas. The United States needs to adopt a new policy that would use military force only as a last resort in the defense of truly vital national interests.

The Cold War has ended, yet the United States continues to use its worldwide military dominance to intervene anywhere and everywhere in an effort to maintain its defense perimeter far forward. In a changed strategic environment in which ostensibly weak terrorist groups might acquire weapons of mass destruction, such an extended defense perimeter may actually increase the catastrophic threat to the American homeland. Even the U.S. Department of Defense admits the problem:

> Indeed, a paradox of the new strategic environment is that American military superiority actually *increases* the threat of nuclear, biological, and chemical attack against us by creating incentives for adversaries to challenge us asymmetrically. These weapons may be used as tools of terrorism against the American people.

But proponents of America's current interventionist foreign policy, such as the *National Review,* ignore the new strategic realities and criticize the proposed policy of military restraint as "preemptively capitulating to the terrorists." Adopting a restrained foreign policy has nothing to do with appeasing terrorists. Terrorist acts are morally outrageous and should be punished whenever possible.

Reducing the motive for terrorists to attack the United States with weapons of mass destruction is not the only reason to adopt a policy of military restraint overseas, although it is a sensible one. In the more benign environment of a post-Cold War world, promiscuous military intervention by the United States—which can result in lost lives, high financial costs, and open-ended commitments—is no longer needed. It is common sense, rather than appeasement, for the United States to adapt its activist Cold War foreign policy to the new strategic environment that requires more restraint overseas.

Fool's Errands?

Gary Dempsey

After NATO's 78-day bombing campaign against Yugoslavia came to a close in June 1999, secretary of state Madeleine K. Albright spoke to U.S. troops preparing to move into Kosovo as peacekeepers. She stressed to them the importance of the U.S. mission: "This is what America is good at: helping people."

Several days later, President Clinton echoed Albright's ideas while touring a refugee camp in northern Macedonia: "We are committed not only to making Kosovo safe, but to helping people rebuild their lives, rebuild their communities."

But is what Clinton and Albright claimed correct? Is the U.S. government really any good at "helping people" in troubled places? America's recent encounters with nation building suggest the contrary. Indeed, Washington said it would bring order to Somalia, but left chaos; it went to Haiti to restore democracy, but produced tyranny; it intervened in Bosnia to reverse the effects of a civil war, but now oversees a peace that is not self-sustaining; and it occupied Kosovo to build a multiethnic democracy, but has instead witnessed widespread ethnic cleansing. That all these attempts at nation building have not actually solved the problems they set out to address seems not to have bothered advocates of this approach to foreign policy.

Gunpoint Democracy

By the time President Clinton entered office in January 1993, foreign policy thinking in Washington had shifted away from focusing on geopolitical containment of the Soviet Union toward redefining U.S. foreign policy for the post-Cold War world. One theme that proved popular with the foreign policy establishment—and that coincidentally

Gary Dempsey is a foreign policy analyst at the Cato Institute.
Gary Dempsey with Roger Fontaine, *Fool's Errands* (Cato Institute, 2001)

required maintaining Cold War era levels of global activism and defense spending—was "promoting democracy." The Clinton administration used the promotion of democracy, or what it called "democratic enlargement," as its clarion call to justify eight years of interventionist foreign policy. In a speech delivered before the UN General Assembly in September 1993, the president proclaimed, "Our overriding purpose must be to expand and strengthen the world's community of market-based democracies. During the Cold War, we fought to contain a threat to the survival of free institutions. Now we seek to enlarge the circle of nations that live under those free institutions."

By June 1993, Secretary of State Warren Christopher had announced in a cable to the U.S. diplomatic corps that the Clinton administration's priority in Somalia would be to transform that nation into a stable democratic member of the world community. "For the first time," explained Christopher, "there will be a sturdy American role to help the United Nations rebuild a viable nation state."

But when 18 U.S. soldiers were killed and 76 were wounded in a Mogadishu firefight several weeks later, Clinton quickly began to distance himself from his nation-building experiment in Somalia. Indeed, he announced that it was not America's responsibility to rebuild Somalia and that Washington had obligations elsewhere.

Although the term "nation building" was exorcised from the Clinton administration's vocabulary after the Somalia debacle, the administration continued to engage in the practice of nation building elsewhere. On September 19, 1994, for example, Clinton dispatched 20,000 U.S. troops to Haiti as part of Operation Uphold Democracy. The mission's objectives, explained the president, were to

> provide a secure environment for the restoration of President [Jean-Bertrand] Aristide and democracy [in Haiti], to begin the work of retraining the police and the military in a professional manner and to facilitate a quick hand-off to the [U.S.-led] United Nations mission so that the work of restoring democracy can be continued, the developmental aid can begin to flow, Haiti can be rebuilt and, in 1995, another free and fair election for president can be held.

In similar fashion, Clinton announced on December 18, 1997, that U.S. troops would not be leaving Bosnia until there were

> joint institutions strong enough to be self-sustaining . . . [the] political parties [had] really given up the so-called state-run media . . . the civilian police [were] large enough, well-trained enough, [and] well-man-

aged enough to do the job it has to do . . . [and] we have confidence that the military is under democratic rule.

Repeatedly tasked with those sorts of missions, defense analysts began to differentiate between "traditional warfighting" and what they had come to dub "military operations other than war." U.S. soldiers and Marines thereafter found that time they formerly used to spend practicing how to execute combat missions was instead dedicated to learning the importance of "indigenous conflict resolution techniques" and how to "work with the [disputing] parties to identify common ground on which to build meaningful dialogue"— which were just two of the many subjects covered in the Pentagon's 1997 Joint Task Force Commander's Handbook for Peace Operations.

Virtuous Power

Another promise Clinton made early in his presidency was to focus more on human rights than did the George H.W. Bush administration. Secretary of State Christopher summarized the administration's thinking,

> The great new focus of our agenda for freedom is this: expanding, consolidating, and defending democratic progress around the world. It is democracy that establishes the civil institutions that replace the power of oppressive regimes. Democracy is the best means not just to gain— but to guarantee—human rights.

In other words, the Clinton administration regarded its democratic enlargement agenda as a means to another goal: the goal of creating an idealistic new world free of widespread inhumanity. President Woodrow Wilson tried to do that more than 80 years ago, and failed. But during the 1990s, the Clinton administration insisted that things were different. Indeed, its view was that Washington faced a special moment in history when the United States and its allies had the military, economic, and political strength to be able to run a foreign policy designed not only to defend American citizens' human rights, but also the human rights of other countries' citizens.

The Clinton administration thus fashioned what might be called a doctrine of "virtuous power": the view that in a properly ordered world, human rights are at the center, and just as legislation—backed by the coercive power of the state—must be enlisted to enforce this vision at home, international norms—backed by U.S. military force—must be applied abroad. The logic behind the administration's thinking was that human rights violations could be greatly reduced, if not eliminated entirely, by creating a just world order in which human rights were elevated to a military priority and a preeminent foreign policy value. After that happens, explained one proponent of the view, the "higher, grander goal that has eluded humanity for centuries—the ideal of justice backed by power"—could become a global reality.

Defining Away Sovereignty

In June 1999, shortly after NATO ended its bombing campaign against Yugoslavia, CNN reporter Wolf Blitzer asked President Clinton if the Kosovo war amounted to a new U.S. foreign policy doctrine. Clinton responded affirmatively. "Whether within or beyond the borders of a country, if the world community has the power to stop it, we ought to stop genocide and ethnic cleansing," he said. Despite initially backing away from the policy implications of that statement, Clinton later reiterated his view, saying that universal human rights is "an important principle . . . that I hope will be applied in the future . . . whether within or beyond the borders of a country."

Whatever the merits of the moral reasoning behind NATO's bombing campaign against Yugoslavia, Washington and the West did cross an important threshold in international politics: the United States and its allies ignored the "great powers" consensus required by the UN Charter and deliberately violated the sovereignty of a country.

Indeed, Clinton administration officials attempted to define away state sovereignty as an obstacle to their "virtuous power" doctrine. When Washington first threatened military action against Yugoslavia in October 1998, a reporter asked Secretary of State Albright, "In the eyes of the United States has [Yugoslav] President [Slobodan] Milosevic forfeited sovereignty over his country?" Albright answered,

> I think that that is an international legal question that I think I don't want to answer in a specific form. . . . [But] I think that it's very important that he understand that as the leader—an elected leader—of a sovereign nation, he has responsibilities not only to his own people but to the international community for trying to pursue civilized behavior.

By January 2000, Deputy Secretary of State Strobe Talbott announced that the United States had "accepted the principle that the way a government treats its own people is not just an `internal matter.' It's the business of the international community."

American officials were not the only ones who were advancing that kind of view. British prime minister Tony Blair, for instance, declared during the Kosovo war, "We are fighting not for territory but for values, for a new internationalism where the brutal repression of whole ethnic groups will no longer be tolerated." After the war, Blair recommended embarking on a "new moral crusade," explaining that the West can now build a "new doctrine of international community" that transcends sovereignty and allows military intervention in defense of human rights.

It would be a mistake, however, to conclude from these examples that those who favor redefining sovereignty reside only on the political left. As with promoting democracy, there are adherents on the right too. For example, William Kristol and other editors at the neoconservative *Weekly Standard* have recommended that sovereignty be made secondary to a U.S. "benevolent global hegemony" that aims to universalize Western values. Indeed, during NATO's air war against Yugoslavia they editorialized,

> The struggle in Kosovo today is about more than human suffering. It is about more even than European stability and NATO's credibility. At stake is the single overriding question of our time: Will the United States and its allies have the will to shape the world in conformance with our interests and our principles, challenging as that task may be?

The Nation Builders

Today's nation builders are brimming with advice on how to build nations, recommending everything from "forging a more equitable distribution of wealth" and "rehabilitating the health [care] sector in postconflict situations" to encouraging "psychosocial healing" and "enfranchisement-based collective identity." The World Bank recommends reconstructing the "enabling conditions" of peacetime society and suggests seven distinct nation-building activities. A report by the Overseas Development Council identifies no fewer than 10 activities that should receive the "early attention" of the nation builder. These include providing a sufficient level of internal security to enable economic recovery; persuading the foreign business community to invest; strengthening the government's capacity to carry out key activities; assisting the return of refugees and internally displaced persons; supporting the rejuvenation of household economies; assisting the recovery of communities; rehabilitating crucial economic infrastructure, such as major roads, bridges, marketplaces, and power-generation facilities; giving priority to the basic needs of social groups and geographic areas most affected by the conflict; removing land mines from critical sites; stabilizing the national currency and rehabilitating financial institutions; and promoting national reconciliation.

Besides the U.S. military, one of the Clinton administration's chief nation-building organs was the U.S. Agency for International Development, which, according to the agency's self-description, "has taken a leading role in promoting and consolidating democracy worldwide." After Clinton took office, USAID came to be dominated by a variety of new nation-building priorities. "One of our main goals is to have concern about gender issues be a part of all of our programs," explained one USAID official in 1994. By Clinton's second term, USAID officials said they planned to "launch an effort to advance compliance with labor codes, particularly with regard to the rights of union organizing, collective bargaining, elimination of child labor, and adherence to work-place health and safety standards." They also said they would seek to develop "human capacity," "stabilize the world population," and protect the global environment for "sustainable development."

The Clinton administration also utilized the National Endowment for Democracy, a little-known foreign-aid program intended to promote democracy abroad. The NED is nominally a private organization, but all of its funds come from the federal treasury. It says its programs are aimed at encouraging "democratic political development." In practice, however, the NED under the Clinton administration took advantage of its quasi-private status to influence foreign elections in ways that would be illegal if a foreign group tried to conduct the same activity in the United States. The NED also supported myriad nation-building programs. In Bosnia, for example, it has been financing an array of human rights and civic organizations that provide "training to local citizens in the areas of conflict prevention and dispute mediation, responsible journalism, micro-enterprise development, and local public administration."

Of course, any description of the Clinton administration's nation-building organs would be incomplete without addressing the specific kind of nations they were repeatedly tasked with creating, namely, nations that embodied American-style pluralism. From Somalia to Haiti to Bosnia to Kosovo, that was the assigned goal. Indeed, the Clinton administration's efforts were all basically aimed at getting large numbers of people to get along with each other, without regard to whether their differences were based on clan, class, religion, or ethnicity. As Clinton's deputy secretary of state Strobe Talbott summarized Washington's view with respect to the Bosnian conflict,

> If there is to be a post-Cold War peace in Europe . . . it must be based on the principle of multiethnic democracy. The United States is one of the first and one of the greatest examples of that principle. What's more, the civic behavior and constitutional structures associated with pluralism are conducive to regional peace and international trade. Hence, it is in our interest that multiethnic democracy ultimately prevails in Europe and elsewhere.

The Clinton administration's enthusiasm for the pluralistic ideal should have been evident from its early emphasis on "multilateralism" and "international community" and its willingness to abandon the longstanding tradition of American troops serving only under the American flag. The administration's pluralistic pretensions, however, became most evident with NATO's bombing campaign against Yugoslavia. On the eve of the first night of air strikes, for example, President Clinton implored, "I want us to live in a world where we get along with each other, with all of our differences." Several weeks later, Clinton explicitly linked his Kosovo policy with his support for domestic hate crimes legislation. "We first have to set an example, as best we can—standing against hate crimes against racial minorities or gays; standing for respect, for diversity." "Second," he said, "we have to act responsibly, recognizing this . . . fleeting position the United States now enjoys of remarkable military, political and economic influence. We have to do what we can to protect the circle of humanity against those who would divide it by dehumanizing the other."

With the end of NATO's bombing campaign, Clinton continued to place the pluralistic ideal at the center of his rhetoric, telling a unit of the Illinois Air National Guard in Chicago,

You have people of Serbian and Albanian descent flying together, proving that we do find strength in our diversity and we come together for the common good. . . . We want people who live in the Balkans to be able to work together the way the people in this unit who come from the Balkans work together.

In practice, explained Vice President Al Gore, that meant that Washington's starting point in Kosovo was that "there must be a genuine recognition of and respect for difference . . . [and] then . . . a transcendence of difference."

Making Excuses

Realist critics largely dismissed such thinking for what it was, global do-goodism masquerading as foreign policy. Johns Hopkins professor Michael Mandelbaum, for example, attacked what he called Clinton's "Mother Teresa" foreign policy, which he said aimed to turn America's national security pursuit "into social work." Similarly, Robert Manning of the Council on Foreign Relations and Patrick Clawson of the Washington Institute for Near East Policy suggested that Clinton's nation-building operations all were "instances of social engineering passing as foreign policy." Despite those criticisms, however, the empirical question is left unanswered: Does nation building even work?

Today's advocates of nation building will usually concede that Washington's recent attempts have either failed or are in the process of failing. Yet that has not dampened their enthusiasm for the practice of nation building. They tend to dismiss the failures by arguing that nation building hasn't really failed, it just hasn't been tried hard enough. Typical of that kind of excuse is an October 28, 1999, report by the Washington- and Brussels-based International Crisis Group. That report first admits that the Dayton Agreement—Washington's blueprint for nation building in Bosnia—is failing. After years of NATO occupation, the report explains, Bosnia

> has three de facto mono-ethnic entities, three separate armies, three separate police forces, and a national government that exists mostly on paper and operates at the mercy of the entities. . . . In addition, two out of the three ethnic groups actively oppose Dayton, and are prepared to wait until such a time as the international community withdraws and the agreement can be laid to rest.

But the report then goes on to assert that Dayton's nation building "can succeed if implemented properly," if only the "NATO-led international force" in Bosnia were to work "more robustly" to "act as an implementing agent." An American official in Bosnia put it more forcefully: "This is only a half dictatorship. We should have made it a full dictatorship."

In the case of Somalia, the excuse is much the same, that nation building would have succeeded if only it had been pursued more vigorously. The commander in charge of the United Nations pullout, for example, told a news conference,

> We didn't have enough forces or resources to disarm the country. That's why Operation Hope can't fulfill all its goals. . . . The international body and contributing nations must be committed enough to accept the violence and loss of life associated with war, and then stay the course.

A nearly identical excuse is given in the case of Haiti. Hugh Byrne and Rachel Neild of the Washington Office on Latin America, for example, concede in a 1997 *Christian Science Monitor* op-ed piece, "The truth is that three years after the intervention, U.S. and international policy in Haiti has been no great success." The aim of America's Haitian policy, to restore democracy and jump-start the economy, has failed.

> Some $2.8 billion in aid—sent or pledged—held out the promise of building infrastructure, modernizing the state, restoring economic growth, and alleviating poverty. There are precious few signs of any of this. Instead, there are rutted roads, a weak and ineffective state, stagnant growth, and poverty. Politically, the picture is no better. A dynamic grass-roots movement that helped topple the [Jean Claude "Baby Doc"] Duvalier dictatorship and elect Mr. Aristide has been sidelined and largely demobilized. Political ambition and opportunism are the order of the day.

But then Byrne and Neild go on to argue that a more vigorous nation-building effort is the answer.

> Now is the time to begin crafting a new, long-term international approach. International donors should commit for the long haul. . . . But greater emphasis should be placed on development in the rural sector, where some two-thirds of Haitians live, and on long-term strategies to create jobs and alleviate the country's crippling burden of poverty.

Lastly, in the case of Kosovo, some analysts are already explaining away the unfolding nation-building failure there by arguing that it would be working if only the United States and NATO had been more assertive in imposing their will in the pursuit of a nation-building agenda. Typical of those holding this view is columnist Georgie Anne Geyer, who blames many of the problems in Kosovo on U.S.-NATO peacekeepers not doing enough: "NATO is bogged down by contortions of excessive protocol, hapless collective decision-making in the European defense establishments and the refusal of Washington to lead and make judgments." Her solution: "A no-nonsense military occupation in the style of Gen. Douglas MacArthur . . . with the military and the civil power combined."

Such arguments, however, are dubious. Because all nation-building missions could conceivably be started earlier or pursued more vigorously, no way exists to directly refute someone who makes such excuses. Moreover, such excuses are self-reinforcing; that is, they employ success, failure, and everything in between as evidence in favor of the nation-building agenda.

False Comparisons

Other advocates of nation building prefer to argue that it succeeded in post-World War II Germany and Japan, so the practice must work if done right. Then Sen. Paul Simon (D-Ill.), for example, endorsed nation building in Somalia in 1993 claiming, "We didn't do too badly in Germany and Japan." Writing in *Commentary*, AEI's Joshua Muravchik similarly claimed,

> Nor should it be doubted that America is capable of using force effectively on behalf of democracy. When the U.S. invaded Grenada in 1983, Sen. Daniel Patrick Moynihan exclaimed: "I don't know that you restore democracy at the point of a bayonet." But that in fact is what we did . . . in Japan [and] Germany . . . after World War II.

But postwar Germany and Japan cannot justifiably be compared with places like Somalia, Haiti, Bosnia, or Kosovo. First of all, it is an abuse of history to imply that Somalia, Haiti, Bosnia, or Kosovo come anywhere close to warranting the same military concern (and commitment of resources) as postwar Germany or Japan. Those four places—even combined—could not build a military-industrial capacity that could threaten the United States and its allies as Germany and Japan both once did. Moreover, the security payoff of rebuilding Germany and Japan—in terms of shoring up Europe and Asia against communist expansion—and the economic payoff—in terms of foreign trade—were critical to the United States. The same cannot be said for Somalia, Haiti, Bosnia, or Kosovo.

Second, the postwar political situations in Germany and Japan were historically unique. Unlike America's recent encounters with nation building, Germany and Japan were totally defeated in war and their leaders thoroughly discredited. In fact, University of Illinois political scientist Richard Merritt explains that the "failure of Nazism and the confusion of potential leaders" in the wake of Germany's unconditional surrender "made the German people receptive to discourse on governance . . . [and] imposed social change." The same cannot be said of Somalia, Haiti, Bosnia, or Kosovo, where the troubling politics and politicians remained constant if not popular. Moreover, says Merritt, even before the war's end, Germans had become amenable to the policy prescriptions Washington and its allies wanted to impose.

> We must consider first the extent to which Germans were predisposed, even before the war's end, to accept the programs that AMG [the American Military Government] and other Tripartite Allies might propose. The data show that substantial numbers of German respondents were disgusted by what the Nazis had done and increasingly realized that Nazi actions were not accidental but were consistent with and even prefigured by Nazi ideology. . . . To some measure, then, AMG enjoyed a ready market for its product.

By the end of the war in the Pacific, the Japanese, too, had become receptive to profound political change in ways not replicated in Somalia, Haiti, Bosnia, and Kosovo. Indeed, according to renowned historian John Dower, the U.S. occupying force "encountered a populace sick of war, contemptuous of the militarists who had led them to disaster, and all but overwhelmed by the difficulties of their present circumstances in a ruined land." The Japanese, moreover, embraced their defeat not as an end, but as a beginning to make a better future. As a result, explains Dower, "the ideals of peace and democracy took root in Japan—not as a borrowed ideology or imposed vision, but as a lived experience and a seized opportunity. . . . It was an extraordinary, and extraordinarily fluid, moment—never seen before in history and, as it turned out, never to be repeated."

Third, with regard to Bosnia and Kosovo specifically, the inhabitants there fought a war with each other. The inhabitants of Germany and Japan did not participate in such communal bloodletting. Perhaps if a third party had tried to force the French to live with the Germans, or the Koreans to live with the Japanese under a single government after the war, then a comparison could be made with Bosnia or Kosovo today. Otherwise, the postwar political situations are radically different.

Fourth, the high level of education and industrial know-how in postwar Germany and Japan facilitated an economic recovery inconceivable in Somalia, Haiti, Bosnia, or Kosovo. Germany also had a strong tradition of the rule of law, property rights, and free trade before the Nazi era. Japan's elite embraced an honorific culture that respected and obeyed the wishes of the victor in battle. Somalia, Haiti, Bosnia, and Kosovo, in contrast, have little in the way of either liberal traditions or cultural attitudes that are agreeable to massive foreign interference.

Despite all the sharp historical differences, the Clinton administration nevertheless spent tens of billions of dollars and huge amounts of diplomatic capital trying to nation build. In one sense, its efforts mirrored those of Britain and France in the late 19th century. Those two powers expended their limited resources and diplomatic energy in areas of secondary importance when their attention should have been devoted to their chief security problem—the rise of Germany. Britain and France may have gained some peripheral security, but they lost their core security. For eight years, the Clinton administration repeated the same mistake, devoting America's limited resources and diplomatic energy to the periphery in Somalia, Haiti, Bosnia, and Kosovo, while ignoring the security concerns that should actually demand a superpower's attention—Russia and China.

Fool's Errands

Putting the excuses and false comparisons aside, several important lessons can be learned from Washington's recent encounters with nation building. One lesson is that nation building is a fool's errand when the American people are unprepared to sacrifice the blood and treasure of their countrymen in a place they consider strategically unimportant; that is, nation building totally unattached from national self-interest is not sustainable if there are casualties. A second lesson is that nation building is a fool's errand if the country in question is not "ripe" for the effort. That is, favorable historical conditions must be in place for nation building to succeed. A third lesson is that nation building is a fool's errand when it perpetuates a "security dilemma" between formerly opposing sides in a bloody dispute; that is, when it preserves an environment in which each side's efforts to increase its own security decreases, or appears to decrease, the security of the other side. A fourth lesson is that nation building is a fool's errand when one of the factions in a place targeted for the effort has not given up its wartime objective; that is, when they are not yet so worn out that they cease believing there is still more to gain by continuing to agitate, provoke, and fight.

However, today's nation builders seem oblivious to the evidence before them. They seem to have chronic trouble distinguishing between what they aspire to attain through their policies from the real world. Hans Morgenthau warned of this tendency more than 50 years ago in *Politics among Nations,* wherein he noted that the true study of politics must take account of "what is" and not focus just on "what should be." The latter is what the nation builders do regularly. Indeed, in their exuberance to solve the world's problems, they often overlook how the world actually works, particularly when it will expose the contradictory patterns and unintended consequences of their actions, such as the way nation building tends to breed dependency and corruption where it is attempted.

Conducting foreign policy on the basis of "what should be," moreover, may be more than just flawed. It could prove unwise as it may end up producing side effects that are detrimental to the security of the United States and its citizens. Indeed, if Washington continues to make a habit of intervening in and remaking other countries, it risks enlarging the substantive number of international matters over which the United States and other nations can disagree, which significantly increases the potential for dispute, armed confrontation, and even war. Such a policy also encourages larger countries to form countervailing military alliances to prevent unchecked U.S. meddling in their backyard, and gives an incentive to smaller and insecure countries to acquire weapons of mass destruction as an insurance policy against Washington's would-be nation builders. Lastly, such a policy risks overstretching the U.S. military and undermining its ability to recruit and retain members. In short, the potential costs associated with nation building are far greater than today's nation builders have grasped.

PART VII

TRADE AND INTERNATIONAL FINANCE

The Globalization of Finance

Alan Greenspan

As a result of very rapid increases in telecommunications and computer-based technologies and products, a dramatic expansion in cross-border financial flows and within countries has emerged. The pace has become truly remarkable. These technology-based developments have so expanded the breadth and depth of markets that governments, even reluctant ones, increasingly have felt they have had little alternative but to deregulate and free up internal credit and financial markets.

In recent years global economic integration has accelerated on a multitude of fronts. While trade liberalization, which has been ongoing for a longer period, has continued, more dramatic changes have occurred in the financial sphere.

World financial markets undoubtedly are far more efficient today than ever before. Changes in communications and information technology, and the new instruments and risk-management techniques they have made possible, enable an ever wider range of financial and nonfinancial firms today to manage their financial risks more effectively. As a consequence, they can now concentrate on managing the economic risks associated with their primary businesses.

The solid profitability of new financial products in the face of their huge proliferation attests to the increasing effectiveness of financial markets in facilitating the flow of trade and direct investment, which are so patently contributing to ever higher standards of living around the world. Complex financial instruments—derivative instruments, in one form or another—are being developed to take advantage of the gains in communications and information technology. Such instruments would not have flourished as they have without the technological advances of the past several decades. They could

Alan Greenspan is chairman of the Federal Reserve Board. This paper is an edited version of his keynote address at the Cato Institute's 15th Annual Monetary Conference, October 14, 1997.

Cato Journal, Vol. 17, No. 3 (Winter 1998)

not be priced properly, the markets they involve could not be arbitraged properly, and the risks they give rise to could not be managed at all, to say nothing of properly, without high-powered data processing and communications capabilities.

New Challenges

Still, for central bankers with responsibilities for financial market stability, the new technologies and new instruments have presented new challenges. Some argue that market dynamics have been altered in ways that increase the likelihood of significant market disruptions. Whatever the merits of this argument, there is a clear sense that the new technologies, and the financial instruments and techniques they have made possible, have strengthened interdependencies between markets and market participants, both within and across national boundaries. As a result, a disturbance in one market segment or one country is likely to be transmitted far more rapidly throughout the world economy than was evident in previous eras.

In earlier generations information moved slowly, constrained by the primitive state of communications. Financial crises in the early 19th century, for example, particularly those associated with the Napoleonic Wars, were often related to military and other events in faraway places. An investor's speculative position could be wiped out by a military setback, and he might not even know about it for days or even weeks, which, from the perspective of central banking today, might be considered bliss.

As the 19th century unfolded, communications speeded up. By the turn of the century, events moved more rapidly, but their speed was at most a crawl by the standard of today's financial markets. The environment now facing the world's central banks—and, of course, private participants in financial markets as well—is characterized by instant communication.

It is worthwhile to trace the roots of this extraordinary expansion of global finance, to assess its benefits and risks, and to suggest some avenues that can usefully be explored in order to contain some of its potentially adverse consequences.

The Roots of Globalization

A global financial system, of course, is not an end in itself. It is the institutional structure that has been developed over the centuries to facilitate the production of goods and services. Accordingly, we can better understand the evolution of today's burgeoning global financial markets by parsing the extraordinary changes that have emerged, in the past century or more, in what we conventionally call the real side of economies: the production of goods and services. The same technological forces currently driving finance were first evident in the production process and have had a profound effect on what we produce, how we produce it, and how it is financed. Technological change or, more generally, ideas have significantly altered the nature of output so that it has become increasingly conceptual and less physical. A much smaller proportion of the measured real gross domestic product constitutes physical bulk today than in past generations.

The increasing substitution of concepts for physical effort in the creation of economic value also has affected how we produce; computer-assisted design systems, machine tools, and inventory control systems provide examples. Offices are now routinely outfitted with high-speed information-processing technology. Because the accretion of knowledge is, with rare exceptions, irreversible, this trend almost surely will continue into the next century and beyond. Value creation at the turn of the 21st century will surely involve the transmission of information and ideas, generally over complex telecommunication networks. That development will create considerably greater flexibility of where services are produced and where employees do their work. A century earlier, transportation of goods to their most value-creating locations served the same purpose for an economy whose value creation still rested heavily on physical, bulky output.

Not unexpectedly, as goods and services have moved across borders, the necessity to finance them has increased dramatically. But what is particularly startling is how large the expansion in cross-border finance has become, relative to the trade it finances. To be sure, much cross-border finance supports investment portfolios, doubtless some largely speculative. But, at bottom, even they are part of the support systems for efficient international movement of goods and services.

The rapid expansion in cross-border banking and finance should not be surprising given the extent to which low-cost information processing and communications technology have improved the ability of customers in one part of the world to avail themselves of borrowing, depositing, or risk-management opportunities offered anywhere in the world on a real-time basis.

Benefits and Risks of Global Finance

These developments enhance the process whereby an excess of saving over investment in one country finds an appropriate outlet in another. In short, they facilitate the drive to equate risk-adjusted rates of return on investments worldwide. They thereby improve the worldwide allocation of scarce capital and, in the process, engender a huge increase in risk dispersion and hedging opportunities.

But there is still evidence of less than full arbitrage of risk-adjusted rates of return on a worldwide basis. This suggests the potential for a far larger world financial system than currently exists. If we can resist protectionist pressures in our societies in the financial arena as well as in the interchange of goods and services, we can look forward to the benefits of the international division of labor on a much larger scale in the 21st century.

What we do not know for sure, but strongly suspect, is that the accelerating expansion of global finance may be indispensable to the continued rapid growth in world trade in goods and services. It is becoming increasingly evident that many layers of financial intermediation will be required if we are to capture the full benefits of our advances in finance. Certainly, the emergence of a highly liquid foreign exchange market has facilitated basic forex transactions, and the availability of more complex hedging strategies enables producers and investors to achieve their desired risk positions. This owes largely to the ability of modern financial products to unbundle complex risks in ways that enable each counterparty to choose the combination of risks necessary to advance its business strategy, and to eschew those that do not. This process enhances cross-border trade in goods and services, facilitates cross-border portfolio investment strategies, enhances the lower-cost financing of real capital formation on a worldwide basis, and, hence, leads to an expansion of international trade and rising standards of living.

But achieving those benefits surely will require the maintenance of a stable macroeconomic environment. An environment conducive to stable product prices and to maintaining sustainable economic growth has become a prime responsibility of governments and, of course, central banks. It was not always thus. In the last comparable period of open international trade a century ago, the gold standard prevailed. The roles of central banks, where they existed (remember the United States did not have one), were then quite different from today.

International stabilization was implemented by more or less automatic gold flows from those financial markets where conditions were lax to those where liquidity was in short supply. To some, myself included, the system appears to have worked rather well. To others, the gold standard was perceived as too rigid or unstable, and in any event the inability to finance discretionary policy, both monetary and fiscal, led first to a further compromise of the gold standard system after World War I, and by the 1930s it had been essentially abandoned.

The fiat money systems that emerged have given considerable power and responsibility to central banks to manage the sovereign credit of nations. Under a gold standard, money creation was at the limit tied to changes in gold reserves. The discretionary range of monetary policy was relatively narrow. Today's central banks have the capability of creating or destroying unlimited supplies of money and credit.

Clearly, how well we take our responsibilities in this modern world has profound implications for participants in financial markets. We provide the backdrop against which participants make their decisions. As a consequence, it is incumbent upon us to endeavor to produce the same noninflationary environment as existed a century ago, if we seek maximum sustainable growth. In this regard, doubtless, the most important development that has occurred in recent years has been the shift from an environment of inflationary expectations built into both business planning and financial contracts toward an environment of lower inflation. It is important that that progress continue and that we maintain a credible long-run commitment to price stability.

While there can be little doubt that the extraordinary changes in global finance on balance have been beneficial in facilitating significant improvements in economic structures and living standards throughout the world, they also have the potential for some negative consequences. In fact, while the speed of transmission of positive economic events has been an important plus for the world economy in recent years, it is becoming increasingly obvious, as evidenced by recent events in Thailand and its neighbors and several years ago in Mexico, that significant macroeconomic policy mistakes also reverberate around the world at a prodigious pace. In any event, technological progress is not reversible. We must learn to live with it.

In the context of rapid changes affecting financial markets, disruptions are inevitable. The turmoil in the European Exchange Rate mechanism in 1992, the plunge in the exchange value of the Mexican peso at the end of 1994 and early 1995, and the recent sharp exchange rate adjustments in a number of Asian economies have shown how the new world of financial trading can punish policy misalignments, actual or perceived, with amazing alacrity. This is new. Even as recently as 15 or 20 years ago, the size of the international financial system was a fraction of what it is today. Contagion effects were more limited, and, thus, breakdowns carried fewer negative consequences. In both new and old environments, the economic consequences of disruptions are minimized if they are not further compounded by financial instability associated with underlying inflation trends.

Maintaining Financial Stability

The recent financial turmoil in some Asian financial markets, and similar events elsewhere previously, confirm that in a world of increasing capital mobility there is a premium on governments maintaining sound macroeconomic policies and allowing exchange rates to provide appropriate signals for the broader pricing structure of the economy.

These countries became vulnerable as markets became increasingly aware of a buildup of excesses, including overvalued exchange rates, bulging current account deficits, and sharp increases in asset values. In many cases, these were the consequence of poor investment judgments in seeking to employ huge increases in portfolios for investment. In some cases, these excesses were fed by unsound real estate and other lending activity by various financial institutions in these countries, which, in turn, undermined the soundness of these countries' financial systems. As a consequence, these countries lost the confidence of both domestic and international investors, with resulting disturbances in their financial markets.

The resort to capital controls to deal with financial market disturbances of the sort a number of emerging economies have experienced would be a step backwards from the trend toward financial
market liberalization, and in the end would not be effective. The
maintenance of financial stability in an environment of global capital
markets, therefore, calls for greater attention by governments to the
soundness of public policy.

Governments are beginning to recognize that the release of timely
and accurate economic and financial data is a critical element to the
maintenance of financial stability. We do not know what the appropriate amount of disclosure is, but it is pretty clear from the Mexican
experience in 1994 and the recent Thai experience that the level of
disclosure was too little. More comprehensive public information on
the financial condition of a country, including current data on commitments by governments to buy or sell currencies in the future and
on nonperforming loans of a country's financial institutions, would
allow investors—both domestic and international—to make more
rational investment decisions. Such disclosure would help to avoid
sudden and sharp reversals in the investment positions of investors
once they become aware of the true status of a country's and a banking system's financial health. More timely and more comprehensive
disclosure of financial data also would help sensitize the principal
economic policymakers of a country to the potential emerging
threats to its financial stability.

Thus, as international financial markets continue to expand, central banks have twin objectives: achieving macroeconomic stability
and a safe and sound financial system that can take advantage of stability while exploiting the inevitable new technological advances.

The changing dynamics of modern global financial systems also
require that central banks address the inevitable increase of systemic
risk. It is probably fair to say that the very efficiency of global financial markets, engendered by the rapid proliferation of financial products, also has the capability of transmitting mistakes at a far faster
pace throughout the financial system in ways that were unknown a
generation ago, and not even remotely imagined in the 19th century.

Today's technology enables single individuals to initiate massive
transactions with very rapid execution. Clearly, not only has the productivity of global finance increased markedly, but so, obviously,
has the ability to generate losses at a previously inconceivable rate.

Moreover, increasing global financial efficiency, by creating the mechanisms for mistakes to ricochet throughout the global financial system, has patently increased the potential for systemic risk. Why not then, one might ask, bar or contain the expansion of global finance by capital controls, transaction taxes, or other market-inhibiting initiatives? Why not return to the less hectic and seemingly less threatening markets of, say, the 1950s?

Endeavoring to thwart technological advance and new knowledge and innovation through the erection of barriers to the spread of knowledge would, as history amply demonstrates, have large, often adverse, unintended consequences. Suppressed markets in one location would be rapidly displaced by others outside the reach of government controls and taxes. Of greater importance, risk taking, so indispensable to the creation of wealth, would undoubtedly be curbed, to the detriment of rising living standards. We cannot turn back the clock on technology—and we should not try to do so.

Rather, we should recognize that, if it is technology that has imparted the current stress to markets, technology can be employed to contain it. Enhancements to financial institutions' internal risk-management systems arguably constitute the most effective countermeasure to the increased potential instability of the global financial system. Improving the efficiency of the world's payment systems is clearly another.

The availability of new technology and new derivative financial instruments clearly has facilitated new, more rigorous approaches to the conceptualization, measurement, and management of risk for such systems. There are, however, limitations to the statistical models used in such systems owing to the necessity of overly simplifying assumptions. Hence, human judgments, based on analytically looser but far more realistic evaluations of what the future may hold, are of critical importance in risk management. Although a sophisticated understanding of statistical modeling techniques is important to risk management, an intimate knowledge of the markets in which an institution trades and of the customers it serves is turning out to be far more important.

In these and other ways, we must assure that our rapidly changing global financial system retains the capacity to contain market shocks. This is a never-ending process that requires never-ending vigilance.

Using the Market for Social Development

Milton Friedman

An episode during an earlier visit to China impressed me strongly with the wide gulf of understanding that separates people immersed in different economic institutions. That gulf makes it extremely important to stress over and over basic principles and ideas that all of us simply take for granted with respect to the system to which we are accustomed. The episode in question occurred when my wife and I had lunch with a deputy minister of one of the government departments who was shortly going to the United States to observe the American economy. Our host wanted help from us on whom to see.

His first question in that connection was, "Who in the United States is in charge of materials distribution?" That question took my wife and me aback. I doubt that any resident of the United States, however unsophisticated about economics, would even think of asking such a question. Yet it was entirely natural for a citizen of a command economy to ask such a question. He is accustomed to a situation in which somebody decides who gets what from whom, whether that be who gets what materials from whom or who gets what wages from whom.

My initial answer was to suggest that he visit the floor of the Chicago Mercantile Exchange, where commodities such as wheat, cotton, silver, and gold are traded. This answer understandably baffled our host, so I went on to elaborate on the fact that there was no single person—or even committee of persons—"in charge of materials distribution." There are a Department of Commerce and a Department of the Interior that are concerned with materials pro-

Milton Friedman is a senior research fellow at the Hoover Institution and the 1976 Nobel laureate in economics. This article is based on his remarks at the Cato Institute conference, "Economic Reform in China," in Shanghai in September 1988.

Cato Policy Report, November/December 1988

duction and distribution in a wholly different way. But they do not determine who gets how much of what. In consequence, I was forced to answer in terms that my host found extremely difficult to comprehend. Needless to say, that is not a criticism of him. Given his background, it is almost inconceivable that he could have understood how the market can distribute a variety of materials among millions of different people for thousands of uses untouched, as an ad might say, by political hands.

The miracle of the market is precisely that out of the chaos of people screaming at one another, making arcane signals with their hands, and fighting on the floor of the Chicago Mercantile Exchange, somehow or other the corner store always seems to have enough bread, the bakery always seems to have enough flour, the miller always seems to have enough wheat, and so on. That is the miracle of the way the market coordinates the activities of millions of people, and does so in a wholly impersonal way through pricing that, if left completely free, does not involve any corruption, bribes, special influence, or need for political mechanisms.

Let me now turn more directly to the topic. In some ways, referring to "the market" puts the discussion on the wrong basis. The market is not a cow to be milked; neither is it a sure-fire cure for all ills. In literal terms, the market is simply a meeting at a specified place and time for the purpose of making deals. Needless to say, "meeting" and "place" are often euphemisms; they do not involve physical getting together. As of the moment, there is a market in foreign exchange that encompasses the world. People get together through satellites, telephones, and so on. Moreover, the deals made in or through a market are not restricted to those involving money, purchases, or sales. Scientists who cooperate with one another in advancing their discipline, whether it be physics, chemistry, economics, or astronomy, are effectively making deals with one another. Their market is a set of interrelated journals, conferences, and so on.

The market is a mechanism that may be mobilized for any number of purposes. Depending on the way it is used, it may contribute to social and economic development or inhibit such development. Using or not using the market is not the crucial distinction. Every society, whether communist, socialist, social democratic, purely capitalist, or what you will, uses the market. Rather, the crucial distinction is private property or no private property. Who are the participants in the market and on whose behalf are they operating? Are the participants government bureaucrats who are operating on behalf of something called the state? Or are they individuals operating directly or indirectly on their own behalf?

That is why, in an earlier paper delivered in China, I advocated the widest possible use of not the market but "free, private markets." The words "free" and "private" are even more important than the word "market."

Many specific problems arise when a society tries to replace a command economy with the invisible hand of the market, of which I shall discuss only a few. Those problems are not restricted to societies that have tried to use command as their basic economic mechanism, such as China and Russia; they also arise in Western economies such as the United States, Great Britain, and Germany, in which command elements have become more extensive over time and in which there are attempts to reverse that process. Eliminating government-owned enterprises in the West, such as the postal service in the United States and railroads and utilities in other countries, raises problems that are identical with those that arise in replacing command and public ownership by voluntary cooperation and private ownership in China, Russia, and so on.

Partial versus Total Decontrol

Introducing a greater role for private market mechanisms in one sector of an economy may be partially or completely frustrated by the limited scope of the change. Consider what has been regarded as a major move toward wider use of the market, namely creation of the European common market and the attempt to achieve free trade among the common market countries. It has now been nearly 40 years since the Schuman plan for a coal and steel community was adopted, yet no observer will dispute that free trade within the common market is still an ideal rather than a reality. The latest bit of evidence is the recent agreement to *really* eliminate all barriers by 1992. Had the initial common market agreement been successful, that would have been achieved many years ago.

What was the problem? Why is there no real United States of Europe? In my view, the answer is that decontrol was adopted even in principle only for goods and services but not for money. The separate countries retained full authority over their national moneys. More important, they refused to adopt a system of freely floating exchange rates—that is, the free exchange of one currency for another at whatever rates of exchange were voluntarily agreed to in free private markets. The refusal to let the private market determine the rates of exchange among currencies was a fatal weakness.

Currently, China is faced with precisely the same problem. But my purpose in discussing it here is not to present again the case for a system of freely floating exchange rates but rather to give a striking illustration of how limiting decontrol or privatization to one area, while not extending it to closely related areas, can largely frustrate the basic objective.

A second example is from the United States. Although nominally private, U.S. airlines were subject to extensive government control with respect to the prices they could charge and the markets they could serve. Deregulation of the airlines in 1978 has resulted in very much enhanced competition, widespread and substantial reduction in prices and increase in the range of services, and, in consequence, major expansion in the volume of traffic. However, while airlines were deregulated, or, as I would prefer to put it, privatized, airports were not. They remain government-owned and -operated. Private enterprise has had no difficulty in producing all the planes the airlines find it profitable to use. The private-enterprise airlines have had no difficulty in finding pilots to fly them and attendants to service them. On the other hand, planes filled with passengers are often delayed because facilities or provisions for landing them at government-run airports are inadequate. Naturally, the government responds by trying to blame the private airlines: it has started requiring them to report delays in meeting their scheduled arrival times and publishing summary reports on the on-time performance of the several airlines. Repeated proposals have been made that, even if government retained the ownership and operation of the airports, at the very least rights to gates, with respect both to number of gates and to the times at which they are to be used, should be auctioned off. Unfortunately, the opposition of airlines that have vested interests in the gates and times assigned to them by government entities has prevented the adoption of even such incomplete reforms. Of course, a far better solution would be to privatize the airports.

A third example is privatizing some areas of manufacturing while keeping the production or pricing of the raw materials under government control.

Let me cite some obvious examples for China. Introduction of a considerable element of privatization in agriculture has produced a remarkable increase in agricultural output and productivity—the most dramatic manifestation of China's success in widening the use of the private market. But it is clear that the very success has created a real problem. The overwhelming majority of the Chinese population is employed in agriculture. Even a relatively small improvement in agricultural productivity obviously means release from agriculture of labor that it is no longer productive to employ. It is in China's interest to use that labor in more productive areas, such as industry. Yet the bulk of industry remains in the command economy; it has not been privatized, deregulated, or fully subjected to the market process.

There has been a real attempt to change the way government-owned enterprises operate. The people in charge have been told to use market mechanisms, and an attempt has been made to provide incentives for them to do so. However, as long as bureaucrats run government-owned industries, their ability to respond to market pressures effectively will be severely limited. In the case of China, the most serious limitation is on their flexibility, their willingness or ability to be venturesome, to undertake risky projects that have a likelihood of failure but a real, if small, chance of spectacular success. Again, the problem is universal. Every study of the United States or the United Kingdom demonstrates that small enterprises—not the megacorporations that are household names—are responsible for most of the new jobs. In China, the scope for such private enterprises is extremely narrow.

A much wider privatization of economic activity would greatly reduce the difficulty of absorbing the workers released from agriculture. Private enterprises would then spring up all over the place to absorb the workforce.

A second example for China is similar to the problem I described for the common market: the difference between the extent of freedom in the production and distribution of goods and services and in the production and distribution of money. The substantial freeing of many prices, particularly those of agricultural and similar goods, has not been accompanied by the privatization of the banking system. As

I understand it, the Chinese government indirectly determines what happens to the money supply through the credits it grants state enterprises. The results include a rapid increase in the quantity of money and, not surprisingly, a rapid upward pressure on prices, so that inflation, both open and repressed, has reared its ugly head.

When should reform be gradual, and when is radical and immediate change appropriate? One alternative is illustrated by the tale of the tortoise and the hare, when the "slow but steady" tortoise reaches the finish line ahead of the much speedier but more erratic hare; the other is illustrated by the maxim, there is no sense in cutting a dog's tail off by inches. This is one of the most difficult problems encountered in widening the scope of the market. Let me illustrate with foreign trade. Suppose a country that has had high levels of tariffs decides to move to a free trade position. The case for moving gradually is clear. Capital has been invested in ways that will no longer represent an effective use of private resources under the new conditions. Much of that capital is in the form of machinery, buildings, human skills, and the like. Is it not clearly both more equitable and more efficient to reduce the tariffs gradually? That would give the owners of specialized resources the opportunity to withdraw their capital gradually and thus would reduce the costs imposed on them by the change.

The case for eliminating the tariff in one fell swoop, that is, for shock treatment, is more subtle, yet at the level of economic efficiency, compelling. Insofar as it is economically efficient to use the specialized resources in the absence of a tariff, they will be used. If any return over marginal cost can be obtained by continuing to use the specialized human and other resources, it is better to get that return than to get nothing. The burden would be imposed on the owners of the specialized resources immediately, but technical disinvestment would proceed only as rapidly as the specialized labor and other resources could be employed more productively elsewhere. On the other hand, gradual reduction in the tariff makes it privately profitable to continue using the specialized resources at a higher level than is socially efficient, thereby imposing unnecessary costs on the community.

Ending an ongoing inflation raises similar problems. Eliminating inflation at one fell swoop, if not anticipated long in advance, may cause widespread capital losses. Long-term contracts entered into

302

with one expectation about the likely rates of inflation may now suddenly be rendered inappropriate. The case on equity grounds for a gradual transition is far stronger for moderate degrees of inflation than for tariffs. The effects of both the prior inflation and its unanticipated ending are more pervasive and affect more people who have not only been harmed rather than benefited by the prior inflation but would be harmed again by its abrupt end. Reducing inflation gradually eases the transition and reduces the cost of achieving noninflationary growth.

However, much depends on the height of the inflation. If inflation is extremely high—at annual rates in triple digits—the situation is very different. Almost all participants in the market will have adjusted their arrangement so that any longstanding commitments are fully indexed. Abrupt disinflation will impose few costs because financial and other institutions have been adapted to radical changes in the rate of inflation—indeed, such adaptations represent a major cost of high and erratic inflation. Gradual elimination is sometimes not even feasible because there is not time enough—the dog will be dead before its extra-long tail can be cut off by inches.

Direct controls over prices—whether general or specific, e.g., on rents or exchange rates—are almost always best ended at once. Margaret Thatcher properly ended exchange-rate controls in Britain overnight and completely. Gradual adjustment only prolongs the harm done by controls and provides unjustified benefits to "insiders." The shortages, queues, and other distortions produced by trying to hold prices below their market level would continue though they might be reduced, and additional problems arise because gradualism encourages speculation about reversal and encourages opponents to seek reversal. A similar proposition holds for attempts to maintain prices above market levels—as is so amply demonstrated by the agricultural policies of the United States, Japan, and the common market.

Overcoming Political Obstacles

This subject has already inevitably intruded into the preceding section. The general issue here is how to overcome political obstacles to widening the market. The danger is not alone that these obstacles will frustrate the attempt to free the market but equally that overcoming political obstacles may destroy the advantages of freeing the market. The challenge is to find ways to overcome obstacles that do not have those effects. The West's experience with privatization is particularly helpful in this connection. Perhaps the most extensive body of experience and the experience that has been most widely analyzed is the British experience with privatization, and I strongly recommend to our Chinese friends seeking to widen the market that they examine the evidence of privatization in Britain.

A simple case from the United States that illustrates the problem is privatizing the post office. The U.S. Postal Service has a monopoly in first-class mail because of the private express statutes, which make it a crime for individuals to offer common-carrier first-class service. Various attempts to do so have only succeeded in prosecution, which has ended the attempts. Privatization has been creeping in at the margin, first in the form of alternate parcel service. The United Parcel Service and other parcel delivery companies have taken over the bulk of the Postal Service's prior business. In addition, private messenger services have developed, of which the best known is Federal Express, which has been so successful that numerous competitors have emerged. Developments that technological advances would have encouraged no matter how postal service was organized have doubtless been speeded up. Examples are electronic mail via computers and telephones and facsimile service, again over telephones. These examples illustrate the ingenuity of private markets in exploiting the opportunities offered by the inefficiency of government enterprises.

Repeated attempts have been made to seek the repeal of the private express statutes so that private individuals and enterprises could compete with the Postal Service. However, such attempts always bring violent protests from the postal employee unions, from the executives of the U.S. Postal Service, and from rural communities that feel they would be deprived of postal service. On the other hand, few people have a strong and concentrated interest leading them to favor repealing the private express statutes. Entrepreneurs who might in fact enter the business if it were open to private entry do not know in advance that they would do so. Hundreds of thousands of people who would doubtless obtain employment in a privately developed postal system do not have the slightest idea that they would do so.

One way to overcome the opposition to privatization, widely used in Britain, is, as described by Robert Poole,

> to identify potential opponents and cut them in on the deal, generally by means of stock ownership. Two specific applications of the principle are (1) employee stock ownership, and (2) popular capitalism. . . .
>
> The opportunity to become shareholders can dramatically change the incentives of unionized civil servants, as illustrated in the case of British Telecom. Union officials denounced the planned privatization of Telecom, telling their members not to purchase the shares which were being offered to them at a discount. Yet in the end, sensing the chance to make money, some 96 percent of the workforce bought shares.

Poole also uses British Telecom to illustrate the second technique, popular capitalism:

> To encourage telephone customers to buy shares, they were offered vouchers granting them a discount on their phone bills if they held their shares for at least six months. And to prevent institutions and large firms from buying up the lion's share, initial purchases were limited to 800 shares per buyer.

A pitfall to be avoided in adopting such expedients is to sweeten the deal by converting a government monopoly into a private monopoly—which may be an improvement but falls far short of the desirable outcome. The U.S. Postal Service illustrates that pitfall as well as the fallacy that mimicking the form of private enterprise can achieve the substance. It was established as a supposedly independent government corporation that would not be subject to direct political influence and that would operate on market principles. That has hardly been the outcome, and understandably so. It remained a monopoly and did not develop a strong private interest in efficiency.

My own favorite form of privatization is not to sell shares of stock at all but to give government-owned enterprises to the citizens. Who, I ask opponents, owns the government enterprises? The answer invariably is, "The public." Well, then, why not make that into a reality rather than a rhetorical flourish? Set up a private corporation and give each citizen one or one hundred shares in it. Let them be free to buy or sell the shares. The shares would soon come into the hands of entrepreneurs who would either maintain the enterprise, for example, the postal system, as a single entity if it was most profitable to do so or break it up into a number of entities if that seemed most profitable.

A final example illustrates the point in another way. The Russians have permitted small private plots in agriculture. Those private plots are estimated to occupy about 3 percent of the arable land in the Soviet Union, and roughly one-third of all domestic food products in the Soviet Union are sold as coming from those private plots. I have chosen my words carefully. I did not say that one-third were "produced on those private plots," because in my opinion that would not be correct. Much of the food sold as coming from the private plots has indeed been produced on them, but I strongly suspect that much has also been diverted from collective farms.

For decades, it has been clear to the rulers of the Soviet Union that they could increase the domestic output of agriculture substantially by increasing the size and role of the private plots. Why have they not done so? Surely not because of ignorance. The answer clearly is that privatization would tend to establish independent centers of power that would reduce the political power of the bureaucracy. The rulers regarded the political price they would have to pay as higher than the economic reward. As of the moment, largely I suspect under the influence of the extraordinary success of such a policy in China, President Gorbachev is talking about a considerable expansion in private plots. It is by no means clear whether he will succeed.

Tyranny of the Status Quo

The problems of overcoming vested interests, of frustrating rent-seeking, apply to almost every attempt to change government policy, whether the change involves privatization, or eliminating military bases, or reducing subsidies, or anything else. The resulting "tyranny of the status quo," as my wife and I entitled a recent book discussing a range of such cases in the United States, is the major reason that political mechanisms are so much less effective than free-market mechanisms in encouraging dynamic change, in producing growth and economic prosperity.

Few simple maxims exist for overcoming the tyranny of the status quo. But there is one that ties in closely with the earlier discussion of gradual versus abrupt change. If a government activity is to be privatized or eliminated, by all means do so completely. Do not compromise by partial privatization or partial reduction. That simply leaves a core of determined opponents who will work diligently and often successfully to reverse the change. The Reagan administration repeatedly attempted, for example, to privatize Amtrak (the railroad passenger service) and to eliminate the Legal Services Corporation. In each case, it settled for a reduction in budget, achieving a fairly transitory victory. On the other hand, the complete abolition of the Civil Aeronautics Board gives far greater hope that airline deregulation is here to stay.

In conclusion, there are better and worse ways to privatize a command economy, but there is no magic formula for shifting painlessly from a command to a voluntary exchange economy. Nonetheless, the potential rewards are so great that, if the shift can be achieved, transitional costs will pale into insignificance. It is a tribute to the current leaders of China that they recognize that the potential gains dwarf the transitional costs and that they are engaged in a serious effort to make the transition. The Chinese people would be the main but by no means the only beneficiaries of the success of this effort. All the peoples of the world would benefit. Peace and widely shared prosperity are the ultimate prizes of the worldwide use of voluntary cooperation as the major means of organizing economic activity.

Free Trade from the Bottom Up

Brink Lindsey

In determining the proper course of future WTO negotiations, it is useful to ask a very basic question at the outset. Namely, why have international trade negotiations in the first place?

The question posed here is addressed to free traders, not protectionists. Of course protectionists oppose trade talks; they do so because they oppose open markets. But just because protectionists are against trade negotiations does not mean that free traders should automatically embrace them.

That suggestion might seem baffling at first, since the cause of free trade and the vehicle of trade negotiations are so inextricably connected in the prevailing conventional wisdom. But if we step back from current preconceptions and examine the underlying economic and political realities, the need to pursue trade liberalization through international negotiations begins to look much less obvious.

In trade negotiations, countries offer to reduce import barriers in exchange for other countries' offers of equivalent reductions. In other words, liberalization at home is made contingent upon liberalization abroad. Indeed, according to the rhetoric of negotiations, removal of domestic protectionist policies is treated as the price to be paid for freer markets elsewhere. Countries "gain" access to other nations' markets in exchange for which they "give up" greater access to their own. Thus, in official GATT parlance, commitments to open one's own market are labeled "concessions" while other countries' commitments to open their markets are labeled "benefits."

The rhetoric of negotiations, however, turns out to be economic nonsense. The overwhelming weight of economic analysis and evi-

Brink Lindsey is director of the Cato Institute's Center for Trade Policy Studies and author of *Against the Dead Hand*.

Cato Journal, Vol. 19, No. 3 (Winter 2000)

dence supports the conclusion that a country benefits from opening its own markets *regardless of what policies other countries choose to pursue.*

Free Trade Is Its Own Reward

The case for free trade at home can be embellished with all kinds of technical complexities, but in the end it boils down to common sense. It is now widely recognized that free markets are indispensable to our prosperity: when people are free to buy from, sell to, and invest in each other's markets as they choose, they are able to achieve far more than when governments attempt to control economic decisions. Given that fact, isn't it obvious that free markets work even better when we widen that circle in which we can buy, sell, and invest? Free trade is nothing more than the extension of free markets across political boundaries. The benefits of free trade are the benefits of *larger* free markets: by multiplying our potential business partners, we multiply the opportunities for creating wealth.

From this perspective, it becomes clear that Americans gain from open U.S. markets even when other countries are relatively closed. The fact that people in other countries are not as free as they should be is no reason to restrict the freedom of Americans. When goods, services, and capital flow over U.S. borders without interference, Americans are able to take full advantage of the opportunities of the international marketplace. We can buy the best and cheapest goods and services the world has to offer; we can sell to the most promising markets; we can choose from the best investment opportunities; and we can tap into the worldwide pool of capital.

In particular, openness to foreign competition boosts American productivity and living standards in two basic ways. First, import penetration causes us to shift resources out of import-competing sectors in which we are relatively less productive and into exporting sectors in which we are relatively more productive. Thus, the workings of comparative advantage raise our nation's overall productivity by allowing us to concentrate on the things we do best.

Second, resistance to import penetration on the part of domestic suppliers causes them to reduce costs, improve quality, and otherwise increase productivity. Thus, even when foreign competitors do not succeed in expanding their market share, the spur of added competition that they provide sharpens the incentives to innovate here at home. For example, Americans today drive much better cars than we did 20 years ago, and not just because many drive imports; American cars are much better today, in large part because the U.S. auto industry was forced to compete at a higher level to stave off an onslaught of Japanese and European competition.

Thus, contrary to the logic of trade negotiations, countries should open their markets as a simple matter of national economic interest. The benefits that come from openness to foreign competition should not be rejected just because other countries insist on sticking with benighted and dysfunctional policies.

Many free traders are familiar with the theoretical case for unilateral liberalization. Nevertheless, they dismiss any alternative to international negotiations as politically impractical. It is widely assumed that countries will undergo the political pain of liberalization only if they get something in return—namely, improved market access abroad, and with it improved business opportunities for exporting firms. According to this view, which enjoys overwhelming acceptance in contemporary U.S. trade policy circles, trade negotiations may be based on economically questionable premises, but for free traders they are the only game in town. Furthermore, in this conventional conception, trade negotiations are dominated by considerations of reciprocity—that is, countries are motivated to liberalize not by the good it will do them, but by the quid pro quo they can win in return.

But this belief, however firmly entrenched, is demonstrably incorrect as a matter of historical fact. Not only *should* countries liberalize because it serves their national economic interest, but in the big picture that is precisely what they *do*.

Why Countries Liberalize

The past couple of decades have witnessed dramatic reductions in trade barriers around the world, and by and large these bold moves toward freer trade have occurred outside the context of trade negotiations. Countries as diverse as Australia, New Zealand, Argentina, Bolivia, Peru, Chile, the Philippines, Thailand, Indonesia, and India have decided unilaterally to forsake the old autarkic model of import substitution in favor of greater integration with the global economy. The driving force for sweeping change in those countries was not tough bargaining or the prospect of a quid pro quo, but rather the realization that protectionism was causing economic stagnation. In other words, protectionist countries have changed their policies to catch up economically with more open countries. When liberalization is unilateral, it goes without saying that considerations of reciprocity play no role; rather, the impetus for reform comes entirely from changing perceptions of national economic interest.

Even when liberalization occurs in the context of negotiations, it often fails to follow the reciprocity model. Consider the case of Mexico, our partner in the North American Free Trade Agreement: Mexico began dismantling protectionist policies on its own in the mid-1980s, and those initial unilateral reforms were actually far more sweeping than the additional reforms it promised under NAFTA. The NAFTA negotiations were then undertaken at Mexico's initiative, despite the fact that it still had more trade barriers than either the United States or Canada and thus relatively more to "give up" than to "gain" through negotiations. Mexico pushed for NAFTA primarily as a means to lock in prior unilateral reforms; the Salinas administration believed that it would be more difficult for future administrations to undo those reforms if they had been made a matter of international obligation. Here again, then, considerations of the national economic interest in liberalization were paramount.

A similar dynamic explains China's bold offer in 1999 of sweeping market-opening commitments in its World Trade Organization accession agreement with the United States. China has been officially seeking membership in the General Agreement on Tariffs and Trade and then WTO for 13 years, over which time negotiations dragged on and on with little progress. Then, suddenly, over the course of a few weeks, China agreed to almost everything the United States had been asking for. Why the change of heart? It seems clear that China's leadership came to the conclusion that a new round of market reforms was necessary to reverse the country's recently flagging economic performance; like Mexico in the NAFTA talks, China endeavored to use international negotiations to ram through needed domestic policy changes and then to insulate those changes from later reversal.

Of course, liberalization does occur as well through conventional reciprocity-driven swapping of "concessions." The point here, though, is this conventional model is not the only, or even the most important, path to liberalization. The real energy propelling liberalization around the world over the past couple of decades has been at the national level. When countries perceive that it is in their economic interest to open their markets, they do so—without especially worrying about what reciprocal offers of market-opening they will get in return. On the other hand, when countries do not believe that liberalization is needed, negotiations are doomed to achieve only marginal gains.

The conventional understanding of trade liberalization can be thought of as a "top-down" vision of international order. In this vision, the relatively open world trading system is imposed from above by international institutions and agreements. This interpretation, however, distorts why countries should liberalize their trade and why they usually do. However at odds with received wisdom, a "bottom-up" vision of international order is actually much more consistent with both economics and political reality. According to the bottom-up view, the bedrock of the relatively liberal international trading system consists of national-level decisions that openness at home is in the national interest. Freedom of international exchange thus flows up from below as a necessary consequence of predominantly unilateral decisions at the national level.

How Trade Talks Can Help

What then is the role for international negotiations and institutions in the bottom-up vision of trade liberalization? When appropriately structured and limited, trade agreements can play an important role in facilitating liberalization and especially in consolidating prior gains.

In the first place, linking liberalization at home with liberalization abroad can greatly strengthen the political prospects of dismantling domestic trade barriers. For one thing, the economic benefits of mutual liberalization are greater than those of unilateral liberalization. Although liberalization pays even if other countries remain protectionist, the payoff is richer still if other countries follow suit. Thus champions of international liberalization have a more appealing product to sell. Furthermore, although reforming protectionist policies brings economic benefits, it usually faces concerted political opposition from affected import-competing interests. If that lobbying pressure can be counteracted by the pro-trade lobbying, not just of import-using interests but also of exporting interests eager for improved access to foreign markets, then the chances of overcoming the opposition are enhanced considerably.

Probably the greatest assistance that international negotiations lend to trade liberalization, though, is in consolidating and institutionalizing prior gains. Once countries have decided to open their markets in the furtherance of their own national self-interest, those decisions can be harder to undo by subsequent protectionist-minded governments if liberalization has been enshrined as an international obligation. Thus, trade agreements can serve to "lock in" reforms by imposing additional political constraints on their reversal. Mexico's pursuit of NAFTA, discussed earlier, was motivated primarily by precisely such considerations. Similarly, the recent defeat of legislation to impose quotas on U.S. steel imports was achieved largely on the ground that such legislation amounted to a blatant violation of U.S. obligations under the WTO agreements.

Avoiding the Pitfalls of Reciprocity

Although trade negotiations can assist the process of liberalization, there are potential drawbacks as well. First, trade negotiations can actually undermine political support for open markets by fostering protectionist misconceptions and thus breeding a hostile political culture. As discussed previously, the conventional "reciprocity" model of trade talks is premised on the protectionist notion that imports are harmful and trade barriers are prized strategic assets. By following this model, trade negotiators and their supporters end up validating the very ideas that give rise to protectionist pressure in the first place.

Because of the reciprocity model, protectionist assumptions and attitudes color every aspect of how trade agreements are currently negotiated and evaluated. Trade negotiators, in the process of championing freer trade, insist that a "bad deal" (i.e., one in which we liberalize more than other countries do) is worse than no deal at all. They oppose domestic reforms outside the context of negotiations on the ground that our own bad policies are "bargaining chips" that should be retained for their exchange value. More ominously, they refer to liberalization without reciprocity as "unilateral disarmament." And when an agreement has been reached, supporters focus on the benefits to exporters, not importers. They tout the benefits of reducing foreign trade barriers, but say little or nothing about the benefits of reducing our own.

By adopting the reciprocity model, free traders forfeit the opportunity to educate the public on the true benefits of open markets. That default was not especially important in the past when trade policy was hammered out in back rooms by experts and insiders. Now, however, trade issues engage the attention and passions of the broader public. And what the public sees in the often heated debates over trade policy is not a contest between true free traders and protectionists, but rather a disagreement between optimistic mercantilists and pessimistic mercantilists. The optimists, the supporters of trade liberalization, highlight the new export opportunities created by opening markets abroad; the pessimists dwell on the supposed threat of increased imports caused by opening markets here. Neither side, though, challenges the fallacious "exports good, imports bad" worldview.

Meanwhile, although free traders push optimism when they are trying to sell trade agreements, they unwittingly corroborate the pessimists' fears when they are actually negotiating those deals. Thus, our trade negotiators never tire of claiming that the U.S. market is the most open in the world. Of course, within the logic of trade negotiations, this is a sensible bargaining position, since it supports the conclusion that the United States should not have to "give in" on this or that issue. The American public, though, hears these claims and many conclude that the United States has been short-changed by past negotiations. Skepticism about future negotiations is therefore understandable. Similarly, U.S. trade negotiators complain incessantly about other countries' trade barriers and their failure to live up to past agreements. Again, this line makes sense at the negotiating table, since it pressures our trade partners to make additional "concessions." The American public hears these repeated complaints, though, and for many they confirm suspicions that the United States is always being out-negotiated or even cheated. Trade liberalization therefore looks like a losing proposition.

Trade policymakers can avoid these pitfalls by abandoning the old "reciprocity" model in favor of a new approach toward international negotiations. Under this new approach, policymakers would explicitly recognize what is in fact the case—namely, that open markets at home are the primary benefit of participating in trade agreements. Such a recognition would create an entirely different negotiating dynamic—it would replace haggling over reciprocity with "coordinated unilateralism."

Unlike in reciprocity-based negotiations, the goal wouldn't be to "win" at the bargaining table by "getting" more than you "give." Rather, the express purpose of negotiations would be for each country to gain by reforming its own policies, but also to maximize that gain by linking reforms to liberalization abroad. Reforming one's own policies would be a central negotiating objective rather than the downside of the transaction, while coordination would strengthen the political case for free trade by adding the benefits of liberalization abroad to those of market-opening at home.

Such an approach still leaves plenty of room for tough bargaining. Under coordinated unilateralism, however, the focus would be on the integrity of the overall agreement, not on any country-by-country tallying of "concessions" given and received. Specifically, the measure of success would be an agreement that reflects a serious international commitment to free-trade principles—as evidenced by the fact that a "critical mass" of countries has agreed to commit to some minimum threshold of liberalization. And in measuring the level of commitment of various countries, what matters is the extent of liberalization agreed to in the end; whether that end result is achieved through new reforms, or simply through an agreement to "lock in" previously made unilateral reforms, should be irrelevant.

Under this approach, if there is not sufficient international interest in meaningful and significant commitments, then no agreement is reached. Countries are then free to continue to liberalize unilaterally. Going it alone will not mean a loss of "bargaining chips" or leverage in subsequent negotiations; if such negotiations do occur in the future, countries will receive full "credit" for any liberalization achieved in the interim.

Although coordinated unilateralism would represent a sharp break from the current rhetoric of trade talks, diverging from current practice would be much less dramatic. In a study of the Uruguay Round negotiations, J. Michael Finger of the World Bank found that the reciprocity model does a very poor job of explaining what actually happened. That model would predict that countries' "net concessions" should be close to zero; in fact, however, an analysis of the tariff commitments of 33 countries shows that net concessions varied dramatically from country to country. Meanwhile, interviews with 10 different negotiating delegations found none that had actually tallied concessions given versus received (either within the tariff negotiations specifically or across the range of all Uruguay Round agreements). There was broad agreement, however, about the importance of ensuring that each country made an "appropriate contribution" to tariff cutting. In this regard, Finger found that countries did receive "credit" for prior unilateral cuts when they agreed to bind their rates at the currently applied levels.

In addition, the coordinated unilateralism model fits very well with the record of the post-Uruguay Round sectoral negotiations—the Information Technology Agreement and the agreements on telecommunications and financial services. For all three agreements the challenge was to enlist a critical mass of countries to agree to particular liberalization thresholds. In all of these talks, the United States exercised significant leverage despite the fact that it already had a zero tariff rate for semiconductors and offered only to lock in current levels of openness in telecommunications and financial services. The lock-in by itself was considered a valuable U.S. contribution by other countries; furthermore, U.S. participation in the agreements gave them legitimacy and thus bolstered other countries' confidence in each other's commitments. Using its leverage, the United States walked away from the financial services talks when it was dissatisfied with some of the offers from key participants; in the end negotiations resumed and a stronger package of commitments was achieved.

So how would coordinated unilateralism differ from the status quo? The difference would be primarily rhetorical, not substantive. But in politics rhetorical changes can be extremely important. In the present case, a shift to coordinated unilateralism would allow trade policymakers to continue to reap the political advantages of international liberalization without at the same time salting the earth with protectionist nonsense.

Keeping Negotiations on Track

The other major problem with trade negotiations, besides their mercantilist assumptions, is that they can veer off in the wrong direction. Instead of reducing government interference in trade and investment flows, misguided international agreements can actually increase such interference. This risk has grown in line with the increasingly ambitious scope of trade negotiations.

The original focus of trade agreements was on border measures that discriminate overtly against foreign goods—namely, tariffs and quantitative restrictions. Over time, though, as tariff levels have fallen and import quotas have been relaxed and eliminated, the scope of trade negotiations has expanded to address nontariff barriers—that is, domestic policies that discriminate against or simply inhibit international commerce. Thus, such areas as product standards, food safety regulation, subsidies, and intellectual property protection have been swept within the purview of trade policy.

As the reach of trade agreements into domestic policy has extended, it has become increasingly plausible to argue that any policy area that "affects" trade—and practically every public policy has some effect on trade—deserves to be included on the trade agenda. In particular, those who call for negotiating international labor and environmental agreements through the WTO are able to make a seductive argument: If the WTO requires national governments to protect the intellectual property rights of software companies and pharmaceutical manufacturers, why shouldn't it require, or at least allow, national governments to protect the environment or the rights of workers? Are these objectives somehow less valuable than the profits of multinational companies?

If such thinking carries the day, there is a serious risk that future trade negotiations will end up doing more harm than good. First, they could create broad new exceptions that allow national governments to close their markets out of social policy considerations—for example, restricting imports from countries that do not guarantee a particular minimum wage or that do require certain air quality standards. Alternatively, trade agreements could impose ill-considered new international regulatory requirements on national governments, compliance with which would then be enforceable through the WTO dispute settlement process.

Such unfortunate developments can be resisted effectively only if free traders remember what makes trade negotiations worth pursuing in the first place. Trade agreements are beneficial insofar as they facilitate the opening up of national markets to foreign competition. If they subvert that objective—whether by conferring international legitimacy on new forms of protectionism or by saddling the world with a new layer of international regulatory bureaucracy—they deserve the opposition, not the support, of believers in free trade.

The risk that trade agreements will wind up increasing rather than decreasing government interference in international markets is heightened considerably by the currently dominant top-down vision of international order. People who believe that a global economy requires a global rule-making body will naturally sympathize with extending the WTO's mandate into any area of plausibly international concern—even when such extension conflicts with the original market-opening purpose of the organization. Even more committed free traders who do not welcome WTO "mission creep" will be influenced to compromise by the top-down viewpoint. To the extent that they believe the world trading system is completely dependent on international negotiations and institutions, they are correspondingly more likely to give in to demands to expand the trade agenda in illiberal directions if that is the only apparent way to keep the "process" moving forward. Just in the past year or so, in the wake of the multiple failures of fast track legislation and then the debacle in Seattle, there has been increasing pressure within elements of the U.S. free-trade camp to make concessions on environmental and labor issues.

From the bottom-up perspective, on the other hand, it is clear that liberalization can proceed if need be without international negotiations—and indeed would be much better off without them if they become infected by anti-market initiatives. Those free-traders who counsel appeasement of environmental and labor activists cite the "bicycle theory" of trade negotiations, according to which the process must either keep moving forward or else collapse into protectionism and conflict. But as trade economist Jagdish Bhagwati has responded, it may be better to fall off the bicycle than to keep pedaling in the wrong direction. And in the end, a credible willingness to accept no agreement rather than a bad agreement may be the best guarantor of avoiding a wrong turn.

Conclusion

The case for trade negotiations from the free-trade perspective is more nuanced than is commonly understood. Negotiations are not required for trade liberalization to occur; after all, the most dramatic progress in market-opening over the past couple of decades has occurred through unilateral reforms at the national level. Furthermore, negotiations, if conducted incorrectly, can actually undermine the free-trade cause.

When structured properly, though, international trade agreements can provide a useful supplement to purely unilateral liberalization. Such agreements can help overcome political obstacles that hinder the opening of markets; also, they can consolidate market-opening gains and make them harder to reverse. The key to maximizing negotiated liberalization's advantages, and avoiding its pitfalls, is found in the bottom-up vision of international economic order. That vision recognizes that countries should and do open their markets largely on the basis of perceived national economic interest. Accordingly, the proper model for trade negotiations is not mercantilist-minded "reciprocity" but rather "coordinated unilateralism."

The Asian Crisis: Why the IMF Should Not Intervene

Ian Vásquez

It is a pleasure to leave Washington to contribute to the discussion about the International Monetary Fund and its role in Asia. I take it as indication that people are genuinely interested in debating the merits of various perspectives as opposed to discussing it because they can derive immediate and direct benefit from advocating one point of view—nobody ever comes to Washington asking not to be bailed out. Usually, the IMF takes a low profile except when there are riots in the capitals of client countries, national currency crises, or when the IMF is asking for more money. Unfortunately, all three factors explain the currently high profile of the Fund.

The emergency atmosphere of the ongoing Asian financial crisis has resulted in bailout packages there totaling about US$117 billion and urgent requests for a massive increase in the IMF's resources. For the United States, the added contribution would be $18 billion, which U.S. Treasury officials insist doesn't cost U.S. taxpayers a dime. Only in Washington can one simultaneously plead for more money and insist, with a straight face, that the contribution is cost-free. Cato Institute chairman William Niskanen, the former head of Reagan's Council of Economic Advisers, put it more accurately when he described the U.S. relationship with the IMF thusly: "U.S. government membership in the IMF is like being a limited partner in a financial firm that makes high-risk loans, pays dividends at a rate lower than that on Treasury bills, and makes large periodic cash calls for additional funds."

But the monetary costs of supporting the IMF are not the most important reasons to oppose more funding. The people who are most

Ian Vásquez is director of the Project on Global Economic Liberty at the Cato Institute. These remarks were presented at Fundación Diálogos, Madrid, Spain, February 25, 1998.

Vital Speeches, April 15, 1998

directly affected by IMF interventions—the world's poor—are those who can least afford it. If the goal is to help developing countries progress economically and to promote a liberal global economy, then the least rich countries can do is deny further funding for the IMF.

Free-market economists have long been critical of the IMF. Mexico-style crises may have brought much attention to the Fund in recent years, but the lending agency's record over the past 50 years has been dismal, as numerous books and studies have documented. The IMF does not appear to have helped countries either achieve self-sustaining growth or to promote market reforms. Despite its poor performance, the IMF has proven to be a remarkably resilient institution. When the system of fixed exchange rates ended in the early 1970s, so did the agency's original mission of maintaining exchange-rate stability by lending to countries experiencing balance-of-payments problems. Instead of closing down, however, the Fund has created new missions for itself with each new crisis, each time expanding its economic influence or resources or both. Those episodes included the oil crises of the 1970s, the Third World debt crisis, the collapse of communism, and now, Mexico-style crises.

Keep in mind that the IMF in theory makes short-term loans in exchange for policy changes in recipient countries. This has not, however, helped countries move to the free market. Instead the Fund has created loan addicts as review of its lending reveals. Eleven nations have been relying on IMF aid for at least 30 years; 32 countries had been borrowers for between 20 and 29 years; and 41 countries had been using IMF credit for between 10 and 19 years. That is not evidence of either the success of the Fund's so-called conditionality or the temporary nature of the Fund's short-term loans.

But the reason we are discussing the IMF today is because of the turmoil in Asia and because of calls for increased funding. Specifically, the money would finance a new fund at the IMF, known as the New Arrangements to Borrow, which would function as a special bailout fund for countries in crisis; and for a general increase in resources, known as a quota increase, which of course would also be used for bailouts. Using the IMF to bail out a country experiencing a currency or debt crisis is a bad idea for three reasons.

Moral Hazard

The first reason is that it creates moral hazard. This is not a minor point, as U.S. Treasury Secretary Robert Rubin has himself recognized. The more the IMF bails out countries, the more we can expect countries to slip into crises in the future because it encourages risky behavior on the part of governments and investors who fully expect that if anything goes wrong, the IMF will come to their rescue.

We've seen the moral hazard problem in the past and we are seeing it today. With every election cycle in the past 20 years, for example, Mexico has experienced a currency crisis caused by irresponsible monetary and fiscal policy. Each episode has been accompanied by U.S. Treasury and IMF bailouts, each time in increasing amounts. In Mexico, everybody has come to expect a financial rescue at the end of each presidential term. And although IMF and U.S. officials had since 1995 claimed the last Mexican bailout a success, its legacy has been the Asian crisis of today—at least in its degree and severity. Indeed, the bailout of Mexico was a signal to the world that if anything went wrong in emerging economies, the IMF would come to investors' rescue. How else can we explain the near doubling of capital flows to East Asia in 1995 alone?

Governments in Asia were not discouraged from maintaining flawed policies as long as lenders kept the capital flowing. Lenders, for their part, behaved imprudently with the knowledge that government money would be used in case of financial troubles. That knowledge by no means meant that investors did not care if a crisis erupted; but it led to the mispricing of risk and a change in the investment calculations of lenders. Thailand, Indonesia, and South Korea, after all, shared some common factors that should have led to more investor caution, but didn't. Those factors included borrowing in foreign currencies and lending in domestic currency under pegged exchange rates; extensively borrowing in the short term while lending in the long term; lack of supervision of borrowers' balance sheets by foreign lenders; government-directed credit; and shaky financial systems. The financial crisis in Asia was created in Asia, but the aggravating effect of moral hazard was extensive. As Michael Prowse of the *Financial Times* commented after the Mexican bailout, "Rubin and Co. wanted to make global capitalism safe for the mutual fund investor. They actually made it far riskier."

An Expensive, Unjust Solution

IMF bailouts of Asian countries are expensive, bureaucratic, and fundamentally unjust solutions to currency crises. In the first place, the financial aid cuts investors' losses rather than allowing them to bear the full responsibility for their decisions. Just as profits should not be socialized when times are good, neither should losses be socialized during difficult times. "The $57 billion committed to Korea," Harvard economist Jeffrey Sachs observes, "didn't help anybody but the banks." Unfortunately for the ordinary Asian citizens who had nothing to do with creating the crisis, they will be forced to pay for the added debt burden imposed by IMF loans.

IMF bailouts pose another burden on ordinary citizens because they don't work very well. The Fund's money goes to governments that have created the crisis to begin with and that have shown themselves to be unwilling or reluctant to introduce necessary reforms. Giving money to such governments does not tend to promote market reforms, it tends to delay them because it takes the pressure off of governments to change their policies. Rather, a suspension of loans will tend to concentrate the minds of policymakers in the various troubled countries. The reason, after all, that there is any talk today of market-reform is not because the IMF has shown up and suggested it is a good and necessary thing. That is fairly obvious. Economic reality is forcing the long-needed change. To the extent that the IMF steps in and provides money, those reforms will not be as forthcoming. Thus, the citizens of recipient Asian nations suffer the added burden of IMF intervention. Not only do they have to pay a greater debt; but they also have to suffer prolonged economic agony that is produced by the Fund's bailouts.

But what about the Fund's "strong conditionality"? Don't the strict conditions of IMF lending ensure that important policy changes will be made? Again, the record of long-term dependency of countries shows that conditionality has not worked well in the past. But besides the Fund's poor record, there is good reason why the IMF has little credibility in imposing its conditions. As we have seen with Russia over the past several years, a country—especially a highly visible one—that does not stick to IMF conditions risks having its loans suspended. When loans are cut off, recipient governments tend to become more serious about reform. Note that the IMF encourages misbehaving governments to introduce reforms by cutting loans off; it is the *cutoff* of credit that induces policy change.

Unfortunately, when policy changes are forthcoming, the IMF resumes lending. Indeed, the IMF has a bureaucratic incentive to lend. It simply cannot afford to watch countries reform on their own because it would risk making the IMF appear irrelevant. The resumption of financial aid starts the process over again and prolongs the period of reform. The Fund's pressure to lend money in order to keep borrowers current on previous loans and to be able to ask for more money is well documented. The IMF's bureaucratic incentive to lend is also well known by both recipient governments and the IMF itself, making the Fund's conditionality that much less credible.

Undermining Superior, Market Solutions

The third reason I oppose IMF bailouts is that they undermine superior, less expensive market solutions. In the absence of an IMF, creditors and debtors would do what creditors and debtors always do in cases of illiquidity or insolvency: they renegotiate debt or enter into bankruptcy procedures. In a world without the IMF, both parties would have an incentive to do so because the alternative, to do nothing, would mean a complete loss. Direct negotiations between private parties and bankruptcy procedures are essential if capitalism is to work. As James Glassman has stated, capitalism without bankruptcy is like Christianity without Hell. IMF bailouts, unfortunately, undermine one of the most important underpinnings of a free economy by overriding the market mechanism. There is simply no reason why international creditors and borrowers should be treated any differently than are lenders and debtors in the domestic market.

Governments would also react differently if no IMF interventions were forthcoming. There would be little alternative to widespread and rapid reforms if policymakers were not shielded from economic reality. Lawrence Lindsey, a former governor of the U.S. Federal Reserve opposed to bailouts, has noted, for example, that, "All of the 'conditions' supposedly negotiated by the IMF will be forced on South Korea by the market." Of course, there is always the possibility that a government would be reluctant to change its ways under any set of circumstances; but that is a possibility that is larger, and indeed has become a reality, under IMF programs.

Conclusion

The U.S. Congress plays a large role in determining the scale of the IMF's influence on the world economy. An increasing number of prominent economists are now calling for an end to IMF bailouts and even its abolition—something to which U.S. congressmen are paying attention. Because the Fund creates moral hazard, causes more harm than good once a crisis does erupt, and undermines superior market solutions, the United States and other major donors should reject further funding for the IMF and in that way vote for a more stable and free global economy. That would send a signal to the world that the Fund's resources are not, in fact, unlimited. Beyond that, wealthy nations should further help the world's poor by dismantling the IMF altogether.

PART VIII

LAW AND LIBERTY

Economic Affairs as Human Affairs

Antonin Scalia

The title of this article—"Economic Affairs as Human Affairs"—is derived from a phrase I recall from the earliest days of my political awareness. Dwight Eisenhower used to insist, with demonstrably successful effect, that he was "a conservative in economic affairs, but a liberal in human affairs." I am sure he meant it to connote nothing more profound than that he represented the best of both Republican and Democratic tradition. But still, that seemed to me a peculiar way to put it—contrasting economic affairs with human affairs as though economics is a science developed for the benefit of dogs or trees; something that has nothing to do with human beings, with their welfare, aspirations, or freedoms.

That, of course, is a pernicious notion, though it represents a turn of mind that characterizes much American political thought. It leads to the conclusion that economic rights and liberties are qualitatively distinct from, and fundamentally inferior to, other noble human values called civil rights, about which we should be more generous. Unless one is a thoroughgoing materialist, there is some appeal to this. Surely the freedom to dispose of one's property as one pleases, for example, is not as high an aspiration as the freedom to think or write or worship as one's conscience dictates. On closer analysis, however, it seems to me that the difference between economic freedoms and what are generally called civil rights turns out to be a difference of degree rather than of kind. Few of us, I suspect, would have much difficulty choosing between the right to own property and the right to receive a Miranda warning.

In any case, in the real world a stark dichotomy between economic freedoms and civil rights does not exist. Human liberties of various

Antonin Scalia, then a judge on the U.S. Court of Appeals, is now a justice of the United States Supreme Court. This paper is an edited version of his remarks at the Cato Institute's conference, "Economic Liberties and the Judiciary," October 26, 1984.

Cato Journal, Vol. 4, No. 3 (Winter 1985)

types are dependent on one another, and it may well be that the most humble of them is indispensable to the others—the firmament, so to speak, upon which the high spires of the most exalted freedoms ultimately rest. I know no society, today or in any era of history, in which high degrees of intellectual and political freedom have flourished side by side with a high degree of state control over the relevant citizen's economic life. The free market, which presupposes relatively broad economic freedom, has historically been the cradle of broad political freedom, and in modern times the demise of economic freedom has been the grave of political freedom as well. The same phenomenon is observable in the small scales of our private lives. As a practical matter, he who controls my economic destiny controls much more of my life as well. Most salaried professionals do not consider themselves "free" to go about wearing sandals and Nehru jackets, or to write letters on any subjects they please to the *New York Times*.

My concern in this essay, however, is not economic liberty in general, but economic liberty and the judiciary. One must approach this topic with the realization that the courts are (in most contexts, at least) hardly disparaging of economic rights and liberties. Although most of the cases you read of in the newspaper may involve busing, or homosexual rights, or the supervision of school districts and mental institutions, the vast bulk of the courts' civil business consists of the vindication of economic rights between private individuals and against the government. Indeed, even the vast bulk of noncriminal "civil rights" cases are really cases involving economic disputes. The legal basis for the plaintiff's claim may be sex discrimination, but what she is really complaining about is that someone did her out of a job. Even the particular court on which I sit, which because of its location probably gets an inordinately large share of civil cases *not* involving economic rights, still finds that the majority of its business consists of enforcing economic rights against the government—the right to conduct business in an unregulated fashion where Congress has authorized no regulation, or the right to receive a fair return upon capital invested in a rate-regulated business. Indeed, some of the economic interests protected by my court are quite rarefied, such as a business's right to remain free of economic competition from a government licensee whose license is defective in a respect having nothing to do with the plaintiff's interests—for example, one radio station's challenge to the license of a competing station on the basis that the latter will produce electronic interference with a third station.

Fundamental or rarefied, the point is that we, the judiciary, do a lot of protecting of economic rights and liberties. The problem that some see is that this protection in the federal courts runs only by and large against the executive branch and not against the Congress. We will ensure that the executive does not impose any constraints upon economic activity which Congress has not authorized; and that where constraints *are* authorized the executive follows statutorily prescribed procedures and that the executive (and, much more rarely, Congress in its prescriptions) follows constitutionally required procedures. But we will never (well, hardly ever) decree that the substance of the congressionally authorized constraint is unlawful. That is to say, we do not provide a *constitutionalized* protection except insofar as matters of process, as opposed to substantive economic rights, are concerned.

There are those who urge reversal of this practice. The main vehicle available—and the only one I address specifically here—is the due process clause of the Fifth and Fourteenth Amendments, which provides that no person shall be deprived of "life, liberty, or property, without due process of law." Although one might suppose that a reference to "process" places limitations only upon the *manner* in which a thing may be done, and not upon the *doing* of it, since at least the late 1800s the federal courts have in fact interpreted these clauses to prohibit the *substance* of certain governmental action, no matter what fair and legitimate procedures attend that substance. Thus, there has come to develop a judicial vocabulary which refers (seemingly redundantly) to "procedural due process" on the one hand, and (seemingly paradoxically) to "substantive due process" on the other hand. Until the mid-1930s, substantive due process rights were extended not merely to what we would now term "civil rights"—for example, the freedom to teach one's child a foreign language if one wishes—but also to a broad range of economic rights—for example, the right to work twelve hours a day if one wishes. Since that time, application of the concept has been consistently expanded in the civil rights field (*Roe v. Wade* is the most controversial recent extension) but entirely eliminated in the field of economic rights. Some urge that it should be resuscitated.

I pause to note at this point, lest I either be credited with what is good in the present system or blamed for what is bad, that it is not up to me. (I did not have to make that disclaimer a few years ago, when I was a law professor.) The Supreme Court decisions rejecting substantive due process in the economic field are clear, unequivocal and current, and as an appellate judge I try to do what I'm told. But I will go beyond that disclaimer and say that in my view the position the Supreme Court has arrived at is good—or at least that the suggestion that it change its position is even worse.

As should be apparent from what I said above, my position is not based on the proposition that economic rights are unimportant. Nor do I necessarily quarrel with the specific nature of the particular economic rights that the most sagacious of the proponents of substantive due process would bring within the protection of the Constitution; were I a legislator, I might well vote for them. Rather, my skepticism arises from misgivings about, first, the effect of such expansion on the behavior of courts in other areas quite separate from economic liberty, and second, the ability of the courts to limit their constitutionalizing to those elements of economic liberty that are sensible. I will say a few words about each.

First, the effect of constitutionalizing substantive economic guarantees on the behavior of the courts in other areas: There is an inevitable connection between judges' ability and willingness to craft substantive due process guarantees in the economic field and their ability and willingness to do it elsewhere. Many believe—and among those many are some of the same people who urge an expansion of economic due process rights—that our system already suffers from relatively recent constitutionalizing, and thus judicializing, of social judgments that ought better be left to the democratic process. The courts, they feel, have come to be regarded as an alternate legislature, whose charge differs from that of the ordinary legislature in the respect that while the latter may enact into law good ideas, the former may enact into law only *unquestionably* good ideas, which, since they *are* so unquestionably good, *must* be part of the Constitution. I would not adopt such an extravagant description of the problem. But I do believe that every era raises its own peculiar threat to constitutional democracy, and that the attitude of mind thus caricatured represents the distinctive threat of our times. And I therefore believe that whatever reinforces rather than challenges that attitude is to that extent undesirable. It seems to me that the reversal of a half-century of judicial restraint in the economic realm comes within that category. In the long run, and perhaps even in the short run, the reinforcement of mistaken and unconstitutional perceptions of the role of the courts in our system far outweighs whatever evils may have accrued from undue judicial abstention in the economic field.

The response to my concern, I suppose, is that the connection I assert between judicial intervention in the economic realm and in other realms can simply not be shown to exist. We have substantive due process aplenty in the field of civil liberties, even while it has been obliterated in the economic field. My rejoinder is simply an abiding faith that logic will out. Litigants before me often characterize the argument that if the court does *w* (which is desirable) then it must logically do *x, y,* and *z* (which are undesirable) as a "parade of horribles"; but in my years at the law I have too often seen the end of the parade come by. There really is an inevitable tug of logical consistency upon human affairs, and especially upon judicial affairs—indeed, that is the only thing that makes the system work. So I must believe that as bad as some feel judicial "activism" has gotten without substantive due process in the economic field, *absent* that memento of judicial humility it might have gotten even worse. And I have little hope that judicial and lawyerly attitudes can be coaxed back to a more restricted view of the courts' role in a democratic society at the same time that we are charging forward on an entirely new front.

Though it is something of an oversimplification, I do not think it unfair to say that this issue presents the moment of truth for many conservatives who have been criticizing the courts in recent years. They must decide whether they really believe, as they have been saying, that the courts are doing too much, or whether they are actually nursing only the less principled grievance that the courts have not been doing what *they* want.

The second reason for my skepticism is the absence of any reason to believe that the courts would limit their constitutionalizing of economic rights to those rights that are sensible. In this regard some conservatives seem to make the same mistake they so persuasively argue the society makes whenever it unthinkingly calls in government regulation to remedy a "market failure." It is first necessary to make sure, they have persuaded us, that the cure is not worse than the disease—that the phenomenon of "government failure," attributable to the fact that the government, like the market, happens to be composed of self-interested human beings, will not leave the last state of the problem worse than the first. It strikes me as peculiar that these same rational free-market proponents will unthinkingly call in the courts as a *deus ex machina* to solve what they perceive as the problems of democratic inadequacy in the field of economic rights. Is there much reason to believe that the courts, if they undertook the task, would do a good job? If economic sophistication is the touchstone, it suffices to observe that these are the folks who developed three-quarters of a century of counterproductive law under the Sherman Act. But perhaps what counts is not economic sophistication, but rather a favoritism—not shared by the political branches of government—toward the institution of property and its protection. I have no doubt that judges once met this qualification. When Madison described them as a "natural aristocracy," I am sure he had in mind an aristocracy of property as well as of manners. But with the proliferation and consequent bureaucratization of the courts, the relative modesty of judicial salaries, and above all the development of lawyers (and hence of judges) through a system of generally available university education which, in this country as in others, more often nurtures collectivist than capitalist philosophy, one would be foolish to look for Daddy Warbucks on the bench.

But, the proponents of constitutionalized economic rights will object, we do not propose an open-ended, unlimited charter to the courts to create economic rights, but would tie the content of those rights to the text of the Constitution and, where the text is itself somewhat open-ended (the due process clause, for example), to established (if recently forgotten) constitutional traditions. As a theoretical matter, that could be done—though it is infinitely more difficult today than it was fifty years ago. Because of the courts' long retirement from the field of constitutional economics, and because of judicial and legislative developments in other fields, the social consensus as to what are the limited, "core" economic rights does not exist today as it perhaps once did. But even if it is theoretically possible for the courts to mark out limits to their intervention, it is hard to be confident that they would do so. We may find ourselves burdened with judicially prescribed economic liberties that are worse than the pre-existing economic bondage. What would you think, for example, of a substantive-due-process, constitutionally guaranteed, economic right of every worker to "just and favourable remuneration ensuring for himself and his family an existence worthy of human dignity?"

Many think this a precept of natural law; why not of the Constitution? A sort of constitutionally prescribed (and thus judicially determined) minimum wage. Lest it be thought fanciful, I have taken the formulation of this right verbatim from Article 23 of the United Nations' Universal Declaration of Human Rights.

Finally, let me suggest that the call for creating (or, if you prefer, "reestablishing") economic constitutional guarantees mistakes the nature and effect of the constitutionalizing process. To some degree, a constitutional guarantee is like a commercial loan: you can only get it if, at the time, you don't really need it. The most important, enduring, and stable portions of the Constitution represent such a deep social consensus that one suspects that if they were entirely eliminated, very little would change. And the converse is also true. A guarantee may appear in the words of the Constitution, but when the society ceases to possess an abiding belief in it, it has no living effect. Consider the fate of the principle expressed in the Tenth Amendment that the federal government is a government of limited powers. I do not suggest that constitutionalization has no effect in helping the society to preserve allegiance to its fundamental principles. That is the whole purpose of a constitution. But the allegiance comes first and the preservation afterwards.

Most of the constitutionalizing of civil rights that the courts have effected in recent years has been at the margins of well-established and deeply held social beliefs. Even *Brown v. Board of Education*, as significant a step as it might have seemed, was only an elaboration of the consequences of the nation's deep belief in the equality of all persons before the law. Where the Court has tried to go further than that (the unsuccessful attempt to eliminate the death penalty, to take one of the currently less controversial examples), the results have been precarious. Unless I have been on the bench so long that I no longer have any feel for popular sentiment, I do not detect the sort of national commitment to most of the economic liberties generally discussed that would enable even an activist court to constitutionalize them. That lack of sentiment may be regrettable, but to seek to develop it by enshrining the unaccepted principles in the Constitution is to place the cart before the horse.

If you are interested in economic liberties, then, the first step is to recall the society to that belief in their importance which (I have no doubt) the founders of the republic shared. That may be no simple task, because the roots of the problem extend as deeply into modern theology as into modern social thought. I remember a conversation with Irving Kristol some years ago, in which he expressed gratitude that his half of the Judeo-Christian heritage had never thought it a sin to be rich. In fact my half never thought it so either. Voluntary poverty, like voluntary celibacy, was a counsel of perfection—but it was not thought that either wealth or marriage was inherently evil, or a condition that the just society should seek to stamp out. But that subtle distinction has assuredly been forgotten, and we live in an age in which many Christians are predisposed to believe that John D. Rockefeller, for all his piety (he founded the University of Chicago as a Baptist institution), is likely to be damned and Ché Guevara, for all his nonbelief, is likely to be among the elect. This suggests that the task of creating what I might call a constitutional ethos of economic liberty is no easy one. But it is the first task.

Judicial Review: Reckoning on Two Kinds of Error

Richard A. Epstein

Antonin Scalia has explained why he believes courts should re-
frain from intervening to protect what are generally described as economic liberties—chiefly, the right to own and use property and the
right to dispose of both property and labor by contract. In so doing,
he has recounted at length all the errors and confusions that beset
courts when they try to vindicate these basic economic rights by constitutional means.

There are powerful reasons why judges may do badly in this endeavor. They are isolated, and they tend to be drawn from political
or social elites. Their competence on economic matters is often limited. When they pass on complex legislation, they often misunderstand its purpose and effect. By any standard, the error rate of their
decisions has been high. I cannot challenge his conclusions simply by
saying that he underestimates the sterling performance of his colleagues on the bench. If the only issue were judicial competence,
Scalia's conclusion would swiftly follow: Since courts cannot master
economic matters, they should adopt a form of judicial laissez faire
that keeps judges' hands off the economic system.

As stated, Scalia's plea for judicial restraint is not a defense of legal anarchy. Instead, it accepts government control over economic
affairs, but guarantees that this control will be exercised by the legislative and executive branches of government (as well as the administrative agencies they have created). By necessity, only political

Richard Epstein is James Parker Hall Professor of Law at the University of Chicago
and an adjunct scholar of the Cato Institute. This paper is an edited version of his remarks at the Cato Institute's conference, "Economic Liberties and the Judiciary," October 26, 1984.

Cato Journal, Vol. 4, No. 3 (Winter 1985)

checks are available to ensure that national policy does not stray too far from the social consensus.

Scalia's position represents the mainstream of American constitutional theory today. My purpose is to take issue with the conventional wisdom. I hope to persuade Scalia to take upon himself, and to pursue energetically, the tasks that our Constitution assigns to him and to other federal judges. Note that in urging this course I speak as an academic who would impose on sitting judges duties more extensive than they are often willing to assume.

In my view, Scalia has addressed only one side of a two-sided problem. He has pointed out the weaknesses of judicial action. But he has not paid sufficient attention to the errors and dangers in unchanneled legislative behavior. The only way to reach a balanced, informed judgment on the intrinsic desirability of judicial control of economic liberties is to consider the *relative* shortcomings of the two institutions—judicial and legislative—that compete for the crown of final authority. The constitutionality of legislation restricting economic liberties cannot be decided solely by appealing to an initial presumption in favor of judicial restraint. Instead, the imperfections of the judicial system must be matched with the imperfections of the political branches of government.

What are the problems with legislation? When we put someone in charge of the collective purse or the police force, we in effect give him a spigot that allows him to tap into other people's property, money, and liberty. The legislator that casts a vote on an appropriations bill is spending not only his own wealth, but everyone else's. When the power of coalition, the power of factions, the power of artifice and strategy come into play, it often turns out that legislatures reach results that (in the long as well as the short run) are far from the social optimum.

To take the limiting case, suppose a group of people have a profound and anxious debate, and then decide, by a bare majority, that the prevailing distribution of wealth is wrong. So the 51 percent decide to condemn, without payment, all the property of the 49 percent. Strict majoritarian principles would allow them to get away with that. But Scalia and others would say, "It cannot be done because the eminent domain clause in our Constitution provides that when government takes private property for public use, it must pay." The winners in a legislative battle may not confiscate the property of the losers.

Now, note the slippery slope. We have identified a form of legislative failure, along with a constitutional provision that seems to respond to that kind of failure. The first step down the slope is the announcement that a particular piece of legislation, even if it reflects the consensus of the population at large, is not going to work. And once we take that step, where in principle do we stop? Suppose we change the dynamics of coalition building, so that it takes 80 percent of the population to confiscate the wealth of the other 20 percent. Does this broader consensus mean that the program is acceptable and can proceed? Or are the perils of faction not indeed, in many ways, even greater in the second case than they were before, since the minority is now more isolated and less able to defend itself in the legislative forum?

Once one starts down the slippery slope, one cannot stop, at least without a theory. Intellectually, we must conclude that much of the impetus behind legislative behavior is to induce forced exchanges—to take from some people more than they get in exchange, in order to provide benefits to those who happen to control the political levers. To some extent this is unavoidable, since we need a system of collective controls in order to operate the police, the courts, the national defense, and so on. And opportunities for abuse in government operations are inseparable from that collective need.

The theory of constitutionalism, as I understand it, tries to find a way to minimize the sum of the abuses that stem from legislative greed on the one hand, and judicial incompetence on the other. There is, by and large, no third alternative to this sorry state of affairs. What I fear is wrong with Scalia's statement of the argument is this: By focusing exclusively on the defects he finds in the judicial part of the process, he tends to ignore the powerful defects that pervade the legislative part of the process. Our Constitution reflects a general distrust toward the political process of government—a high degree of risk aversion. That is why it wisely spreads the powers of government among different institutions through a system of checks and balances. To provide no (or at least no effective) check on the legislature's power to regulate economic liberties is to concentrate power in ways that are inconsistent with the need to diversify risk. To allow courts to strike down legislation, but never to pass it, helps to control political abuse without undermining the distinctive features of the separate branches of government. Once we realize that all human institutions (being peopled by people) are prey to error, the only thing we can hope to do is to minimize those errors so that the productive activities of society can go forward as little hampered as possible.

Thus far I have been discussing general political theory: How is it that one would want to organize a constitution? But we do not have to talk about constitutions in the round and in the abstract. We have an actual constitution, and since it is a written one, we can check to see how it handles the particular problem of protecting economic liberties.

To listen to my colleague—and to the many other advocates of judicial restraint—one would almost think that the Constitution contained only the following kinds of provisions: those organizing a judiciary, a legislature, and an executive; and those providing for separation of powers, checks and balances, and so on. All those devices—efforts to divide and conquer the governing power—are efforts to limit the abuses of factions. But they are not the only provisions our Constitution contains. It also contains many broad and powerful clauses designed to limit the jurisdiction of both federal and state governments. The commerce clause, at least in its original conception, comes to mind. Other clauses are designed to limit what the states and the federal government can do within the scope of their admitted powers. These include the eminent domain clause (which always bound the federal government and since the Civil War amendments has bound the states as well), the contracts clause, the privileges and immunities clause found both in the original Constitution and the Fourteenth Amendment, the equal protection clause, and due process.

These provisions are not curlicues on the margins of the document; they are not without force or consequence. They are provisions designed to preserve definite boundaries between public and private ordering. Take the question of minimum wages. The principle of freedom of contract—that parties should be free to set wage terms as they see fit—is, given the contracts clause, on a collision course with that sort of legislative regulation of the economy. So it is with the eminent domain question discussed above. Many of the particular provisions of the Constitution are designed to deal with the very kinds of questions that political theory indicates to be sources of our enormous uneasiness and distrust of the legislative process.

The next question is, how have these constitutional provisions been interpreted in actual practice? A key element is the "rational basis" test, which holds that so long as there is some "plausible" or "conceivable" justification for the challenged legislation, it is invulnerable to constitutional attack. Under the guise of this test, judges have decided that the last thing they will do is look hard and analytically at any political institution, at any legislative action, that regulates economic affairs. It turns out that Scalia's position, already stated even more forcefully by the Supreme Court itself, completely abandons the idea that serious intellectual discussion can yield right and wrong answers on matters of political organization and constitutional interpretation. Courts simply give up before they try, and embrace an appalling sort of ethical noncognitivism. Anything legislatures do is as good as anything else they might have done; we cannot decide what is right or wrong, so it is up to Congress and the states to determine the limitations of their own power—which, of course, totally subverts the original constitutional arrangement of limited government.

Part of the explanation for the judiciary's poor performance now becomes clear. When courts do not try, they cannot succeed. When they use transparent arguments to justify dubious legislation, they cannot raise the level of debate. When courts (following the lead of the Supreme Court) hold that the state has the right to say X, when they know X is wrong, they fritter away their own political authority on an indefensible cause.

But can matters ever be this clear? In some instances it has seemed that no conceivable interpretation of the constitutional text could generate or justify the results that the Supreme Court has been prepared to reach. Take its decision in *Hawaiian Housing Authority v. Midkiff* (1984). There is a good reason why the constitutional clause restricting the seizure of property by eminent domain contains a provision specifying that the seizure must be for public use. The last thing one needs a government for is to arrange a set of coerced transfers between A and B when voluntary markets can arrange the same transfers without the abuses of faction. For the most part, this means that when we want the government to take property, we want it to do so in order to generate a public good, some nonexclusive benefit, that a private market cannot generate. Legislation (like that challenged in *Midkiff*) that simply takes land and transfers it from landlords to tenants, or the reverse, constitutes the paradigmatic transaction that the eminent domain clause was designed to prohibit. So when the Court sustained the Hawaiian statute, it declared the central wrong to be perfectly legal. The justices stood the Constitution on its head. They said, in effect, that although the eminent domain clause must have been put there for some purpose, we cannot figure out what that purpose might be, so we might as well read it out of the document and act as if it had never existed.

The courts have shown the same pattern of behavior in other cases. For example, it seems clear today that they will no longer construe the police power to protect private contracts of any sort—even when those contracts complied with all applicable rules at the time of their formation. What does a clause that prohibits impairing the obligation of contracts mean? Today, it turns out (with only minor exaggeration) that a legislature can simply decide to nullify contractual provisions on the grounds that this legally imposed breach of contract makes one of the contracting parties better off than it was before. If that is the only test, then every contract is vulnerable to judicial nullification.

This judicial deference in the protection of economic rights has enormous costs. The moment courts allow all private rights to become unstable and subject to collective (legislative) determination, all of the general productive activities of society will have to take on a new form. People will no longer be able to plan private arrangements secure in the knowledge of their social protection. Instead, they will take the same attitude toward domestic investment that they take toward foreign investment. Assuming that their enterprise will be confiscated within a certain number of years, domestic investors will make only those investments with a high rate of return and short payout period, so that when they see confiscation coming, they will be able to run. To be sure, the probability of expropriation is greater in many foreign contracts than it is in the United States. But given our record of price controls and selective industry regulation, it is clear that the once great protections we enjoyed have been compromised, and for no desirable social goal.

I submit that this is not what we want legislatures to do. It is wrongheaded to argue that, because an auditor cannot hope to correct every abuse in the Defense Department's procurement policies, he should therefore refuse to go after the $5,000 coffee pot—or that because a judge cannot hope to correct every infringement of economic liberties, he should therefore refuse to go after large-lot zoning restrictions. There are many blatantly inappropriate statutes that cry out for a quick and easy kill. Striking them down puts no particular strain on the judiciary. To invalidate a statute, a judge need not make complex factual determinations or continually supervise large branches of the federal government. He need not take over school boards, try to run prisons or mental hospitals, or demand that Congress appropriate funds. He need only say that, in certain circumstances, the government cannot do something—period—while in other circumstances, it can, but must pay those people on whom it imposes a disproportionate burden.

Government exists, after all, because the market's ability to organize forced exchanges is limited. We need to collect taxes, to impose regulations, to assign rights and liabilities through a centralized process, but only for limited public purposes. Our guiding principle should derive from our Lockean tradition—a tradition that speaks about justice and natural rights, a tradition that understands the importance of the autonomy of the person, and respects it in religion, in speech, and in ordinary day-to-day affairs. When government wishes to encroach on those rights in order to discharge its collective functions, it must give all the individuals on whom it imposes its obligations a fair equivalent in exchange. It may be that it is not always possible to measure that equivalence. Possibly we cannot achieve the goal of full compensation and simultaneously provide the collective goods. I am prepared to debate at great length where the proper margins are with respect to the application of this general principle. What I am not prepared to say is that we can organize our society on the belief that the question I just posed is not worth asking. Consequently, when the government announces that it has provided a comparable benefit, courts should not take its word on faith, when everything in the record points indubitably to the opposite conclusion.

When one compares the original Constitution with the present state of judicial interpretation, the real issue becomes not how to protect the status quo, but what kinds of incremental adjustments should be made in order to shift the balance back toward the original design. On this question, we can say two things. First, at the very least, we do not want to remove what feeble protection still remains for economic liberties. Any further judicial abdication in this area will only invite further legislative intrigue and more irresponsible legislation. Yet recent Supreme Court decisions have tended to invite just that. Second, since courts are bound to some extent by a larger social reality, we cannot pretend that the New Deal never happened. Rather, we must strive to regain sight of the proper objectives of con-

343

stitutional government and the proper distribution of powers between the legislatures and the courts, so as to come up with the kinds of incremental adjustments that might help us to restore the proper constitutional balance.

Judicial restraint is fine when it keeps courts from intervening in areas where they have no business intervening. But the world always has two kinds of errors: the error of commission (type I) and the error of omission (type II). In the context of our discussion, type I error refers to the probability of judicial intervention to protect economic rights when such intervention is not justified by constitutional provisions. And type II error refers to the probability of forgoing judicial intervention to protect economic liberties when such intervention is justified. This second type of error—the failure to intervene when there is strong textual authority and constitutional theory—cannot be ignored.

What Scalia has, in effect, argued for is to minimize type I error. We run our system by being most afraid of intervention where it is not appropriate. My view is that we should minimize both types of error. One only has to read the opinions of the Supreme Court on economic liberties and property rights to realize that these opinions are intellectually incoherent and that some movement in the direction of judicial activism is clearly indicated. The only sensible disagreement is over the nature, the intensity, and the duration of the shift.

At this point, the division of power within the legal system is not in an advantageous equilibrium. If the judiciary continues on the path of self-restraint with respect to economic liberties, we will continue to suffer social and institutional losses that could have been reduced by the prudent judicial control that would result from taking the constitutional protections of economic liberties at their face value.

The Constitutional Protection of Economic Freedom

Paul Craig Roberts

A person born in one of the Western democracies before the turn of the century was born a private individual. He was born into a world where his existence was attested by his mere physical presence—without documents, forms, permits, licenses, orders, lists of currency carried in and out, identity cards, draft cards, ration cards, exit stamps, customs declarations, questionnaires, tax forms, reports in multiplicate, Social Security number, or other authentications of his being, birth, nationality, status, beliefs, creed or right to be, enter, leave, move about, work, trade, purchase, dwell. He was born into a world where a person could travel anywhere on the face of the earth, except Russia and Turkey, without need of a passport, visa, or identity card. He was born into a world of freedom of movement of people, money, and ideas. A confident 19th-century futurology predicted that the 20th century would find him freer still.

But by World War I, the world into which that person was born was already in decline. The period since then has been one of autonomy not of the individual, but of the state. He was born in a century that pulled down walls, and he lived out his life in the century of the wall builders. Whether made from iron, or from barbed wire, mine fields, and machine-gun towers, or from paper—the barbed wire of documents—20th-century walls are byproducts of the universal bureaucratization of life. In place of the 19th century's autonomous individual, to whom some romanticized that all things were permitted, we have the 20th century's autonomous state, to which, as Dostoevsky predicted and Lenin declared, all things *are* permitted.

Paul Craig Roberts was a distinguished fellow at the Cato Institute and is the John M. Olin Fellow at the Institute for Political Economy.
Cato Policy Report, May/June 1986

The private individual is a recent and precarious invention. A central question of our time is whether he is a mere momentary caprice of history.

Many people take private individuals for granted, and they will find what I am saying farfetched. But private individuals do not exist in the Soviet Union, where the claims of the state are total and even art and literature must be subservient. Neither do private individuals exist in many of the emerging nations, where change consists only of replacing the subordination of the person to his tribe or caste with subordination to the modern activist state.

The Private-Property Revolution

Private individuals did not exist in ancient Egypt, and they were not prevalent in the Europe of the Middle Ages. Private individuals were the creation of the social revolution that created private property. This social revolution and the reaction to it comprise the social, economic, political, and intellectual history of Western civilization from the 12th century through the present. The revolution began with the Inclosures in the 12th century and attained its greatest flowering in the 19th century. Prior to the appearance of private property and private individuals, there were only the rulers and the ruled, the lords and the serfs.

A serf was a person who did not own his own labor. Although he was not himself owned by another—that is, he could not be bought and sold like a slave—the feudal state had rights over the serf's labor. A serf owed a certain amount of his working time to the state. Over time and regions this obligation seems to have averaged about one-third of a serf's working life.

In turn, the serf had use-rights in the land. The social revolution that abolished the serf's use-rights in the land abolished the state's use-rights in the serf's labor. The social revolution that created private property in land and capital created private property in labor. Serfdom disappeared as wages appeared. As Karl Marx recognized, "Wages and private property are identical."

Reaction to this great social revolution began immediately, and over most of the course of the revolution, reaction was identified with conservatism. But what was really happening was that as different groups—landowners, merchants, capitalists, and laborers—

attained specific private-property rights in land, trade, capital, and labor, respectively, each group had an incentive to gain control of the state as a means of advancing its specific property rights at the expense of others. A "reactionary" was merely whoever had control of the state at a given point in time and was defending his interests against the interests of others. As different groups in different times gained control of the state, each in turn passed from the offensive to the defensive and automatically became conservatives, which meant they wanted to conserve their interests. But no group trusted the state as such; no group felt its property rights secure unless it controlled the state. Each group identified progress with the advancement of its own property rights.

Historians have often confused this strife among property interests with an alleged reaction of property against democracy. But whichever property group was in power, it tended to see democracy as the right of others to vote away its property. Democracy was thus limited to voting by members of the groups whose property interests were dominant. This greatly limited the power of government because any claim to act in the public interest was quickly recognized for what it was—a cover for the dominant private interests.

Although each property group had an accurate assessment of the threat of government to its interests, each group mistakenly saw its interests as divergent from the interests of others. However, despite the strife among its beneficiaries, the social revolution of private property was inexorable, and the real reactionaries were swept aside.

Marx's Counterrevolution

But the revolution was never quite completed. Just as, through the influence of Adam Smith and others, the various property groups began to realize their common interests and unite against government per se, Karl Marx began a new counterattack against the ongoing revolution. Marx knew exactly what he was reacting to: private individuals. According to Marx, man is individualized only through the creation of private property: "Man originally appears as a generic being, a tribal being, a herd animal." Private property "makes the herd animal superfluous and dissolves the herd."

According to Marx, the private individual is rootless, powerless, alienated, and unfree. As an individual actor, he must bear the con-

347

sequences of his own action; yet he has no control over his life because he is affected by, but has no control over, the actions of others. Thus, the divergent actions of private individuals produce consequences beyond the control of all, and a private individual is the victim of his own individuality. He only appears to be free.

Marx's solution was to do away with the private individual and reduce him to a herd animal. Herd animals do not act as individuals and therefore do not have to bear uncontrolled consequences of private actions. Instead, they act as a community, or the state acts for the community.

Marx's counterattack provided the basis for political movements in the 20th century that have rolled back economic freedom. As Marx and his followers translated his argument for the masses, it came out: "It is not government that exploits, but private property." To Lenin, to Mussolini, to Hitler, to European socialists and statists of all hues and to their counterparts in the United States, this meant that progress could be realized only through government. The strife this century between the various statists has overshadowed their agreement that government action is the instrument of progress.

The Success of the Reactionaries

The success of the reactionary forces in this century can be summed up in simple economic terms. By 1929, government in the United States had established a claim to 12 percent of the national income. By 1960, the government's claim had grown to 33 percent. By 1984, it had expanded to 42.5 percent. In relative terms, the position of a U.S. citizen today is worse than that of a medieval serf who owed the state only one-third of his working time.

The statists owe their success partly to capital accumulation and technological change, which raised national income over time. If people are better off in absolute terms, they may not notice that they are worse off in relative terms. But statists owe their success mainly to the power of reaction in the 20th century. It is striking that it has required little more than a half century to reverse a social revolution that has been in motion since the 12th century. When a "progressive" says that we cannot repeal the 20th century, all he is saying is that 20th-century statist reactionaries have repealed the 19th and 18th centuries and have us on the road back to serfdom.

Many may reject this parallel. They may say that the United States has a democratic government controlled by the people and that high taxes and big government merely reflect the voters' demands for public goods in the public interest. Such an argument is reassuring but problematical; the income tax, for example, was voted in under one guise and retained under another. Furthermore, it was the action of a past generation. For us it is an inherited obligation, as were feudal dues for others, and it is seen that way by the Internal Revenue Service.

When the U.S. government brought in the income tax in 1914, it gave assurances that it would fall only on the rich. Initially, the personal income-tax burden rested on only 357,515 people—less than one-half of 1 percent of the population—whose incomes were much greater than average. The tax rates ranged from 1 percent to 7 percent. Only income in excess of $186,500 (in today's dollars) encountered the first surtax bracket of 2 percent, and the top tax bracket of 7 percent was encountered only by income in excess of $4.6 million (in today's dollars). The personal income tax soon found its way into the lower brackets as income thresholds were lowered and tax rates were raised. The growth of the personal income tax can be summarized succinctly: between 1914 and 1982, the population grew 137 percent but the number of individual tax returns grew by 26,666 percent.

For the past decade and a half, taxes in the United States have grown much faster than wages or prices. From 1970 to 1983, the average wage rose 148 percent, the consumer price index rose 157 percent, and the tax burden rose 241 percent. The 241 percent growth in the tax bite exceeded the 233 percent growth in the total production of goods and services (GNP) and the 226 percent growth in total national income. Taxes far outpace the growth in real income. During 1984, federal receipts grew by 12.4 percent. The entire economy grew by 7.2 percent, and 3.9 percent of that growth was a result of inflation rather than an actual increase in the production of goods and services. Last year, U.S. taxpayers paid $151.4 billion more in taxes than they spent on the three basic necessities of food, clothing, and housing.

All of us have been born to the statist gospels. As recent experience under the Reagan administration has shown, clamors for tax reduction are translated into proposals for tax reform, which are further transformed into proposals for securing more revenues for government.

Constitutional Protection

Even in a real democracy there is a great deal of propaganda in the term "self rule." Wise people know this, and they endeavor to protect themselves from their government by constraining it with a constitution. The U.S. Constitution provides protections for civil liberties and economic freedoms.

Unfortunately, the guarantees of economic liberty have not held up as well as the guarantees of civil liberty. Over time, the courts have emasculated many of the economic guarantees; and regulation and control of the economy have become commonplace as barriers to government growth have fallen. The constitutional amendment that made possible the personal income tax in 1914 provided the government with a source of enormous revenues. This mechanism, together with the government's assumed regulatory powers, has produced such a strong central power that who controls the government is often a matter of economic life or death.

Many people, especially intellectuals, mistakenly believe that the encroachment of the state on economic freedom is synonymous with an increase in economic justice. They have this illusion because they believe, perhaps erroneously, that whereas the feudal state redistributed income from the poor to the rich, the modern democracy redistributes income from the rich to the poor. They overlook the fact that in neither conception of the state does the individual own the fruits of his own labor.

Any doctrine of progress that depends merely upon which income class is being exploited suffers from serious moral deficiencies. Indeed, the progressive income tax—the mainstay of "economic justice"—seems almost atavistic in permitting discrimination on the basis of size and source of income and marital status when all other forms of personal discrimination, such as race, sex, and age, are strictly prohibited.

It would be a mistake to interpret the position taken here as one of cynicism and hopelessness. It is no more cynical than the position taken by the Founding Fathers of the U.S. Constitution, who knew that government, whatever its form, is by nature rapacious and that even a limited government must be bound by a carefully crafted constitution. They went wrong only in not anticipating the income tax.

In the late 18th century, when the U.S. Constitution was drawn up, the idea of an income tax would have been dismissed as feudal. The notion that a constitutional democracy would enserf its citizenry with an income tax was too farfetched to warrant specific constitutional protection. Nevertheless, although the income tax was not banned specifically by name and by constitutional provision, efforts to enact an income tax prior to 1914 were ruled unconstitutional, and it required a constitutional amendment in the United States to reestablish a feudal relationship between the people and the state.

Taxes and the Constitution

Today, having witnessed constitutional governments grow in size and power far beyond the scope of the absolute monarchies of the past, we have learned that taxation should be treated explicitly as a constitutional issue. An income tax should be explicitly prohibited on the grounds that it is a direct violation of economic liberty. At the same time, the demands of the modern rapacious state for revenues must be acknowledged. The Constitution should specify both the form and the amount of taxation that are permissible. I would recommend a uniform value-added or expenditure tax, and I would specify that at no time could the revenues of the state exceed 20 percent of the national income.

Such constitutional protections do not preclude the redistribution of income. When governments are large, as modern governments are, income redistribution takes place primarily through the expenditure side of the budget. It is certainly possible to design government spending programs or income-transfer and income-support programs such that only the poor can qualify for them. A proportionate tax paid by all but spent only on the poor is redistributive. Indeed, even a regressive income tax can, through the expenditure side of the budget, result in the redistribution of income from rich to poor. Therefore, there is no honest reason for the ideological left to resist the constitutional protection of economic liberty.

Indeed, there is every economic reason for the left to support it. During most of our history, we had no income tax and no social safety net. Nevertheless, we absorbed wave after wave of penniless immigrants while the poverty level in the United States simultaneously declined. Today, we are being overrun by illegal aliens, who, not being citizens, do not qualify for welfare benefits or income-redistribution programs. They come and work and prosper. They have

351

gained enough political clout to have bills introduced in Congress that would grant them citizenship. Sooner or later, these bills will pass. There are millions of illegal aliens in the United States, and none of them have found income redistribution necessary for their success. The people who cannot get anywhere seem to be that part of the native population that is born into welfare programs.

Of course, a government could always evade a constitutional limit on revenues by running budget deficits and financing them by borrowing or printing money. Therefore, it could be appropriate to constitutionally limit expenditures in addition to revenues and to specify that borrowing be limited to capital projects that add to productive social investment.

A constitution that prohibited the direct taxation of income and placed a limit on the government's claim to the national income would be a wondrous document. It would displace the U.S. Constitution as the model for the free world. It would revive the spirit and culture of freedom everywhere in the worn-out West, and it would infuse the country so blessed with principles that could make it the greatest nation on earth.

National Emergency and the Erosion of Private Property Rights

Robert Higgs and Charlotte Twight

Only an emergency can justify repression.

—Justice Brandeis

The scope of private property rights in the United States has been greatly reduced during the 20th century. Much of the reduction occurred episodically, as governmental officials took control of economic affairs during national emergencies—mainly wars, depressions, and actual or threatened strikes in critical industries. Derogations from private rights that occurred during national emergencies often remained after the crises had passed. A "ratchet" took hold. People adjusted first their actions, then their thinking, to accommodate themselves to emergency governmental controls.. Later, lacking the previous degree of public support, private property rights failed to regain their pre-crisis scope.

Emergency restrictions of private property rights are by no means of concern only to historians of the growth of governmental power. Today, emergency restrictions limit many private rights, and many more sweeping restrictions could be lawfully imposed at the President's discretion. The possibility is real. Like several presidents before him, Ronald Reagan has dipped repeatedly into the government's reservoir of emergency economic powers. The potential exists for the greatly expanded use—and abuse—of such powers.

Robert Higgs is editor of the *Independent Review* and author of *Crisis and Leviathan*. Charlotte Twight is a professor of economics at Boise State University, a lawyer, and the author of *Dependent on D.C.: The Rise of Federal Control over the Lives of Ordinary Americans*.

Cato Journal, Vol. 6, No. 3 (Winter 1987)

Presuppositions

Rulers prefer more power to less, but in a liberal democracy the rulers are constrained by institutions that sustain private rights. Specifically, private property rights place the power of resource allocation in the hands of private citizens, thereby limiting the capacity of governmental officials to shape the economy. Governmental officials have interests of their own, which are not necessarily representative of or even in harmony with the interests of people outside government. Therefore, the rulers and the ruled normally struggle in various ways to determine who will control the use of resources. The greater the scope of private property rights, the more limited is the capacity of the rulers to achieve the ends they prefer at the expense of those preferred by the citizenry.

But citizens rely on the government for certain essential services, especially for the maintenance of social order and the protection of life and property; this dependence episodically creates opportunities for governments to take over previously private rights. If national emergencies did not just happen from time to time, governmental officials would be tempted to create them. In a genuine emergency, citizens are exceptionally willing to surrender their rights to governmental officials who offer plausible promises that they will restore social order, national security, or economic prosperity by wielding extraordinary powers. War, as Randolph Bourne aptly expressed it, is "the health of the state." Business depressions also promote robust government, as do nationwide strikes in strategic industries, especially those involving essential means of transportation or communication. Under modern ideological conditions—that is, if people insist that governments "do something" to rectify perceived socio-economic problems—national emergencies invariably witness a transfer of economic rights from private citizens to governmental officials.

For several reasons, rights taken over by governmental officials during an emergency are unlikely to revert fully to their previous holders when normal times return. First, during the emergency the government learns how to operate its command-and-control system more successfully; that is, how to get necessary information, how to resolve competing claims on resources, and how to placate and respond to the complaints of politically influential aggrieved parties. Second, the imposition of a less-than comprehensive system of controls—for example, regulating the economy but not the exercise of

354

religious or political rights—discredits the conservative all-or-nothing warnings that normally inhibit governmental takeovers of private economic rights by representing them as steps toward totalitarianism. Third, many people discover, not only in the government's bureaus but in the more regulated "private" sector, that the controlled economy offers its own characteristic avenues to personal success. Those who travel happily along these avenues naturally come to regard the entire system in which they thrive as essentially desirable. Some who adapt only out of necessity are eventually won over. Of course, during the emergency the government does all it can to justify its exercise of new powers, trumpeting the necessity and virtues of its controls, belittling the attendant costs and inequities, and defaming those who criticize its policies. Such propaganda is especially likely to hit its targets during a crisis, when the dogs of patriotism howl at their loudest and citizens rally more closely around the flag. Opponents of the government's emergency measures can be stigmatized as "slackers" or "draft-dodgers" or worse; in extreme cases, they may be imprisoned, deported, or deprived of normal civil liberties.

A great emergency, therefore, produces a ratchet: At an early stage the government, responding to an urgent and widespread insistence that it "do something," takes over rights previously held by private citizens; when the crisis wanes, public attitudes—the dominant ideology, some would say—have been so altered by the experience of governmental controls and the pervasive adaptations of behavior and thinking to those controls that public support for the recovery of the private rights is insufficient to produce their full restoration. While the hard residues of crisis-spawned laws, administrative agencies, and constitutional pronouncements are important, ultimately the most significant consequence of the emergency experience is the ideological change it fosters. As William Graham Sumner wrote, "it is not possible to experiment with a society and just drop the experiment whenever we choose. The experiment enters into the life of the society and never can be got out again."

How Emergencies Eroded Private Rights Historically

At the turn of the 20th century, Americans enjoyed a wide scope of private property rights. The prevailing ideology of both elites and masses greatly emphasized economic liberty. As James Bryce observed, the typical American regarded the "right to the enjoyment of what he has earned" as "primordial and sacred." Most Americans believed that all governmental authorities "ought to be strictly limited" and "the less of government the better."

Federal officials and judges typically acted in conformity with the belief that government ought to be confined to protective functions, refraining from redistributionist policies and leaving citizens free to conduct their economic affairs as they pleased. There were exceptions, of course, but they only highlight how limited the government, especially the federal government, was as a rule. In *Allgeyer v. Louisiana* (1897), the Supreme Court articulated the prevailing sentiment, declaring that the Constitution protects

> not only the right of the citizen to be free from the mere physical restraint of his person . . . but . . . the right of the citizen to be free in the enjoyment of all his faculties; to be free to use them in all lawful ways; to live and work where he will; to earn his livelihood by any lawful calling; to pursue any livelihood or avocation, and for that purpose to enter into all contracts which may be proper, necessary, and essential to his carrying out [these purposes] to a successful conclusion.

When citizens were guaranteed such extensive freedom of contract, governments had little ability to fix prices and wages, restrict hours or other conditions of employment, compel collective bargaining, regulate the locations of enterprises, or set aside the terms of private agreements; nor did governments have much justification for increasing the burden of taxation. Although governments, especially at the state and local levels, increased their economic functions somewhat during the late 19th and early 20th centuries and, more importantly, the dominant ideology gradually became more sympathetic to more-than-minimal government, the economy remained essentially a market system as late as 1914.

In a violent break with American tradition, private property rights were suppressed on a wide scale during World War I. In 1916, in anticipation of a future state of war, Congress granted the President emergency powers to seize materials, plants, and transport systems. During the year and a half of official U.S. belligerency that followed, the federal government took over the railroad, ocean shipping, telephone, and telegraph industries; suspended the gold standard and controlled all international exchanges of goods and financial assets; commandeered hundreds of manufacturing plants; entered into massive economic enterprises on its own account in such varied departments as shipbuilding, wheat and sugar trading, and building construction; lent huge sums to businesses directly or indirectly; regulated the private issuance of securities; established official priorities for the use of transport facilities, food, fuel, and many other goods; fixed the prices of dozens of important commodities; intervened in hundreds of labor disputes; and conscripted nearly three million men into the army. In short, the government extensively attenuated or destroyed private rights, creating what some contemporaries called "war socialism." The Supreme Court did nothing to restrain the government's suppression of private rights; evidently, constitutional war powers covered all cases.

Although most private rights were restored after the war, not all were. Tax rates remained higher, the tax structure was more "progressive," and the income tax became a much more important source of federal revenues relative to traditional consumption taxes. The Transportation Act of 1920, by which the government relinquished its emergency control of the railroads, came close to nationalizing them; government remained in the ocean-shipping business; and the War Finance Corporation episodically participated in the credit markets until 1925. Most significantly, the war left a legacy of ideological change. As Bernard Baruch observed, the war experience convinced many prominent businessmen and others that "government direction of the economy need not be inefficient or undemocratic, and suggested that in time of danger it was imperative."

The next "time of danger" was occasioned not by war but by the Great Depression, a national catastrophe that Justice Brandeis called "an emergency more serious than war." After three years of widespread bankruptcies, foreclosures, and bank failures, and of rapidly falling income and massively rising unemployment, it seemed that the market economy would never recover. All classes of Americans increasingly clamored for relief.

Recalling how the government had wielded sweeping emergency powers to manage the economy during the war, many politically influential people believed that similar governmental controls could be used effectively to "fight" the depression. In 1933, the federal government launched a fleet of emergency measures: huge work-relief projects; a program to cartelize virtually all industries; abandonment of the gold standard and prohibition of private domestic monetary transactions in gold; price and production controls in agriculture; detailed regulation of securities markets; extensive federal intrusion into labor markets and union-management relations; federal production and sale of electrical power; and, before the New Deal had spent itself in 1938, a multitude of federal insurance and credit programs, Social Security pensions and welfare payments, the minimum wage, national unemployment insurance, and many other forms of governmental intervention in the market economy.

For a while the Supreme Court resisted. The National Industrial Recovery Act and the first Agricultural Adjustment Act, centerpieces of the early New Deal, were declared unconstitutional. But the Court was of two minds. In 1934, in *Nebbia v. New York*, it upheld an emergency-inspired state law fixing milk prices and imposing criminal sanctions on those who transacted at lower prices. The Court ruled (1934) that "neither property rights nor contract rights are absolute." In 1935, in the *Norman* case, sustaining the government's crisis-induced abrogation of the gold standard, the Court put private contractual rights in a clearly inferior position (1935): "There is no constitutional ground for denying to the Congress the power expressly to prohibit and invalidate contracts although previously made, and valid when made, when they interfere with the carrying out of the [monetary] policy it is free to adopt."

After vacillating during 1934–36, sometimes sustaining and sometimes striking down the government's unprecedented derogations from private property rights, the Court caved in completely in 1937. Since then it has maintained that virtually any state or federal governmental interference with private property rights is constitutional. Only a law that is manifestly arbitrary and lacking any imaginable relation to a public purpose will be disallowed. In a bloodless revolution, the U.S. Supreme Court overturned constitutional protections of private property rights that had existed for 150 years.

The justices were only registering the ideological transformation going on around them. The Great Depression deeply discredited longstanding beliefs in individualism, private property rights, free markets, and limited government. The New Deal gave desperate people money, jobs, and protection from market competition, for which they were grateful. More importantly, it taught many people, including a new generation of Americans who had no personal experience with anything else, to value collectivist policies and governmental promises of economic security.

Drawing on the collectivist programs and sentiments of World War I and the New Deal, the federal government during World War II built an unprecedented apparatus of economic control. Political scientist Clinton L. Rossiter concluded: "Of all the time-honored Anglo-Saxon liberties, the freedom of contract took the worst beating in the war." Governmental authorities drafted 10 million men for service in the armed forces; allocated strategic materials; established priorities for the use of transport, food, fuel, and other goods; commandeered plants and sometimes whole industries; fixed prices and rents; rationed many consumer goods; and built and operated entire new industries. In short, the free market virtually disappeared during 1942–45.

While private property rights were being suppressed, the Supreme Court only approved. As Justice Douglas wrote in *Bowles v. Willingham* (1944), a case involving rent controls, "where Congress has provided for judicial review after the regulations or orders have been made effective it has done all that due process under the war emergency requires." But Justice Roberts, dissenting in a related case, *Yakus v. United States* (1944), correctly described the judicial review as "a solemn farce." The government simply did as it pleased, showing no regard for private property rights. As Rossiter commented, "the Court, too, likes to win wars." Even when the government herded some 110,000 persons of Japanese descent, two-thirds of them U.S. citizens, into concentration camps, the Court stood aside, declaring the peremptory imprisonment of these innocent persons "in the crisis of war" to be "not wholly beyond the limits of the Constitution" (*Hirabayashi v. United States,* 1943). Where, one wonders, *are* the constitutional limits on governmental invasion of private rights during emergencies? During World War II, not even the most elementary private rights could withstand the government's determination to exercise emergency powers.

Enduring legacies of the war include the Employment Act of 1946, which committed the federal government to a policy of ongoing macroeconomic management; the Taft-Hartley Act of 1947, which preserved many of the federal powers first stipulated in the War Labor Disputes Act of 1943; and the Selective Service Act of 1948, which extended into peacetime the military conscription by which the government had coercively obtained the bulk of its military manpower at below-market rates during the war. The emergency rationale held sway. As a congressman said during the debate on the peacetime draft bill, "What we propose to do today is, under ordinary conditions, contrary to our traditions. . . . We are not living in an ordinary time. . . . We are living in a world of fear, of chaos, of uncertainty. . . ."

Most significantly, as Calvin B. Hoover observed, the war experience "conditioned [businessmen] to accept a degree of governmental intervention and control after the war which they had deeply resented prior to it." Even under the pro-business Eisenhower administration, no serious attempt was made to overthrow the economic controls inherited from past emergencies. Having so greatly adjusted their actions and their thinking to the emergency suppression of private property rights, most Americans seemed to fear a return to a free market regime more than they feared the denial of private rights, actual and potential, under the postwar politico-economic arrangements.

How Emergency Powers Continue to Be Exercised

Until the late 1970s, unrevoked presidential declarations of national emergency, left over from long-past crises, continued to sustain extraordinary governmental authority. As late as 1976 the national emergencies declared by Roosevelt in 1933 and by Truman in 1950 had not been terminated. After the end of the Korean War, even though economic and political conditions in the United States were often as normal as possible in an age of Cold War and nuclear weapons, the government continued to use a fictitious emergency rationale to augment its statutory power—and thereby to diminish the scope of private property rights.

Few people worried about the emergency-spawned powers until the Nixon years. President Nixon himself added to the perpetual official crisis by declaring national emergencies in order to deal with the postal workers' strike in 1970 and the balance-of-payments "crisis" in 1971. These declarations remained unrevoked when their precipitating crises passed. Only when the Watergate scandal and Nixon's impoundment of congressionally authorized funds engendered widespread fear of an imperial presidency did Congress begin to investigate seriously the web of governmental authority spun on the pillars of unrevoked executive declarations of national emergency.

In 1973, the Senate created a Special Committee on the Termination of the National Emergency (subsequently redesignated the Special Committee on National Emergencies and Delegated Emergency Powers) to investigate the matter and to propose reforms. Ascertaining the continued existence of four presidential declarations of national emergency, the Special Committee reported:

> These proclamations give force to 470 provisions of Federal law. . . . taken together, [they] confer enough authority to rule the country without reference to normal constitutional processes. Under the powers delegated by these statutes, the President may: seize property; organize and control the means of production; seize commodities; assign military forces abroad; institute martial law; seize and control all transportation and communication; regulate the operation of private enterprise; restrict travel; and, in a plethora of particular ways, control the lives of all American citizens.

Yet, there was no statutory definition of what constitutes an emergency; as with the fabled emperor's clothes, the assertion could belie the reality. As its investigation proceeded, the committee repeatedly voiced concern about both the longevity of the claimed emergencies and the use of a single national emergency decree to effectuate widely scattered emergency powers wholly unrelated to the emergency at hand.

Despite post-Watergate concerns about emergency executive powers, those powers live on. President Carter and President Reagan have declared national emergencies repeatedly to impose sweeping economic restrictions on the dealings of Americans with citizens of other nations, including Iran, Nicaragua, South Africa, and Libya. Most recently, invoking the National Emergencies Act (NEA) and the International Emergency Economic Powers Act (IEEPA), President Reagan declared a national emergency to warrant a prohibition of the economic activities of Americans in Libya and ordered all U.S. citizens residing in Libya to leave or face criminal sanctions. Also under claim of national emergency, President Reagan recently used the IEEPA to sustain an important trade restriction, the Export Administration Act, for more than a year during which Congress had allowed it to expire.

The Libyan episode is particularly revealing of the fundamental issues involved in recent emergency declarations. Although the President and the popular press invite us to view the restrictions as impinging on the Libyan government, in reality the emergency decrees restrict the rights of American citizens. In an Executive Order 12543 dated January 7, 1986, President Reagan explicitly forbade U.S. citizens to engage in

(a) The import into the United States of any goods or services of Libyan origin . . .;

(b) The export to Libya of any goods, technology (including technical data or other information) or services from the United States . . .;

(c) Any transaction by a United States person relating to transportation to or from Libya; . . . or the sale in the United States by any person holding authority under the Federal Aviation Act of any transportation by air which includes any stop in Libya;

(d) The purchase by any United States person of goods for export from Libya to any country;

(e) The performance by any United States person of any contract in support of an industrial or other commercial or governmental project in Libya;

(f) The grant or extension of credits or loans by any United States person to the Government of Libya, its instrumentalities and controlled entities;

(g) Any transaction by a United States person relating to travel by any United States citizen or permanent resident alien to Libya, or to activities by any such person within Libya, after the date of this Order, other than transactions necessary to effect such person's departure from Libya . . .; and

(h) Any transaction by any United States person which evades or avoids, or has the purpose of evading or avoiding, any of the prohibitions set forth in this Order.

Whatever one's views of the events that prompted the President's actions, one cannot escape the conclusion that the economic activities of *Americans*, not Libyans, are controlled directly by the emergency restrictions. It became evident that the valuable investments of Americans in plants and equipment stood a good chance of being relinquished to the Libyan government, without compensation, by the terms of the President's executive order.

Caught in its own snare, the Reagan administration changed the program, making exceptions to and deferrals of its original orders in hopes of avoiding the enormous financial gains to Qadhafi's regime that rigid enforcement of the edicts would create. While observing the government's confused thrashing, one might well have reflected on who was supposed to suffer as a result of the emergency economic sanctions and on whether or not such suffering could reasonably be expected to result from such restrictions of American rights. These events prompt one to wonder about what events might provoke a charismatic President to impose sanctions that selectively restrict the property rights of an unpopular subgroup of Americans—such as the Japanese-Americans in 1942—under the pretext of emergency.

The Constitutionality of Emergency Powers

Are emergency powers constitutional? The short answer is yes. One sense of "constitutional" is whatever the government makes a practice of doing. Since the federal government took emergency action to head off the threatened railroad strike in 1916, it has repeatedly exercised emergency powers. To conduct a practice for 70 years is to establish that it is not simply an aberration.

Another meaning of "constitutional" is whatever accords with the U.S. Constitution. Ours is a written document that completely enumerates the powers that may be exercised by the federal government. The Tenth Amendment guarantees that powers not explicitly assigned to the central government nor prohibited to the state governments belong to the states and the people. The Constitution makes no provision for the exercise of emergency powers. Evidently, it was meant to govern the actions of federal authorities in foul weather as well as in fair. How, then, has it been possible for federal officials to exercise—eventually as a matter of routine—extraordinary powers for which the Constitution provides no warrant?

The answer lies in a third meaning of "constitutional"; that is, whatever the Supreme Court allows. The Court has ruled on several occasions on the permissibility of emergency powers; these decisions constitute a melancholy chapter of constitutional history, a record of evasion and capitulation of the judicial function against which many justices on the minority side have objected.

The first modern ruling, still a leading precedent, was handed down in *Wilson v. New* (1917), a case arising from a challenge to the government's emergency appeasement of the railroad unions during a railroad strike in 1916. By a 5–4 margin, the justices upheld the government's actions. Speaking for the Court, Chief Justice White argued that the Adamson Act, establishing the eight-hour workday for railroad employees, was a legitimate exercise of the legislative will "to the end that no individual dispute or difference might bring ruin to the vast interests concerned in the movement of interstate commerce. . . ." The dispute, he observed, "if not remedied, would leave the public helpless, the whole people ruined and all the homes of the land submitted to a danger of the most serious character."

The Chief Justice repeatedly emphasized the gravity of the circumstances prompting the Adamson Act: "the impediment and destruction of interstate commerce which was threatened" and "the infinite injury to the public interest which was imminent." Oddly, he took pains to *deny* that the emergency *per se* gave rise to the government's authority under the act: "although an emergency may not call into life a [constitutional] power which has never lived," he reasoned, "nevertheless emergency may afford a reason for the exertion of a living power already enjoyed." In view of the unprecedented character of the government's actions, White's distinction was a most delicate one; not everyone could see the sense of it.

The dissenting justices declared that emergency conditions, however threatening, could not excuse the denial of constitutional rights. In their view, the Constitution had been adopted to protect private property *especially* under such conditions. "The suggestion," wrote Justice Pitney, that the Adamson Act "was passed to prevent a threatened strike . . . amounts to no more than saying that it was enacted to take care of an emergency. But an emergency can neither create a power nor excuse a defiance of the limitations upon the powers of the Government." Despite their strong arguments, the dissenters could do no more than register their dissatisfaction. The majority's curious doctrine, that emergencies may call forth extraordinary powers from some previously untapped yet still legitimate reservoir, carried the day and established the precedent.

A broad construction of the war powers excused the government's suppression of private rights during World War I, but legal challenges persisted into the postwar era. In the spring of 1921, the Supreme Court ruled that a rent-control ordinance that Congress had imposed in late 1919 in the District of Columbia—"its provisions were made necessary by emergencies growing out of the war"—"was not, in the prevailing circumstances, an unconstitutional restriction of the owner's dominion and right of contract or a taking of his property for a use not public." The ruling, which emphasized the temporariness of the disputed rent controls, seemed to the dissenters to open the door to all kinds of governmental restrictions of the private right of contract. "As a power in government," wrote Justice McKenna, "if it exist at all, it is perennial and universal. . . . necessarily, if one contract can be disregarded in the public interest every contract can be. . . . other exigencies may come to the Government making necessary other appeals." Indeed they would.

Early in 1934 the Court issued what is perhaps the classic decision on the emergency powers of government and the protection to be afforded or withheld from private property rights during economic crises (*Home Building and Loan Association v. Blaisdell*, 1934). The case involved a legislative moratorium—one of 25 such state laws enacted during 1932–33—on mortgage foreclosures. A statute approved by the government of Minnesota on April 18, 1933, under ominous pressures by indebted farmers, declared an economic emergency and extended temporarily the period during which creditors were prevented from foreclosing on and selling mortgaged real estate. At the discretion of local courts the owners of foreclosed property could be allowed up to two years to redeem their property. During the extended redemption period the mortgagor was required to pay the mortgagee what amounted to rent, but the mortgagee was deprived of the right to take control over the property. The Home Building and Loan Association of Minneapolis challenged the law as an unconstitutional impairment of the obligation of contract. Its position was upheld by a county court but overturned by the state supreme court; the case then came before the U.S. Supreme Court on appeal.

The main issue was whether emergency conditions justified the exercise of otherwise unconstitutional powers by a state government. The most compelling precedents for an affirmative answer were *Wilson v. New* and the 1921 rent-control cases. The force of the rent-control decisions was uncertain, however, as Justice Holmes had previously declared that "they went to the very verge of the law" (*Pennsylvania Coal Company v. Mahon*, 1921). Counsel for the state of Minnesota conceded that "in normal times and under normal conditions" the state's moratorium law would be unconstitutional. "But these," he urged, "are not normal times nor normal conditions. A great economic emergency has arisen in which the State has been compelled to invoke the police power. . . ." The justices would have to decide again whether or not an emergency altered the protections of the Constitution and, if so, what qualified as an emergency. Their decision could have wide repercussions, because virtually all of the important federal statutes enacted during Franklin D. Roosevelt's first 100 days had appealed to emergency conditions, evidently with an eye toward the Supreme Court.

Although the Court upheld the Minnesota moratorium law and by implication all the others, it failed to clarify whether or not an emergency justified setting aside the constitutional protection of private property rights. Perhaps the most important aspect of the decision is simply that state infringement of contractual obligations was validated. Paradoxically, however, the Court *denied* that it had sustained the Minnesota statute because of emergency. "Emergency does not create power," said Chief Justice Hughes, speaking for the five-man majority. "Emergency does not increase granted power or remove or diminish the restrictions imposed upon power granted or reserved." What could be plainer? Yet, wrote Hughes, referring to the slippery doctrine enunciated in *Wilson v. New*, "while emergency does not create power, emergency may furnish the occasion for the exercise of power." The prohibition of governmental intervention guaranteed by the Contracts Clause, he added, "is not an absolute one and is not to be read with literal exactness like a mathematical formula. . . . The economic interests of the State may justify the exercise of its continuing and dominant protective power notwithstanding interference with contracts." Any doubts about the capaciousness of the police powers of the state government and the implied limitation on the protection of private contractual rights, he believed, should have been removed by the rent-control decisions, where "the relief afforded was temporary and conditional . . . sustained because of the emergency." The Chief Justice insisted that "the reservation of the reasonable exercise of the protective power of the State is read into all contracts. . . ." He concluded: "An emergency existed in Minnesota which furnished a proper occasion for the exercise of the reserved power of the State to protect the vital interests of the community."

The four dissenting justices disagreed emphatically. "He simply closes his eyes to the necessary implications of the decision," said their spokesman, Justice Sutherland, "who fails to see in it the potentiality of future gradual but ever-advancing encroachments upon the sanctity of private and public contracts." The correct doctrine, they believed, was to be found in the classic decision of *Ex parte Milligan* (1866), which declared constitutional guarantees and restrictions to be absolutely invariant with respect to emergencies or any other social conditions. Quoting from a considerable collection of historical works, Sutherland established that the framers had intended the Contracts Clause to apply *"primarily and especially"* during economic crises; a crisis similar to the current depression had provoked them to add it to the Constitution in the first place. "The present exigency is nothing new," Sutherland pointed out. The rent-control decisions were dismissed as too weakly justified at the time and as dealing with a matter too dissimilar to the present one to afford a binding precedent.

The dissenters on the Court rejected Hughes's sophistical distinction between genuine emergency powers and reserved powers brought into play by emergency conditions:

> The question is not whether an emergency furnishes the occasion for the exercise of that state power, but whether an emergency furnishes an occasion for the relaxation of the restrictions upon the power imposed by the contract impairment clause; and the difficulty is that the contract impairment clause forbids state action under any circumstances, if it have the effect of impairing the obligation of contracts. . . . The Minnesota statute either impairs the obligation of contracts or it does not. If it does not, the occasion to which it relates becomes immaterial, since then the passage of the statute is the exercise of a normal, unrestricted, state power and requires no special occasion to render it effective. If it does, the emergency no more furnishes a proper occasion for its exercise than if the emergency were non-existent. And so, while, in form, the suggested distinction seems to put us forward in a straight line, in reality it simply carries us back in a circle, like bewildered travelers lost in a wood.

The dissenting opinion concluded: "If the provisions of the Constitution be not upheld when they pinch as well as when they comfort, they may as well be abandoned." The dissenters feared that the Court, to facilitate the extraordinary governmental measures being implemented at all levels, had begun to abandon the Constitution by embracing a reinterpretation so sweeping as to effectively destroy the traditional understanding and force of the constitutional protection of private rights.

During the Korean War, the Court had another occasion to consider its doctrine regarding emergency powers. President Truman, placed in an uncomfortable political position by a deadlocked union-management dispute that threatened a nationwide strike, directed the Secretary of Commerce in April 1952 to seize and operate several steel mills. The owners obtained an injunction to prevent the seizure. The Supreme Court upheld the injunction by a 6–3 vote in the *Youngstown* case decided June 2, 1952.

Although the Court denied Truman—by that time a very unpopular President—a power previously exercised freely by Wilson and FDR, the decision did not impose a restriction on the *government's* power to take private property in an emergency; it restrained only a *presidential* taking without specific statutory authorization. As Justice Black said in announcing the majority's opinion, "This is a job for the Nation's lawmakers, not for its military authorities." In a concurring opinion, Justice Jackson emphasized "the ease, expedition and safety with which Congress can grant and has granted large emergency powers." Neither the majority nor the minority gave any weight to private property rights. While the majority objected only to Truman's presidential high-handedness, the minority grumbled that "such a [presidential] power of seizure has been accepted throughout our history." The Constitution was read in this case, as in many others, not as a bulwark against governmental oppression of private citizens but as the institutional setting within which high officials in the different branches of government conduct their internecine struggles for supremacy.

Conclusion

The history of the United States in the 20th century provides strong evidence that derogations from private property rights in a liberal democracy occur chiefly during national emergencies and that, once curtailed, private rights seldom regain their previous scope. The pattern should not be surprising. Crisis clearly alters the expected benefits and costs of curtailment of private rights on both sides of the political equation. A fearful public, ideologically predisposed to believe in the efficacy of governmental action, insists that the government "do something" to diminish the threat, perceiving the benefits of such action to be immediate and direct and the costs to be remote and largely external. This public perception is nurtured by those who, for material or ideological reasons, would use the occasion to further their economic or political aims. From a cost-benefit perspective, governmental officials experience reduced political costs and increased political benefits from curtailing private rights in crisis as compared to non-crisis conditions.

As people adjust to the crisis-expanded role of government, many variables change in ways that diminish the likelihood that the post-crisis retrenchment of the government will restore private rights to their previous scope. Private citizens discover that governmental action in a liberal democracy need not lead to the establishment of totalitarianism, as some conservatives have predicted. Governmental officials develop the bureaucratic technology to administer their controls less abrasively and more effectively. Many people find the politically and economically rewarding paths to personal advancement unique to systems powered by discretionary governmental authority. Thus, history is irrevocably altered by the crisis-induced expansion of governmental authority. The change is consolidated and compounded as new generations never experience the broader realm of private rights that once prevailed. For the younger generations, the status quo is the current, high degree of governmental power; for them there is no personal experience and, therefore, no genuine appreciation of the old regime.

The legal legacies of crisis tilt the polity in the same direction: Statutes, regulations, and judicial decisions expressing and facilitating expanded governmental powers become embedded in the law as well as in the public's consciousness. The plethora of crisis-engendered statutes and judicial decisions attests to the magnitude of this aspect of the politico-economic dynamics. The discretionary nature of governmental powers thereby created provides an easy avenue to their expanded use in future situations that the public perceives, or can be induced to perceive, as "crises."

Thus, private property rights, historically truncated during national emergencies, remain vulnerable to further erosion during future crises. Attempts to restrain the abuse of emergency powers have not eliminated the ratcheting effect of actual or purported emergency in augmenting governmental power. Only the respite of non-crisis affords time to contemplate and forestall the threat to liberty and private property rights inherent in the emergency psychology of the public and its exploitation by governmental officials.

The Forgotten Ninth and Tenth Amendments

Roger Pilon

It is unremarkable that a section of the American Bar Association, even the Section of Individual Rights and Responsibilities, should title the final session of its program commemorating the bicentennial of the Bill of Rights "The Forgotten Ninth and Tenth Amendments." As Randy Barnett and Suzanna Sherry have reminded us, those amendments were meant to secure the higher law that stands behind the Constitution. Yet within 30 years of the drafting of the Bill of Rights, adjudication based on the concept of a higher law all but disappeared in this country.

It was something of a surprise, then, when Justice Arthur Goldberg drew upon the Ninth Amendment in 1965 to find a right to privacy, which helped the Court to strike down a Connecticut statute forbidding the sale of contraceptive devices. Although the Ninth Amendment has since been cited in over 1,000 cases, in all but one of those cases it has played only a supporting role. As for the Tenth Amendment, after a brief revival in 1976, the Court reversed itself only nine years later. Thus, if not entirely forgotten, the Ninth and Tenth Amendments today are hardly alive and well.

Our ambivalence toward the demise of those amendments could not be better illustrated than by comparing the debate that four years ago surrounded the nomination of Judge Robert Bork to the Supreme Court with the debate that today surrounds the nomination of Judge Clarence Thomas. When Bork likened the Ninth Amendment to an inkblot that afforded judges no guidance in interpreting the Consti-

Roger Pilon is vice president for legal affairs and director of the Center for Constitutional Studies at the Cato Institute. This is a revised version of remarks he delivered on August 13, 1991, at the annual meeting of the American Bar Association in Atlanta, Georgia.

Cato Policy Report, September/October 1991

tution, he was supported by conservatives but roundly condemned by liberals. Unlike Bork, Thomas believes that the Ninth Amendment points to the higher law that ought to guide judges in their adjudication, yet he too has been generally supported by conservatives but eyed with suspicion by liberals.

Although a large part of that ambivalence is simple politics, there are deeper issues that help to explain why the Ninth and Tenth Amendments and the higher law they reflect have played so limited a role in our legal history. Before examining those issues, however, we need first to review briefly what the amendments meant to the men who wrote them. We will then be in a position to ask what led to their demise and what must be done to restore them.

The Original Understanding

Addressed to our rights, the Ninth Amendment states, "The enumeration in the Constitution of certain rights shall not be construed to deny or disparage others retained by the people." By contrast, the Tenth Amendment speaks to powers: "The powers not delegated to the United States by the Constitution, nor prohibited by it to the States, are reserved to the States respectively, or to the people."

Coming at the conclusion of the founding period—and, quite literally, at the conclusion of the original Constitution and the Bill of Rights—the Ninth and Tenth Amendments can be thought to have summed up that period and those documents. In the Declaration of Independence, the Founders set forth the essence of the higher law: the primacy of the individual; the principle of moral equality, defined by our equal natural rights; and the idea that government, resting on consent, is created not to give us rights but to secure the rights we already have. Through a written constitution, the founding generation then authorized the institutions and powers of government they thought would best secure their rights. Finally, to help ensure that end, they added a bill of rights. And they concluded that document by returning to first principles. Thus the Ninth Amendment makes it clear that the rights enumerated in our founding documents are not the only rights we have, while the Tenth Amendment makes it equally clear that the powers delegated to the federal government are its only powers. Rights were both enumerated and unenumerated; powers, intended to secure those rights, were strictly enumerated.

The debates that surrounded the adoption of the Bill of Rights only reinforce this plain reading of the document's final members. As calls for a bill of rights intensified during the ratification period, those who opposed such a bill objected that it was unnecessary because the Constitution was already a bill of rights. "Why declare that things shall not be done which there is no power to do?" asked Alexander Hamilton. James Wilson reinforced that point by observing that "every thing which is not given is reserved." Moreover, a bill of rights might even prove dangerous, the opponents continued. First, since it is impossible to enumerate all of our rights, enumerating certain rights might be construed as surrendering the rest. And second, declaring as rights what everyone knows to be rights might trivialize all rights, even those that are enumerated.

When a bill of rights proved necessary to ratification, the Ninth and Tenth Amendments were written to guard against those dangers, making it clear that the enumeration of certain rights was not meant to deny or disparage others and that powers were meant to be limited to those that were enumerated. After reviewing the ratification debates, Sherry concludes that "the founding generation envisioned natural rights beyond those protected by the first eight amendments" and that "the framers of the Bill of Rights did not expect the Constitution to be read, as the sole source of fundamental law." Indeed, if the Framers intended unenumerated rights to be protected *without* a bill of rights, how can we imagine that those rights were meant to be any less secure *with* a bill of rights?

Those conclusions are at direct variance with modern constitutional thought, of course, save for in a fairly limited range of cases. Today even liberals call upon judges to find rights within "the four corners" of the Constitution—admittedly, by interpreting its language liberally—while conservatives urge judges to read the document more or less literally—to guard against importing into it their own values. Almost never do modern judges, whether liberal or conservative, purport to go "beyond" the Constitution. When we add the general presumption, which has arisen over the years, that legislation is constitutional—and the expansion of that presumption, especially through the Commerce Clause, to a wide range of activities the Founders would never have imagined—the result amounts almost to the inversion of the Founders' presumptions: enumerated rights, unenumerated powers. Modern practice, in short, runs directly counter to the practice Sherry discerned in her review of the first 30 years of American constitutional jurisprudence: "there is no case during this period in which the courts have upheld an act contrary to natural law on the ground that the law was not in conflict with any constitutional provision."

Legitimacy and the Loss of Confidence

How did we get to this point—where conservatives read the Constitution almost literally, save for the forgotten Ninth and Tenth Amendments, while liberals do the same, save to get the rights or powers they want by stretching the text to the breaking point? Why is it, in short, that the modern mind is so reluctant to repair to the higher law that the Founders thought would inform the broad language of the Constitution, including the Ninth and Tenth Amendments?

The answers to those questions are many, but they all come down to a concern for legitimacy and to a loss of confidence, especially among the judiciary, about the genuine foundations of legitimacy. In a nutshell, over the past two centuries we have seen the foundations of legitimacy shift ever so gradually but ever so clearly from reason to popular will. We have moved, that is, from a constitution of reason to a constitution of will.

Plainly, the Founders thought political legitimacy, including the legitimacy of judicial review, was rooted not in any conception of value or political ends, much less in democratic will, but in the theory of natural rights. The Declaration states that theory as succinctly as it has ever been stated, grounding its self-evident truths in "the Laws of Nature and of Nature's God." Couched in the language of the day, that was simply another way of saying, with John Locke, that the Declaration's principles were grounded in "Reason."

No sooner had those principles been declared, however, than they came under attack. Perhaps the most strident of the critics was Jeremy Bentham, the father of British utilitarianism, who wrote in 1791 that talk of natural rights was "simple nonsense: natural and imprescriptible rights, rhetorical nonsense,—nonsense upon stilts." Bentham stood in a long line of moral skeptics, stretching from antiquity to today, each of whom argued the impossibility of legitimacy yet had his own second-best solution to the problem of legitimacy.

In time, not surprisingly, those skeptics took their toll on the American judiciary. Playing upon the all-too-human tendency toward self-doubt, they undermined judicial belief in natural rights and propelled judges toward other rationales. With their faith shaken, judges turned naturally to the "clearest" source of law—the written text—and toward a theory that might lend legitimacy to that text. Plainly, the simplest such theory, the easiest to comprehend, held that the Constitution was legitimate because it represented the will of the sovereign, the American people. Thus did the twin premises of legal positivism and democratic rationale take root. Never mind that the Framers had restrained popular will at every turn. When construing the text not as reflecting higher law, which would require judicial understanding and insight to interpret, but as mere positive law, only a theory of sovereignty could lend legitimacy to that text, and the theory of popular sovereignty was as good as—in fact, better than—any other. It lent itself, moreover, to an ever-greater latitude for majoritarian will, which of course has been taken advantage of.

Those conceptual shifts took place only over time, of course. Moreover, they manifested themselves as a fundamental jurisprudential shift only much later, with the New Deal Court. Until then, majoritarian demands had not been so extensive as to lead to the kind of judicial crisis that arose during the New Deal. Nevertheless, the foundations for crisis were being laid all along, especially during the Progressive Era. It was then, in fact, that a crucial shift took place in our conception of government, when we stopped thinking of government as a necessary evil, created to secure our rights, and started thinking of it instead as an instrument for doing good.

The importance of that reconceptualization of government cannot be overstated. It led eventually to what Robert Summers has called America's leading theory of law, "pragmatic instrumentalism," which conceives law to be a practical instrument for accomplishing social goals. With the rise of industrialization and urbanization and the social problems that ensued, with the influence of German idealism and progressive theories of good government conducted by career civil servants, the forces were in place for a fundamental transition in our conception of law—from rights-based to policy-driven law, from judge-made to statutory law, from the law of reason to the law of will. Indeed, it remained only for the judiciary to catch up to modern, progressive thought.

But the New Deal Court was slow to catch up. In fact, not until President Roosevelt threatened to pack the Court with six additional members did it finally get the majoritarian message. Once it did, however, the floodgates were opened. With the Court stepping aside, with its systematic deference to the political branches, those branches were able to move on with their social agenda, unrestrained by any "rights" that might stand in the way of their pursuit of the social good. But to be thus restrained and deferential the Court needed a rationale. After all, for most of its history it had stood athwart the majoritarian engine, albeit by teasing rights out of the text of the Constitution rather than finding them in its higher law background. What now could justify the Court's doing not even that—and permitting unheard of powers besides? In short, what could justify its ignoring both the Ninth and Tenth Amendments?

Justice Stone provided that rationale in 1938 in *Carolene Products*, especially in his famous footnote 4, wherein he distinguished "fundamental" rights—relating to political participation and to "discrete and insular minorities" that might be restricted from such participation—from other, presumably "non-fundamental" rights. Legislative interference with the former, he said, should receive strict judicial scrutiny, whereas interference with the latter, especially with rights exercised in ordinary commercial transactions, should be presumed to be constitutional if it rests upon some rational basis. That dual theory of rights and two-tiered theory of judicial review, aimed at enhancing political participation, are nowhere to be found in the Constitution, of course, nor are they any part of its higher law background. Rather, they were invented out of whole cloth, for political reasons, to enable the New Deal state, its roots in the Progressive Era, to proceed with its political and economic agenda. Unenumerated rights were ignored. Unenumerated powers were allowed—all in the name of the sovereign will.

The transition that had begun a century and more before was now nearly complete; what remained was simply the episodic expansion of "fundamental rights," drawn not from higher law but from "evolving social values." The democratic rationale that had lent legitimacy to a constitution conceived as mere positive law, as a product of sovereign will, now served as the filter through which the document's very terms came to be understood and given a largely political cast. No longer conversant with the higher law of reason, s could at least understand the ordinary law of will, and whether the commands of that will conflicted with explicit restraints in the Constitution, constraints that were themselves construed as intended to enhance political participation. Defending that "politicization" of the Constitution, John Hart Ely has put the matter straightforwardly: "unblocking stoppages in the democratic process is what judicial review ought preeminently to be about." Indeed, the theory of *Carolene Products* has been called a "great and modern charter for ordering the relations between judges and other agencies of government."

It is not a little ironic, of course, that modern liberals, who expanded the state through Progressive Era regulation, New Deal welfare programs, and Great Society egalitarian efforts, ignoring in the process the unenumerated rights of the Ninth Amendment and the limited powers of the Tenth Amendment, should today be searching the Ninth Amendment for pockets of protection from the ubiquitous state they created. Nor is it without irony that modern conservatives, purporting to rest their constitutional jurisprudence on the intentions of the Framers, should ignore the Framers' intent when it comes to the Ninth and Tenth Amendments and rely instead on the political jurisprudence of the New Deal Court to enable lawmakers at every level of government to regulate our personal lives in countless ways—the theory being that our rights to those lives are nowhere to be found in the Constitution. Because both liberals and conservatives have today bought into the will theory of constitutional legitimacy, neither privacy nor property is secure.

Restoring the Vision

The Founders got it right. They understood that in the end, legitimacy is a function of reason, not of political will. To be sure, it takes some act of political will—or at least some manifestation of political recognition—to get a legal regime going. In the American context, that is what ratification was all about. But that is *all* that ratification was about. That original consent could hardly have made legitimate the terms and relationships that were ratified—as consent to a contract makes legitimate, among the consenting parties, the terms and relationships that are thereby authorized. Ratification could not

376

have done that because its effects, in establishing the legal regime, reached far beyond the ratifying parties. Indeed, the ratifiers purported to be binding not simply themselves but succeeding generations as well. They could not have done that if they had not gotten it right—right as a matter of *substance*. But that substantive legitimacy is a function not of process but of the higher law of reason. Freedom of religion and the right to property are legitimate not because the ratifiers *declared* them to be so—through an act of political will—but because they are *natural* rights. Indeed, those rights would be legitimate even if the ratifying generation had declared them *not* to be so.

If we are to restore the vision of the Founders, the vision of individual liberty and limited government that the Ninth and Tenth Amendments were meant to secure, the first thing we must do is disabuse ourselves of the idea that democratic will per se imparts any real measure of legitimacy. Democratic process may decide an issue, with the majority prevailing over the minority. But that hardly makes the product of that process legitimate. Majority decisions to redistribute property, for example, or to prohibit nonviolent associations, which so many modern statutes do, are simply illegitimate, however large the majority behind them. They are legally illegitimate because they violate the rights protected by the Ninth Amendment (at least) and proceed from powers the Tenth Amendment was meant to make clear were never given. And they are morally illegitimate because in no way do they conform to the higher law that stands behind the Constitution, the theory of natural rights that was meant to inform the document's broad language, guiding judges in their review of such political acts.

When properly understood, then, that review does not require judges to go "beyond" the Constitution. If the document is law by virtue of having been ratified, and if the original understanding was that the text was to be interpreted by reference to principles of a higher law, then judges who repair to those principles for guidance can hardly be said to be acting beyond the scope of their authority. So far is this from judicial "activism" as to be precisely the opposite: a judge whose misguided "restraint" precludes him from carrying out his full responsibilities—like a judge whose misguided "activism" takes him truly beyond the theory of natural rights—is in fact an "activist," finding powers, in effect, that have nowhere been given. The responsibility of the judge is to apply the Constitution as it was meant to be applied—indeed, as it was applied in the early years of the nation.

To do that, however, the judiciary must not only disabuse itself of its misguided belief in the legitimating power of majoritarian will; it must also affirmatively inform itself about the character and content of the higher law. In an age inclined toward moral skepticism, that will not be easy. Nevertheless, it can be done. Indeed, the Founders had a fairly consistent, correct, and confident understanding of that law. Nor is it surprising that they did, since they took their counsel from a fairly commonsense understanding and appreciation of reason.

The primacy of the individual. The idea of moral equality, defined by equal rights. The ultimate grounding of rights in property and promise—not in need, or want, or aspiration, or any other evaluative notion. The presumption in favor of the voluntary, private realm. The suspicion of public power. Those are the elements of the higher law, of the free society, of the vision the Ninth and Tenth Amendments were meant to secure. It is a vision the modern judiciary would do well to revisit.

Dissolving the Inkblot: Privacy as Property Right

Sheldon Richman

No question in jurisprudence is as muddled as that of privacy. Conservatives refuse to recognize a general legal right to privacy. Big-government liberals misconstrue the concept and apply it arbitrarily and opportunistically. They would protect a woman's decision to abort a fetus but not two business competitors who wished to discuss their pricing strategies.

The dominant liberal and conservative approaches to privacy are unsatisfactory because they are essentially unprincipled. Liberals, such as Laurence Tribe, envision a right of privacy radiating from express provisions of the Constitution, but that right is so narrow that it is self-subverting. Conservatives, such as Robert Bork, reject that vision of a right to privacy because they believe that the method used to find it will allow judges to invent rights. Conservatives seem to assume that there is no alternative vision. But there is an alternative vision, one that derives privacy rights from a Lockean framework based on each person's property in his own life, liberty, and estate.

The Liberal-Conservative Debate

The right of privacy as a legal matter moved onto its current track in 1890 in a famous *Harvard Law Review* article by Louis Brandeis and Samuel D. Warren. Previously, the right to privacy had been seen in England and America as derived from the right to property and the right to make contracts. Brandeis and Warren thought that view too restrictive (it could not stop newspaper gossip columnists) and spec-

Sheldon Richman was a senior editor at the Cato Institute and is now editor of *Ideas on Liberty*.
Cato Policy Report, January/February 1993

ulated that what underlay older court decisions was a general right to be left alone. "The principle," they wrote, "is in reality not the principle of private property, but that of an inviolate personality." According to that view, the principle manifests itself, for example, in the right of a person to control disclosure of facts about himself even when those facts have been lawfully discovered by others. The right to privacy was thus loosened from its property anchor and allowed to float more or less free. Brandeis and Warren's splitting of privacy and property foreshadowed future invidious divisions of rights by various Supreme Courts, divisions that once favored narrowly construed economic over noneconomic rights but that since the New Deal have done the opposite.

The landmark privacy case in American constitutional jurisprudence is *Griswold v. Connecticut* (1965), in which the U.S. Supreme Court struck down a Connecticut law prohibiting the use of contraceptives. In the *Griswold* decision the separation of privacy and property is palpable, as can be seen in Justice Arthur Goldberg's concurring opinion. "Certainly the safeguarding of the home does not follow merely from the sanctity of property rights. The home derives its pre-eminence as the seat of family life."

Although not the first case to protect some notion of a right to privacy, *Griswold* shaped subsequent Court thinking and led directly to *Roe v. Wade* (1973), which established a limited constitutional right to abortion. It also set the terms that, ironically, led a conservative-dominated Court to uphold a Georgia law against sodomy in *Bowers v. Hardwick* (1986).

In *Griswold*, Justice William O. Douglas found that the ban on the use of contraceptives by married couples unconstitutionally intruded into a "zone of privacy"—the marital relationship—that is implied by a combination of several express guarantees in the Constitution. Douglas, writing for the majority, penned an immortal phrase when he stated that "specific guarantees in the Bill of Rights have penumbras, formed by emanations from those guarantees that help give them life and substance."

Using Court precedents, Douglas argued for a right of privacy as one of those penumbral rights.

> Various guarantees create zones of privacy. The right of association contained in the penumbra of the First Amendment is one, as we have seen. The Third Amendment in its prohibition against the quartering of sol-

diers "in any house" in time of peace without the consent of the owner is another facet of that privacy. The Fourth Amendment explicitly affirms the "right of the people to be secure in their persons, houses, papers, and effects, against unreasonable searches and seizures." The Fifth Amendment in its Self-Incrimination Clause enables the citizen to create a zone of privacy which government may not force him to surrender to his detriment. The Ninth Amendment provides: "The enumeration in the Constitution, of certain rights, shall not be construed to deny or disparage others retained by the people."

In his concurring opinion in *Griswold*, Goldberg cited Justice Brandeis's dissent in *Olmstead v. United States* (1928). The Framers, Brandeis wrote, "conferred, as against the government, the right to be let alone—the most comprehensive of rights and the right most valued by civilized men." According to Goldberg, only "fundamental rights" were protected in the zones of privacy. To the question, Which rights are fundamental? Goldberg replied that judges should not turn to their personal notions. "Rather, they must look to the 'traditions and [collective] conscience of our people' to determine whether a principle is 'so rooted [there] . . . as to be ranked as fundamental.'"

Other concurring justices preferred to strike the Connecticut law on the ground that it violated the section of the Fourteenth Amendment that prohibits states from depriving persons of life, liberty, or property without due process of law. Those justices revived the old, and unfortunately abandoned, idea of substantive due process, but they applied it only to noneconomic rights.

For a majority of the Supreme Court, it was but a short jump from *Griswold* to the controversial ruling on abortion in *Roe*. Justice Harry Blackmun, writing for the majority, said, "This right of privacy . . . is broad enough to encompass a woman's decision whether or not to terminate her pregnancy." Yet Blackmun disagreed with the appellants that the woman's right is absolute. He wrote that the state "may properly assert important interests" related to, among other things, the protection of potential life and that "at some point in pregnancy, these respective interests become sufficiently compelling to sustain regulation of the factors that govern the abortion decision."

The minority opinions in *Griswold* went to the heart of Douglas's and Goldberg's methods. Justice Hugo Black disputed the substitution of the "broad, abstract and ambiguous" term "privacy" for the more concrete language of the express guarantees in the Bill of

Rights. "I like my privacy as well as the next one, but I am neverthe-less compelled to admit that government has a right to invade it un-less prohibited by some specific constitutional provision." Similarly, Justice Potter Stewart wrote, "With all deference, I can find no such general right of privacy in the Bill of Rights, in any other part of the Constitution, or in any case ever before decided by this Court."

It is the liberals' ad hoc reasoning in those cases that gives plausi-bility to the criticism of the liberal Court by Robert Bork and other conservatives. In *The Tempting of America*, Bork notes that the concern with marriage in *Griswold* was later dropped in *Eisentadt v. Baird* (1972) when the issue shifted to the use of contraceptives by unmar-ried people. Given the mercurial way in which the liberals incre-mentally unveiled their right to privacy, it was impossible to know what would come next.

Bork does not object to the idea of penumbras emanating from the Bill of Rights; he just does not believe that any of the statutes stricken in the privacy cases violated so-called penumbral rights. Nor does he wish to defend the anti-contraception statute. His focus is on the le-gal argument and how it creates "an unconfinable judicial power." "No matter what your moral views on any of these matters [dealt with in the privacy cases]," he writes, "nothing in the Constitution addresses them."

To the liberal claim that laws against contraception and abortion fall to the due process clause of the Fourteenth Amendment, Bork re-sponds that due process refers only to procedures and that "sub-stantive due process" is a contradiction in terms. Finally, Bork finds no case for privacy in the Ninth Amendment, which he says is as ob-scure as it would be had an inkblot covered it on the original parch-ment.

Where the Liberals and Conservatives Go Wrong

To understand where the Court's majority went wrong in *Gris-wold*, one must distinguish the method of interpretation from its ap-plication. Douglas's method was to look for the logical implications (which is how I read "penumbras formed by emanations") of the ex-press guarantees in the Bill of Rights. As Douglas put it when he agreed with an earlier Court that the right of association can be found in the First Amendment, "While it is not expressly included in the First Amendment its existence is necessary in making the express guarantees fully meaningful."

That is sound as far as it goes. The problem is not the penumbras but that Douglas found only what he wanted to find and no more. (In 1965 he found a right to marital privacy, but in 1942 in *Wickard v. Filburn* he could not find a right to grow wheat on one's own land even for one's own use.) For Douglas, the penumbras contained so-called personal, noneconomic rights relating to speech, press, religion, and the like. Yet other zones of privacy are logically covered by the same guarantees that Douglas used; those zones relate to economic activities. Since the Constitution refers to property several times, it is hard to see how a right to privacy emanating from those guarantees can exclude commercial matters, such as a discussion of prices by competitors. Besides, all "personal rights" require the use of property, if only a place to stand, and hence are "economic rights" as well. One cannot distinguish economic from personal rights on the ground that only the former have third-party effects. So do personal rights. Bork is correct when he says in reference to sodomy that "knowledge that an activity is taking place is a harm to those who find it profoundly immoral." The point is that it is a "harm" (a subjective state in someone who objects) that does not violate anyone's rights. The same is true of price "fixing." (The Constitution's interstate commerce clause is not properly read as a plenary power to regulate commerce since it is constrained by other clauses.)

The arbitrariness of Douglas's reasoning in *Griswold* can be seen in his "notions of privacy surrounding the marriage relationship." As he put it, the case concerned "a law which, in forbidding the *use* of contraceptives rather than regulating their manufacture or sale, seeks to achieve its goals by means having a maximum destructive impact upon that relationship." He apparently would have had no problem with a ban on only manufacture or sale because enforcement would not have required searches of the marital bedroom.

Note the arbitrariness: First, the marital relationship was deserving of protection, but commercial relationships were not. Second, for Douglas, some ways of intruding on the marital relationship were apparently permissible, as long as they had less than "maximum destructive impact" on the relationship. While the state may not barge into the bedroom looking for contraceptives, it may outlaw their manufacture and sale to make sure they never get to the bedroom.

But that is only a less hamhanded form of disrupting the marital relationship.

Third, Douglas excluded unmarried couples from protection. It was left to a later Court to extend the protection to them. In *Eisenstadt* the Court broadened the right to privacy on the ground that a married couple consists of *individuals,* and all individuals, married or not, face the fundamental decision of whether or not to have children.

The conservatives have their problems as well. Stewart and Bork demand to know what specific guarantees in the Bill of Rights are violated by a state law against contraception or abortion. They do not accept the holistic reading of the Constitution that the identification of penumbral rights entails. "Nobody has ever quarreled with the proposition that certain zones or aspects of privacy or freedom are protected by the Constitution," writes Bork. But finding those zones in particular guarantees is not the same as finding a general right of privacy in the penumbras, which, Bork says, only creates a "loose canon in the law." The *Roe* Court "did not even feel obliged to settle the question of where the right of privacy or the subsidiary right to abort is to be attached to the Constitution's text," Bork complains. He finds the various references to implicit liberty and the nation's traditions "pretty vaporous stuff."

Thus, he applauds the Court's upholding of a Georgia law against sodomy in *Bowers* (1986). The conservative majority refused to apply the principles of the earlier privacy cases because homosexual sodomy had nothing to do with family, marriage, procreation, or the nation's history and tradition. (The liberals were hoist with their own petard. As does unpopular speech, untraditional ways of living most need protection.)

Bork's real objection is to any holistic reading of the Constitution. Instead, he favors what John Hart Ely called a "clause-bound interpretation." The idea is to read each guarantee in the Bill of Rights as if no others existed, taking care not to acquire any cumulative sense of what the Framers had in mind. That is a dubious theory of interpretation, but in at least one case Bork is not "clause-bound" enough: he prefers to read the Constitution as if the Ninth Amendment were not there. (Conversely, the liberals who abhor clause-boundedness do not mind reading the commerce clause that way. That clause must be read in the full context of the general protection accorded property in the Constitution.)

Finally, the conservatives reject substantive due process, which they see as a contradiction in terms that authorizes judges to legislate. If the term sounds odd, it would be odder still to dismiss the idea. As Roger Pilon writes, "By 'law' [in due process of law] the drafters could hardly have meant mere legislation or the guarantee would have been all but empty." In other words, if a legislature may "duly" pass any substantive law it wishes, life, liberty, and property are hardly secure. Substantive due process is an indispensable restraint on legislative caprice.

Thus, both the liberals and the conservatives misunderstand privacy. The conservatives engage in a narrow and unnatural reading of the Constitution in order to avoid seeing what they do not wish to see, while the liberals find in the Constitution not penumbras but a Rorschach test that reveals only what they wish to see. In both cases it comes down to an inkblot. Both approaches allow their adherents to disparage most freedoms and exalt the few freedoms allowed by their respective moral and political philosophies.

Propertarian Privacy

Fortunately, there is a coherent, objective alternative to the liberals' arbitrary right of privacy and the conservatives' crabbed, clause-bound notion of constitutional freedom. It is a model of privacy re-anchored in natural property rights (beginning with self-ownership). That the propertarian model of privacy has the full force of the Constitution behind it is evident in the purposes listed in the preamble to the Constitution, in the recurring express references to property, and in the protection of unenumerated rights in the Ninth Amendment.

The notion of propertarian privacy is unabashedly based on a holistic reading of the Constitution. As Justice John Marshal Harlan said, the rights in the Bill of Rights are not a "series of isolated points" but "a rational continuum." When one begins with the preamble; proceeds through the delegation of limited federal powers and on through the Bill of Rights, including the guarantee of unenumerated rights and the Tenth Amendment's reiteration of the limitation of federal power; and winds up at the Fourteenth Amendment's limit on state governments—and when one reads all that against the "higher law background"—one cannot reasonably deny that the document is meant to protect persons, their liberty, and their property. Privacy, the realm beyond the reach of forcible intervention, is inherent in and inseparable from that intent. If property is not a sanctuary from entreaty and command, what is it? The Founding Fathers understood that.

The propertarian approach to privacy is not only morally sound, it also has an impeccable case-law pedigree. As noted, before 1890 privacy was not separated from property. For example, in his opinion in *Boyd v. United States* (1886), a search and seizure case involving a businessman, Justice Joseph Bradley wrote that the constitutional guarantees securing people in their persons, houses, papers, and effects transcend the concrete case and "apply to all invasions on the part of government and its employes of the sanctity of a man's home and the privacies of life. It is not the breaking of his doors, and the rummaging in his drawers, that constitutes the essence of the offense; but it is the invasion of his indefeasible right of personal security, personal liberty and private property."

More recently, that model of privacy was invoked by Justice John Paul Stevens. In *Moore v. East Cleveland* (1977), in which the Court struck down a zoning law that prohibited a woman from living with two grandsons who were not brothers, Stevens, in a concurring opinion, said that the test to be applied was "whether East Cleveland's housing ordinance is a permissible restriction on [Mrs. Moore's] right to use her property as she sees fit." There was no need to resort to vaporous (as Bork puts it) freedoms "deeply rooted in this Nation's history and tradition."

And in his *Bowers* dissent, Blackmun argued that the law against sodomy violated (quoting Charles Fried) the "moral fact that a person *belongs* to himself and not others nor to the society as a whole" (emphasis added). But as Stephen Macedo suggests, Blackmun weakened his argument by resorting to the vague Brandeisian freedom "to define one's identity."

Propertarian privacy has all the advantages of the big-government liberals' contrived right of privacy and none of the disadvantages. It is not a warrant for judges to do whatever they wish. To determine whether one has a right of privacy with respect to some act, a judge need only ask what the property rights are. Thus, the use of contraceptives is protected because each party owns himself or herself (the first property right) and at least one owns the contraceptive device. No rights are violated. The same is true for the woman who wishes to live with her grandsons and for persons who engage in consensual homosexual sodomy, use drugs or pornography, grow wheat on their land, buy the services of a prostitute, or "fix" prices with business competitors. Those actions are perfectly consistent with property rights. (In fact, competitors cannot "fix" prices; they can only agree to *ask* the same price. Buyers are free to abstain from purchasing or to purchase from someone who is not a party to the agreement.)

On the other hand, child abuse, even in one's home, is not protected because the child is a self-owner. (As to abortion, the salient fact is that the fetus comes into existence inside the body of a self-owner. Philosopher Judith Jarvis Thomson has argued that the issue of fetal rights distracts from the more fundamental issue of whether the state may force a woman to be an incubator.)

The property rights standard makes distinguishing privacy violations from nonviolations a matter of principle. For example, an employer tells a prospective employee that he may not smoke—even at home—if he takes the job. Violation of privacy? Contrary to the ACLU's position, no. As a condition to a voluntary exchange, it violates no rights. The prospective employee can turn down the job.

Another example: A private firm compiles a computer data base on consumers in order to rent it to direct marketers. Privacy violation? Not if the information was originally provided freely by the consumers (or otherwise lawfully obtained) and all contractual restrictions are observed. But if information was given confidentially, divulgence should be actionable. To be sure, data can be misappropriated, stolen by computer hackers, or used in ways that violate contractual obligations. That is why there are criminal and civil courts.

(Incidentally, people naively and too readily give up personal information to private firms. The computer columnist Jim Seymour writes that he routinely ignores questions on applications, "and I can't recall a single incident, in 20 years, when I was refused whatever I was seeking simply because I didn't fill in every blank on the form.")

The liberal and conservative obfuscation of the privacy issue has led to a constitutional miasma that threatens to violate natural rights by construing the right to privacy either too broadly or too narrowly. Propertarian privacy dispels the miasma to reveal the clear path laid out by the Founding Fathers more than 200 years ago.

Clinton's Chilling Constitutional Legacy

Nadine Strossen

The rule of law is not simply about order and regularity, but about justice as well. And central to that substantive side of the rule of law is respect for the rights of speech and privacy. To the extent that governments abuse such basic rights, they cannot claim to be operating under the rule of law. Regrettably, the Clinton administration's record in this regard leaves much to be desired.

A single essay cannot do justice to the injustices that the Clinton administration has perpetrated through its far-ranging assaults on free speech and privacy. This chapter will instead provide what Adlai Stevenson once called a "fan-dance discussion": the point of the discussion, like the point of the fan, is not to cover the subject but rather to draw attention to it. I hasten to stress that the American Civil Liberties Union (ACLU) is staunchly nonpartisan. The ACLU has never endorsed or opposed any candidate or official. The ACLU does endorse and oppose particular positions on matters involving civil liberties. From that perspective, I am not aware of any candidate or official whose overall civil liberties record is not mixed—positive on some issues, negative on others.

Thus, in fairness to Clinton, before I focus on the dark side of his civil liberties record, I should note that he has earned especially high ACLU ratings in such important areas as religious liberty and reproductive freedom.

Clinton's Mixed Civil Rights Record

In noting Clinton's positive contributions to human rights, I am deliberately omitting one important area in which he often claims—and

Nadine Strossen is a professor at New York Law School and president of the American Civil Liberties Union.
The Rule of Law in the Wake of Clinton, ed. Roger Pilon (Cato Institute, 2000)

388

gets—kudos: racial justice. To be sure, Clinton has staunchly opposed racial discrimination and segregation. All told, though, his administration's policies have perpetuated discrimination, subjugation, and even disenfranchisement on the basis of race. That is because one of the major sources of racial injustice today is the "War on Crime"—and, in particular, the "War on Drugs"—and Clinton is one of the most militant crime and drug "warriors" we have ever seen. As one commentator observed in 1997: "The Clinton Administration is waging [the drug war] more intensely than its predecessors, having spent a record $15 billion on drug enforcement [in 1996] and added federal death penalties for so-called drug kingpins." Marijuana-related arrests alone—88 percent of which are for mere possession—have risen 80 percent during the Clinton presidency, reaching a record high of 695,200 in 1997.

The Clinton-championed drug policies inherently violate the whole panoply of our most cherished rights, but none more than the right not to be discriminated against on the basis of race or skin color. It is bad enough that any adult should be imprisoned for voluntarily ingesting anything into his or her own body, but it is even worse when those who are imprisoned for such "consensual crimes" are disproportionately selected on the basis of their skin color—which is precisely what happens.

Consider just a few of the shocking statistics. African-Americans constitute 13 percent of the country's population and 13 percent of its drug users. In other words, as every government study confirms, African-Americans use drugs in the same proportion as members of other racial groups. Yet, when we turn from those who use drugs to those who are arrested for such use, the African-American representation jumps to 37 percent. Worse yet, when we consider those who are convicted for drug use, the African-American representation climbs still higher, to 55 percent. And when we look at the drug users who are sentenced to prison, the African-American contingent soars all the way up to 74 percent. In sum, African-Americans are 13 percent of our total drug users, but 74 percent of our imprisoned drug users.

In light of such statistics, many commentators have concluded that the War on Drugs would more accurately be called the "War on the Constitution" or the "War on Racial Minorities." Our Commander in Chief in such a war can hardly claim the mantle of racial justice. As strongly as Bill Clinton may feel about civil rights and racial justice— and I am not questioning what appear to be his deep-seated commitments in these areas—he apparently feels even more strongly about being viewed as "tough on crime" and on drugs. One official's description of the Justice Department's overriding goal during the Clinton administration was "to make the president look tough on crime and worry about everything else, including civil liberties, later."

In his zeal to look tough, Bill Clinton has refused to support even modest steps to correct even the most egregious examples of the racial discrimination that is endemic in the drug war. In particular, the Clinton administration rejected a recommendation of the U.S. Sentencing Commission—which can hardly be accused of being "soft on crime"—to eliminate the racially biased, 100-fold disparity between sentences meted out for crack and those meted out for powdered cocaine, which are pharmacologically identical and produce the same effect on the body. Despite the chemical identity of those two forms of cocaine, a mandatory five-year minimum sentence is now imposed for possessing five grams of crack, which is used mostly by African-Americans and Latinos, whereas the same mandatory minimum is not triggered for possession of powder cocaine until the amount rises to 500 grams. In the words of one commentator, this disparity "hammers poor blacks while treating rich whites with kid gloves."

Even after such discriminatory sentences have been duly served, their racially repressive results are compounded by the widespread disenfranchisement of convicted felons. All states but four disenfranchise anyone convicted of a felony. The result is that, nationwide, a shocking 14 percent of all African-American men are stripped of the fundamental right to vote, and in some southern states that number soars to 30 percent—mostly due to our discriminatory drug laws and their discriminatory enforcement patterns. In short, the Jim Crow deprivation of voting rights that the Voting Rights Act of 1965 remedied has been reinstated by the War on Drugs. How, then, can Chief Drug Warrior Clinton be viewed fairly as a civil rights champion?

Overview of Clinton's Anti–Civil Liberties Legacy

Despite Clinton's positive civil liberties accomplishments in some areas, his overall record is not good—and that is the most diplomatic way to phrase it. Many respected liberal, civil libertarian commentators have been more blunt in describing Clinton's net "contributions" concerning our precious individual rights. Such criticism cannot be dismissed as partisan sniping. For example, *Washington Post* columnist Richard Cohen concluded that Clinton's major historic legacy is that "under his presidency the civil liberties of Americans were diminished." Likewise, John Heilemann wrote a cover story in *Wired* magazine that described the civil liberties record of "Big Brother Bill," to quote the title, as "breathtaking in both the breadth and depth of its awfulness."

From a historical perspective, Heilemann wrote, "So atrocious is Clinton's record, it can plausibly be argued that he is the worst civil liberties president since Richard Nixon." But *New York Times* columnist Anthony Lewis thought that historical comparison was unfair—unfair to Richard Nixon. In his view, we have to go back even further in history to find some fair anti-civil-liberties competition for Bill Clinton. Lewis concluded that "Bill Clinton has the worst civil liberties record of any president in at least 60 years." Even that is an understatement according to another seasoned journalist—Nat Hentoff of the *Village Voice* and *Washington Post*. Hentoff has concluded that no other American president "has done so much damage to constitutional liberties as Bill Clinton." Obviously, those are strong statements. Unfortunately, they are not hyperbolic. Clinton's assaults on liberty will have ongoing adverse consequences long after he leaves office.

The harsh verdicts I have quoted appeared in essays describing a long litany of specific civil liberties violations. If I had to single out one especially damaging type of abuse from this "embarrassment of riches," I would opt for the series of Clinton-championed measures that cut back on access to the courts and judicial review for many constitutional claims. In 1996, the ACLU issued a special report on those "court-stripping measures." To be sure, the Republican Congress played its part in passing these measures. But they could not have been enacted or enforced without the active support of the Clinton administration, which has defended them against constitutional challenges in the courts, as well as Congress. These judicial door-closing laws will cause the greatest long-range harm to constitutional rights because they remove the ultimate safety net that our system provides for our rights: the federal courts, with their relative insulation from the majoritarian pressures that at least tempt elected officials to ignore constitutional principles.

Anthony Lewis has been a particularly persistent critic of the many new court-stripping statutes that the Clinton administration successfully promoted. In one column, Lewis put these measures in historic perspective:

> The worst aspect of [Bill Clinton's] Presidency . . . is his appalling record on constitutional rights. The Clinton years have seen, among other things, a series of measures stripping the courts of their power to protect individuals from official abuse—the power that has been the key to American freedom. There has been nothing like it since the Radical Republicans, after the Civil War, acted to keep the courts from holding the occupation of the South to constitutional standards.

Clinton's Anti-Privacy Activism

One of the foremost, internationally respected experts on technology and privacy, Marc Rotenberg, the founder and executive director of the Electronic Privacy Information Center (EPIC), has assessed President Clinton's record in the following way: "Not since Richard Nixon wiretapped his political opponents has there been an administration with less regard for the privacy rights of American citizens."

Widespread press and public concern about Clinton's anti-privacy policies were first triggered by the 1996 Filegate scandal. Even FBI Director Louis Freeh condemned the "egregious violations of privacy" involved in that episode, in which White House officials ordered and obtained from the FBI 900 confidential personnel files of Republican appointees. At the time, the ACLU not only condemned Filegate itself but also issued a report that put the incident in context, stressing that it was part of a much larger, although much less publicized, pattern of pervasive privacy predations by the Clinton administration. In particular, this administration has constantly pushed to collect increasing categories of personal information from and about Americans for the government's ever-expanding electronic databases. The Clinton data-collection engine has extended even to personal information that most of us consider especially sensitive—medical and financial information.

Too often, these new databases have been created as part of major legislative initiatives, so they have not attracted the attention they deserve. One notable example is the 1996 welfare reform legislation, which requires all employers to collect personal information about all new employees, creating a massive new database that will include almost all of us who work—in other words, almost all of us.

Another example is the Clinton health care initiative. All of the hoopla about other aspects of that ill-fated plan obscured its call for a unique national identification number and collection of medical records on every health care recipient. Again, of course, that means on everyone. To be sure, the whole health care proposal went down in flames, but the Clinton administration is still supporting its data-collection concept. In November 1999 the Department of Health and Human Services issued regulations that give government agents more access to our medical records.

Yet one more new, nationwide Clinton-sponsored database is the "sex offender" registry. Not only did Clinton champion such a registry on the national level, he also waved the carrot of federal funding to spur similar registries in all fifty states. In some especially tragic instances, these registries have ruined the lives of people who had long ago been convicted of private consensual acts that have since been decriminalized, including homosexual sex and sex with a younger teenager. In other words, one type of privacy violation—punishing private, personal relationships—has been compounded by another—telling the world about those relationships.

In addition to initiating and supporting new databases, the Clinton administration has also pushed for expanded government power to intercept our communications and snoop into our data. Far from letting us pursue the potential of new communications technology to protect our privacy, the president has instead done the opposite—tried to co-opt the technology to promote government surveillance through electronic communications of all of our movements and expressions. The Clinton administration has been determined to distort the design and development of new communications technologies, from cell phones to computers, to turn them into tracking devices—tracking not only our bodies, but also our minds.

The most notorious examples are the Communications Assistance for Law Enforcement Act (CALEA) and the series of "Clipper Chip" initiatives. Those measures constitute government commandeering of cellular and computer communications, respectively, to facilitate government spying on individuals who may not even be suspected of any illicit activity. That would be analogous to the government's requiring all builders to install bugs in the walls of new homes and office buildings. As one ACLU analysis concluded, "If the Clinton administration has its way, Big Brother [will be] permanently hard-wired into the country's communications infrastructure." Robyn Blumner, a former ACLU leader who is now a syndicated columnist, summed up Clinton's data-gathering initiatives this way: "Clinton's willingness to abandon privacy rights puts the Filegate scandal in perspective—just another day at the White House."

"Clinton vs. the First Amendment"

Clinton's anti-free-speech record was dissected in the most damning detail in a *New York Times Magazine* cover story by one of the most prominent First Amendment lawyers in the country, Floyd Abrams. The title says it all: "Clinton vs. the First Amendment." The article began by describing a case whose name says it all: *ACLU v. Reno.* That case culminated in the Supreme Court's landmark 1997 ruling striking down the first federal Internet censorship law, which the Clinton administration championed. Even more telling is the fact that we now have to call that case *ACLU v. Reno I,* since Clinton subsequently championed and signed the second federal Internet censorship law, which the ACLU also promptly challenged in a case called *ACLU v. Reno II.*

Floyd Abrams's article exhaustively analyzes not only Clinton's efforts to censor the Internet but also dozens of other instances in which he led or capitulated in restraints on freedom of speech and of the press. This is how Abrams summarized the overall pattern: "Time and again, the Administration has opposed serious First Amendment claims in court, acquiesced in serious First Amendment damage by legislation and ignored First Amendment limits in its own conduct. Even when the Administration has raised First Amendment concerns, it has done so haltingly and briefly."

Although Abrams acknowledged several counterexamples to the Clinton administration's generally weak free-speech stances—most important, the administration's opposition to the flag-desecration constitutional amendment—his analysis showed that such pro-free-speech actions were the "exceptions."

Moreover, one of the good grades—more accurately, the absence of a demerit—that Abrams awards the Clinton administration overlooks its negative record in the pertinent area. Specifically, Abrams gives positive credit to Bill Clinton on the ground that "he has said nothing as shameful about civil liberties issues as did former President George Bush in his McCarthyite attack on Michael Dukakis as a 'card-carrying member of the A.C.L.U.'" That statement is literally true concerning Clinton's own public pronouncements, but it is not true concerning at least one top-level spokesperson and policy adviser on his White House staff, Rahm Emanuel. Emanuel notoriously did play the anti-ACLU card, apparently with at least the tacit blessing of the president. John Heilemann detailed this strategy in *Wired* magazine:

> In March 1996, the ACLU's press person in Washington received a call from a reporter at *U.S. News & World Report* asking for a comment on the fact that "the White House is saying that it's moderate because it opposes the ACLU on this whole list of issues." [ACLU Washington Office Director] Laura Murphy's reaction was instant: "I said, 'Oh, no, we're back to card-carrying days and George Bush, only this time the Democrat is going after us.'" When the story appeared, a quote from the White House's Rahm Emanuel seemed to confirm Murphy's fears. "We protect victims first and make criminals pay for their crimes," Emanuel declared. "That may get us in the crosshairs of the ACLU, but those are our principles."
>
> A few weeks later, . . . Murphy saw Emanuel at Ron Brown's funeral. "I went up to him and said, 'What are you doing?'" Murphy recalls. "I said, 'Lay off the ACLU.'" . . . And he said, 'Yeah, yeah, beat me, beat me—I love it when you beat up on me. Come on, say it publicly. It's good for us if you fight us.' . . ."
>
> For his part, Emanuel recalls saying no such thing to Murphy. He also insists that he sees no mileage in goading the ACLU into assailing Clinton—a claim which was undercut somewhat when another White House aide referred, unprompted, to the ACLU-baiting strategy as "the Rahm Emanuel theory of the universe."

Given the foregoing facts, Floyd Abrams was overly generous toward the Clinton administration's civil liberties record when he assumed that it was untainted by ACLU-bashing. Even taking that "false positive" into account, though, his net assessment of the "Administration's entire First Amendment record" is still negative: "Sum it up this way: Lee Atwater would have admired it; Dick Morris may yet claim credit for it; and Bill Clinton should know better."

Perpetuating Personal Power vs. Protecting Principles or Promoting Public Policies

The overarching theme that captures Clinton's overall civil liberties transgressions, including in the free speech and privacy areas, is that they seem animated not by ignorance of constitutional principles but rather by a brazen disregard for those principles. Accordingly, the critics of Clinton's constitutional sins—including his liberal critics—repeatedly describe those infractions with terms such as "cavalier" and "blithe." As Nat Hentoff put it, "There is a chilling insouciance in Clinton's elbowing the Constitution out of the way." In other words, what is especially distressing is not that Clinton is wrong-headed in his thinking about constitutional rights; it is, rather, that he seems not to think about those rights at all.

What is even more distressing is that this casual disregard seems in turn to reflect not an overweening concern for the kinds of countervailing public policy goals that have motivated many other politicians to compromise the Constitution—for example, fighting Communism or crime or terrorism. Instead, Clinton's "countervailing concern" seems to be nothing more than perpetuating his own power for its own sake. Bad enough to sell your birthrights—and ours—for the proverbial mess of pottage. Even worse is selling them for the chance to go on selling them.

Again, this theme is consistently sounded by civil libertarian and liberal commentators when they deplore Clinton's anti-constitutional record. Anthony Lewis echoed Floyd Abrams in observing that Clinton's civil liberties record "is so disappointing because he knows better." He added, "Clinton will not stand on principle when he thinks he might be damaged politically. In the end he is interested in only one thing: his own survival." In another column, Lewis castigated Clinton's constant scapegoating of civil liberties as especially unwarranted, given the absence of any real countervailing public policy concern akin to the former Communist bogeyman:

> The Soviet threat, which used to be the excuse for shoving the Constitution aside, is gone. Even in the worst days of the Red Scare we did not strip the courts of their protective power. Why are we legislating in panic now? Why, especially, is the President indifferent to constitutional rights and their protection by the courts?

Richard Cohen made the same point this way: "When it comes to political courage, Clinton has mastered only half the concept. . . .

When it comes to civil liberties: he will do nothing to endan⌣ reelection." Maureen Dowd captured the same theme with one of her trademark quips: "Clinton moved from the left wing to the right wing because what he really believes in is the West Wing."

Although those perspectives seem persuasive as far as they go, they do not go far enough to explain Clinton's continued reckless disregard for constitutional rights even after he could no longer run for office and even after his political popularity had reached record levels. To my mind, that is the sorriest aspect of his sorry record—not just selling our rights for his political survival but giving away so many of our rights outright, for nothing. Here is John Heilemann's damning dissection of this pattern:

> The notion that Clinton "knows better" rests on the assumption that the president possesses principles that are independent of political calculation—and on civil liberties, at least, there exists virtually no evidence to support that assumption. It is perfectly possible that a lifetime of shameless compromise has left Clinton incapable of even identifying a civil liberty, let alone fighting for one.

Congressional Coconspirators Notwithstanding, Clinton Deserves Much Blame

As noted, many of the administration's violations were not the sole responsibility of Bill Clinton or his administration. All of the legislative violations required the complicity of Congress, of course. Certainly, too many members of Congress, on both sides of the aisle, have turned a blind eye to important civil liberties, including in the areas of free speech and privacy. One illustration is the federal cybercensorship legislation referred to above. Both federal laws that suppress cyberspeech passed by overwhelming bipartisan majorities in both houses of Congress.

Notwithstanding Congress's passage of the two national Internet censorship laws—the Communications Decency Act (CDA) and the Child Online Protection Act (COPA)—Bill Clinton has also played essential enabling roles in the ongoing effort to "dumb down" the Internet to a level acceptable to the most intolerant parents of the most immature children. Bill Clinton did not have to sign the laws. Nor did his Justice Department have to defend the laws in court, let alone seek Supreme Court review of the unanimous lower court rulings against the first of those laws.

Neither did Clinton have to go out of his way to champion that law, even after federal judges had resoundingly repudiated it. After the first such ruling—unanimously supported by three federal judges, two of whom were Bush appointees—the president himself continued his pro-censorship pandering, declaring, "Our Constitution allows us to help parents by enforcing this act to prevent children from being exposed to objectionable material."

Regarding still other anti–civil liberties legislation, Clinton's role was even more central; commentators believe that Congress would not have passed such legislation if the president had made an effort to stop it. Moreover, some of the most damaging laws were initially proposed, and consistently pushed, by Clinton himself. For these reasons, too—in addition to the sense that "he should know better"—Clinton does deserve special blame for so many of the civil liberties setbacks while he has been in office, even those in which he did have coconspirators.

One especially egregious set of civil liberties abuses was contained in the administration's own "Omnibus Counter-Terrorism Act," which the ACLU immediately denounced as the "Ominous Counter-Constitution Act." It was proposed in the wake of the Oklahoma City bombing as an ostensible response to that and other instances of "terrorism." In fact, though, the legislation itself caused more damage to our cherished American way of life than any terrorism has ever done. This Clinton initiative, therefore, called to mind that sage warning by Benjamin Franklin: "Those who would give up essential liberty to purchase a little temporary safety deserve neither liberty nor safety."

Given Clinton's determination to appear tough on crime and on terrorism, that warning too often has proven prophetic throughout his presidency. The misnamed "anti-terrorism" law was staved off for a year by an ideologically broad coalition of citizens' groups—ranging from the ACLU to the Cato Institute to the NRA. Ultimately, though, most of its anti-rights agenda was enacted, thanks in large measure to persistent pressure from the Clinton administration. Those civil liberties nightmares range from gutting the time-honored writ of habeas corpus, which Alexander Hamilton hailed as the greatest liberty of all, to permitting sweeping, "roving" wiretaps (taps of any phone a suspect might use), to authorizing deportations on the basis of secret evidence, to outlawing association with any group that the government, at its sole discretion, might choose to brand as "terrorists."

The Clinton administration bears the brunt of the blame for all of those devastating assaults on cherished constitutional rights. Those abuses were documented and decried by Anthony Lewis in a series of columns throughout the Clinton years. A quote from one such column tells the all-too-typical tale:

> The Republican Congress . . . initiated some of the attacks. . . . But President Clinton did not resist them as other Presidents have. And he proposed some of the measures trampling on constitutional protections. Much of the worst has happened [due to the Clinton-sponsored] counterterrorism . . . law. One [feature] had nothing to do with terrorism: a provision gutting the power of Federal courts to examine state criminal convictions, on writs of habeas corpus, to make sure there was no violation of constitutional rights. The Senate might well have moderated the habeas corpus provision if the President had put up a fight. But he broke a promise and gave way.

Conclusion

Anthony Lewis sounded an important note at the end of yet another column condemning Clinton's constitutional abuses. He raised this rhetorical question about Clinton's historical legacy: "Does Bill Clinton really want to be remembered as the president who sold out habeas corpus?" I would add, does Clinton really want to be remembered, more generally, as the president who sold out so many other constitutional rights?

This volume will contribute to the vital task of chronicling Clinton's record undermining the rule of law—of which his anti-rights record is so fundamental a part. That task promotes two important interrelated purposes. First, we must set the record straight—by documenting in detail the enduring damage the Clinton administration has done to our precious rights. That is an essential prerequisite to the second, more forward-looking mission: to repair that damage by taking the necessary countermeasures to restore the rule of law and the rights it secures.

The War on Drugs

David Boaz and Timothy Lynch

Ours is a federal republic. The federal government has only the powers granted to it in the Constitution. And the United States has a tradition of individual liberty, vigorous civil society, and limited government. Identification of a problem does not mean that the government ought to undertake to solve it, and the fact that a problem occurs in more than one state does not mean that it is a proper subject for federal policy.

Perhaps no area more clearly demonstrates the bad consequences of not following such rules than does drug prohibition. The long federal experiment in prohibition of marijuana, cocaine, heroin, and other drugs has given us crime and corruption combined with a manifest failure to stop the use of drugs or reduce their availability to children.

In the 1920s Congress experimented with the prohibition of alcohol. On February 20, 1933, a new Congress acknowledged the failure of alcohol prohibition and sent the Twenty-First Amendment to the states. Congress recognized that Prohibition had failed to stop drinking and had increased prison populations and violent crime. By the end of 1933, national Prohibition was history, though many states continued to outlaw or severely restrict the sale of liquor.

Today Congress confronts a similarly failed prohibition policy. Futile efforts to enforce prohibition have been pursued even more vigorously in the 1980s and 1990s than they were in the 1920s. Total federal expenditures for the first 10 years of Prohibition amounted to $88 million—about $733 million in 1993 dollars. Drug enforcement costs about $19 billion a year now in federal spending alone.

David Boaz is executive vice president of the Cato Institute and author of *Libertarianism: A Primer*. Timothy Lynch is director of the Cato Institute's Project on Criminal Justice.

Cato Handbook for Congress (Cato Institute, 2001)

Those billions have had some effect. Total drug arrests are now more than 1.5 million a year. Since 1989 more people have been incarcerated for drug offenses than for all violent crimes combined. There are now about 400,000 drug offenders in jails and prisons, and more than 60 percent of the federal prison population consists of drug offenders

Yet, as was the case during Prohibition, all the arrests and incarcerations haven't stopped the use and abuse of drugs, or the drug trade, or the crime associated with black-market transactions. Cocaine and heroin supplies are up; the more our Customs agents interdict, the more smugglers import. And most tragic, the crime rate has soared. Despite the good news about crime in the past few years, crime rates remain at unprecedented levels.

As for discouraging young people from using drugs, the massive federal effort has largely been a dud. Despite the soaring expenditures on anti-drug efforts, about half the students in the United States in 1995 tried an illegal drug before they graduated from high school. Every year from 1975 to 1995, at least 82 percent of high school seniors said they found marijuana "fairly easy" or "very easy" to obtain. During that same period, according to federal statistics of dubious reliability, teenage marijuana use fell dramatically and then rose significantly, suggesting that cultural factors have more effect than the "war on drugs."

The manifest failure of drug prohibition explains why more and more people—from Nobel laureate Milton Friedman and conservative columnist William F. Buckley Jr. to former secretary of state George Shultz, Minnesota governor Jesse Ventura, and New Mexico governor Gary Johnson—have argued that drug prohibition actually causes more crime and other harms than it prevents.

Repeal the Controlled Substances Act

The United States is a federal republic, and Congress should deal with drug prohibition the way it dealt with alcohol prohibition. The Twenty-First Amendment did not actually legalize the sale of alcohol; it simply repealed the federal prohibition and returned to the several states the authority to set alcohol policy. States took the opportunity to design diverse liquor policies that were in tune with the preferences of their citizens. After 1933 three states and hundreds of counties continued to practice prohibition. Other states chose various forms of alcohol legalization.

The single most important law that Congress must repeal is the Controlled Substances Act of 1970. That law is probably the most far-reaching federal statute in American history, since it asserts federal jurisdiction over every drug offense in the United States, no matter how small or local in scope. Once that law is removed from the statute books, Congress should move to abolish the Drug Enforcement Administration and repeal all of the other federal drug laws.

There are a number of reasons why Congress should end the federal government's war on drugs. First and foremost, the federal drug laws are constitutionally dubious. As previously noted, the federal government can exercise only the powers that have been delegated to it. The Tenth Amendment reserves all other powers to the states or to the people. However misguided the alcohol prohibitionists turned out to have been, they deserve credit for honoring our constitutional system by seeking a constitutional amendment that would explicitly authorize a national policy on the sale of alcohol. Congress never asked the American people for additional constitutional powers to declare a war on drug consumers. That usurpation of power is something that few politicians or their court intellectuals wish to discuss.

Second, drug prohibition creates high levels of crime. Addicts are forced to commit crimes to pay for a habit that would be easily affordable if it were legal. Police sources have estimated that as much as half the property crime in some major cities is committed by drug users. More dramatic, because drugs are illegal, participants in the drug trade cannot go to court to settle disputes, whether between buyer and seller or between rival sellers. When black-market contracts are breached, the result is often some form of violent sanction, which usually leads to retaliation and then open warfare in the streets.

Our capital city, Washington, D.C., has become known as the "murder capital" even though it is the most heavily policed city in the United States. Make no mistake about it, the annual carnage that accounts for America's still shockingly high murder rates has nothing to do with the mind-altering effects of a marijuana cigarette or a crack pipe. It is instead one of the grim and bitter consequences of an ideological crusade whose proponents will not yet admit defeat.

Third, drug prohibition channels more than $40 billion a year into the criminal underworld. Alcohol prohibition drove reputable companies into other industries or out of business altogether, which paved the way for mobsters to make millions in the black market. If drugs were legal, organized crime would stand to lose billions of dollars, and drugs would be sold by legitimate businesses in an open marketplace.

Fourth, drug prohibition is a classic example of throwing money at a problem. The federal government spends some $19 billion to enforce the drug laws every year—all to no avail. For years drug war bureaucrats have been tailoring their budget requests to the latest news reports. When drug use goes up, taxpayers are told the government needs more money so that it can redouble its efforts against a rising drug scourge. When drug use goes down, taxpayers are told that it would be a big mistake to curtail spending just when progress is being made. Good news or bad, spending levels must be maintained or increased.

Fifth, the drug laws are responsible for widespread social upheaval. "Law and order" politicians too often fail to recognize that some laws can actually cause societal disorder. A simple example will illustrate that phenomenon. Right now our college campuses are relatively calm and peaceful, but imagine what would happen if Congress were to institute military conscription in order to wage a war against a dictator in the Middle East. Campuses across the country would likely erupt in protest—even though Congress did not desire that result. The drug laws happen to have different "disordering" effects. Perhaps the most obvious has been turning our cities into battlefields and upending the normal social order.

Drug prohibition has created a criminal subculture in our inner cities. The immense profits to be had from a black-market business make drug dealing the most lucrative endeavor for many people, especially those who care least about getting on the wrong side of the law.

Drug dealers become the most visibly successful people in inner-city communities, the ones with money and clothes and cars. Social order is turned upside down when the most successful people in a community are criminals. The drug war makes peace and prosperity virtually impossible in inner cities.

Students of American history will someday ponder the question of how today's elected officials could readily admit to the mistaken policy of alcohol prohibition in the 1920s but recklessly pursue a policy of drug prohibition. Indeed, the only historical lesson that recent presidents and Congresses seem to have drawn from Prohibition is that government should not try to outlaw the sale of booze. One of the broader lessons that they should have learned is this: prohibition laws should be judged according to their real-world effects, not their promised benefits. If the 107th Congress will subject the federal drug laws to that standard, it will recognize that the drug war is not the answer to problems associated with drug use.

Respect State Initiatives

The failures of drug prohibition are becoming obvious to more and more Americans. A particularly tragic consequence of the stepped-up war on drugs is the refusal to allow sick people to use marijuana as medicine. Prohibitionists insist that marijuana is not good medicine, or at least that there are legal alternatives to marijuana that are equally good. Those who believe that individuals should make their own decisions, not have their decisions made for them by Washington bureaucracies, would simply say that that's a decision for patients and their doctors to make. But in fact there is good medical evidence of the therapeutic value of marijuana—despite the difficulty of doing adequate research on an illegal drug. A recent National Institutes of Health panel concluded that smoking marijuana may help treat a number of conditions, including nausea and pain. It can be particularly effective in improving the appetite of AIDS and cancer patients. The drug could also assist people who fail to respond to traditional remedies.

More than 70 percent of U.S. cancer specialists in one survey said they would prescribe marijuana if it were legal; nearly half said they had urged their patients to break the law to acquire the drug. The British Medical Association reports that nearly 70 percent of its members believe marijuana should be available for therapeutic use. Even President George Bush's Office of National Drug Control Policy criticized the Department of Health and Human Services for closing its special medical marijuana program.

Whatever the actual value of medical marijuana, the relevant fact for federal policymakers is that in 1996 the voters of California and Arizona authorized physicians licensed in those states to recommend the use of medical marijuana to seriously ill and terminally ill patients residing in the states, without being subject to civil and criminal penalties.

In response to those referenda, however, the Clinton administration announced, without any intervening authorization from

Congress, that any physician recommending or prescribing medicinal marijuana under state law would be prosecuted. In the February 11, 1997, *Federal Register*, the Office of National Drug Control Policy announced that federal policy would be as follows: (1) physicians who recommend and prescribe medicinal marijuana to patients in conformity with state law and patients who use such marijuana will be prosecuted; (2) physicians who recommend and prescribe medicinal marijuana to patients in conformity with state law will be excluded from Medicare and Medicaid; and (3) physicians who recommend and prescribe medicinal marijuana to patients in conformity with state law will have their scheduled-drug DEA registrations revoked.

The announced federal policy also encourages state and local enforcement officials to arrest and prosecute physicians suspected of prescribing or recommending medicinal marijuana and to arrest and prosecute patients who use such marijuana. And adding insult to injury, the policy also encourages the Internal Revenue Service to issue a revenue ruling disallowing any medical deduction for medical marijuana lawfully obtained under state law.

Clearly, this is a blatant effort by the federal government to impose a national policy on the people in the states in question, people who have already voted for a contrary policy. Federal officials do not agree with the policy the people have chosen; they mean to override it, local rule notwithstanding—just as the Clinton administration has tried to do in other cases, such as the California initiatives dealing with racial preferences and state benefits for immigrants.

Congress and the administration should respect the decisions of the voters in Arizona and California, and in the other states where such initiatives passed in subsequent years. One of the benefits of a federal republic is that different policies may be tried in different states. One of the benefits of our Constitution is that it limits the power of the federal government to impose one policy on the several states.

Repeal Mandatory Minimums

The common law in England and America has always relied on judges and juries to decide cases and set punishments. Under our modern system, of course, many crimes are defined by the legislature, and appropriate penalties are defined by statute. However, mandatory minimum sentences and rigid sentencing guidelines shift too much power to legislators and regulators who are not involved in particular cases. They turn judges into clerks and prevent judges from weighing all the facts and circumstances in setting appropriate sentences. In addition, mandatory minimums for nonviolent first-time drug offenders result in sentences grotesquely disproportionate to the gravity of the offenses.

Rather than extend mandatory minimum sentences to further crimes, Congress should repeal mandatory minimums and let judges perform their traditional function of weighing the facts and setting appropriate sentences.

Conclusion

Drug abuse is a problem for those involved in it and for their families and friends. But it is better dealt with as a moral and medical than as a criminal problem—"a problem for the surgeon general, not the attorney general," as former Baltimore mayor Kurt Schmoke puts it.

The United States is a federal republic, and Congress should deal with drug prohibition the way it dealt with alcohol prohibition. The Twenty-First Amendment did not actually legalize the sale of alcohol; it simply repealed the federal prohibition and returned to the several states the authority to set alcohol policy. States took the opportunity to design diverse liquor policies that were in tune with the preferences of their citizens. After 1933 three states and hundreds of counties continued to practice prohibition. Other states chose various forms of alcohol legalization.

Congress should repeal the Controlled Substances Act of 1970, shut down the Drug Enforcement Administration, and let the states set their own policies with regard to currently illegal drugs. They would do well to treat marijuana, cocaine, and heroin the way most states now treat alcohol: It should be legal for licensed stores to sell such drugs to adults. Drug sales to children, like alcohol sales to children, should remain illegal. Driving under the influence of drugs should be illegal.

With such a policy, Congress would acknowledge that our current drug policies have failed. It would restore authority to the states, as the Founders envisioned. It would save taxpayers' money. And it would give the states the power to experiment with drug policies and perhaps devise more successful rules.

Repeal of prohibition would take the astronomical profits out of the drug business and destroy the drug kingpins who terrorize parts of our cities. It would reduce crime even more dramatically than did the repeal of alcohol prohibition. Not only would there be less crime; reform would also free police to concentrate on robbery, burglary, and violent crime.

The war on drugs has lasted longer than Prohibition, longer than the Vietnam War. But there is no light at the end of this tunnel. Prohibition has failed, again, and should be repealed, again.

PART IX

DEMOCRACY AND CULTURE

Myths of Individualism

Tom G. Palmer

It has recently been asserted that libertarians, or classical liberals, actually think that "individual agents are fully formed and their value preferences are in place prior to and outside of any society." They "ignore robust social scientific evidence about the ill effects of isolation," and, yet more shocking, they "actively oppose the notion of 'shared values' or the idea of 'the common good.'" I am quoting from the 1995 presidential address of Professor Amitai Etzioni to the American Sociological Association (*American Sociological Review,* February 1996). As a frequent talk show guest and as editor of the journal *The Responsive Community,* Etzioni has come to some public prominence as a publicist for a political movement known as communitarianism.

Etzioni is hardly alone in making such charges. They come from both left and right. From the left, *Washington Post* columnist E. J. Dionne Jr. argued in his book *Why Americans Hate Politics* that "the growing popularity of the libertarian cause suggested that many Americans had even given up on the possibility of a 'common good'" and, in a recent essay in the *Washington Post Magazine,* that "the libertarian emphasis on the freewheeling individual seems to assume that individuals come into the world as fully formed adults who should be held responsible for their actions from the moment of birth." From the right, the late Russell Kirk, in a vitriolic article titled "Libertarians: The Chirping Sectaries," claimed that "the perennial libertarian, like Satan, can bear no authority, temporal or spiritual" and that "the libertarian does not venerate ancient beliefs and customs, or the natural world, or his country, or the immortal spark in his fellow men."

Tom G. Palmer is a senior fellow at the Cato Institute.
Cato Policy Report, September/October 1996

More politely, Sen. Dan Coats (R-Ind.) and David Brooks of the *Weekly Standard* have excoriated libertarians for allegedly ignoring the value of community. Defending his proposal for more federal programs to "rebuild" community, Coats wrote that his bill is "self-consciously conservative, not purely libertarian. It recognizes, not only individual rights, but the contribution of groups rebuilding the social and moral infrastructure of their neighborhoods." The implication is that individual rights are somehow incompatible with participation in groups or neighborhoods.

Such charges, which are coming with increasing frequency from those opposed to classical liberal ideals, are never substantiated by quotations from classical liberals; nor is any evidence offered that those who favor individual liberty and limited constitutional government actually think as charged by Etzioni and his echoes. Absurd charges often made and not rebutted can come to be accepted as truths, so it is imperative that Etzioni and others be called to account for their distortions.

Atomistic Individualism

Etzioni, Dionne, Kirk, and others have set up a straw man, the "atomistic individualist." The charge of atomism is a staple of academic libertarian thumping. For example, Harvard's Michael Sandel, in *Democracy's Discontent,* asserts that libertarian ideas rest on an "image of the self as free and independent, unencumbered by aims and attachments it does not choose for itself . . . freed from the sanctions of custom and tradition and inherited status, unbound by moral ties antecedent to choice." And philosopher Charles Taylor claims that, because libertarians believe in individual rights and abstract principles, they believe in "the self-sufficiency of man alone, or, if you prefer, of the individual." Those are updated versions of an old attack on classical liberalism, according to which classical liberals posited "abstract individuals" as the basis of their views about justice.

Those claims are nonsense. No one believes that you will ever find "man alone" or that there are actually "abstract individuals." Rather, classical liberals and libertarians argue that the *system of justice* should abstract from the concrete characteristics of individuals. Thus, when an individual comes before a court, her height, color, wealth, social standing, and religion are normally irrelevant to questions of justice. That is what equality before the law means; it does not mean that no one actually *has* a particular height, skin color, or religious belief. Abstraction is a mental process used to discern what is essential or relevant to a problem; it does not require a belief in abstract entities.

It is precisely because neither individuals nor small groups can be fully self-sufficient that cooperation is necessary to human survival and flourishing. And because cooperation takes place among countless individuals unknown to each other, the rules governing that interaction are abstract in nature. Abstract rules, which establish in advance what we may expect of one another, make cooperation possible on a wide scale.

No reasonable person could possibly believe that individuals are fully formed outside society—in isolation, if you will. That would mean that no one could have had any parents, cousins, friends, personal heroes, or even neighbors. Obviously, all of us have been influenced by those around us. What libertarians assert is simply that differences among normal adults do not imply different fundamental rights.

Sources and Limits of Obligations

Libertarianism is not at base a metaphysical theory about the primacy of the individual over the abstract, much less an absurd theory about "abstract individuals." Nor is it an anomic rejection of traditions, as Kirk and some conservatives have charged. Rather, it is a political theory that emerged in response to the growth of unlimited state power. Libertarianism draws its strength from a powerful fusion of a normative theory about the moral and political sources and limits of obligations and a positive theory explaining the sources of order: each person has the right to be free, and free persons can produce order spontaneously, without a commanding power over them.

What of Dionne's patently absurd characterization of libertarianism: "individuals come into the world as fully formed adults who should be held responsible for their actions from the moment of birth"? Libertarians recognize the difference between adults and children, as well as differences between normal adults and adults who are insane or mentally hindered. Guardians are necessary for children and abnormal adults, because they cannot make responsible choices for themselves. But there is no obvious reason for holding that some adults are entitled to make choices for other normal adults, as paternalists of both left and right believe. Libertarians argue that no adult has the right to impose choices on other normal adults, except in abnormal circumstances, such as when one person finds another unconscious and administers medical assistance or calls an ambulance.

What distinguishes libertarianism from other views of political morality is principally its theory of *enforceable* obligations. Some obligations, such as the obligation to write a thank-you note to one's host after a dinner party, are not normally enforceable by law. Others, such as the obligation not to punch a disagreeable critic in the nose or to pay for a pair of shoes before walking out of the store in them, are. Obligations may be universal or particular. Individuals, whoever and wherever they may be (i.e., in abstraction from particular circumstances), have an enforceable obligation to all other persons: not to harm them in their lives, liberties, health, or possessions. In John Locke's terms, "Being all equal and independent, no one ought to harm another in his life, health, liberty, or possessions." All individuals have the right that others not harm them in their enjoyment of those goods. The rights and the obligations are correlative and, being both universal and "negative" in character, are capable under normal circumstances of being enjoyed by all simultaneously. It is the *universality* of the human right not to be killed, injured, or robbed that is at the base of the libertarian view, and one need not posit an "abstract individual" to assert the universality of that right. It is precisely his veneration for the "immortal spark in his fellow men" that leads the libertarian to defend individual rights.

Those obligations are universal, but what about "particular" obligations? As I write this, I am sitting in a coffee house and have just ordered another coffee. I have freely undertaken the particular obligation to pay for the coffee: I have transferred a property right to a certain amount of my money to the owner of the coffee shop, and she has transferred the property right to the cup of coffee to me. Libertarians typically argue that particular obligations, at least under normal circumstances, must be created by consent; they cannot be unilaterally imposed by others. Equality of rights means that some

414

people cannot simply impose obligations on others, for the moral agency and rights of those others would then be violated. Communitarians, on the other hand, argue that we all are born with many particular obligations, such as to give to this body of persons—called a state or, more nebulously, a nation, community, or folk—so much money, so much obedience, or even one's life. And they argue that those particular obligations can be coercively enforced. In fact, according to communitarians such as Taylor and Sandel, I am actually *constituted as a person*, not only by the facts of my upbringing and my experiences, but by a set of very particular unchosen obligations.

To repeat, communitarians maintain that we are constituted as persons by our particular obligations, and therefore those obligations cannot be a matter of choice. Yet that is a mere assertion and cannot substitute for an *argument* that one is obligated to others; it is no justification for coercion. One might well ask, If an individual is born with the obligation to obey, who is born with the right to command? If one wants a coherent theory of obligations, there must be someone, whether an individual or a group, with the right to the fulfillment of the obligation. If I am constituted as a person by my obligation to obey, who is constituted as a person by the right to obedience? Such a theory of obligation may have been coherent in an age of God-kings, but it seems rather out of place in the modern world.

To sum up, no reasonable person believes in the existence of abstract individuals, and the true dispute between libertarians and communitarians is not about individualism as such but about the source of particular obligations, whether imposed or freely assumed.

Groups and Common Goods

A theory of obligation focusing on individuals does *not* mean that there is no such "thing" as society or that we cannot speak meaningfully of groups. The fact that there are trees does not mean that we cannot speak of forests, after all. Society is not merely a collection of individuals, nor is it some "bigger or better" thing separate from them. Just as a building is not a pile of bricks but the bricks *and* the relationships among them, society is not a person, with his own rights, but many individuals *and* the complex set of relationships among them.

A moment's reflection makes it clear that claims that libertarians reject "shared values" and the "common good" are incoherent. If libertarians share the value of liberty (at a minimum), then they cannot "actively oppose the notion of 'shared values,'" and if libertarians believe that we will all be better off if we enjoy freedom, then they have not "given up on the possibility of 'a common good,'" for a central part of their efforts is to assert what the common good is! In response to Kirk's claim that libertarians reject tradition, let me point out that libertarians defend a tradition of liberty that is the fruit of thousands of years of human history. In addition, pure traditionalism is incoherent, for traditions may clash, and then one has no guide to right action. Generally, the statement that libertarians "reject tradition" is both tasteless and absurd. Libertarians follow religious traditions, family traditions, ethnic traditions, and social traditions such as courtesy and even respect for others, which is evidently not a tradition Kirk thought it necessary to maintain.

The libertarian case for individual liberty, which has been so distorted by communitarian critics, is simple and reasonable. It is obvious that different individuals require different things to live good, healthy, and virtuous lives. Despite their common nature, people are materially and numerically individuated, and we have needs that differ. So, how far does our common good extend?

Karl Marx, an early and especially brilliant and biting communitarian critic of libertarianism, asserted that civil society is based on a "decomposition of man" such that man's "essence is no longer in community but in difference"; under socialism, in contrast, man would realize his nature as a "species being." Accordingly, socialists believe that collective provision of everything is appropriate; in a truly socialized state, we would all enjoy the same common good and conflict simply would not occur. Communitarians are typically much more cautious, but despite a lot of talk they rarely tell us much about what our common good might be. The communitarian philosopher Alasdair MacIntyre, for instance, in his influential book *After Virtue,* insists for 219 pages that there is a "good life for man" that must be pursued in common and then rather lamely concludes that "the good life for man is the life spent in seeking for the good life for man."

A familiar claim is that providing retirement security through the state is an element of the common good, for it "brings all of us together." But who is included in "all of us"? Actuarial data show that African-American males who have paid the same taxes into the Social Security system as have Caucasian males over their working lives stand to get back about half as much. Further, more black than white males will die before they receive a single penny, meaning all of their money has gone to benefit others and none of their "investments" are available to their families. In other words, they are being robbed for the benefit of nonblack retirees. Are African-American males part of the "all of us" who are enjoying a common good, or are they victims of the "common good" of others? (As readers of this magazine should know, all would be better off under a privatized system, which leads libertarians to assert the common good of freedom to choose among retirement systems.) All too often, claims about the "common good" serve as covers for quite selfish attempts to secure private goods; as the classical liberal Austrian novelist Robert Musil noted in his great work *The Man without Qualities*, "Nowadays only criminals dare to harm others without philosophy."

Libertarians recognize the inevitable pluralism of the modern world and for that reason assert that individual liberty is at least part of the common good. They also understand the absolute necessity of cooperation for the attainment of one's ends; a solitary individual could never actually *be* "self-sufficient," which is precisely why we must have rules—governing property and contracts, for example—to make peaceful cooperation possible and why we institute government to enforce those rules. The common good is a system of justice that allows all to live together in harmony and peace; a common good more extensive than that tends to be, not a common good for "all of us," but a common good for some of us at the expense of others of us. (There is another sense, understood by every parent, to the term "self-sufficiency." Parents normally desire that their children acquire the virtue of "pulling their own weight" and not subsisting as scroungers, layabouts, moochers, or parasites. That is a necessary condition of self-respect; Taylor and other critics of libertarianism often confuse the virtue of self-sufficiency with the impossible condition of never relying on or cooperating with others.)

The issue of the common good is related to the beliefs of communitarians regarding the personality or the separate existence of groups. Both are part and parcel of a fundamentally unscientific and irrational view of politics that tends to personalize institutions and groups, such as the state or nation or society. Instead of enriching political science and avoiding the alleged naiveté of libertarian individualism, as communitarians claim, however, the personification thesis obscures matters and prevents us from asking the interesting questions with which scientific inquiry begins. No one ever put the matter quite as well as the classical liberal historian Parker T. Moon of Columbia University in his study of 19th-century European imperialism, *Imperialism and World Politics*:

> Language often obscures truth. More than is ordinarily realized, our eyes are blinded to the facts of international relations by tricks of the tongue. When one uses the simple monosyllable "France" one thinks of France as a unit, an entity. When to avoid awkward repetition we use a personal pronoun in referring to a country—when for example we say "France sent *her* troops to conquer Tunis"—we impute not only unity but personality to the country. The very words conceal the facts and make international relations a glamorous drama in which personalized nations are the actors, and all too easily we forget the flesh-and-blood men and women who are the true actors. How different it would be if we had no such word as "France," and had to say instead—thirty-eight million men, women and children of very diversified interests and beliefs, inhabiting 218,000 square miles of territory! Then we should more accurately describe the Tunis expedition in some such way as this: "A few of these thirty-eight million persons sent thirty thousand others to conquer Tunis." This way of putting the fact immediately suggests a question, or rather a series of questions. Who are the "few"? Why did they send the thirty thousand to Tunis? And why did these obey?

Group personification obscures, rather than illuminates, important political questions. Those questions, centering mostly around the explanation of complex political phenomena and the assignment of moral responsibility, simply cannot be addressed within the confines of group personification, which drapes a cloak of mysticism around the actions of policymakers, thus allowing some to use "philosophy"—and mystical philosophy, at that—to harm others.

Libertarians are separated from communitarians by differences on important issues, notably whether coercion is necessary to maintain community, solidarity, friendship, love, and the other things that make life worth living and that can be enjoyed only in common with others. Those differences cannot be swept away a priori; their resolution is not furthered by shameless distortion, absurd characterizations, or petty name-calling.

Rights and Responsibilities

David Boaz

A journalist asked me recently what I thought of a proposal of self-styled communitarians to "suspend for a while the minting of new rights." How many ways, I thought, does that get it wrong? Communitarians seem to see rights as little boxes; when you have too many, the room gets full. In my view, we have only one right—or an infinite number. The one fundamental human right is the right to live your life as you choose so long as you don't infringe on the equal rights of others.

But that one right has infinite implications. As James Wilson, a signer of the Constitution, said in response to a proposal that a bill of rights be added to the Constitution: "Enumerate all the rights of man! I am sure, sirs, that no gentleman in the late Convention would have attempted such a thing." After all, a person has a right to wear a hat—or not; to marry, or not; to grow beans, or apples; or to open a haberdashery. It is impossible to enumerate a priori all the rights we have; we usually go to the trouble of identifying them only when someone proposes to limit one or another. Treating rights as tangible claims that must be limited in number gets the whole concept wrong.

Every right carries with it a correlative responsibility. My right to speak freely implies your responsibility not to censor me. Your right to private property implies my responsibility not to steal it, or to force you to use it in the way I demand. In short, the protection of my rights entails my respecting the rights of others. So why do I feel uncomfortable when I hear communitarians talk about "rights and responsibilities"? The problem is that there are three senses of the term "responsibility," which are frequently confused.

David Boaz is executive vice president of the Cato Institute and author of *Libertarianism: A Primer*.

Cato Policy Report, January/February 1994

First, there are the responsibilities noted above, the obligations that correlate with other people's rights.

Second, there are the "responsibilities" that some would insist that we assume as a prerequisite to exercising our rights. This sense, frequently found in communitarian writings, echoes the *ancien régime* approach, the notion of rights as privileges that we retain only so long as we use them responsibly. That idea degrades the American tradition of individualism. It implies that we have our rights only so long as someone—the government, in practice—approves of the way we use them. In fact, as the Declaration of Independence tells us, humans have rights before they enter into governments, which are created for the very purpose of *protecting* those rights.

Conservatives as well as communitarians sometimes fall into that way of thinking. Our friend Stuart Butler of the Heritage Foundation defends government-mandated health insurance on the ground that "freedom also implies responsibility." But if the government can *require* us to act in the way it deems responsible by buying health insurance, what kind of freedom do we have?

People rarely try to take our rights when they think we are using them responsibly. No one tries to censor popular, mainstream speech; it is obscene or radical speech that is frequently threatened. We must defend even the irresponsible use of rights *because* they're rights and not privileges. Governments never begin by taking away the rights of average citizens and taxpayers. But by establishing legal precedents through attacks on the rights of despised groups, governments lay the groundwork for the narrowing of everyone's rights.

Third, there are the moral responsibilities that we have outside the realm of rights. It is frequently charged—famously by communitarian philosopher Mary Ann Glendon—that "the language of rights is morally incomplete." Of course it is; rights pertain only to a certain domain of morality, a narrow domain in fact, not to all of morality. Rights establish certain minimal standards for our treatment of each other: we must not kill, rape, rob, or otherwise initiate force against each other. That leaves a great many options to be dealt with by other theories of morality. But that fact doesn't mean that the idea of rights is invalid or incomplete *in the domain where it applies*; it just means that most of the decisions we make every day involve choices that are only broadly circumscribed by the obligation to respect each other's rights.

Libertarians are often charged with ignoring or even rejecting moral responsibilities. There may be some truth to the first charge. Libertarians obviously spend most of their time defending liberty and thus criticizing government. They leave it to others to explore moral obligations and exhort people to assume them. Why is that? I see two reasons. First, there is the question of specialization. We do not demand of the AIDS researcher, Why aren't you searching for a cure for cancer as well? With government as big as it is, libertarians find the task of limiting its size thoroughly time-consuming. Second, libertarians have noticed that too many nonlibertarians want to legally enforce every moral virtue. As Bill Niskanen puts it, welfare-state liberals fail to distinguish between a virtue and a requirement, while contemporary conservatives fail to distinguish between a sin and a crime. (The unique contribution of communitarians to the current debate may be that they make both of those grievous errors.)

When libertarians omit moral values from their social analysis, however, they are ignoring the lessons taught by all their intellectual mentors. Adam Smith wrote *The Theory of Moral Sentiments.* F. A. Hayek stressed the importance of morals and tradition. Ayn Rand set out a fairly strict code of personal ethics. Thomas Szasz's work challenges the reductionists and behaviorists with a commitment to the old ideas of good and bad, right and wrong, and responsibility for one's choices. Charles Murray emphasizes the value and indeed the necessity of community and responsibility. Libertarians should do more to make clear the role of moral responsibility in their philosophy. However, they will rightly continue to emphasize that government can undermine the values necessary for a free society—honesty, self-reliance, reason, thrift, education, tolerance, discipline, property, contract, and family—but it cannot instill them.

The Right to Do as You Please and Take the Consequences

P. J. O'Rourke

The Cato Institute has an unusual political cause—no political cause whatsoever. We are here tonight to dedicate ourselves to that cause, to dedicate ourselves, in other words, to . . . nothing.

We have no ideology, no agenda, no catechism, no dialectic, no plan for humanity. We have no "vision thing," as our ex-president would say, or, as our current president would say, we have no Hillary.

All we have is the belief that people should do what they want to do, unless it causes harm to other people. And that had better be clear and provable harm. No nonsense about second-hand smoke or hurtful, insensitive language, please.

I don't know what's good for you. You don't know what's good for me. We don't know what's good for mankind. And it sometimes seems as though we're the only people who don't. It may well be that gathered here in this room tonight are all the people in the world who don't want to tell all the people in the world what to do.

That is because we believe in freedom. Freedom—what this country was established upon, what the Constitution was written to defend, what the Civil War was fought to perfect.

Freedom is not empowerment. Empowerment is what the Serbs have in Bosnia. Anybody can grab a gun and be empowered. It's not entitlement. An entitlement is what people on welfare get, and how free are they? It's not an endlessly expanding list of rights—the "right" to education, the "right" to health care, the "right" to food and housing.

P. J. O'Rourke is the Mencken Research Fellow of the Cato Institute and the author of numerous books, including *Parliament of Whores*. He delivered these remarks at the banquet celebrating the opening of the Cato Institute's new building on May 6, 1993.

Cato Policy Report, July/August 1993

That's not freedom; that's dependence. Those aren't rights; those are rations of slavery—hay and a barn for human cattle.

There is only one basic human right, the right to do as you damn well please. And with it comes the only basic human duty, the duty to take the consequences.

So we have here tonight a kind of anti-matter protest—an unpolitical nondemonstration by deeply uncommitted inactivists. We are part of a huge invisible picket line that circles the White House 24 hours a day. We are participants in an enormous nonmarch on Washington—millions and millions of Americans *not* descending on the nation's capital to demand *nothing* from the U.S. government. To demand nothing, that is, except the one thing that no government in history has been able to do—leave us alone.

There are just two rules of governance in a free society: mind your own business and keep your hands to yourself. Bill, keep your hands to yourself. Hillary, mind your own business.

We have a group of incredibly silly people in the White House right now, people who think government works. Or that government *would* work if you got some really bright young kids from Yale to run it.

We're being governed by dorm-room bull session. The Clinton administration is over there right now pulling an all-nighter in the West Wing. They think, if they can just stay up late enough, they can create a healthy economy and bring peace to the former Yugoslavia.

The Clinton administration is groping to decrease government spending by increasing the amount of money we give to the government to spend.

Health care is too expensive, so the Clinton administration is putting a high-powered corporation lawyer in charge of making it cheaper. (This is what I always do when I want to spend less money—hire a lawyer from Yale.) If you think health care is expensive now, wait until you see what it costs when it's free.

The Clinton administration is putting together a program to let college graduates work to pay off their school tuition. As if this were some genius idea. It's called *getting a job*. Most folks do that when they get out of college, unless, of course, they happen to become governor of Arkansas.

And the Clinton administration launched an attack on people in Texas because those people were religious nuts with guns. Hell, this country was *founded* by religious nuts with guns. Who does Bill Clinton think stepped ashore on Plymouth Rock? Peace Corps volunteers? Or maybe the people in Texas were attacked because of child abuse. But, if child abuse was the issue, why didn't Janet Reno tear gas Woody Allen?

You know, if government were a product, selling it would be illegal.

Government is a health hazard. Governments have killed many more people than cigarettes or unbuckled seat belts ever have.

Government contains impure ingredients—as anybody who's looked at Congress can tell you.

On the basis of Bill Clinton's 1992 campaign promises, I think we can say that government practices deceptive advertising.

And the merest glance at the federal budget is enough to convict government of perjury, extortion, and fraud.

There, ladies and gentlemen, you have the Cato Institute in a nutshell: government should be against the law. Term limits aren't enough. We need jail.

Are Libertarians Anti-Government?

David Boaz

For the past several years, especially since the Oklahoma City bombing, the national media have focused a lot of attention on "anti-government" extremists. Libertarians, who are critical of a great deal that government does, have unfortunately but perhaps understandably been tossed into the "anti-government" camp by many journalists.

There are two problems with this identification. The first and most obvious is that many of the so-called anti-government groups are racist or violent or both, and being identified with them verges on libel.

The second and ultimately more important problem is that libertarians are not, in any serious sense, "anti-government." It's understandable that journalists might refer to people who often criticize both incumbent officeholders and government programs as "anti-government," but the term is misleading.

A government is a set of institutions through which we adjudicate our disputes, defend our rights, and provide for certain common needs. It derives its authority, at some level and in some way, from the consent of the governed.

Libertarians want people to be able to live peacefully together in civil society. Cooperation is better than coercion. Peaceful coexistence and voluntary cooperation require an institution to protect us from outside threats, deter or punish criminals, and settle the disputes that will inevitably arise among neighbors—a government, in short. Thus, to criticize a wide range of the activities undertaken by federal and state governments—from Social Security to drug prohibition to out-of-control taxation—is not to be "anti-government." It is simply to insist that what we want is a limited government that attends to its necessary and proper functions.

David Boaz is executive vice president of the Cato Institute and author of *Libertarianism: A Primer.*

Cato Policy Report, July/August 1998

But if libertarians are not "anti-government," then how do we describe the kind of government that libertarians support? One formulation found in the media is that "libertarians support weak government." That has a certain appeal. But consider a prominent case of "weak government." Numerous reports have told us recently about the weakness of the Russian government. Not only does it have trouble raising taxes and paying its still numerous employees, it has trouble deterring or punishing criminals. It is in fact too weak to carry out its legitimate functions. The Russian government is a failure on two counts: it is massive, clumsy, overextended, and virtually unconstrained in scope, yet too weak to perform its essential job. (Residents of many American cities may find that description a bit too close for comfort.)

Not "weak government," then. How about "small government"? Lots of people, including many libertarians, like that phrase to describe libertarian views. And it has a certain plausibility. We rail against "big government," so we must prefer small government, or "less government." Of course, we wouldn't want a government too small to deter military threats or apprehend criminals. And *Washington Post* columnist E. J. Dionne Jr. offers us this comparison: "a dictatorship in which the government provides no social security, health, welfare or pension programs of any kind" and "levies relatively low taxes that go almost entirely toward the support of large military and secret police forces that regularly kill or jail people for their political or religious views" or "a democracy with open elections and full freedom of speech and religion [which] levies higher taxes than the dictatorship to support an extensive welfare state."

"The first country might technically have a 'smaller government,'" Dionne writes, "but it undoubtedly is *not* a free society. The second country would have a 'bigger government,' but it *is* indeed a free society."

Now there are several problems with this comparison, not least Dionne's apparent view that high taxes don't limit the freedom of those forced to pay them. But our concern here is the term "smaller government." Measured as a percentage of GDP or by the number of employees, the second government may well be larger than the first. Measured by its power and control over individuals and society, however, the first government is doubtless larger. Thus, as long as the term is properly understood, it's reasonable for libertarians to endorse "smaller government." But Dionne's criticism should remind us that the term may not be well understood.

So if we're not anti-government, and not really for weak or small government, how should we describe the libertarian position? To answer that question, we need to go back to the Declaration of Independence and the Constitution. Libertarians generally support a government formed by the consent of the governed and designed to achieve certain limited purposes. Both the form of government and the limits on its powers should be specified in a constitution, and the challenge in any society is to keep government constrained and limited so that individuals can prosper and solve problems in a free and civil society.

Thus libertarians are not "anti-government." Libertarians support limited, constitutional government—limited not just in size but, of far greater importance, in the scope of its powers.

Creating a World of Free Men

Dick Armey

Fifty years after *The Road to Serfdom,* the closing thought of F. A. Hayek's great treatise (as expressed in the highly influential *Reader's Digest* condensation) still rings true: "The guiding principle of any attempt to create a world of free men is this. A policy of freedom for the individual is the only truly progressive policy."

Sometimes we forget how radical this statement was in 1944. Hayek's little book evoked contempt from his fellow intellectuals. To suggest, in the midst of the Second World War, that central planning does not work and is generally self-defeating and dangerous was a dramatic statement that the political class could not accept. To argue that government should be so limited as to be able to do little beyond protecting life, liberty, and property was antiquated, eccentric, even bizarre. And yet, today, looking back over the decades, who would say that the socialists and central planners were right, and Hayek wrong?

Events, of course, have proved him prophetic. Indeed, he had the good fortune to live long enough not only to see national socialism smashed but also to see Soviet socialism relegated to the ash heap of history. And I'd like to think he is up there somewhere tonight smiling down on us, as big government liberalism follows those two great, tragic "isms" into oblivion.

What was it that so enraged left-wingers about Hayek? It was the assertion that liberal paternalism is just as dangerous to humanity in the long run as fascism or communism. Liberalism, he argued, differs from those evil systems only in degree, not in kind. Hayek was a humble man, genuinely humble before reality. And that humility

Rep. Dick Armey (R-Tex.), Majority Leader of the House of Representatives, delivered these remarks at the dedication of the Cato Institute's F. A. Hayek Auditorium on May 9, 1995.

Cato Policy Report, July/August 1995

gave his words the boldness of honesty and the audacity of truth. And the liberals could not forgive him.

Reading back over *The Road to Serfdom,* I could not help thinking of the old quip that a conservative is someone who says, "I'll believe it when I see it," and a liberal is someone who says, "I'll see it when I believe it." While Hayek always called himself a liberal in the classical sense of "one who is for liberty," he was truly conservative in the sense I'm talking about. He never thought human nature or the constitution of reality could be changed or reshaped by force of will. He was a rarity, an intellectually honest man in an intellectually dishonest age. What an ideal name for an auditorium dedicated to the promotion of human freedom.

And what an ideal think tank to have helping our new majority transform Washington. Your devotion to truth, like that of Hayek, has cast you as mavericks. It has put you at odds with the received opinions of the conventional left and right. But it is that principled consistency that has made the Cato Institute so "hot" these days. I mean, who would have imagined, a year ago, that the leaders of Congress would be looking to those crazy libertarians over at Cato for advice? Who could have imagined we would be discussing abolishing whole programs, turning others back to the states, repealing ill-conceived laws, and dismantling cabinet agencies, just as you've always recommended?

You have been successful because you believe what Hayek never ceased to point out—and indeed what the entire 20th century makes plain—that freedom, and only freedom, works.

What a hopeful time this is. Socialism is finished. The liberal welfare state is passé. And I'm more optimistic than I've ever dared to be that we are entering a new era of limited government. Congress is run by Americans who believe ordinary people can be trusted to spend their own money and make their own decisions. We will send power back from the hallowed halls of Congress to the more hallowed kitchen tables of America, where night after night families bow their heads in thanks and make decisions about education, charity, jobs, spending, debt, and personal behavior with a wisdom and a compassion that no agency head, no cabinet secretary, no member of Congress could ever match.

Just today, we shook the foundations of Washington by doing something that hasn't been done for a quarter century. We proposed a balanced budget.

429

True to our word, and despite the skeptics, we've produced a specific, detailed plan to balance the budget in seven years. And we get there with real spending cuts. No accounting gimmicks. No tax increases. In Hayekian fashion, we asked basic questions: Does the typical American family really need a Department of Commerce? Could our children learn without an Education Department? Could the Republic survive without a National Endowment for the Arts? Would the economy grind to a halt without an Interstate Commerce Commission?

While this budget faces a tough road, we believe the American people demand no less, for the sake of freedom. Americans want not just a smaller government, but the government of the Framers of the Constitution. And that's what we intend to restore.

Can I give you a peek at where we're headed? Just look at Estonia. Three years ago that tiny republic was a typical, ex-Soviet basket case, with negative growth, staggering unemployment, and skyrocketing inflation. But in late 1992 Prime Minister Mart Laar's reform government decided to throw the dice. They abolished all tariffs. They privatized 90 percent of state-owned enterprises. They scrapped every last subsidy, right down to farm subsidies. To create a sound money supply, they threw out the worthless ruble and created a new local currency, pegged to the German mark. Here's my favorite part: They established a flat tax. And yes, they balanced their national budget.

What's the result? Today, the Estonian economy is growing at a vigorous 6 percent a year, twice America's growth rate. Unemployment is just 2 percent. Inflation has collapsed from 1,000 percent to 40. Sixty thousand new private businesses have sprung up in a population of only two million.

Mart Laar came to my office the other day to recount his country's remarkable transformation. He described a nation of people who are harder working, more virtuous—yes, more virtuous, because the market punishes immorality—and more hopeful about the future than they've ever been in their history. I asked Mr. Laar where his government got the idea for those reforms. Do you know what he replied? He said, "We read Milton Friedman and F. A. Hayek."

Ladies and gentlemen, if Estonia is not a vindication of everything we believe in—from free trade to privatization to sound money to balanced budgets—I am at a loss as to how else one *could* validate our ideas. To quote my friend and hero, Thomas Sowell, we don't have *faith* that freedom works. We have evidence.

And by the way, if I can advertise for a moment, it turns out Estonians *love* their flat tax. They like the postcard-size return. Compliance has actually gone up. People are willing to pay their taxes voluntarily now, because they feel the system is fair. Their only complaint: They think the rate is too high. But of course, there's an easy way to cure that.

And speaking of taxes, isn't it amazing that the debate over how we restructure America's tax system for the next century is coming down to a contest between a flat tax and a consumption tax? How far we've come.

As I say, I'm hopeful for the future of freedom. But I do have concerns. Let me just mention one. More and more these days, immigrants are being viewed as if they were the source of America's problems. It seems the old Malthusian notion that people are a drain is making one of its regular revivals. Well, it's good to know Cato has always held fast against that misguided teaching. At a time when some are turning against immigrants, you continue to view them as human beings, in Julian Simon's beautiful phrase, as the ultimate resource.

Anti-immigration has always been ironic, because throughout our history newcomers have been a source of strength, not weakness. America still attracts the world's best talent. And surely that is no liability. Think of it. We can avail ourselves of much of the world's intellectual wealth simply by opening our doors. America never has to grow old. We can always take in new talent and new ideas and new blood. No ruling elite can dominate us for very long, because we always have younger, smarter, more entrepreneurial spirits willing and eager to move up.

The impulse to limit immigration is really a manifestation of the protectionist impulse. And it's misguided. It's a desire to use government's monopoly of coercive power to benefit oneself at the expense of somebody else. And that, as Hayek taught us, is self-defeating. But the biggest problem with the closed-border idea is that it embraces the liberals' world view. And thus it leads logically down the path to bigger government.

Should we have an orderly immigration policy? Of course.

Should we give the Border Patrol the appropriate tools? Of course.

But in so doing, should we infringe on the personal liberties of law-abiding Americans? Absolutely not.

We need immigration reform. But our goal should be to make immigration more orderly, not more restrictive.

We have too many immigrants coming here to get on welfare. But the reasonable response is not to build a police state. It's to shrink the welfare state.

We have an educational system that no longer promotes assimilation. But the sensible response is not to exclude foreign children. It's to scrap multiculturalism in the schools and give parents real school choice.

Should we reduce *legal* immigration? Well, I'm hard-pressed to think of a single problem that would be solved by shutting off the supply of willing and eager new Americans. If anything, in the spirit of Hayek, we should be thinking about *increasing* legal immigration.

Should we turn private employers into auxiliary border guards? I think unfunded mandates are bad enough without that.

And as for a national ID card, which I understand the administration is considering, let me just say this. I oppose it. And I will fight it. Let me be clear here. What some are calling a "national computer registry" is just a euphemism for a national ID card. And any system in which Americans would be forced to possess such a card, for any reason, is an abomination and wholly at odds with the American tradition of individual freedom.

Lest I close on such a defiant note, let me leave you by saying how much comfort it gives me to know that when it comes to that issue, as so many others, we'll be able to count on our good friends at Cato.

The coming months promise major battles with the liberals over spending, taxes, crime, education, the environment, welfare, property rights, and a hundred other issues. And, as always, Cato will be there for us, arming our legions of righteousness with facts, statistics, policy briefs, and four-color charts.

For like the great man we are celebrating tonight, you have the boldness of honesty and the audacity of truth. You believe, as he always reminded us, that true human progress lies, not in power or planning, but in markets and the rule of law. It is with those safeguards, and those alone, that we may dare hope to avoid the road to serfdom and "create a world of free men."

Is Our Culture in Decline?

Tyler Cowen

The "culture wars" and recent debates over the National Endowment for the Arts reflect deep disagreements about the health of contemporary culture. The current wave of cultural pessimism, expressed in various forms by both the left and the right, suggests that our culture is experiencing corruption and decline. The left concludes that government support for the arts is needed, while the right often favors government support for traditional culture. But a review of the evidence offers strong reasons for cultural optimism and confidence that a modern commercial society will stimulate artistic creativity and diversity.

The music of Bach, Mozart, Haydn, and Beethoven is more accessible to today's listeners than it was to the listeners of the 18th or 19th centuries. Modern concertgoers can sample an unparalleled range of musical periods, instruments, and styles. Even relatively obscure composers have their material stocked in music superstores, which are common in both American cities and suburbs. A small Tower Records outlet will offer at least 10,000 classical music titles, and the largest Tower branch in Manhattan has over 22,000 titles. The Naxos label markets excellent performances of the classics for as little as $5.99 for 70 minutes of music. Music of all kinds—both old and new—is available in great profusion.

Movies, including many silents, can be rented on videocassette very cheaply, or on laser disks for those who want higher quality picture and sound. Modern video stores, run on a private for-profit basis, are libraries full of classic works.

New and definitive editions of many literary works, or better translations, are published regularly. The Bible and Plato, two fa-

Tyler Cowen is a professor of economics at George Mason University and the author of *In Praise of Commercial Culture.*

Cato Policy Report, September/October 1998

vorites of many cultural pessimists, continue to be reissued in new editions, while the classics are available in cheap paperback. Television, video stores, and bookstores give modern fans better access to the works of Shakespeare than the Elizabethans had.

Literacy and reading are two areas where the modern world comes in for especially harsh criticism, but even here the trends are largely positive. Between 1970 and 1990 the measured world literacy rate for adults rose from 61.5 to 73.5 percent. The industrialized countries increased their literacy rate from 93.8 to 96.7 percent over that period. American illiteracy was far worse 100 years ago or even in the middle of this century. Consistent with those trends, the average American buys more than twice as many books today as in 1947. The number of bookstores has jumped nearly 10-fold, and their average size has increased dramatically. Book superstores are now commonplace.

Contrary to many claims, television and the Internet are not killing the book. The printed word offers unique modes of story-telling and analysis that other media have not replaced. Television and the Internet often complement reading and stimulate reader interest in books, instead of replacing them. Today a wide variety of talented writers is actively publishing and transcending traditional genre boundaries.

Art museums and art museum attendance are booming. Blockbuster art exhibitions travel the world and bring great paintings to increasing numbers of viewers. Earlier in this century, most Americans outside New York had few means of viewing high-quality art. Art publishing is doing well; even minor painters now have published catalogs full of high-quality color plates.

Live performance of the arts has flourished as well. From 1965 to 1990 America grew from having 58 symphony orchestras to having nearly 300, from 27 opera companies to more than 150, and from 22 nonprofit regional theaters to 500. Contemporary Western culture, especially in the United States, is flourishing.

Markets Spur Innovation

The market economy continually spurs new artistic innovations. Arguing the worth of particular contemporary creations is more difficult, given the tendencies for disagreement about the culture of the present day (Mozart was controversial in his time, but few dispute his merits today). Modern creators, however, have offered many deep and lasting creations, which are universal in their scope and significant in their import. Those creations delight and enrich large numbers of intelligent fans and influence subsequent artists. We can fully expect many modern and contemporary works to stand the test of time, just as earlier works have, even if we cannot identify exactly which ones.

The most impressive creations of contemporary culture include cinema, rock 'n' roll, Pop Art and Minimalism, modern dance, jazz, genre fiction, and the modern biography, to give but a few examples. The skylines of Manhattan, Chicago, and Hong Kong were financed and designed almost entirely by the private sector. The exact contents of a list of important contemporary creations will vary with taste, but our culture provides a wide variety of styles, aesthetics, and moods. An individual need not have a very particular set of preferences to love contemporary creations. The 20th century is not only the age of intellectual, atonal music; it is also the age of Buddy Holly and Steven Spielberg, both life-affirming and celebratory creators.

New musical genres continue to blossom. Our century has seen the development of blues, soul, rhythm and blues, jazz, ragtime, swing, rock, country and western, rap, and bluegrass, as well as more recent forms of electronic music. Some of the most significant modern artists are still around, playing and recording for our enjoyment. We can hear Bob Dylan and the Rolling Stones in concert, still in good form, even if not at their youthful peak.

Film is the art of the 20th century, par excellence. It combines drama, music, and high technology to entertain and inspire large audiences. Moviegoers all around the world want to see American films. Some movie buffs complain that "they don't make 'em like they used to," but the best American films of the last 20 years—my list would include *The Thin Blue Line, Blue Velvet, Basic Instinct, Schindler's List, Dangerous Liaisons, L.A. Confidential, Titanic,* and *The Truman Show*—belie that opinion. (The viewer who disagrees with my list will have no trouble coming up with his or her own favorites.) Art movies and independent films show continued vitality.

New or newly deregulated technologies are likely to induce further cultural innovations. Cable television is expanding rapidly and breaking down the hegemony of the networks. Eventually viewers will be able to choose from hundreds of channels. Cable already offers the world's greatest movies; the modern drama of sporting events; large doses of popular music; and high arts such as ballet, theater, and classical music. Viewers can take a class in Shakespeare without leaving their living rooms or use foreign-language channels to learn languages, thereby enlarging their access to the world's cultural treasures.

Cable is not the only new artistic medium. We can only guess at the development of the Web, Virtual Reality technologies, and Hypertext, both as means for delivering older creations and as new media for future works.

Finally, quasi-artistic activities are blossoming like never before. Fashion, decoration, cuisine, sports, product design, computer graphics, and commercial art—to give just a few examples—continue to flourish and grow. As recently as 20 years ago, Thai food was not available in most American cities; now Thai restaurants dot the suburbs as well. Although those fields are not art in the narrow sense, they bring beauty and drama into our lives. A beautifully decorated home or a luxurious shopping mall delights us and appeals to our aesthetic sense. The question "What is art?" has become less meaningful with the growing diversity of capitalist production.

Markets and Contemporary Culture

It is no accident that contemporary culture has flourished in our wealthy society. Most of the great cultural movements of the past— those of Athens, Rome, early China, the Islamic empire, the Italian Renaissance, and 19th-century Europe—like 20th-century modernism, occurred in societies that were relatively wealthy and commercial for their time. Today, most important works in film, music, literature, painting, and sculpture are sold as commodities. Contemporary art is capitalist art, and the history of art has been a history of the struggle to establish markets.

Creators have the best chance of living from their work in a wealthy, capitalist society. Both artists and audiences have more leisure time and are freed from tiresome physical labor. The larger size of the market supports a greater diversity of products, in both artistic and nonartistic realms. Not surprisingly, the number of individuals who work as full-time creators has risen steadily for centuries.

Capitalism increases the independence of the artist from the immediate demands of the culture-consuming public. The wealth of a market economy funds alternative sources of financial support, such as private foundations, universities, bequests from wealthy relatives, and day jobs. Those sources of funding allow artists to invest in skills, undertake long-term projects, and control their fate. Ironically, artists who care about art, rather than money, have the best chance in a system based on money and commercial incentives.

Wealthy societies give artists the greatest chance of financial independence and thus creative independence. Beethoven wrote, "I am not out to be a musical usurer as you think, who writes only to become rich, by no means! Yet, I love an independent life, and this I cannot have without a small income." In other cases, income also allows artists to purchase the materials necessary for artistic creation, such as paint and canvas or, in the case of Damien Hirst, sharks and formaldehyde.

We should not disapprove of artists who produce for money. The painters and sculptors of the Italian Renaissance were businessmen who produced for profit and negotiated hard bargains. Mozart wrote, "Believe me, my sole purpose is to make as much money as possible; for after good health it is the best thing to have." Capitalism allows artists to commercialize their product and sell to large numbers, if they so wish, thereby mobilizing greed in the service of creativity.

Finally, many arts depend on the technological innovations delivered by capitalism. We take paper for granted, but in earlier eras its expense significantly limited the output of both writers and artists. Photography, cinema, and electronic reproduction of music were not possible until relatively recent times. Advances in medicine allow artists to live to older ages, and birth control allows many female creators to manage their careers more effectively.

The economist William J. Baumol has argued that the performing arts suffer from a "cost disease" because they do not enjoy the benefits of technical progress as much as other industries do. Baumol notes that it took 40 minutes of work to produce a Mozart string quartet in 1780, and it still would take 40 minutes today. Baumol, however, underestimates the progressive nature of artistic production. Electronic reproduction, in the forms of recording and radio, has improved the productivity of musicians by allowing them to reach larger audiences. Today's string quartet travels by airplane rather than by stagecoach or train. A string quartet in 1780 could play Mozart, but today's string quartet can play Beethoven, Bartok, and the Beatles' "Eleanor Rigby" as well.

Cultural Pessimism and Its Appeal

Many cultural commentators take explicitly pessimistic views. Neo-Marxists and critics of mass culture, such as the Frankfurt School, believe that markets degrade culture. In their view, the commodification of culture lowers artistic quality and corrupts artists. They identify market culture with the production of low-quality television programs for the masses. The influence of that view, of course, has extended well beyond the radical left. Many neoliberal writers share the concerns of the Frankfurt School, even though their politics are far more moderate. Neil Postman argues that modern technology and media are destroying literacy. Herbert Schiller titled his book *Culture, Inc.: The Corporate Takeover of Public Expression.*

The political correctness movement identifies capitalistic culture with the suppression of minorities and women. Some multiculturalists argue that market exchange leads to a globalized, homogenized culture of the least common denominator. Marshall McLuhan wrote of the "global village," in which we all consume the same products. In response to those fears, cultural protectionism is practiced around the world, especially in countries such as France and Canada that fear American influence. No American representative was invited to the recent Ottawa conference on cultural protectionism, on the ostensible grounds that America has no cabinet-level culture minister—which is one reason why American culture has proven so formidable.

On the right, many neoconservatives believe that our culture is in a sorry state, as a reflection of more general trends of permissiveness, crime, and loss of respect for tradition. Allan Bloom, Daniel Bell, Irving Kristol, and Robert Bork have all written critiques of culture under capitalism. They argue that capitalistic culture gives insufficient support to traditional values.

Yet Western culture has been on an upswing since at least the year 1000. Both innovation and preservation of the past have blossomed. Why then has cultural pessimism had so much influence?

Cognitive biases induce observers to grant cultural pessimism more plausibility than it deserves. The pessimists focus on the decline of what they already appreciate, and neglect the rise of what is yet to come. It is easy to perceive the loss of what we know and harder to discern new developments and surprises. Even if long-term trends are positive, culture may appear to be deteriorating.

Observers often judge present culture against the very best of past culture, causing the present to appear lacking in contrast. But comparing the best of the past against the entirety of the present is unfair. No matter how vital contemporary culture may be, our favorite novels, movies, and recordings were not all produced just yesterday. Anyone's favorite epochs, including those of the cultural optimist, will lie at some point in the past. As a result, each field will appear to have declined, given that some superior era lies behind us in each case. Yet we should not conclude that creativity is drying up or slowing down. Rather, the past contains more accumulated achievement than does any single moment in time, such as the present. Furthermore, cultural pessimism will appear increasingly persuasive, precisely because the world continues to produce creative works. With every passing year, the entire past contains an increasing amount of culture, relative to the present.

We also consume contemporary culture less efficiently than we consume the culture of the past. Eighteenth-century music critics did not commonly understand that Haydn and Mozart were categorically superior to Gluck, Cherubini, Cimarosa, and Gretry. Years of debate and listening were needed for the truth to become obvious. Similarly, we cannot yet identify the truly worthy and seminal performers in modern popular music or contemporary art. It takes decades, and sometimes even centuries, to separate the cultural wheat from the chaff.

Most great creators, even those who now strike us as conservative, faced considerable opposition in their day. The French Impressionists were rejected by the artistic mainstream of their day and considered ridiculously unstructured. Mozart's music was considered incredibly dissonant by many of his contemporaries. One critic charged Anton Bruckner with being "the greatest living musical peril, a tonal Antichrist . . . [who] composes nothing but high treason, revolution and murder . . . poisoned with the sulphur of Hell."

Older audiences often cannot appreciate new and innovative cultural products. Many individuals devote their maximum attention to culture in their youth. Between the ages of 15 and 25, for instance, the mind is receptive to new influences, individuals are searching for their identity, and, more often than not, they are rebelling against their elders. For many individuals, those years are a formative period for cultural taste. Over time, however, marriage, children, and jobs crowd out the opportunity to discover new products. Therefore, in the eyes of many individuals, culture appears to be drying up and declining, which creates yet further support for pessimism.

Some individuals hold pessimistic attitudes to support their elitism. Elitists need to feel that they belong to a privileged minority. Contemporary culture, however, is massive in size, diverse in scope, and widely disseminated. Elitists have a hard time sustaining their self-images if they admit that our culture is wonderful and vibrant. Celebrating the dynamism of modern creations ascribes aesthetic virtues and insights to a very large class of artistic producers and consumers—contra elitism.

The diversity of modern culture implies that much trash will be produced, providing fodder for pessimism and elitism. We should keep these low-quality outputs in perspective and view them as a luxury that only diverse and wealthy societies can afford.

Some kinds of cultural pessimism spring from lack of imagination. Cultural pessimism and "resource pessimism" share common roots in this regard. Resource pessimism is the view, effectively criticized by Julian Simon, that the world will run out of resources in the near future. Resource pessimists focus on one kind of resource, such as oil, and see only so many years' supply remaining. They fail to see that the world could procure energy by different means in the future. Many cultural pessimists hold analogous attitudes. The West has developed certain great art forms, such as epic poetry, classical drama, and the symphony. Those forms have been "exhausted," at least in terms of the taste of the pessimist, implying cultural decline. Yet we should not look for cultural innovation to recur in the same areas over time; if anything, we should expect the exact opposite. There is no 20th-century Homer or Aeschylus, but we do have Alfred Hitchcock, Duke Ellington, and Frank Lloyd Wright.

Cultural pessimism has been around as long as culture. Pessimistic attacks have been leveled for centuries, although the target has changed frequently. Many moralists and philosophers, including Plato, criticized theater and poetry for their corrupting influence.

Books became a target after the onset of publishing. Eighteenth-century pessimists accused novels of preventing readers from thinking, preaching disobedience to parents (note the contradictory charges), undermining women's sense of subservience, breaking down class distinctions, and making readers sick. Libraries, especially privately run circulating libraries, were another target. Edward Mangin remarked in 1808, "There is scarcely a street of the metropolis, or a village in the country, in which a circulating library may not be found: nor is there a corner of the empire, where the English language is understood, that has not suffered from the effects of this institution."

In the 18th and 19th centuries the targets included epistolary romances, newspapers, opera, the music hall, photography, and instrumental virtuosi, such as Liszt and Paganini. The 20th century brought the scapegoats of radio, movies, modern art, professional sports, the automobile, television, rhythm and blues, rock 'n' roll, comic books, MTV music videos, and rap music. Each new medium or genre has been accused of corrupting youth and promoting excess sensuality, political subversion, and moral relativism.

My version of cultural optimism offers a contrasting perspective. Capitalist art consists fundamentally of bringing the consumer and producer together. Therein lies its exhilarating, challenging, and poetic nature. Marketplace art is about the meeting of minds and hearts. We should not deplore our culture, as do the pessimists. Rather, we should recognize its fundamentally capitalist nature, which implies creativity, entertainment, innovation, and above all diversity.

Affirmative Action Can't Be Mended

Walter E. Williams

For the last several decades, affirmative action has been the basic component of the civil rights agenda. But affirmative action, in the form of racial preferences, has worn out its political welcome. In Gallup Polls, between 1987 and 1990, people were asked if they agreed with the statement: "We should make every effort to improve the position of blacks and other minorities even if it means giving them preferential treatment." More than 70 percent of the respondents opposed preferential treatment while only 24 percent supported it. Among blacks, 66 percent opposed preferential treatment and 32 percent supported it.

The rejection of racial preferences by the broad public and increasingly by the Supreme Court has been partially recognized by even supporters of affirmative action. While they have not forsaken their goals, they have begun to distance themselves from some of the language of affirmative action. Thus, many business, government, and university affirmative action offices have been renamed "equity offices." Racial preferences are increasingly referred to as "diversity multiculturalism." What is it about affirmative action that gives rise to its contentiousness?

For the most part, post-World War II America has supported civil rights for blacks. Indeed, if we stick to the uncorrupted concept of civil rights, we can safely say that the civil rights struggle for blacks is over and won. Civil rights properly refer to rights, held simultaneously among individuals, to be treated equally in the eyes of the law, make contracts, sue and be sued, give evidence, associate and travel freely, and vote. There was a time when blacks did not fully

Walter Williams is the John M. Olin Distinguished Professor of Economics and former department chairman at George Mason University.
Cato Journal, Vol. 17, No. 1 (Spring/Summer 1997)

enjoy those rights. With the yeoman-like work of civil rights organizations and decent Americans, both black and white, who fought lengthy court, legislative, and street battles, civil rights have been successfully secured for blacks. No small part of that success was due to a morally compelling appeal to America's civil libertarian tradition of private property, rule of law, and limited government.

Today's corrupted vision of civil rights attacks that civil libertarian tradition. Principles of private property rights, rule of law, freedom of association, and limited government are greeted with contempt. As such, the agenda of today's civil rights organizations conceptually differs little from yesteryear's restrictions that were the targets of the earlier civil rights struggle. Yesteryear civil rights organizations fought *against* the use of race in hiring, access to public schools, and university admissions. Today, civil rights organizations fight *for* the use of race in hiring, access to public schools, and university admissions. Yesteryear, civil rights organizations fought *against* restricted association in the forms of racially segregated schools, libraries, and private organizations. Today, they fight *for* restricted associations. They use state power, not unlike the racists they fought, to enforce racial associations they deem desirable. They protest that blacks should be a certain percentage of a company's workforce or clientele, a certain percentage of a student body, and even a certain percentage of an advertiser's models.

Civil rights organizations, in their successful struggle against state-sanctioned segregation, have lost sight of what it means to be truly committed to liberty, especially the freedom of association. The true test of that commitment does not come when we allow people to be free to associate in ways we deem appropriate. The true test is when we allow people to form those voluntary associations we deem offensive. It is the same principle we apply to our commitment to free speech. What tests our commitment to free speech is our willingness to permit people the freedom to say things we find offensive.

Zero-Sum Games

The tragedy of America's civil rights movement is that it has substituted today's government-backed racial favoritism in the allocation of resources for yesterday's legal and extralegal racial favoritism. In doing so, civil rights leaders fail to realize that government allocation of resources produces the kind of conflict that does not arise with market allocation of resources. Part of the reason is that any government allocation of resources, including racial preferential treatment, is a zero-sum game.

A zero-sum game is defined as any transaction where one person's gain necessarily results in another person's loss. The simplest example of a zero-sum game is poker. A winner's gain is matched precisely by the losses of one or more persons. In this respect, the only essential difference between affirmative action and poker is that in poker participation is voluntary. Another difference is the loser is readily identifiable, a point to which I will return later.

The University of California, Berkeley's affirmative action program for blacks captures the essence of a zero-sum game. Blacks are admitted with considerably lower average SAT scores (952) than the typical white (1232) and Asian student (1254). Between UCLA and UC Berkeley, more than 2,000 white and Asian straight A students are turned away in order to provide spaces for black and Hispanic students. The admissions gains by blacks are exactly matched by admissions losses by white and Asian students. Thus, any preferential treatment program results in a zero-sum game almost by definition.

More generally, government allocation of resources is a zero-sum game primarily because government has no resources of its very own. When government gives some citizens food stamps, crop subsidies, or disaster relief payments, the recipients of the largesse gain. Losers are identified by asking: where does government acquire the resources to confer the largesse? In order for government to give to some citizens, it must through intimidation, threats, and coercion take from other citizens. Those who lose the rights to their earnings, to finance government largesse, are the losers.

Government-mandated racial preferential treatment programs produce a similar result. When government creates a special advantage for one ethnic group, it necessarily comes at the expense of other ethnic groups for whom government simultaneously creates a special disadvantage in the form of reduced alternatives. If a college or employer has X amount of positions, and R of them have been set aside for blacks or some other group, that necessarily means there are $(X - R)$ fewer positions for which other ethnic groups might compete. At a time when there were restrictions against blacks, that operated in favor of whites, those restrictions translated into a reduced opportunity set for blacks. It is a zero-sum game independent of the race or ethnicity of the winners and losers.

Our courts have a blind-sided vision of the zero-sum game. They have upheld discriminatory racial preferences in hiring but have resisted discriminatory racial preferences in job layoffs. An example is the U.S. Supreme Court's ruling in *Wygant v. Jackson Board of Education* (1986), where a teacher union's collective-bargaining agreement protected black teachers from job layoffs in order to maintain racial balance. Subsequently, as a result of that agreement, the Jackson County School Board laid off white teachers having greater seniority while black teachers with less seniority were retained.

A lower court upheld the constitutionality of the collective bargaining agreement by finding that racial preferences in layoffs were a permissible means to remedy societal discrimination. White teachers petitioned the U.S. Supreme Court, claiming their constitutional rights under the Equal Protection clause were violated. The Court found in their favor. Justice Lewis F. Powell delivered the opinion saying, "While hiring goals impose a diffuse burden, only closing one of several opportunities, layoffs impose the entire burden of achieving racial equity on particular individuals, often resulting in serious disruption of their lives. The burden is too intrusive."

In *Wygant*, the Supreme Court recognized the illegitimacy of creating a special privilege for one citizen (a black teacher) that comes at the expense and disadvantage of another citizen (a white teacher). However, the Court made a false distinction when it stated that "hiring goals impose a diffuse burden [while] . . . layoffs impose the entire burden . . . on particular individuals."

There is no conceptual distinction in the outcome of the zero-sum game whether it is played on the layoff or the hiring side of the labor market. If a company plans to lay off X amount of workers and decides that R of them will have their jobs protected because of race, that means the group of workers that may be laid off have $(X - R)$ fewer job retention opportunities. The diffuseness to which Justice Powell refers is not diffuseness at all. It is simply that the victims of hiring preferences are less visible than victims of layoff preferences as in the case of *Wygant*. The petitioners in *Wygant* were identifiable people who could not be covered up as "society." That differs from the cases of hiring and college admissions racial preferences where those who face a reduced opportunity set tend to be unidentifiable to the courts, other people, and even to themselves. Since they are invisible victims, the Supreme Court and others can blithely say racial hiring goals (and admission goals) impose a diffuse burden.

Tentative Victim Identification

In California, voters passed the California Civil Rights Initiative of 1996 (CCRI) that says: "The state shall not discriminate against, or grant preferential treatment to, any individual or group on the basis of race, sex, color, ethnicity, or national origin in the operation of public employment, public education, or public contracting." Therefore, California public universities can no longer have preferential admission policies that include race as a factor in deciding whom to admit. As a result, the UCLA School of Law reported accepting only 21 black applicants for its fall 1997 class—a drop of 80 percent from the previous year, in which 108 black applicants were accepted. At the UC Berkeley Boalt Hall School of Law, only 14 of the 792 students accepted for the fall 1997 class are black, down from 75 the previous year. At the UCLA School of Law, white enrollment increased by 14 percent for the fall 1997 term and Asian enrollment rose by 7 percent. At UC Berkeley, enrollment of white law students increased by 12 percent and Asian law students increased by 18 percent.

For illustrative purposes, let us pretend that CCRI had not been adopted and the UCLA School of Law accepted 108 black students as it had in 1996 and UC Berkeley accepted 75. That being the case, 83 more blacks would be accepted to UCLA Law School for the 1997–98 academic year and 61 more blacks would be accepted to UC Berkeley's Law School. Clearly, the preferential admissions program, at least in terms of being accepted to these law schools, benefits blacks. However, that benefit is not without costs. With preferential admission programs in place, both UCLA and UC Berkeley law schools would have had to turn away 144 white and Asian students, with higher academic credentials, in order to have room for black students.

In the case of UC Berkeley's preferential admissions for blacks, those whites and Asians who have significantly higher SAT scores and grades than the admitted blacks are victims of reverse discrimination. However, in the eyes of the courts, others, and possibly themselves, they are invisible victims. In other words, no one can tell for sure who among those turned away would have gained entry to UC Berkeley were it not for the preferential treatment given to blacks.

The basic problem of zero-sum games (those of an involuntary nature) is that they are politically and socially unstable. In the case of UCLA and UC Berkeley, two of California's most prestigious universities, one would not expect parents to permanently tolerate seeing their children work hard to meet the university's admission standards only to be denied admission because of racial preference programs. Since the University of California is a taxpayer-subsidized system, one suspects that sooner or later parents and others would begin to register complaints and seek termination of racial preferences in admissions. That is precisely much of the political motivation behind Proposition 209.

Affirmative Action and Supply

An important focus of affirmative action is statistical underrepresentation of different racial and ethnic groups on college and university campuses. If the percentages of blacks and Mexican-Americans, for example, are not at a level deemed appropriate by a court, administrative agency, or university administrator, racial preference programs are instituted. The inference made from the underrepresentation argument is that, in the absence of racial discrimination, groups would be represented on college campuses in proportion to their numbers in the relevant population. In making that argument, little attention is paid to the supply issue—that is, to the pool of students available that meet the standards or qualifications of the university in question.

In 1985, fewer than 1,032 blacks scored 600 and above on the verbal portion of the SAT and 1,907 scored 600 and above on the quantitative portion of the examination. There are roughly 58 elite colleges and universities with student body average composite SAT scores of 1200 and above. If blacks scoring 600 or higher on the quantitative portion of the SAT (assuming their performance on the verbal portion of the examination gave them a composite SAT score of 1200 or higher) were recruited to elite colleges and universities, there would be less than 33 black students available per university. At none of those universities would blacks be represented according to their numbers in the population.

There is no evidence that suggests that university admissions offices practice racial discrimination by turning away blacks with SAT scores of 1200 or higher. In reality, there are not enough blacks to be admitted to leading colleges and universities on the same terms as other students, such that their numbers in the campus population bear any resemblance to their numbers in the general population.

Attempts by affirmative action programs to increase the percent of blacks admitted to top schools, regardless of whether blacks match the academic characteristics of the general student body, often produce disastrous results. In order to meet affirmative action guidelines, leading colleges and universities recruit and admit black students whose academic qualifications are well below the norm for other students. For example, of the 317 black students admitted to UC Berkeley in 1985, all were admitted under affirmative action criteria rather than academic qualifications. Those students had an average SAT score of 952 compared to the national average of 900 among all students. However, their SAT scores were well below UC Berkeley's average of nearly 1200. More than 70 percent of the black students failed to graduate from UC Berkeley.

Not far from UC Berkeley is San Jose State University, not one of the top-tier colleges, but nonetheless respectable. More than 70 percent of its black students fail to graduate. The black students who might have been successful at San Jose State University have been recruited to UC Berkeley and elsewhere where they have been made artificial failures. This pattern is one of the consequences of trying to use racial preferences to make a student body reflect the relative importance of different ethnic groups in the general population. There is a mismatch between black student qualifications and those of other students when the wrong students are recruited to the wrong universities.

There is no question that preferential admissions is unjust to both white and Asian students who may be qualified but are turned away to make room for less-qualified students in the "right" ethnic group. However, viewed from a solely black self-interest point of view, the question should be asked whether such affirmative action programs serve the best interests of blacks. Is there such an abundance of black students who score above the national average on the SAT, such as those admitted to UC Berkeley, that blacks as a group can afford to have those students turned into artificial failures in the name of diversity, multiculturalism, or racial justice? The affirmative action debate needs to go beyond simply an issue of whether blacks are benefited at the expense of whites. Whites and Asians who are turned away to accommodate blacks are still better off than the blacks who were admitted. After all, graduating from the university of one's second choice is preferable to flunking out of the university of one's first choice.

To the extent racial preferences in admission produce an academic mismatch of students, the critics of California's Proposition 209 may be unnecessarily alarmed, assuming their concern is with black students actually graduating from college. If black students, who score 952 on the SAT, are not admitted to UC Berkeley, that does not mean that they cannot gain admittance to one of America's 3,000 other colleges. It means that they will gain admittance to some other college where their academic characteristics will be more similar to those of their peers. There will not be as much of an academic mismatch. To the extent this is true, we may see an *increase* in black graduation rates. Moreover, if black students find themselves more similar to their white peers in terms of college grades and graduation honors, they are less likely to feel academically isolated and harbor feelings of low self-esteem.

Affirmative Action and Justice

Aside from any other question, we might ask what case can be made for the morality or justice of turning away more highly credentialed white and Asian students so as to be able to admit more blacks? Clearly, blacks as a group have suffered past injustices, including discrimination in college and university admissions. However, that fact does not spontaneously yield sensible policy proposals for today. The fact is that a special privilege cannot be created for one person without creating a special disadvantage for another. In the case of preferential admissions at UCLA and UC Berkeley, a special privilege for black students translates into a special disadvantage for white and Asian students. Thus, we must ask what have those individual white and Asian students done to deserve punishment? Were they at all responsible for the injustices, either in the past or present, suffered by blacks? If, as so often is the case, the justification for preferential treatment is to redress past grievances, how just is it to have a policy where a black of today is helped by punishing a white of today for what a white of yesterday did to a black of yesterday? Such an idea becomes even more questionable in light of the fact that so many whites and Asians cannot trace the American part of their ancestry back as much as two or three generations.

Affirmative Action and Racial Resentment

In addition to the injustices that are a result of preferential treatment, such treatment has given rise to racial resentment where it otherwise might not exist. While few people support racial resentment and its manifestations, if one sees some of affirmative action's flagrant attacks on fairness and equality before the law, one can readily understand why resentment is on the rise.

In the summer of 1995, the Federal Aviation Administration (FAA) published a "diversity handbook" that said, "The merit promotion process is but one means of filling vacancies, which need not be utilized if it will not promote your diversity goals." In that spirit, one FAA job announcement said, "Applicants who meet the qualification requirements . . . cannot be considered for this position. . . . Only those applicants who do not meet the Office of Personnel Management requirements . . . will be eligible to compete."

According to a General Accounting Office report that evaluated complaints of discrimination by Asian-Americans, prestigious universities such as UCLA, UC Berkeley, MIT, and the University of Wisconsin have engaged in systematic discrimination in the failure to admit highly qualified Asian students in order to admit relatively unqualified black and Hispanic students.

In Memphis, Tennessee, a white police officer ranked 59th out of 209 applicants for 75 available positions as police sergeant, but he did not get promoted. Black officers, with lower overall test scores than he, were moved ahead of him and promoted to sergeant. Over a two-year period, 43 candidates with lower scores were moved ahead of him and made sergeant.

There is little need to recite the litany of racial preference instances that are clear violations of commonly agreed upon standards of justice and fair play. But the dangers of racial preferences go beyond matters of justice and fair play. They lead to increased group polarization ranging from political backlash to mob violence and civil war as seen in other countries. The difference between the United States and those countries is that racial preferences have not produced the same level of violence. However, they have produced polarization and resentment.

Affirmative action proponents cling to the notion that racial discrimination satisfactorily explains black/white socioeconomic differences. While every vestige of racial discrimination has not been eliminated in our society, current social discrimination cannot begin to explain all that affirmative action proponents purport it explains. Rather than focusing our attention on discrimination, a higher payoff can be realized by focusing on real factors such as fraudulent education, family disintegration, and hostile economic climates in black neighborhoods. Even if affirmative action was not a violation of justice and fair play, was not a zero-sum game, was not racially polarizing, it is a poor cover-up for the real work that needs to be done.

The Future of Liberty

Edward H. Crane

It is estimated that, in 1772 when there were 775,000,000 people inhabiting the world, only about 33,000,000 of them lived under relatively free governments. Some 95 percent of humanity lived lives described by historian Arthur Young as those of "miserable slaves of despotic tyrants." As late as 1848, according to Stanley Engerman, in Austria serfs were about 72 percent of the population, and in Hungary about 50 percent. From that perspective, we've come a long way.

Another measure: worldwide per capita income (in constant dollars) was $100 in 1800; by 1900 it was about $500; next year it will be about $5,000; and by the end of this century some estimates put it in excess of $40,000, or higher than the average Western income of today. It could, of course, turn out to be much greater even than that.

In addition, any long-term assessment of human liberty has to take into account the collapse of communism. Hundreds of millions of people today are free from the yoke of communist totalitarianism under which they labored just a decade or so ago. The change has been dramatic, even in Russia, despite all its difficulties. For those nations that have really moved toward capitalism, the past decade has been nothing short of exhilarating. As *Business Week* noted a couple of months ago, for instance, "Poland has enjoyed brisk economic growth for most of the decade because it chose radical reform, and despite the pain, stuck with it."

The only remaining communist country of any consequence is China, which for all its human rights failings is nevertheless clearly headed in a capitalist direction. The Associated Press recently distributed a photo of a protester in Tiananmen Square sporting an umbrella painted with the slogan "Privatize. Give all state property to

Edward H. Crane is founder and president of the Cato Institute.
Cato Policy Report, January/February 2000

the people." He was arrested, to be sure, but when such subversive ideas are alive in the land, the end is near for the thugs in Beijing.

And not all of the Chinese leaders are thugs. A couple of years ago in Shanghai José Piñera and I met with an official from Beijing who had been charged with responsibility for creating a public pension system in China. Sun Jianyong convinced us that he was a great admirer of the Chilean system because of the higher income at retirement, the economic boost from increased savings, and, he said, because it gave people the dignity of not depending on the state for their retirement income. Some communist he!

Speaking of the collapse of communism, I think one of the clear indications that liberty has the long-term momentum today is the so-called Third Way. Because, believe me, Bill Clinton, Tony Blair, and those other European politicians wouldn't be adopting that phrase—the Third Way—if socialism wasn't as thoroughly discredited as it is. They are leftists who are trying desperately to hide that fact from the voters. To a large degree they've succeeded. But such deceit won't be successful over the long haul as it becomes increasingly evident that, whatever they call themselves, they always end up promoting more state intrusion into civil society. The Third Way politicians are trying to sugarcoat statism in the rhetoric of free markets and reinventing government, but in the Information Age they are sooner or later—sooner, probably—going to be exposed for the statists that they are.

Domestic Policy Reform

I mentioned the interest in China in setting up a private, individually capitalized pension system. There is, of course, tremendous interest in doing so in the United States as well, in large part because of the work of the Cato Institute, the Heritage Foundation, and the National Center for Policy Analysis, each of which is indebted to the incredible work of the Johnny Appleseed of pension reform, José Piñera. Even if we live in an era of Bill Clinton and George W. Bush, the fact is that, by any objective standard, classical liberal ideas are making remarkable progress in the national policy debate. Privatizing Social Security is supported by two-thirds of the population of the United States, and people under 50 support it nearly unanimously. Men and women; Republicans, Democrats, and Independents; union workers; blacks, whites, Asians, and Hispanics all overwhelmingly favor replacing Social Security, the centerpiece of the

New Deal. When asked whether government or individual workers should invest the funds in a privatized system, by a margin of nearly five to one Americans say individuals should be allowed to invest on their own. They also say the present government-run pay-as-you-go system is riskier than the market. This is all from a Zogby International poll that Cato released in September 1999.

In looking over those poll results, by the way, I was reminded of a 1998 poll from the Pew Research Center that asked government officials this question: "Do Americans know enough about issues to form wise opinions about what should be done?" Here are the results: Thirty-one percent of members of Congress said yes, 47 percent said no. Thirteen percent of presidential appointees said yes, and 77 percent said no. Civil servants also are disdainful of the American people, with 14 percent saying the public can form wise decisions and a whopping 81 percent saying no, they can't. The huge gulf between the political class and the people in the United States, it seems to me, is another advance indicator of political change.

Getting back to Social Security, it's true that neither political party has yet had the courage to call for complete privatization, but that's what the people want and Social Security reform may well turn out to be a decisive issue in the presidential campaign. Piñera, who is working with Cato in our efforts in that regard, has already succeeded in bringing some form of privatization to pension systems in no fewer than eight Latin American countries. To achieve such a thing in the United States would not only dramatically change our political dynamics in a very favorable direction; it would also put tremendous pressure on the European Union and Japan to follow suit. They cannot survive forever with public pension systems that feature unfunded liabilities of 200 or 300 percent of gross domestic product.

There are other significant policy gains evident in the United States today—which is not to say that we've attained all our goals, but progress is clearly being made. Today the education monopoly is under attack as never before. The teachers' unions are in rapid retreat, throwing charter schools at the discontented masses in the hopes of placating them before they tear down the walls of the monopoly. Ten years ago the unions were impervious to criticism.

In the area of health care, there is a growing understanding that it's the third-party-payer system, whether government or low-deductible insurance coverage, that's to blame for bureaucratized and expensive health care in America. Hillary Clinton's effort to sell the Canadian system as the model for the United States broke down when it became common knowledge that Canadians travel south when they have serious health problems, despite the deficiencies of the U.S. system. There is a serious effort under way now to expand medical savings accounts and, indeed, to separate health insurance from employment through equal tax treatment, something a growing number of major corporations in the United States now favor. All of this undermines efforts to socialize medicine in the United States.

On other policy fronts, the welfare establishment has never really recovered from the assault on its hegemony by Charles Murray's *Losing Ground* and today lives with the reality that welfare is no longer a federal entitlement. People clearly understand the counterproductive nature of the dole and are determined to hold their fellow citizens responsible for their own actions, as they largely did before the advent of the paternalistic Great Society programs of the 1960s.

Taxes and Trade

There is also a growing consensus that scrapping the 9,000-plus-page U.S. Internal Revenue Code would be a good thing to do. Tax simplification is something to which all politicians now must at least pay lip service. At Cato we frequently have forums on the flat tax or replacing the income tax altogether with a retail sales tax. It is virtually impossible to get politicians or even someone from the IRS to defend the current system at these events. Radical simplification of the tax code not only would be good economically; it would also end the patronizing policies of politicians who now use the tax code to socially engineer citizen behavior. Simplification would increase support for the movement to sharply reduce taxation in America. We are making progress in this area, including creating a consensus to abolish both the capital gains tax and the death tax.

Finally, trade policy has clearly been on a positive trend in the United States for decades. Free traders have won the intellectual battle. The United States today has lower tariffs, as measured by the ratio of tariff income to the value of imports, than at any time in our history. In 1929 with the Smoot-Hawley tariff, that number stood at nearly 60 percent. Today it is less than 4 percent. Furthermore, trade and foreign investment income as a percentage of the GDP of the

United States is at an all-time high of 30 percent, when as recently as 30 years ago it was only 15 percent of GDP. Internationally, a large number of countries—ranging from Chile to Mexico, Argentina, Australia, New Zealand, the transition countries of Central and Eastern Europe, and even, to a certain degree, India—are following suit, as, indeed, they must if they're to prosper in the new global economy.

One other positive development in the United States has been a series of court decisions that may portend the end of a very sorry history of jurisprudence dating back to 1937 when Franklin Roosevelt threatened to pack the Supreme Court unless it agreed to ignore its clear constitutional responsibilities and capitulate to his grand social schemes. In a sort of early Public Choice analysis, Thomas Jefferson once wrote, "The natural progress of things is for government to gain ground and for liberty to yield." Jefferson and most of the American Founders understood very well that there is an inherent tendency for the state to expand—the statist imperative, if you will. Without some kind of institutional constraints, in our case the Constitution, the majoritarian instinct in a democracy would naturally lead to the tendrils of the state reaching into every corner of civil society.

As, indeed, they pretty much have since 1937. But that all may be changing. The father of the Constitution, James Madison, said that the courts were to be the "bulwark of our liberties" against the inevitable majoritarian onslaught from the two political branches of the national government. In recent years the federal courts have once again started defending property rights; have been firm in support of free speech rights; have told Congress not to delegate its power to unelected bureaucrats; and have even resurrected the essence of the Constitution, the Doctrine of Enumerated Powers, according to which, if a power is not specifically delegated to the national government, it is reserved to the states or to the people. A renaissance of respect for the Constitution, which seems to be taking place, is imperative if the prospects for liberty are to be positive.

The Information Age

So, in conventional terms, the prospects for liberty are, if you stand back far enough, pretty bright. But there are at work other forces that augur even more brightly for a global future with far less political society and far more civil society. I speak, of course, of the Information

Age and the two most dramatic things it brings to society: widespread, diversified, and instantaneous knowledge and, on the financial side of the ledger, what Richard McKenzie and Dwight Lee call "quicksilver capital"—the ability of capital to move anywhere in the world with the click of a mouse.

At the Cato Institute we prefer to discuss the political battle—that is, the individual's relationship to the state—in terms of civil society versus political society, rather than liberal versus conservative or even libertarian. In a civil society you make the choices about your life—how to spend your money, where to send your children to school, and so forth. In a political society, based as it is on coercion, somebody else—a politician or a bureaucrat—makes those decisions. The goal, it seems to us, should be to minimize the role of political society consistent with protection of our individual liberties.

Well, it turns out that political society historically has derived its power from three main sources: geographic territory, which is to say land; control of the flow and nature of information because knowledge is power; and control over capital flows and the value of a nation's currency. The Information Age is eating away at those three sources of power just as surely as the sun rises in the east.

Geographic territory and natural resources, as Hong Kong let anyone who was paying attention know decades ago, become increasingly irrelevant with the advent of the new global economy made possible by the information revolution in knowledge and finance. Indeed, the computer-challenged Soviet Union ended up finding geographic territory a liability in its contest with the information-rich West. A book called *The Lexus and the Olive Tree* by the chief foreign correspondent of the *New York Times*, Thomas Friedman, spent several months on the bestseller list in 1998. Friedman is something of an Al Gore Democrat, and his policy prescriptions range from more money for the International Monetary Fund to more environmental regulation. But the first half of the book is really terrific. He says countries today face the "Golden Straitjacket," by which he means that, in order to benefit from the new global economy, nations must play by certain rules. Here's what he writes:

> To fit into the Golden Straitjacket a country must either adopt, or be seen as moving toward, the following golden rules: making the private sector the primary engine of its economic growth, maintaining a low rate of inflation and price stability, shrinking the size of its state bu-

457

reaucracy, maintaining as close to a balanced budget as possible, if not a surplus, eliminating or lowering tariffs on imported goods, removing restrictions on foreign investment, getting rid of quotas and domestic monopolies, increasing exports, privatizing state-owned industries and utilities, deregulating capital markets, making its currency convertible, opening its industries, stock, and bond markets to direct foreign ownership and investment, deregulating its economy to promote as much domestic competition as possible, eliminating government corruption, subsidies and kickbacks as much as possible, opening its banking and telecommunications systems to private ownership and competition, and allowing its citizens to choose from an array of competing pension options and foreign-run pension and mutual funds. . . . As your country puts on the Golden Straitjacket, two things tend to happen: your economy grows and your politics shrinks.

Not bad for a liberal Democrat. Friedman's analysis of the nature of the new global economy is brilliant. So brilliant, in fact, that much of the analysis is reminiscent of Walter Wriston's wonderful 1991 book, *The Twilight of Sovereignty*. That book, written in anticipation of the Internet, has to be one of the most thoughtful, prescient books of all time. Wriston simply saw things the rest of us couldn't.

In it he writes: "Intellectual capital is becoming relatively more important than physical capital. Indeed, the new source of wealth is not material, it is information, knowledge applied to work to create value. The pursuit of wealth is now largely the pursuit of information." And in competition with the private sector today, government can't possibly keep up in the pursuit of information. Individuals are being empowered irrespective of borders, irrespective of what politicians have done throughout the sorry history of government domination of society, which is happily coming to an end—hence Wriston's title.

One of the great sources of power for the state has been its ability to control capital flows by regulating major financial institutions. But one of the great aspects of the information revolution has been disintermediation—the decreasing need for middlemen—and the increasing ability of people to deal with one another directly, anywhere on the globe. Consider, for instance, the fact that in 1997 the singer David Bowie raised $55 million in capital on the basis of his projected royalties. The ability of capital markets to securitize virtually any future income flow, combined with the ability of companies to set up operations virtually anywhere on the globe, means that developing nations are in for explosive growth in the next century and that the IMF and World Bank bureaucrats can start looking for honest work.

Richard Rahn writes in his book *The End of Money*, "The world's people will be neither truly prosperous nor free unless governments retreat from their seemingly never-ending desire to control the production and use of money." He then goes on to persuasively demonstrate that governments have no choice but to give up that control. Private, digital, encrypted money is already a reality, and it will become the norm early in the 21st century. Nations that wish to preserve their sovereignty will do so only in a superficial sense, and then only by pursuing policies of very low taxation and free and open trade.

Information Age Politics

We live in interesting times. When the Agricultural Age turned into the Industrial Age, virtually no one was aware of what was happening. But as the Industrial Age turns into the Information Age, by definition virtually everyone is aware of it. It was estimated that by the end of 1999 some 100 million Americans would be plugged into the Internet. *Wired* magazine has dubbed "Netizens" those individuals who participate on the Net. In a classic 1997 article in *Wired*, Jon Katz wrote:

> The Digital Nation constitutes a new social class. Its citizens are young, educated, affluent. They inhabit wired institutions and industries—universities, computer and telecom companies, Wall Street and financial outfits, the media. . . . Some of their common values are clear: they tend to be libertarian, materialistic, tolerant, rational, technologically adept, disconnected from conventional political organizations—like the Republican or Democratic parties—and from narrow labels like liberal or conservative. . . . The digital young, from Silicon Valley entrepreneurs to college students, have a nearly universal contempt for government's ability to work; they think it's wasteful and clueless. On the Net, government is rarely seen as an instrument of positive change or social good. Politicians are assumed to be manipulative or ill-informed, unable to affect reform or find solutions, forced to lie to survive.

Katz went on to suggest that the Netizen community will fuse technology with politics in such a manner as to advance civil society. I think he's right. The twilight of sovereignty means the dawning of a new age of liberty and the empowerment of the individual. The world is moving toward pluralism, capitalism, and civil society. That will take time, but it will happen. It will happen because as the world community grows, as we get to know one another and work with one another around the globe, independent of the political process, civil society will flourish. Increasingly, citizens groups and policy institutes, not political parties, will lead the way. I'm reminded of that famous quote from the French politician Alexandre Ledru-Rollin, who said during the Paris revolt of 1848, "There go the people. I must follow them, for I am their leader." Politicians and political society are not the answer. The great American experiment in civil society, predicated on respect for the dignity of individual human beings, free from the grasping hands of politicians, is the answer.

Cato Institute

Founded in 1977, the Cato Institute is a public policy research foundation dedicated to broadening the parameters of policy debate to allow consideration of more options that are consistent with the traditional American principles of limited government, individual liberty, and peace. To that end, the Institute strives to achieve greater involvement of the intelligent, concerned lay public in questions of policy and the proper role of government.

The Institute is named for *Cato's Letters*, libertarian pamphlets that were widely read in the American Colonies in the early 18th century and played a major role in laying the philosophical foundation for the American Revolution.

Despite the achievement of the nation's Founders, today virtually no aspect of life is free from government encroachment. A pervasive intolerance for individual rights is shown by government's arbitrary intrusions into private economic transactions and its disregard for civil liberties.

To counter that trend, the Cato Institute undertakes an extensive publications program that addresses the complete spectrum of policy issues. Books, monographs, and shorter studies are commissioned to examine the federal budget, Social Security, regulation, military spending, international trade, and myriad other issues. Major policy conferences are held throughout the year, from which papers are published thrice yearly in the *Cato Journal*. The Institute also publishes the quarterly magazine *Regulation*.

In order to maintain its independence, the Cato Institute accepts no government funding. Contributions are received from foundations, corporations, and individuals, and other revenue is generated from the sale of publications. The Institute is a nonprofit, tax-exempt, educational foundation under Section 501(c)3 of the Internal Revenue Code.

CATO INSTITUTE
1000 Massachusetts Ave., N.W.
Washington, D.C. 20001